Time Out

Budapest

timeout.com/budapest

Published by Time Out Guides Ltd, a wholly owned subsidiary of Time Out Group Ltd.
Time Out and the Time Out logo are trademarks of Time Out Group Ltd.

© Time Out Group Ltd 2007
Previous editions 1996, 1998, 1999, 2003, 2005.

10 9 8 7 6 5 4 3 2 1

This edition first published in Great Britain in 2007 by Ebury Publishing
A Random House Group Company
20 Vauxhall Bridge Road, London SW1V 2SA

Random House Australia Pty Limited 20 Alfred Street, Milsons Point, Sydney, New South Wales 2061, Australia
Random House New Zealand Limited 18 Poland Road, Glenfield, Auckland 10, New Zealand
Random House South Africa (Pty) Limited Isle of Houghton, Corner Boundary
Road & Carse O'Gowrie, Houghton 2198, South Africa

Random House UK Limited Reg. No. 954009

For further distribution details, see www.timeout.com

ISBN 10: 1-84670-027-2
ISBN 13: 978184670 0279

A CIP catalogue record for this book is available from the British Library

Printed and bound by Firmengruppe APPL, aprinta druck, Wemding, Germany

The Random House Group Limited makes every effort to ensure that the papers used in our books are made from trees
that have been legally sourced from well-managed and credibly certified forests. Our paper procurement policy can be
found on www.rbooks.co.uk/environment.

Time Out Guides Limited
Universal House
251 Tottenham Court Road
London W1T 7AB
Tel + 44 (0)20 7813 3000
Fax + 44 (0)20 7813 6001
Email guides@timeout.com
www.timeout.com

Editorial

Editor Peterjon Cresswell
Listings Editors Sue Foy, Natalia Jánossy, Kreet Paljas
Proofreader Simon Cropper
Indexer Sally Davies

Managing Director Peter Fiennes
Financial Director Gareth Garner
Editorial Director Ruth Jarvis
Deputy Series Editor Dominic Earle
Editorial Manager Holly Pick
Assistant Management Accountant Ija Krasnikova

Design

Art Director Scott Moore
Art Editor Pinelope Kourmouzoglou
Senior Designer Henry Elphick
Graphic Designer Gemma Doyle
Junior Graphic Designer Kei Ishimaru
Digital Imaging Simon Foster
Ad Make-up Jodi Sher

Picture Desk

Picture Editor Jael Marschner
Deputy Picture Editor Tracey Kerrigan
Picture Researcher Helen McFarland

Advertising

Sales Director Mark Phillips
International Advertising Manager Kasimir Berger
International Sales Consultant Ross Canadé
International Sales Executive Charlie Sokol
Advertising Sales (Budapest) Julia Béres
Advertising Assistant Kate Staddon

Marketing

Group Marketing Director John Luck
Marketing Manager Yvonne Poon
Sales and Marketing Director North America Lisa Levinson

Production

Group Production Director Mark Lamond
Production Manager Brendan McKeown
Production Coordinator Caroline Bradford
Production Controller Susan Whittaker

Time Out Group

Chairman Tony Elliott
Financial Director Richard Waterlow
Group General Manager/Director Nichola Coulthard
Time Out Magazine Ltd MD Richard Waterlow
Time Out Communications Ltd MD David Pepper
Time Out International MD Cathy Runciman
Group Art Director John Oakey
Group IT Director Simon Chappell

Contributors

Introduction Peterjon Cresswell. **History** Gwen Jones, Desmond McGrath, Bob Cohen. **Budapest Today** Matt Higginson.
Hungarian Identity Gwen Jones. **Where to Stay** Tibor Sáringer. **Sightseeing** Tom Popper, Dave Rimmer, Bob Cohen, Maria
Bredican. **Restaurants** Tom Popper, Bob Cohen. **Cafés & Bars** Tom Popper, Peterjon Cresswell, Bob Cohen. **Shops & Services**
Tibor Sáringer, Bob Cohen. **Festivals & Events** Sue Foy, Peterjon Cresswell. **Baths** Matt Higginson, Chris Condon, Dave
Rimmer. **Children** Ildikó Lázár. **Film** Natalia Jánossy. **Galleries** Reuben & Maja Fowkes. **Gay & Lesbian** Tibor Sáringer.
Music: Classical & Opera Steven Loy. **Music: Rock, Roots & Jazz** Ágnes Molnár, Bob Cohen. **Nightlife** Tom Popper. **Sport
& Fitness** Peterjon Cresswell, Steve Anthony. **Theatre & Dance** Steve Anthony. **Trips Out of Town** Peterjon Cresswell,Tom
Popper, Dave Rimmer. **Directory** Natalia Jánossy.

Maps john@jsgraphics.co.uk.

Photography by Fumie Suzuki, except page 12 Hulton Deutsch Collection/Corbis; page 19 Roger-Viollet/Rex Features;
page 20 akg-images/Erich Lessing; page 22 Rex Features; page 143 Ferenc Novotta; page 159 Hadley Kincade;
page 171 Dávid Lukács; page 190 Katie Sandor.
The following images were provided by the featured establishments/artists: pages 36, 48, 50, 185, 203.

The Editor would like to thank all contributors to previous editions of *Time Out Budapest*, whose work forms the basis
for parts of this book.

Contents

Introduction

Few European capitals have the grace and grandeur of Budapest. Then again, few have a backdrop as spectacular as the Danube, panoramically dividing inescapably bourgeois Buda from business-like Pest. The river offers its most spectacular cityscape here, midway between the Black Forest and the Black Sea.

The metropolis around it was created in majestic style in a wave of 19th-century nationalist endeavour under the dual Habsburg Monarchy. Ornate coffeehouses, sumptuous spas, an opera house, continental Europe's first underground line along a tree-lined boulevard modelled on the Champs-Elysées – Budapest was a capital to contend with. Lofty stations served the empire, great temples to the train age when Budapest was the hub linking Bratislava, Bucharest, the Balkans and Vienna. It still is. Gaze at the main departure board in Keleti station and exotic destinations beckon: Belgrade, Berlin, Kiev, Krakow, Moscow, Paris, Prague, Sarajevo, Split, Thessaloniki and Trieste.

Yet the city directly connected to half of Europe changed dramatically in the century or more since the rail network was built to radiate around it. The Budapest that emerged from devastating global conflict, Holocaust and four decades of Communist decay still had all its faculties if not all its facilities. A rich cultural and intellectual life thrived even though there was no national theatre, orchestras were poorly funded and there wasn't much of an independent film industry to speak of.

In the rush to catch up and rejoin Europe in the 21st century, Budapest has built shiny malls, bridges, five-star hotels, a new national theatre and airport terminals. It has regained its Habsburg heritage – the Gresham Palace, the New York Palace, the Corinthia Grand Royal – and given it a modern makeover with all chic cons. Today's leading domestic filmmakers have a name on the international circuit, and the classical scene is flourishing. Local designers line up their creations on downtown Deák Ferenc utca. Adventurous chefs and restaurateurs are making up for decades of stodge and stasis. Nights out can still be orgiastically open-ended but now come with a fancy umbrella in the cocktail glass, finely selected musical treats and raffia seating.

But that's not why the Hungarian capital has so many aficionados, so many return visitors. Raffish drinks, raucous beats and raffia seats you can get in Ljubljana or London. What draws you here is what's hidden amid the Habsburg olive-and-marzipan façades, some still scarred from 1945 or 1956. Within this disappearing world of Coronation-era shopfronts, on dusty, downtown streets and in communal courtyards, is a civilised society in which men still raise their trilbies to passing ladies, Gypsy violinists carry their cases between assignments and chess is an outdoor social pastime.

The language for all this satisfyingly lazy interaction is notably alien, giving the impression that you've landed on some wacko planet whose natives are friendly – and demonstrably attractive – but who can only express themselves in gobbledegook.

In a bland, brand-named Europe, where no one plays grand piano in the café of the main station, such refined individuality stands out. It could be 1907, it could be 1957, it could be 2007, it might even be 2057. But it couldn't be anywhere else but Budapest.

ABOUT TIME OUT CITY GUIDES

This is the sixth edition of *Time Out Budapest*, one of an expanding series of Time Out City Guides produced by the people behind the successful listings magazines in London, New York and Chicago. Our guides are written and updated by resident experts who have striven to provide you with the most up-to-date information you'll need to explore the city.

THE LIE OF THE LAND

Budapest is well signposted. Every street (*utca* or *u.*), road (*út*), square (*tér*), embankment (*rakpart*), parade (*sétány*), alley (*fasor*), lane (*köz*) and roundabout (*körtér*) is clearly indicated, also giving the house numbers contained within that particular block. Budapest is also divided into 23 districts, *kerületek*, indicated by a Roman numeral before the street name. Postcodes are written in four figures, the middle two indicating the district: 1051 is District V. In listings we've used the Roman numeral because it's easier for finding your way around town. For an overview of the districts, *see p54*. Wherever possible, a map reference has been provided for every venue listed, indicating the page and grid reference at which it can be found on the Budapest street maps, *see pp245-250*.

ESSENTIAL INFORMATION

For all the practical information you might need for visiting the city – emergency phone numbers, visa and customs information and the lowdown on the transport network in and around Budapest – turn to the Directory chapter. You'll find it at the back of this guide, starting on page 217.

THE LOWDOWN ON THE LISTINGS

We have tried to make this guide as useful as possible. Addresses, telephone numbers, websites, transport information, opening times, admission prices and credit card details are included in our listings, all checked at the time we went to press. However, in a city like Budapest, opening hours can change. We would advise you to phone ahead to check particulars. While every effort has been made to ensure the accuracy of the information contained here, the publishers cannot accept responsibility for any errors it may contain.

PRICES AND PAYMENT

The Hungarian currency is the forint – the euro is not expected to be adopted until 2010, at least. Prices throughout this guide are given in forints (Ft), and euros (€) for hotels. The prices we've supplied should be treated as guidelines, not gospel. If they vary wildly from those quoted, please let us know. We have noted whether

venues take credit cards, but have listed only the major ones – American Express (AmEx), Diners Club (DC), MasterCard (MC) and Visa (V).

TELEPHONE NUMBERS

To call Budapest from abroad, dial +36 and then 1, then the number given in this guide. To call Budapest from anywhere else in Hungary, dial access code 06, then 1, then the number. Some numbers given in this guide are mobile ones – generally beginning with 06 20, 06 30 or 06 70. These are indicated by the word *mobile* after them. From abroad or a foreign mobile, you must dial +36 then the 20, 30 or 70, then the number. These calls may be expensive. From a Hungarian mobile or landline, simply call the whole number beginning with 06. To call other places in Hungary from Budapest, dial 06 followed by the area code, then the number. For more on telephones and codes, *see p233*.

MAPS

The map section at the back of this book includes an overview map of Budapest, street maps and a map of the transport system. The maps start on page 243 and now pinpoint specific locations of hotels (❶), restaurants (❶) and bars and cafés (❶).

LET US KNOW WHAT YOU THINK

We hope you enjoy *Time Out Budapest*, and we'd like to know what you think of it. We welcome tips for places that you consider we should include in future editions of the guide and take notice of your criticism of our choices. Email us with your feedback at guides@timeout.com.

There is an online version of this book, along with guides to over 100 international cities, at **www.timeout.com**.

Airline flights are one of the biggest producers of the global warming gas CO_2. But with **The CarbonNeutral Company** you can make your travel a little greener.

Go to **www.carbonneutral.com** to calculate your flight emissions then 'neutralise' them through international projects which save exactly the same amount of carbon dioxide.

Contact us at **shop@carbonneutral.com** or call into the office on **0870 199 99 88** for more details.

CarbonNeutral®flights

In Context

Features

Matthias Church.

Budapest in ruins after 1945. *See p20.*

History

Buda and Pest – a tale of two cities.

The twin settlements of Buda and Pest developed separately on opposite sides of the Danube. Leafy, hilly Buda still seems like a quiet, provincial retreat from the dusty bustle of Pest across the river. Pest is the stage for the city's commercial, political and cultural life, where careers are made, strangers become friends and the future takes shape. Set on a vast plain, it seems open to all possibilities.

The fault line is more than a psychological one. Budapest sits on an ancient geological rift, a line of least resistance that drew the waters of the Danube south in their search for a resting place. It's too deep to disturb amalgamated Budapest today, but the fault line ensured that the hills stayed on one side and the level plain on the other. When the first humans arrived here, some half a million years ago, those hills were seen as prime real estate, a defensible settlement with a fabulous view. Later still, the plain of Pest proved the ideal greenfield site for the extensive urban expansion that took place in the late 19th and early 20th centuries.

The earliest human history in what is now Hungary consisted of agricultural communities around the River Tisza, where large neolithic sites have been discovered. During the first millennium BC, Illyrian populations shared the plains with groups of Celtic peoples, known as the Eravi. They settled by the natural springs of Buda; excavations have unearthed a Celtic site on Gellért Hill, and remains at Óbuda, an area conquered by the Romans in 35 BC.

The region entered written history when it was officially incorporated into the Roman Empire in 14 BC under the name Pannonia. Known to the Romans as Aquincum, Buda was a modest trading town on the far edge of the empire. Today, you can see Roman ruins at the Aquincum Museum, including an old amphitheatre. More Roman ruins can be seen by the Danube in Pest, at Március 15 tér.

Meanwhile, political and cyclical climatic changes in Central Asia were inducing the first of a series of westward migrations in what is called either the 'Age of Barbarians' or the

'Age of Migrations'. In 430 the Huns, a Central Asian confederacy of Turkic-speaking nomads, burst into Europe. Under Attila, they defeated the Romans and vassals alike. Attila returned to Pannonia in 453 without sacking Rome, but died mysteriously on the night of his wedding to Princess Ildikó. Legend has it that he's buried near the River Tisza, in eastern Hungary.

The Huns then returned to their homelands (*see p14* **Sons of the Hun**). Next came the Avars, then the Bulgars, Turkic peoples from the Volga steppes. Meanwhile, the lands west of the Danube were being populated by more sedentary, agricultural Slavs, closely related to today's Slovenians.

WHERE DID THEY COME FROM?

The exact origin of the Hungarian people is unknown – and the subject of much debate. We do know that Magyar is a branch of the Finno-Ugric language group, a subgroup of the Altaic language family of Finns, Turks, Mongolians and many Siberian peoples. The earliest Hungarian homeland was in the dense forests between the River Volga and the Urals.

These proto-Hungarians moved south into the central Volga region around 500 BC. In the first centuries AD, the Hungarians came into contact with Turkic cultures pushing west, but historically speaking, the Magyars first made a name for themselves in the seventh and eighth centuries as vassals of the Turkic-speaking Khazar Empire between the Black and Caspian Seas. By the 800s the Hungarians were based in today's Ukraine and had begun raiding deep into Frankish Europe. St Cyril described the horde of Magyars he met in 860 as *luporum more ululantes*, 'howling in the manner of wolves'. Faced with a howling gang from Asia pillaging the Holy Roman Empire, Western Christendom amended the Catholic mass with: 'Lord save us from sin and the Hungarians'.

While the main Magyar armies spent the spring of 895 raiding Europe, their villages were devastated by Bulgars and Pechenegs. The surviving tribes of Magyars, led by their king, Árpád, fled across the Verecke pass in the northern Carpathians and on to the Hungarian plain. Meeting little resistance from the local Slavs, Goths and Avars, the Hungarians pushed their competitors, the Bulgars, south of the Danube, and began raiding as far west as France, Germany and northern Spain. They continued to plunder Western Europe until they were defeated by the German King Otto I at the Battle of Augsburg in 955.

Retiring to the Pannonian plain, the Hungarians realised that an alliance with a major power might be a good idea. This would mean having to deal with the Christian church.

THE FOUNDING OF THE NATION

Hungary was poised between the Byzantine Orthodox and Roman churches when King Géza, Árpád's grandson, requested missionaries be sent from Rome to convert the Magyars to the Western church, still trumpeted as a decision to be 'linked with the West'. Géza was baptised with his son, Vajk, who took the name István (Stephen) upon his accession to the Hungarian throne at Esztergom on Christmas Day in 1000.

King Stephen didn't have an easy time convincing his countrymen. Tribes loyal to the older, shamanic religion led a revolt in 1006. One consequence was the death of Venetian missionary St Gellért, put into a spiked barrel and rolled down Gellért Hill by miffed Magyar traditionalists. Stephen quickly crushed the revolt and set about destroying the power of the chieftains by appropriating their land and setting up a new class of nobles. He minted coins, forged alliances, built castles and put Hungary on the road to a feudal society. He was canonised in 1083.

> ## 'In 1241 the invasion of the Mongol hordes devastated Hungary. Towns were sacked, crops burned and regions depopulated.'

Stephen's son, Imre, died young, and the next 200 years saw many struggles for the throne of the House of Árpád, a preferred tactic being to blind potential rivals. Despite this, Stephen's successors consolidated and expanded the kingdom, conquering as far as Dalmatia. At home, tribal revolts were common.

The tensions between the landowning nobility and the office of the king were eventually settled by the signing of the 'Golden Bull' under King András in 1222. It recognised the nobility as the 'Hungarian Nation', granted them an exemption from taxation and laid the framework for an annual assembly of nobles, called the Diet. This was to be held in Rákos meadow in Pest; the annual gathering of the nation's high and mighty provided a push that helped Pest develop into a central market town.

In 1241 the invasion of the Mongol hordes devastated Hungary. Towns were sacked, crops burned and regions depopulated. The invaders chased King Béla IV as far south as Dalmatia, only to return east a year later in the wake of the death of the Great Khan.

Béla built a series of castles, including the one in Buda, that gradually would come to dominate the Magyar realm.

Sons of the Hun

Soon after your arrival in Budapest, one factor will begin to clash with your initial impression of the city as the most cosmopolitan of EU capitals. It begins with your cab driver. His name is Attila. Drop your bags at the hotel – the concierge is named Attila. Your waiter introduces himself – Attila again. Chat up the waitress at the bar (address Attila utca). She hands you her phone number. She's called Ildikó, after the bride of Attila. Attila as in Attila the Hun. The Scourge of God.

Yes, upstanding members of the EU still name children after a brutal nomadic Asian chieftain who, 1,500 years after he terrified Christendom and nearly sacked a greatly diminished Rome, remains something of a national hero. Could it be that these polite citizens descend from the Huns who invaded Europe in AD 370? The same Huns who put the dark into the Dark Ages, dispersing after the death of Attila consummating his marriage to Ildikó in AD 453?

Some Hungarians think so. But then some Hungarians also think that the Magyars are descended from the Sumerians, the survivors of Atlantis and even ancient Hawaiians. Put all these theories together and the theology of the Hungarian Hun Minority Council starts to make sense. Formed in Szombathely, the council has begun to petition the present-day Hungarian government to recognise them as true descendants of Attila's horde. 'Today's Huns are peaceful and gentle ... we have nothing to do with bloodshed or bows and arrows,' says György Kisfaludi, the current Hun chief. He finds the best place to collect signatures from emergent neo-Huns is among the fans of Ferencváros, Hungary's right-wing football club. Today's Huns can also be chic in a barbarian sort of way. The small town of Tápiószentmárton, claiming to be the burial place of Attila, is now seeking foreign investment for 'Attila's Palace Hotel and Conference Center Resort'.

Why the sudden re-emergence of the Huns? One idea is the 1.5 million euros awarded to each recognised minority in Hungary for them to open an office and apply for future EU funding. Another is the odd attraction that dressing up in pointy felt hats and living in yurts holds for many of Hungary's wacky right wing, which has its roots in the rightist pan-Turanian movements of the 1930s, themselves a myth-seeking alternative to Aryan-centric Nazism.

In truth, there is little concrete evidence directly linking modern Magyars to the ancient Hun confederacy. The Huns were one of several Turkic central Asian nomadic confederacies to migrate west. Subsequent migrations of Asian nomads included the Avars, Bulgars, and eventually the On-Ogurs, or the Ten Arrows Confederation, with whom the Uralic-speaking Magyars were confederated in the 9th century. 'Onogury' entered the language as 'Hungary'.

JUSTICE AND PROGRESS

When Béla's son, András III, died without leaving an heir, the House of Árpád came to its end. The Hungarian crown eventually settled on the head of Charles Robert of Anjou in 1310, inaugurating 200 years of stability. Charles Robert and his son, Louis the Great, made Hungary into one of the great powers of medieval Europe, a position financed by gold and silver from mines in Slovakia and Transylvania. Their successor was Sigismund of Luxembourg, convenor of the Council of Constance and eventually the Holy Roman Emperor. The ruthless, wily, twice-married Sigismund died heirless in 1437.

Meanwhile, the threat lay to the south, where the remorseless expansion of the Ottoman Empire in the Balkans was finally stemmed by János Hunyadi, a Transylvanian prince who regained control of Belgrade in 1456. Church bells rang all over Europe. Hunyadi's death then led to a bloody struggle for the throne, until in 1458 one of his sons, Mátyás, found himself king by default at the age of 16.

With Mátyás, known to Western historians as Matthias Corvinus, Buda became the focus of Hungarian society. He undertook building within Buda Castle and constructed a palace at Visegrád. Among his achievements was the Royal Library, one of the world's largest. It is said that Mátyás roamed the countryside, disguised as a peasant, seeking out injustices in the feudal system. Even today, his name symbolises good governance. 'Mátyás is dead,' goes the saying, 'and justice died with him'.

Further afield, Mátyás halted the Ottoman advance in Bosnia while expanding his empire to the north. His chief instrument of war, a highly efficient one, was the multi-ethnic Black Army of mercenaries. With his own standing army, a rarity for the time, Mátyás didn't have to depend on the nobles for recruits.

When Mátyás died heirless in 1490, the legacy of culture and order he'd built collapsed. The nobles resented him as a strong leader who could dispense with their services, and chose a weak successor. They appropriated land and taxes, sold his library and dismissed the Black Army. Hungary has never won a war since. In 1514 the Pope ordered a new crusade against the Turks. Hungary's peasantry, under the leadership of György Dózsa, rallied near Pest and turned against the nobles. They were quickly defeated. Dózsa was burned on a hot iron throne and his followers were made to bite into his roasting flesh. The nobility also voted in the Tripartum Law, reducing the peasantry to serfdom and forbidding them to bear arms. Their timing could not have been worse.

TURKISH CONTROL

When the young Hungarian King Lajos II, with 10,000 armoured knights, met the Turkish cavalry on the swampy plains of Mohács on 29 August 1526, some 80,000 Ottoman *spahi* cavalrymen routed the Hungarians in under less than two hours. Lajos drowned in a muddy stream, weighed down by heavy armour. The Turks then turned north, sacking and burning Buda. They retreated briefly, but returned in 1541 to occupy the castle. Buda became the seat of power in Ottoman Hungary and the country was divided into three. A rump Hungary ruled by the Habsburgs existed in the west and north. The Turks controlled the heartland with Transylvania nominally independent as a principality largely under Turkish control. Buda developed into a provincial Ottoman town. Matthias Church was converted into a mosque, and the hot springs inspired the construction of Turkish baths.

Pest was a village mostly populated by Magyars. Few Hungarians resided in Buda, since there were no churches there. As the Reformation made itself felt throughout the Hungarian region, anti-clericalism and the wariness of the Catholic Habsburgs among petty nobles made Hungary a rich recruiting ground for Protestant reform. The austere tenets of Calvinism found eager adherents across the Puszta.

The Ottoman defeat at the Siege of Vienna in 1683 saw the end of their threat to Christian Europe. In 1686 the Habsburgs attacked their stronghold at Buda Castle and took the city after a brutal six-week siege. Buda was again reduced to a pile of rubble, while Pest was virtually depopulated. After a further decade of war, the Turks lost their Hungarian realm, confirmed in writing at the Peace of Karlowitz in 1699. This marked the decline of the Ottomans – and the rise of the Habsburgs.

HABSBURG RULE

Life under the Habsburgs was harsh. They suspended the constitution and placed Hungary under military occupation. Severe Counter-Reformation measures were undertaken to guarantee the nobles' loyalty, including the sale of Protestant pastors as galley slaves in Naples.

In 1703 the Hungarians rebelled, led by the Transylvanian magnate Ferenc Rákóczi II. His rag-tag army kept up the fight for eight years before it was overwhelmed by Habsburg might. Rákóczi died in Turkish exile. To prevent further rebellion, the Austrians blew up every castle in the country and ordered that the walls of each fortified town and church be dismantled. The Szatmár Accord of 1711 saw Hungary recognise Habsburg rule; the Habsburgs in turn recognised Hungary's constitution and feudal Diet. The privileges of the landed gentry, who ran the administration by elected committee, would remain in place until after World War I.

As peace took hold and reconstruction got under way, Buda and Pest began to acquire a Central European character. The reign of the Maria Theresa (1740-80) marked the integration of Austria and Hungary. Hungary's nobility began to look to Vienna as the centre of power. Meanwhile, the peasants still impoverished serfs, using medieval technology. Hungary was still an agricultural backwater feeding an ever more industrialised Austria.

In Buda, a baroque city of German-speaking officialdom emerged from the Ottoman occupation. Pest developed into a commercial centre for the grain and livestock produced on the Hungarian plains and shipped along the Danube. As immigrants arrived from other Habsburg domains, Jews began moving in from from Bohemia and Galicia, settling in Pest, just beyond the dismantled city walls in what is today District VII. This neighbourhood became the centre of Hungarian Jewry, and is still the most complete Jewish quarter remaining in Eastern Europe.

THE AGE OF REFORM

Repercussions of the French Revolution were felt all across Europe, even in Hungary. A conspiracy of Hungarian Jacobins was nipped in the bud, and its leaders were executed near Déli station on land still known as the 'Field of Blood' (Vérmező). Their ideas gained an audience through the Hungarian-language writings of Ferenc Kazinczy. As the 19th century dawned, Hungarians eagerly embraced their own tongue as a revolutionary and literary language, even if it was only spoken by peasants and by nobles in the Calvinist east. Hungarian now began to unite people as 'Hungarian' and not 'Habsburg'.

This period is known as the Reform. Buda and Pest perked up under the Embellishment Act, an 1808 law which began to develop the city according to modern ideas. After the floods in 1838, Pest was redesigned along a pattern of concentric-ringed boulevards. The key figure was Count István Széchenyi, who sought to bring Hungary out of its semi-feudal state and into the world of industrialisation, credit finance and middle-class gentility. While he championed the ideal of development within the Habsburg Empire, other members of the Diet were not convinced. Lajos Kossuth, a minor noble of Slovak origin, was the eloquent voice of nationalist sentiment against Austrian rule. His popular appeal to the powerful middle gentry saw Széchenyi overshadowed.

Pressure on Habsburg internal affairs elsewhere led to a lessening of repression in 1839, and a reform-oriented liberal Diet was convened, led by Ferenc Deák. Kossuth lambasted the Austrian administration. The debate grew until civil nationalist uprisings spread across Europe in 1848, threatening the old monarchical order. On 3 March Kossuth delivered a parliamentary speech demanding a separate Hungarian ministry and an end to tax privileges for land-owning nobles.

On 15 March Kossuth met with the cream of Hungarian dissident liberals in the Pilvax coffeehouse to develop a revolutionary strategy. Among the rebels was the poet Sándor Petőfi who, later that day, famously read his newly penned poem *Nemzeti dal* ('National Song') on the steps of the National Museum – an event still commemorated every 15 March on Revolution Day.

A proposal for a liberalised constitution, giving Hungary far-reaching autonomy, was dispatched to Vienna that day and consented to by the frightened imperial government. On 7 April the Emperor sanctioned a Hungarian Ministry headed by Count Lajos Batthyány, and including Kossuth, Széchenyi and Deák. Hungarian was made the language of state; freedom of the press, assembly and religion were granted; noble privileges were curtailed; and peasants were emancipated from serfdom.

This might have satisfied some, but Kossuth wanted a separate fiscal and army structure. The new Diet went against the Emperor and voted in funding for the creation of a 200,000-man army. Kossuth's tactic was short-sighted. Hungary's minorities comprised over 50 per cent of the population, but they essentially lost all rights under the new constitution. This made it easy for Vienna to encourage a Croatian invasion of Hungary to induce a compromise, and soon the entire region was at war. Buda and Pest fell early to the Austrian army and the

Hungarian government moved to Debrecen while fighting continued. By the spring of 1849, the Hungarian troops had the upper hand.

Emperor Franz Joseph appealed to the Tsar of Russia for help. With Russian troops, the rebellion was quickly, and brutally, crushed, and Kossuth fled to Turkey. Petőfi was killed on a battlefield in Transylvania. The Hungarian generals were executed, an event celebrated by Austrian officers clinking beer glasses, a custom that was socially taboo in Hungary until the late 20th century.

THE BUILDING OF BUDAPEST

With the crushing of the rebellion, Hungarian prisoners had to construct an Austrian military redoubt, the Citadella, atop Gellért Hill. Its guns were intended to deter any future Hungarian attempts to dislodge Habsburg power.

The Austrians' military defeat in Italy in 1859, however, made accommodation with the Magyars a political necessity. In Pest, the remnants of the Liberal Party coalesced around Ferenc Deák, who published a basis for reconciliation with the Austrians in 1865. The *Ausgleich*, or Compromise, of 1867 made Hungary more like an equal partner in the Habsburg Empire. Austria-Hungary was to be a single entity with two governments and two parliaments, although ruled by Habsburg royalty, who would recognise the legitimacy of the crown of St Stephen. For the first time since 1526, Hungarians were again rulers of modern-day Slovakia, Transylvania, northern Serbia and northern Croatia as far as the Adriatic.

The year 1867 also saw a law guaranteeing civic and legal equality to Jews, whose status was unique in the region. Many arrived from Poland and Russia, their know-how driving on industry and construction. This half-century until World War I is known as the Golden Age. Buda, Óbuda and Pest were officially united as Budapest in 1873. Pest boomed with urban development projects, such as Andrássy út and the Nagykörút, which linked once separate districts. Pest became the hub of a rail system bringing many in from the country. Even today, Hungarians refer to Budapest simply as '*Pest*'.

Landowners deserted the countryside to man the vast bureaucracy needed to administer the state-run railway, schools, hospitals and post service. The city's population rose from 280,000 in 1867 to almost a million in 1914; by 1900 Budapest was the sixth largest city in Europe. The language of administration was Hungarian. The boom came with the Magyarisation policies of Prime Minister Kálmán Tisza (1875-90). He feared the Austrians could endanger Hungary's newly strengthened position by finding leverage among the non-Hungarian minorities

Budapest's **Basilica** was one of the landmark architectural projects of the Golden Age.

of the empire, just as in 1848. His response was a programme to assimilate the assorted Croats, Slovaks and Romanians of the Hungarian realm. He declared that all schools would have to teach in Hungarian, and attempts were made to make Magyar the language of the churches. The policy laid the groundwork for the minority unrest that would cost Hungary dear in 1918 and still festers among Hungary's neighbours. Hungarian became the linguistic ticket to success in Budapest. A lively cultural life began to flourish, as artists, writers and politicians exchanged ideas in the coffeehouses of Pest.

THE GOLDEN AGE

Emperor Franz Joseph, on the 25th anniversary of the 1867 agreement, decreed that Budapest was to be a capital equal to that of Vienna. The city became the focus of a new sense of national pride and, to mark the millennial anniversary of Árpád's invasion, a huge fair was planned.

The celebration in the City Park incorporated continental Europe's first underground railway, which ran to a gargantuan memorial to Árpád and his chieftains. An exhibition hall was built and today houses the Agriculture Museum. Nearby, at the Wampetics Gardens, famous chef Károly Gundel prepared traditional cuisine with French flair. Hungarian food became the culinary fad of the new century.

It was also the golden age of Hungarian literature and arts. Mór Jókai was one of the most widely translated novelists in the world. Endre Ady's volume of new poetry, *Új versek*, sparked a veritable literary explosion. Béla Bartók and Zoltán Kodály created the study of ethnomusicology, composing masterpieces of modern music based on Magyar folk traditions, while architects such as Ödön Lechner drew on Magyar motifs for the art nouveau buildings sprouting up around the city. Budapest was also at the forefront of cinema and photography, and became the in-spot for the holidaymaking aristocracy of Europe.

The new Parliament building, opened in 1902, was the largest in the world, naively anticipating a long and prosperous rule. Politics, however, began to take an ominous turn. Working-class unrest first asserted itself in the great May Day demonstration of 1890, and its influence grew over the next decade. Ageing Liberals were challenged by newer right-wing elements who introduced Austrian-influenced anti-Semitism, previously alien to Hungarian life, into political dialogue. Meanwhile, Hungary's high-handed administration of non-Magyars fuelled resentment and nationalism. Slavs and Romanians headed in droves for Paris or America, where their modest political voice could be heard. To the south, the idea of a South Slav ('Yugoslav') nation gained credence. The vast edifice of the revived Hungarian kingdom rested on rotten foundations.

After the assassination of Archduke Franz Ferdinand in Sarajevo, Austria-Hungary gave Serbia the ultimatum that would make World War I inevitable. Budapest, initially opposed to the ultimatum, changed tack when Germany supported Austria-Hungary. Although no fighting took place on its soil, Hungary suffered enormously. Rampant inflation, food shortages and high casualities among the 3.5 million soldiers sent to fight brought the nation to its knees. Worse was to follow.

COLLAPSE AND DIVISION

As World War I came to an end, so did the Austro-Hungarian Empire. When Hungary declared its independence as a republic on 16 November 1918, the country was faced with unsympathetic neighbours aligned with France. No clear lines existed at the border, policed by Serbian and Romanian troops from the 'Little Entente', masterminded by Czech foreign minister Edvard Beneš and supported by France. At the post-war negotiations outside Paris, Hungarian diplomatic efforts fell on deaf ears. Hungary's poor treatment of minorities was a perfectly good argument for ethnic self-determination, the guiding principle behind the redrawing of Europe.

On 21 March 1919 the Hungarian Soviet Republic was declared by Béla Kun, who formed a Red Army and sent emissaries to the new Soviet Union. Moscow did nothing in response. Czech and Romanian armed forces entered a Hungary in chaos. As severe food shortages swept the nation, the Romanian army occupied Budapest on 3 August 1919. Kun and his ministers fled, most of them never to return.

Admiral Miklós Horthy entered Budapest at the head of 25,000 Hungarian troops. The weeks that followed were known as the 'White Terror', as Communists and Jews were killed for their collaboration, real or otherwise, with the Kun regime. On 25 January 1920 Hungarian national elections brought in a Christian-right coalition parliament, with Admiral Horthy as regent. Hungary was now a monarchy without a king, led by an admiral without a navy.

On 4 June 1920 the Treaty of Trianon was signed at Versailles. Hungary lost 72 per cent of its territory and a third of its native population. Refugees clogged Budapest, unemployment raged and the economy came to a virtual standstill. *See p19* **The terrible treaty**.

A new political coalition came to power under Count Gábor Bethlen, a skilful conservative. He kept left and right in check

and worked abroad to gain international credit and sympathy. Budapest continued to be the focus of national development. Financial stability returned, although after the crash of 1929, labour discontent rose, Bethlen resigned and Horthy appointed right-wing Gyula Gömbös as prime minister. His anti-Semitic appeals became more and more the accepted political tone.

Budapest between the wars was not quite as dark as its politics. During this so-called Silver Age, Hungary's spas and casinos became the playground of high society. The coffeehouses still provided the base for an active literary clique. Avant-gardists grouped around Lajos Kassák and his Bauhaus-influenced journal *Ma* (*Today*), while the theatre and cinema boomed. Hollywood moguls swarmed into Budapest to sign up actors, directors and cinematographers.

But society was coming apart. The Jews were the first to feel the change when access to higher education and certain professions was curtailed under the Numerus Clausus law in 1928. Gömbös dreamed of a fascist Hungarian-Italian-German 'axis' (his term), and worked to bring Hungary closer to Nazi Germany in the hope of reversing Trianon. German investment gained influential friends and Oktogon was renamed Mussolini tér. The second Vienna Award in 1938 returned a part of Slovakia to Hungary, and in 1940 Hungary was awarded most of Transylvania. Artists and intellectuals fled to Paris and America.

NO WAY OUT

When war began, all was not rosy between the Hungarians and the Germans. Gömbös had died and the new prime minister, Count Pál Teleki, who mistrusted the Nazis, worked to keep Hungary out of combat, resisting German demands for the deportation of Jews. When Hungary invaded Yugoslavia with the Germans in 1941, Teleki, an Anglophile of the old school, did the noble thing and committed suicide.

Hungary's participation on the Russian front was disastrous. The Russians wiped out the entire Hungarian second army in January 1943, effectively ending Hungary's involvement in the war. German troops entered Hungary in March 1944. Officials resisted German demands for more Jewish deportations, but that became harder when Adolf Eichmann moved his SS headquarters to Buda. Jews were herded into the Ghetto in District VII, while the nearby Astoria hotel served as Nazi headquarters.

In October 1944 Admiral Horthy made a speech calling for an armistice. The SS responded by kidnapping his son. After Horthy had been ousted, German troops occupied Buda Castle. The Nazi puppet Ferenc Szálasi and his

The terrible treaty

The Trianon treaty, signed at Versailles on 4 June 1920, set in ink the borders of the new Hungarian Republic after the collapse of the Austro-Hungarian Empire. Hungary was reduced by almost three-quarters. Hungarians to this day feel that they were singled out for the most punitive treatment.

As World War I ended, the victors (France, the USA and Great Britain) set up treaty commissions to deal with the peace settlements. Hungary was widely believed to have been one of the root causes of the war. Since 1867, Hungary had controlled much of the Carpathian basin with a repressive policy of forced Magyar education and bureaucracy that caused deep resentment among ethnic groups. Point ten of President Wilson's programme called for autonomy for the peoples of Austro-Hungary but not for its outright dismemberment as a political entity. Even so, Czechoslovakia declared its independence on 26 October 1918; the South Slavs, Yugoslavia, quickly followed.

When Hungary declared its independence as a republic on 16 November 1918, no clear demarcation existed at the borders, defined by the ceasefire lines. Troops of the 'Little Entente' supported by France – Serbs, Czechs and Romanians – camped at frontier towns.

In Paris, the peacemakers were resolved to uphold promises made to bring Romania into the war. The French were intent on taking strategic rail lines out of Hungarian hands. The Magyar towns of Szatmár (Satu Mare), Nagyvárad (Oradea) and Temesvár (Timisoara) were all on a major line. The charming British-born Queen Marie of Romania also lobbied for the Romanian cause. The Treaty Commission soon assigned Romania land in the Banat, Bukovina, Bessarabia and Transylvania.

Under the new administration of Prime Minister Mihály Károlyi, Hungarians refused to accept that the dissolution of the Austro-Hungarian Empire should affect the historical notion that the nation of Hungary comprised the Carpathian basin. When the Allies showed their resolve to give two-thirds of Hungary's territory to neighbouring states, Károlyi resigned and the Communists took over.

After their short, disastrous rule, and takeover by Admiral Miklós Horthy, Hungary was invited to Versailles on 1 December 1919. It sent a delegation in January 1920 after elections confirming Horthy as regent.

It was already too late, the de facto borders all but set. The Little Entente lobby prevailed over an ailing Wilson (and Lloyd George), who vainly argued for a fairer decision. Hungarian delegates Count Apponyi, István Bethlen and Pál Teleki walked out on 4 June, having failed to turn the tide. The treaty was signed on behalf of Hungary that day by Labour Minister Ágost Bénárd and envoy Alfréd Drasche-Lázár. These are the borders still in place today.

Budapest **1956**. *See p21.*

fascist Arrow Cross Party took control of Hungary. Extra trains were put on to take Budapest's Jews to Auschwitz. Arrow Cross thugs raided the ghettos, marched Jews to the Danube and shot them. Many survivors owed their lives to Raoul Wallenberg, a Swedish diplomat posted in Budapest. He had safe houses set up and issued fake Swedish passports. He negotiated with German officers and pulled Jews off trains bound for Auschwitz. When the Soviets surrounded Pest, Wallenberg drove to meet them. He was never seen again. Moscow claimed he died in 1947, but Gulag survivors reported seeing him in the 1970s. Two memorials stand to him in Budapest.

The Russians closed in on Budapest, and Allied bombing levelled industrial Angyalföld and Zugló in Pest. The Germans made a last-ditch stand in November 1944. Citizens were caught in the crossfire of an artillery battle that lasted months, killing many more civilians than combatants. The Russians advanced in bloody door-to-door fighting – bullet holes can still be seen on some Pest buildings. By the time the Russians took control of Pest – raping as they went – the Nazis had entrenched themselves around Castle Hill. While Russian tanks could easily control Pest's boulevards, the fighting in Buda's twisting, medieval streets was hellish.

When the Germans finally surrendered on 4 April 1945, and the citizens emerged from their cellars, the castle was in ruins, and not one bridge was left standing over the Danube.

SOVIET SOCIETY
Rebuilding the capital would occupy its citizens for 30 years. The task of restoring order fell to the Soviet military government, which placed loyal Hungarian Communists in all positions of power. Nevertheless, the election of November 1945 was won by the Smallholders, the only legitimate pre-war political party still in existence. Even with blatant vote-rigging, the Communists only garnered 17 per cent, but Soviets insisted they remain in power. The monarchy was abolished and a Hungarian Republic proclaimed. Two weeks later the Paris Peace treaty was signed, compounding the loss of land under Trianon by granting a slice of eastern Hungary to the USSR. Communist authorities controlling the Interior Ministry set up a secret police force, the ÁVH (later ÁVO), run by László Rajk, to root out dissent. Many were picked up off the streets, sent to the Soviet Union and never heard from again.

Changes in the social fabric of Budapest were also part of post-war city planning. Budapest neighbourhoods lost some of their social identity as the Communists tried to homogenise areas in the pursuit of a classless society. Flats went to whoever the local council chose. Schools and factories were nationalised. A plan was put forward to collectivise landholdings, neutralising the Smallholders' Party. The Communist hold on Hungary was complete.

In 1949 the scales of power tipped in favour of Moscow loyalists, led by Mátyás Rákosi. Old-time party members – among them László Rajk – were tried as spies and executed. Rákosi fostered a cult of personality. By the early 1950s Hungary was one of the dimmest lights along the Iron Curtain. Informers were everywhere, classic Hungarian books were banned, church leaders imprisoned and middle-class families persecuted as class enemies.

A brief respite came with Stalin's death in 1953. Rákosi was removed from office and replaced with Imre Nagy, a more humane communist with a sense of sympathy for Hungarian national ideals. It didn't last long. Rákosi, backed by Moscow, accused Nagy of 'deviationism' and came back into power in 1955.

ARISE, HUNGARIANS

In June 1956 intellectuals began to criticise the Rákosi regime, using the forum of the Petőfi Writers' Circle for unprecedented free debate. The Kremlin, now led by Khrushchev, recalled Rákosi to Moscow 'for health reasons', but replaced him with the equally despicable Ernő Gerő. The breaking point came in October.

The Uprising that erupted on Tuesday 23 October had been brewing but wasn't planned. Students had gathered at Petőfi tér and at the statue of the 1848 Polish General Bem to express solidarity with reforms in Poland and to demand change in Hungary. Thousands of workers joined in. An angry crowd pulled down a statue of Stalin near the City Park. Others gathered at the radio building on Bródy Sándor utca to broadcast their demands. The ÁVH began shooting from the roof. Police and soldiers then attacked the ÁVH, and fighting broke out. The Uprising had begun.

In response, Imre Nagy was reinstated as prime minister. Addressing a crowd of 200,000 outside Parliament, he gave a cautious speech that didn't curtail the rising tide. Fighting continued, political prisoners were freed and General Maléter pledged army loyalty to the new government. Confusion reigned. Nagy dithered. Moscow dithered. Nagy declined Soviet help and called the Uprising 'democratic'. Soviet troops pulled out of Hungary.

For the next five days Hungary floated in the euphoria of liberation. Daily life assumed a kind of normality and Radio Free Europe promised Western aid.

With the distraction of the Suez Canal crisis, Moscow retaliated. On 1 November Soviet forces entered Hungary. General Maléter was arrested, sidelining the army, and Soviet tanks re-entered Budapest. Civilians defended gallantly at the Kilián barracks at Üllői út and the Corvin passage nearby. In Buda, students spread oil on the cobbled streets and pulled grenades on strings underneath the stalled tanks. Resistance proved futile. Nagy took refuge in the Yugoslav embassy, but was later handed over to the Soviets. Thousands were sent to prison and 200,000 fled Hungary. Nagy was executed in secret in 1958 and buried in a hidden grave at Plot 301 of Új köztemető.

GOULASH COMMUNISM

The stranglehold that followed the suppression of the 1956 Uprising lasted until the 1960s, when amnesties were granted and János Kádár, the new man installed by the Soviet Union, began a policy of reconciliation. His was a tricky balancing act between hard-line Communism and appeasing the population. Abroad, Hungary maintained a strong Cold War stance and toed the Moscow line; at home, Hungarians enjoyed a higher standard of living than most of Soviet Eastern Europe. Life under Kádár meant food in the shops but censorship and 'psychological hospital' for dissenters. By the 1960s, the aftermath of World War II and 1956 had been cleared away. Historic buildings were restored, museums replaced ministerial buildings in Buda. Tourism began to grow, although Western visitors were still followed around by government spies after dinner.

Kádár's balancing act reached giddy heights in 1968. When Czechoslovakia irked the Soviets with the reforms of the Prague Spring, Hungarian troops loyally participated in the invasion. At the same time, Kádár introduced his 'New Economic Mechanism', a radical new economic reform that broke with previous hard-line Communist theory and laid the ground for modest entrepreneurship.

By the 1980s flaws in 'Goulash Communism' grew harder to ignore. Hungary became more dependent on foreign trade and inflation rose. Hungary's relationship with its Warsaw Pact neighbours was beginning to show signs of strain. A number of writers started to test the limits of open criticism, and Hungary became the centre of Eastern Europe's boom in banned *samizdat* literature. Younger party members began to take positions of power. Known as the 'Miskolc Mafia', after the town where they'd begun their political careers, many, such as Prime Minister Károly Grósz and his successor Miklós Németh, openly tolerated debate and 'market Socialism'.

The summer of '89

All over Eastern Europe the phrase 'Since The Changes' alludes to the birth of a new era 20 years ago. To be in Budapest in the summer of 1989 was to be at the centre of the revolution, sitting in the box seats of a historical arena watching the final play of a great game begun in 1945. Everyone knew the Soviet empire was collapsing. Nobody, however, quite knew what would replace it.

During the 1980s there had been loud whispers within Hungary's Communist Party of the need for reform. Economic liberalisation and measured privatisation in the 1980s had been introduced. *Samizdat* journals became so commonplace that they were no longer banned – one popular contributor was current Budapest mayor Gábor Demszky. It was a common sight to see plaster-spattered proletarian workers chugging beers while poring over the latest literary reviews from long-exiled Hungarian poets like George Faludy.

Starting in May 1989, events began rapidly tumbling towards a momentous summer. Reform-minded party members, locked into

an ideological battle with hardliners, declared that political parties could be formed to discuss the possibility of free elections. In June 250,000 people gathered in Budapest's Heroes' Square to rebury the remains of Imre Nagy, the hero of the 1956 Uprising. One of the most reform-minded members of the government was foreign minister Gyula Horn, who was manoeuvring for more open diplomatic relations between neighbours Hungary and Austria.

Teetering at the brink of a capitalism they barely understood, Hungarians spent the seminal summer of 1989 clutching a newspaper in one hand and a wad of black-market Deutsche Marks in the other. As travel restrictions eased, the sleepy Austrian border town of Nickelsdorf became a riotous traffic jam of consumerism, as Hungarians flooded over to buy Western televisions, refrigerators and jeans. Previously forbidden pornographic magazines flooded news kiosks. Casinos, previously open only to foreign tourists, now tempted Hungarians to learn how fast a fortune could be made – and lost.

The average worker's wage was about US$60 a month, with the currency stable at Ft47 to the dollar. A black market in western currencies flourished. Bread cost Ft1, beer Ft6. Dinner out with too much wine could be had downtown for about $1.30. Ft100 was easily enough for a wild weekend, a punk concert at famed dive the Blue Box to hear Nagy Ferö and his band Beatrice or bizarre genius Vaszlavik Petőfi Gazember – both now ageing right-wing icons. Foreign residents were still rare – there was a modest number of native-speaking English teachers in Budapest at the time. Most knew each other from drinking at the Fregatt Pub in Molnár utca.

Gaps appeared in the barbed wire at the Austrian border. East Germans, sensing a change in the air and able to travel freely to Hungary, flocked south 'on holiday'. So many crammed into the West German embassy in Budapest seeking asylum, the building was forced to close. Locals, always delighted to cock a snook at the Communists, would wait at train stations to offer the 'holidaymakers' home stays, taxi drivers offered free rides to the borders and those who had nowhere else to go would sleep out on Margaret Island and party with the local womenfolk. The authorities housed 'German guests' at the Young Communist Summer Camp in the Buda Hills. 'Picnics' were held near the border and East Germans sneaked over after nightfall.

By the third week of August, so great was the mass movement that Horn successfully arranged for a ceremonially snipping of the border with his Austrian counterpart, Alois Mock (*pictured*). The line dividing Hungary and Austria, East and West, was no more. It was as significant, if not as sexy, as the fall of the Berlin Wall.

1989 was a charmed moment, filled with promise and possibility. As autumn approached, everyone realised that the changes would not be crushed by Soviet tanks. The Germans left, the Berlin Wall fell, Romania erupted in violent revolution. The government allowed free elections. Almost as quickly, the euphoria gave way to privatisation, the 'Wild East' economic development and corruption of the early 1990s – and the same old politicians.

THE FIRST DOMINO

With the opening of the border with Austria, Hungary tipped over the first domino, bringing about the collapse of Communism in Eastern Europe. (*See left* **The summer of '89**.) The Communist Party changed its name to the Hungarian Socialist Party and declared that it was running in the elections.

All talk was focused on new-found freedoms, democracy and market capitalism. Many were quick to position themselves in the emerging economic picture. Others found themselves confused by yet another upheaval in history. The elections of March 1990 brought in a coalition led by the Hungarian Democratic Forum (MDF), a mixed bag of nationalist and conservative views. The 'change of system' (*rendszerváltás*) saw the face of Budapest change as new businesses opened and the city's classy old neon disappear. Street names were changed. Lenin Boulevard and Marx Square were no longer, and their respective statues and monuments were removed out to Statue Park. A law forbade public display of 'symbols of tyranny', such as red stars or swastikas.

Many found opportunities working in Western businesses. But the boom didn't materialise. Unemployment rose as state industries were privatised or shut down, inflation ruined savings and incomes, and people were made homeless. For many, the standard of living dropped below pre-1989 levels, when prices had been fixed and services subsidised by the state.

BITTER PILL, BITTER POLITICS

Nostalgia for more stable and affordable times helped the 1994 election triumph of the Socialist Party, led by Gyula Horn, the man who, as Communist foreign minister, had opened the borders in 1989. The Socialists, along with their coalition partners the Free Democrats, prescribed belt-tightening: more privatisation and devaluations of the local forint. They slashed social funding and hiked energy prices to set Hungary up for EU membership.

Foreign investors loved it, and the revived Budapest stock exchange enjoyed two years as the world's fastest growing stock market. As the currency and the banks were stabilised, many companies made Budapest their regional centre. Shiny office blocks and business centres, rendered less obnoxious by height restrictions, settled among their crusty brick-and-plaster elders. New malls finished off the corner shop.

Hungarians, particularly those in the countryside, baulked. In 1998, voters turned to a third party, the Young Democrats (FIDESZ), founded and led by the charismatic Viktor Orbán. Born out of a late-1980s student activist group, this party initially adopted a liberal stance, then swung right as the Democratic Forum splintered. The change was marked by the addition of 'Hungarian Middle Class Party' to the official moniker. Orbán began promoting pre-war Christian-national values, taking the crown of St Stephen out of the National Museum, floating it up the Danube for a consecration ceremony in Esztergom Cathedral, then installing it in Parliament. Relations between state and city reached a nadir, as cosmopolitan Budapest was viewed as 'non-Magyar', just as it had been a century earlier.

> **'Hungary joined the EU on 1 May 2004, a change that brought some stability to Hungary's economic affairs. It could not stabilise Hungarian politics.'**

FIDESZ reordered the political landscape in stark bipolar terms, bringing a new level of bitterness to debate ahead of the 2002 elections. The divisive strategy backfired, and voters reinstated the Socialists, under the leadership of Prime Minister Péter Medgyessy, a former banker and finance minister in the old regime. He was in charge when Hungary joined the European Union on 1 May 2004, a change that brought some stability to Hungary's economic affairs. It could not stabilise Hungarian politics. After the revelation that he had worked as a counterespionage agent for the Communist-era Ministry for Internal Affairs, Medgyessy was forced out in August 2004. He was replaced by Ferenc Gyurcsány, a former Young Communist turned billionaire. Socialists hoped that one of the richest people in Hungary would have the appeal needed to win the 2006 elections.

FIDESZ suffered a setback in December 2004 when the public did not support its referendum to give citizenship to people with Hungarian ancestry who were born beyond Hungary's borders. Still, by 2005, FIDESZ was ahead in popularity polls, and it seemed likely that the April 2006 elections would bring another change of regime. Despite FIDESZ gaining a slim majority in the first round, the Socialists surprised everyone by narrowly winning the second. They entered into a coalition with the liberal Alliance of Free Democrats (SZDSZ) and proceeded to plan public sector and welfare reform along Blairite lines. Faced with a grave foreign debt and trade deficit levels, and a deeply polarised electorate, the government's hand is always tied by EU and IMF demands for frugality.

RED, WHITE AND GREEN RIOT

The salami hit the fan in September 2006, when a private speech given in May by Gyurcsány to party members was leaked to the press. In his frank talk, Gyurcsány admitted that the party had 'screwed up', and that they had 'lied morning, noon and night' about policy in order to win a second term. Peaceful demonstrations became ugly almost overnight, resulting in by far the worst violence Hungary had seen since 1989. Right-wing football fans and bruisers joined forces to attack the Hungarian State TV headquarters. Mayhem hit the streets of Budapest and other cities. Demonstrators called for Gyurcsány's resignation and a fresh round of national elections. President László Solyom's appeals for unity disappointed those on the right who had hoped he would throw his lot in against Gyurcsány.

The Socialists got a sound beating at the October municipal elections, but Gyurcsány, whose paper coffin took pride of place at the protestors' tents outside Parliament, won a parliamentary vote of confidence on 6 October. Downtown was cleared for the official commemorations of the 1956 Uprising on 23 October, which passed without incident until the last visiting dignitaries had left the area. Earlier that day, protestors had commandeered a tank conveniently on display outside Mayor Demszky's offices, and chugged off down the streets around Deák tér until they ran out of petrol. This was not a revolution, but it was televised: every single minute of the violence has been photographed, videoed and blogged.

Orbán, who had not endorsed the riots, led FIDESZ supporters in mass rallies and candlelit vigils on 4 November, the anniversary of the invasion of the Soviet troops. The planned occupation of central Budapest by farmers in a caravan of tractors failed to materialise. Although order was restored, tensions did not dissipate. Gyurcsány's government set in motion plans to introduce university tuition fees and selected health service charges, both unpopular. The seriously peeved are never far from a national holiday on which to take to the streets: the anniversary of the 1848 revolution on 15 March 2007 provided such an occasion. The security cordon at Kossuth tér was dismantled in person on 19 March by Viktor Orbán and other FIDESZ dignitaries, citing re-enactment of the demolition of the Berlin Wall in 1989.

For the next couple of years at least, it looks as if national holidays (15 March, 20 August, 23 October, 4 November) are going to be highly stressful flashpoints that can easily produce gridlock and public disorder on the streets of central Budapest.

Key events

c1000 BC Celtic tribes inhabit Danube Basin.
c500 BC Proto-Hungarians begin migration.
35 BC Romans conquer Pannonia.
6 AD Pannonians rebel against Romans.
430-52 Huns make Hungary their base for European excursions.
700-850 Hungarians serve as vassals of the Khazar Empire in southern Russia.
895 King Árpád leads Hungarians across Carpathians into the Danube Basin.
955 King Otto I of Bavaria defeats Hungarians at Augsburg, ending period of Hungarian raids.
972 King Géza and his son Vajk convert to Christianity.
1000 Vajk enthroned as King István (Stephen) with a crown donated by the Pope.
1006 Revolt of pagan Hungarian leaders.
1066 First written example of Hungarian.
1222 'Golden Bull' signed by nobles at Rákos meadow, defining the Hungarian nation.
1241 Mongol invasion.
1243 King Béla IV decrees the building of fortified towns. Buda gains in importance.
1301 House of Árpád ends.
1396 Hungarians defeated by Ottoman Turks at Nicopolis.
1456 Hunyadi defeats Turks at Belgrade.
1458 Hunyadi's son Mátyás crowned King of Hungary. Buda's first 'Golden Age'.
1490 King Mátyás dies, leading to chaos between nobles and peasants.
1514 Peasants revolt, unsuccessfully. Peasantry reduced to serfdom.
1526 Turks led by Suliman the Magnificent defeat Hungarians at Mohács, then burn Buda.
1541 Buda occupied by Turks.
1683 Turks defeated at Siege of Vienna.
1686 Habsburgs defeat Turks at Siege of Buda. Buda destroyed.
1699 Turks relinquish claims to Hungary.
1703 Hungarians led by Ferenc Rákóczi rebel unsuccessfully against the Austrians.
1723 Habsburgs claim right to rule Hungary.
1808 The Embellishment Act sets guidelines for the urban development of Buda and Pest.
1839-49 Construction of the Chain Bridge.
1848 Hungarians rebel unsuccessfully.
1867 *Ausgleich* signed, uniting Austria and Hungary as imperial equals.
1873 Pest, Buda, Óbuda united as Budapest.
1896 Budapest hosts Millennial Exhibition.
1914 Austria-Hungary enters World War I.
1918 Austria-Hungary loses World War I. Hungary declares independence from Austria.

1919 Shortlived Soviet Republic under Béla Kun. Romanian army occupies Budapest. Return of Admiral Horthy.
1920 Treaty of Trianon is signed. Hungary loses two-thirds of its territory.
1938 Hungary, allied with Nazi Germany, receives a part of Slovakia under the second Vienna Award.
1940 Hungary awarded most of Transylvania. Troops assist Nazi invasion of Yugoslavia.
1943 Hungarian army defeated by Russians.
1944 Horthy ousted. Jews murdered and deported by Arrow Cross Party.
1945 Red Army captures Budapest.
1946 Hungarian monarchy abolished and a Hungarian People's Republic declared.
1948 Land ownership collectivised.
1949 Mátyás Rákosi, Communist chief, executes other Communist Party leaders.
1953 Stalin dies. Rákosi replaced by Imre Nagy, then by Ernő Gerő.
1956 Hungarians revolt against Soviet occupation. Hungarian Socialist State proclaimed by Imre Nagy, but Russian tanks move in. János Kádár placed in power.
1963 Kádár declares a partial amnesty for those jailed for their role in the 1956 revolt.
1968 Hungary aids Russia in crushing the Prague Spring. Kádár institutes his 'New Economic Mechanism'.
1989 Kádár dies. Reform Communists promise free elections. East Germans flee via Hungary. Communist Party is defunct.
1990 Hungarian elections elect conservative government headed by Hungarian Democratic Forum (MDF). Hungary is declared a Republic.
1994 Socialist Party trounces MDF in the second democratic election. Gyula Horn is named prime minister.
1998 Elections replace Socialists with FIDESZ-led coalition. Viktor Orbán is new PM.
1999 Hungary joins NATO.
2002 Bitter election run-offs see Socialists return to power under Péter Medgyessy.
2004 Celebrations to mark EU accession on 1 May. Megyessy forced out of office. Ferenc Gyurcsány becomes Prime Minister.
2006 Narrow win for the Socialists at the elections. A private speech by Gyurcsány to colleagues that his party had 'lied morning, noon and night' to win the vote is leaked. Protests in Budapest and other towns.
2007 Another public demonstration on Revolution Day, 15 March.

Millenáris Park.

Budapest Today

Flawed masterpiece overseen by a five-time mayor.

Budapest is home to 2.2 million people, nearly a quarter of Hungary's population. It is the seat of government, the civil service and the judiciary, the focal point of mass media, the hub of the national transport system and the driving force behind the country's economy. It's a modern, cosmopolitan city, an EU capital complete with all the trappings of globalisation. It's a city of high culture, a party town and a metropolis of 23 heterogeneous districts. It's stunning and scruffy at the same time – here 19th-century buildings nestle up to 1920s Bauhaus design. Filling the cavities are the façades of modern-day capitalism.

Yet, no matter how strong the forces of modernisation, history is always with you in Budapest, the city at the core of the collapse of the Habsburg and Soviet empires, and with unenviable front row seats for the rise and fall of the Third Reich. Go further back and the city was also at the sharp end when the Ottomans crumbled. This is a place where history is so close you can put your finger in the bullet holes.

A century after the great building boom driven by the Hungarian Millennial celebrations of 1896, the wealthy travellers are back and well catered for at superbly renovated five-star landmarks of the Habsburg era – the Corinthia Grand Hotel Royal, the Gresham Palace and the New York Palace. Spa hotels abound, as do high-end restaurants and grand coffeehouses.

It's not just the wealthy that are enjoying reborn Budapest. Since 2005, budget airlines have made Budapest an easy and affordable destination for all. In 2006, over 2.5 million people visited Budapest, including 250,000 from the UK, behind those from Germany and the US. This is compared to 100,000 UK visitors in 1999. Budapest is back on the radar. Three- and four-star hotels are opening all over Pest, and there's a thriving trade in rented apartments. A significant number of visitors come back to buy flats in the city, particularly Irish and Brits.

This transformation has not come without a social cost. A trip from verdant, affluent Rószadomb in Buda down to District VIII

Meet the mayor

It is impossible to separate the story of modern Budapest from that of Gábor Demszky. Elected in 1990 as the first mayor of the post-Communist city, he is the longest-serving incumbent of any European capital. And while he has many vociferous critics – locals routinely shout his name in vain when stuck in a traffic jam – it's his name on the ballot paper that they have ticked with near clockwork regularity. Demszky has all but ruled out running in 2010, preferring instead to concentrate on the job in hand. 'Of course I would like Budapest to remain a liberal city after 2010,' he says, partly referring to his political party, the SZDSZ Liberals, 'but my biggest concern today is to make these upcoming years in office successful'.

Demszky was speaking after his narrow win at the 2006 polls, during the time of a heavy right-wing backlash against perceived Socialist corruption, and riots on the streets. It was his fifth consecutive victory.

Born on 4 August 1952 in Budapest, the son of two economists, Demszky became a leading figure in Hungary's political underground in the late 1970s and 1980s. His politics first landed him in trouble with the authorities in 1972 when he was suspended from his law studies at ELTE University for 'participating in political conspiracy', a year he spent driving a taxi and working as a librarian. In 1979, as a founding member of a fund for the poor and signatory of a declaration supporting Václav Havel's Charter 77 movement, he earned himself a ban on foreign travel and any further publishing. Unbowed, from 1981 he was instrumental in writing, publishing and disseminating samizdat material, an activity that in 1983 led to a six-month suspended jail sentence. As Hungary's Socialist leadership softened, in 1988 Demszky emerged from the underground to co-found the Association of Free Democrats (SZDSZ), a coalition partner in the current government.

Urbane, intelligent and immediately recognisable by any Hungarian with even the shakiest grip of current affairs, this avowed liberal has overseen much of Budapest's recent civic improvements: 'I consider Budapest as not only the capital of Hungary but also the cultural, economic and financial capital of the region as a whole. We must keep developing the city's infrastructure and continue with the renovation work so that Budapest can stay a truly great European capital'. His pride is almost tangible.

Memorably, in a televised debate in the run-up to the 2006 elections, Demszky outpointed a rival by asking him to state the cost of a ticket on the Budapest metro. He could not. Public transport has always been a major concern. Some 60 per cent of the population and its suburbs travel on the system on a daily basis, one of the highest usage rates in Europe. 'The city desperately needs the fourth metro line,' says Demszky, suggesting that not only will it get the often gridlocked city moving again, but will lower air pollution by reducing traffic jams. Preparatory work is also under way on a fifth line, to connect the south-east suburban railway station on Csepel island to Szentendre station way up in the north-west.

While committed to a frenetic building programme underground, Demszky has visions of traffic-free calm above ground: 'In the long run, I think that the real solution is to make downtown pedestrianised. One of the aims of 'The Heart of the City' programme is to give back the city centre to pedestrians and increase green space'.

Promotion and support of culture have also been paramount. 'We work hard to make Budapest one of the most exciting and diverse cities in Europe,' he says, naming the City's sponsorship of the **Budapest Festival Orchestra** as a particular highlight. He also mentions the **Budapest Spring Festival** (*see p156*) and the **Sziget festival** (*see p159* **Budapest's biggest bash**) as events the city is more than happy to fund. 'In 2011 Hungary is going to hold the EU presidency. Our aim is to make Budapest the capital of Europe, and culture will definitely play an important role.'

Asked to name his greatest achievements, Demszky is quick to note that he still has time to add to them, but says environmental projects are closest to his heart. 'It may not be spectacular, but the Budapest Central Sewage Works, when ready in 2010, will mean that the Danube will no longer only be blue in Strauss' waltz. We can finally give back the river to whom it belongs: Budapesters.' New parks and housing renovations – on which the municipality spends some Ft1.2 billion a year – are further notable accomplishments.

in Pest, a distance of no more than five miles, will give you a vivid illustration of the increasing gap between rich and poor, between those who caught the bus to the EU and modernity and those left clutching an out-of-date ticket. Your ride, though, will be courtesy of one of the best, cheapest and most integrated public transport systems in the world, and with little risk of street crime en route.

As radical as the changes have been since 1989, Budapest has lost much of its dynamism. In the last century, Budapest produced giants in the worlds of science, mathematics, music, cinema, photography, sport and literature. Today, the city's main contribution to the world of entertainment is hard-core pornography. Much of Budapest's 20th-century creativity was borne out of hardship and necessity. Many figures were victims of political or religious persecution. These same factors no longer apply. There is a sense that Budapest's future looks far more bland than its past.

Today, people simply want to live in a tranquil and affluent European city. As a leading cultural commentator wrote in leading daily *Népszabadság* at the time of the 2006 riots, all Hungary and Hungarians really wanted was to be 'normal'.

BACK TO THE FUTURE

For all the political instability of the last ten years, Budapest has had one constant: Gábor Demszky, a dissident of the 1980s and mayor of the city since 1990. *See p27* **Meet the mayor**. Under Demszky, fiscal discipline, long-term planning and intelligent financing have delivered a steady stream of public works projects. New water mains, tram tracks and road reconstruction projects have been completed, and two new bridges span the Danube. Downtown areas have been zoned free of traffic, adding energy and commerce to sleepy neighbourhoods. Town hall politics are as grubby in Budapest as elsewhere, but Demszky is perceived to be above the bickering. But even he was not able to do anything about the four-year delay in starting Budapest's fourth metro line after the centre-right won national elections in 1998. The new line linking south-west Buda to north-east Pest will be completed by 2010. Plans for a fifth are also well advanced as is a direct rail connection to Ferihegy airport. Budapest is gunning for the right to stage the 2020 Olympic Games. Locals had hopes of hosting football's 2012 European Championships, but the vote in April 2007 went to Poland and the Ukraine.

Improvements to the transport infrastructure have not run smoothly as smoothly as expected either. New Siemens Combino trams were

Downtown Budapest, rats and all.

supplied to the city at a cost of Ft36 billion to run on the nos.4/6 route along the Nagykörút, but a combination of design faults and a failure to upgrade the electric lines meant that the last tram was delivered in March 2007 rather than 2005. *See p56* **The curse of the Combinos**. The head of Budapest transport was forced to resign in late 2006 after 13 years in charge.

While the majority of its citizens struggle under a hefty tax burden, the city is awash with money, much of it foreign. Israeli, Irish and German private investors are transforming grubby downtown streets with high-end residential developments. The city council, though its Valuable Heritage Protection Assistance programme, has been giving grants to finance work on buildings around town since 1993. The result is that previously blighted areas such as the District IX north of the Nagykörút are now home to social housing, landscaped parks and new amenities.

While it constantly changes, and no matter how quickly it moves towards 21st-century homogenisation, Budapest and its people retain an individual style and stubbornness unique within Europe. Budapest has endured sporadic invasion and foreign rule for two millennia; it will take more than international property development to crush its spirit.

Hungarian Identity

Princes, paupers and projectiles.

Almost exactly 50 years on from the 1956 Uprising, images of Hungarians throwing projectiles at Budapest riot police were once again beamed around the globe. A speech made by Prime Minister Ferenc Gyurcsány to Socialist party activists in May 2006, in which he admitted that his government had lied to win a second term, was leaked to the press on 17 September. All hell broke loose. On 18 September, the first night of the riots, almost 150 people were hospitalised, more than two-thirds of whom were policemen.

To many commentators outside Hungary, the post-Communist bubble had suddenly burst; despite the rumbling corruption scandals

characteristic to all post-Communist societies, the Magyars seemed to have been the poster-boy for successful transition to a democratic market economy. Inside the country, however, while the ferocity of a small minority intent on setting fire to anything in sight was mostly a source of shame, the underlying tensions were all too familiar. These date at least as far back as the mid 1980s, and the division was roughly set along nationalist-conservative and liberal-cosmopolitan lines.

Ostensibly, protestors were demanding that Ferenc Gyurcsány resign because he was a liar. What really happened was that he had been caught in the act of admitting he and his party had lied, sexing up the health of the economy when Hungary had the largest domestic deficit in the European Union. His party, the Hungarian Socialists (MSZP), are the reformed Communist party, and therefore the heirs to a very unpleasant legacy.

"Only in Hungary have pensioners and far-right thugs joined forces to commandeer tanks on the street."

Since 1989, successive governments have danced around the hard sell that is drastic welfare reform, preferring to line their own pockets while making fiscally implausible election pledges. Here's the rub: everyone in Hungary knows that politicians lie morning, noon and night. Here, as in other recent EU accession states, it's almost expected. Growing social inequality, coming to terms with new European identities and politicians telling porkies are the order of the day. Only in Hungary, however, have pensioners and far-right thugs joined forces to commandeer tanks on the street. The rallying cry in Budapest was for the removal of one lying politician from power, but what was really at stake was a set of pent-up frustrations, rooted in the strange and far trickier world of Hungarian identity.

THEM AND US
For starters, and certainly one of the first things you'll notice, is that Hungarian bears no relation to anything you've ever seen or heard before. Knowledge of other tongues – French, German, Russian – will not help you here one jot. Hungarian belongs to the Uralic language family, stranded here in the Carpathian Basin for 1,100 years, far from its distant brethren in Siberia, and surrounded by speakers of Slavic, Romance and Germanic tongues. Its 13 million speakers here and in the surrounding countries dispense with such frivolities as separate pronouns for he and she, prepositions or the verb 'to have', and instead enjoy the delights of vowel harmony, definite and indefinite verb conjugations, agglutination and, the scourge of computer fonts everywhere, the double umlaut. This linguistic isolation (although Finnish and Estonian are sort of 93rd cousins) produces an obsession with uniqueness, and its offspring, a big, bouncing siege mentality. Protective of their impenetrable language as if it were a rare species of exotic flower that can only survive in a hothouse, Hungarians tend to feel proud of, yet at the same time isolated by, the gilded cage

that is Hungarian. If you can imagine an inferiority complex that is at the same time a superiority complex, and vice versa, then you're getting close.

From Slovenia to Estonia, and everywhere in between, there's not one single ex-Eastern Bloc country that doesn't claim to be the heart of Europe, a bridge between East and West. Here, Hungarians are no different from their neighbours, but they also like to distinguish themselves from what they perceive as the chaotic Balkans, and staid Austria and Bohemia. They also enjoy a denominational split between Catholics (about 54 per cent) and Protestants (about 20 per cent, most of whom are Calvinist, and who tend to be more concentrated in the eastern part of the country), although religion is not something that dominates many people's lives. There's also the eternal rural/urban divide. Either some sinful capital in a neighbouring state is leeching off the oppressed countryside and neglecting Hungarian minorities; or backwards provincials are obstructing Hungary's potential to become a modern, European country, by banging on ad nauseum about historic injustices. There's also the pull of the East. All kinds of esoteric notions surround Hungary's eastern origins: runes, shamans, ancient Sumeria and dilettante linguistics. It seems that the widening gap between rich and poor, and political polarisation, make a fertile breeding ground for crackpot theorists of all persuasions.

1956 AND ALL THAT
Coming to terms with the more recent past is still extremely painful for those old enough to remember the Communist system (and even for those who aren't). There's a lot of unfinished business here, and very little in the way of neutral terminology knocking about. Talking about history is a verbal minefield, thanks to the enforced silence of the Communist era. Hungary's Axis membership, and its Holocaust, could only ever be spoken about in code; the events of 1956 were not publicly mentioned for decades, which means that there's disagreement over whether it was an uprising, a revolt or a revolution, although everyone agrees it wasn't a 'counter-revolution', as the Kádár regime termed it; while the round-table talks of 1989 that led to the Communists vacating power and arranging multi-party elections might be referred to using any one of three remarkably similar but subtly different words referring to régime change. Again, almost everyone agrees it was not a revolution.

The grievances of those who suffered before, under and after Communism have never been sensibly addressed by the political elite, all of

whom, whether ex- or anti-Communist, have done quite nicely from neo-liberal economics. With freedom of speech comes the desire for closure and consensus, but both seem elusive for the time being.

Sadly, the memory of 1956 divides rather than unites. It's hardly surprising, then, that the protestors who demonstrated peacefully, as well as those who stormed around in neo-Nazi garb, presented themselves as the 2006 remake of the 1956 revolution that never was. Although the stakes are politically and emotionally high, there are signs that amnesia, complicity and denial are finally being dealt with openly.

> **"Political rhetoric has lost any anchor in reality, bad news in a small country packed with hotheads and self-appointed experts."**

Hungarian politics basically boils down to a contest between winners and losers, princes and paupers, except that each side claims to be the pauper on the moral high ground, accusing the other of wielding power in a most irresponsible, self-serving fashion. Political rhetoric has lost any anchor in reality, bad news in a small country packed with hotheads and self-appointed experts, with a wealthy elite and

millions who'd give anything to stop worrying about money and go on holiday to Greece instead. Newspaper journalism is either subservient or impossibly boring, most TV stations opt for trash, and while quite a few booze, bathe or blog the blues away, many choose just to shut up, or change the subject.

Budapest is comfortable with extremes. Its architecture encompasses Turkish and Bauhaus, Habsburg and Socialist. The number of homeless people and fancy Western cars rises exponentially every year. You might immerse yourself in the healing waters of a spa before heading off to the poolside bar for a greasy *lángos* snack of fried dough, a strong brandy and a cigarette. The extremes are also there under the surface: the current opposition's point-blank refusal to accept that they lost two elections in a row; the political tug-of-war over the fourth metro line; the controversy over the House of Terror on Andrássy út.

Whatever the debate, national holidays from now on will be marked by marches, protests and the potential for flare-ups. Of course, visitors to Budapest need not don flak jackets or blue helmets. There's way too much fun to be had to get bogged down in the intricacies of Hungarian politics. Plenty of English speakers have lived in the city for years without noticing that the society is polarised. But if you do find yourself nursing a beer while your friends talk politics (the verb for this national pastime is *politizálni*), you can settle in for a long night.

Where to Stay

Where to Stay   **35**

Features

Danubius Hotel Gellért. *See p44*.

Clean water. It's the most basic human necessity. Yet one third of all poverty related deaths are caused by drinking dirty water. Saying *I'm in* means you're part of a growing movement that's fighting the injustice of poverty. Your £8 a month can help bring safe water to some of the world's poorest people. We can do this. We *can* end poverty. Are you in?

shouldn't everyone get clean water? I don't think that's too much to ask for

Let's end poverty together.
Text 'WATER' and your name to 87099 to give £8 a month.

Standard text rates apply. Registered charity No.202918

oxfam.org.uk

I'm in

α Oxfam

Sarite Morales, Greenwich

Where to Stay

New boutique and spa venues complement landmark grandeur.

The post-millennial building boom has not abated. Budapest is not just recreating the splendour of its landmark buildings, but constructing purpose-built hotels for a new clientele who would not have come here had high-end hoteliers not recently redefined local five-star and boutique service. The spacious, neo-classical **Corinthia Grand Hotel Royal** pioneered luxury standards at an original location, the once unfashionable Nagykörút; the Four Season's deservedly hyped Jugendstil **Gresham Palace** followed suit downtown, and the Boscolo's neo-Baroque **New York Palace** (*see p48* **So good they built it twice**), a local legend, has brought an opulent heritage building to the present in the way only Italian design can – again on the Nagykörút. Despite concerns whether Budapest does have enough elsewhere to spoil the weary traveller, the historic **Rác** Turkish baths are being integrated into a luxury spa hotel, the Baglioni Budapest (www.baglionihotels.com), to be opened in 2008. In the meantime, the **Marriott** is renovating its property inside and out, while

the other, older five-star houses are in the middle of lesser refurbishment projects. The steel-and-glass **Kempinski Corvinus**, serene **Le Méridien**, the brown **InterContinental** and the Castle-nestled **Hilton** do corporate business, but **Starlight Suites** offers twice the space and basic services for the individual guest on a shoestring – a trail blazed by the trendy **art'otel** in 2000.

Five-star palaces are not the only fresh arrivals in town. 2007 brought seven new boutique hotels, the overhaul of **Danubius Hotels** venues and standards in newly acquired three-star hotels by the **Mellow Mood Group**. **Lánchíd 19** boasts the best panorama and design detail; down in Pest, near the Nagykörút, the **Atrium** features a five-storey-long second hand from a clock. *See p43* **Boutique Budapest**.

And then there are spa hotels, a Budapest speciality. Along with the famous, faded **Gellért**, there are well-established alternatives on Margaret Island and in outer Pest. Nearly all top-end hotels now feature spa facilities. *See p50* **Spa city**.

Service has improved across the board, with a new generation of English- or German-speaking staff, capable of smiling, that are taking over from the old guard.

TIPS, BOOKING AND PRICES

Online booking now has thematic search functions – by category, district or facility. There is a comprehensive catalogue of accommodation, albeit no booking resource, at www.hotelinfo.hu where you can also check out conditions and purchase of the **Hungary Card** (www.hungarycard.hu), which affords you discount on accommodation as well as other practical services. To book, use the Hungarian National Tourist Office's own www.hungarytourism.hu or private portals www.booking.hu, www.hotels.hu, www.ohb.hu, www.travelport.hu and www.travelstore.hu. It's possible to reserve your room on arriving at Ferihegy airport. Both terminals have a service desk with a select list of hotels on offer at rates

The best Hotels

For art nouveau elegance
Danubius Hotel Gellért. *See p44.*

For a Danube view
Four Seasons Gresham Palace. *See p39.*

For a dirty weekend
art'otel. *See p36.*

For high design
Lánchíd 19. *See p41.*

For outdoor sports
Petneházy Club Hotel. *See p44.*

For sleeping on the cheap
Citadella Hotel. *See p49.*

For spa treatments
Danubius Health Spa Resort Margitsziget. *See p39.*

For spotting film stars
Marriott Hotel Budapest. *See p39.*

❶ Green numbers given in this chapter correspond to the location of each hotel on the street maps. *See pp245-250.*

generally below walk-in prices. You will be required to pay 10-20 per cent of the rate at the desk, and the rest at the hotel. There is no commission charge. At Keleti train station, **Wasteels** books primarily modest three-star hotels and apartments, mostly in the vicinity of the station itself; the accommodation service is only offered on weekdays.

In town, for a full list of places to stay, pick up a catalogue at the Hungarian National Tourist Office's **Tourinform** offices (*see p234*). **Hotel Service** operates a booking office where practically any type of accommodation is available, from hotel rooms to private rooms and apartments. Again, no booking fee. **Express Travel** and **IBUSZ**, two full-service travel agencies, offer special rates at their partner hotels, but will book any specific location with no commission fee.

High season runs from late spring to early autumn, with rates gauged accordingly. At Christmas they can hit rock bottom, with the New Year shooting them back up. The **Spring Festival** in March hikes prices, and the **Grand Prix** (usually the second weekend of August) does terrible things to rates and availability.

Smoking rooms are now fewer and fewer; international TV stations, internet access, Wi-Fi (sometimes free of charge), lifts and air-conditioning are now basic to most hotels.

Prices are usually quoted in forints, euros or dollars. Prices here are listed in euros, which in 2007 trade at around Ft250. Rates include tax and breakfast unless otherwise noted.

The prices given are for a **double room** at low and high season. Allowing for the occasional online bargain, we have classified hotels into four categories: **deluxe** (above €200); **expensive** (€150-€200); **moderate** (€100-€150); and **budget** (below €100). Some may straddle two or three categories.

Booking

City Centre Apartments

VIII.Szentkirályi utca 5 (317 1456, 06 30 251 6121 mobile/www.citycentreapartments.hu). M2 Astoria/ bus 7. **Open** 8am-10pm Mon-Fri; or by appointment. **Credit** AmEx, DC, MC, V. **Map** p249 G6.
City Centre Apartments offer a good inventory of apartments in residential buildings across Budapest, with various auxiliary concierge-type services.

Expressz

V.Semmelweis utca 4 (266 6188/fax 235 0177). M2 Astoria/bus 7. **Open** 8.30am-4.30pm Mon-Fri. **No credit cards**. **Map** p249 F6.
Reserves rooms in any of Budapest's hotels, private rooms, *panziók* or apartments with no commission charge – often giving you a better rate than you would get if approaching the hotel directly.

Hotel Service

V.Apáczai Csere János utca 3 (266 8042). M1 Vörösmarty tér/tram 2. **Open** 9am-8pm daily. **No credit cards**. **Map** p249 C4.
Books lodging at any of Budapest's hotels, private rooms, *panziók* or apartments free of charge. You will often get a more favourable price here than if you reserve accommodation before you travel.

IBUSZ

V.Ferenciek tere 10 (Hotels & panziók 485 2716/ fax 342 2594; rooms & apartments 485 2767/ 485 2769/fax 337 1205/www.ibusz.hu). M3 Ferenciek tere/bus 7. **Open** 9am-5.30pm Mon-Fri; 9am-noon Sat. **Credit** MC, V. **Map** p249 E6.
Both apartment and hotel booking here offer better than walk-in rates. No booking fee.

Tourinform

V.Sütő utca 2 (318 8718/fax 488 8661/www. hungarytourism.hu). M1, M2, M3 Deák tér. **Open** 8am-8pm daily. **No credit cards**. **Map** p249 E5.
No room bookings, but handy for comprehensive hotel information. The telephone is manned 24/7. **Other locations**: I.Szentháromság tér; VI.Liszt Ferenc tér 11; Ferihegy Airport terminals 1, 2A & 2B.

Deluxe

Buda

art'otel

I.Bem rakpart 16-19 (487 9487/fax 487 9488/ www.artotel.de/budapest). M2 Batthyány tér/bus 86. **Rates** €125-€320 double. **Credit** AmEx, DC, MC, V. **Map** p245 C4 ①
Budapest's first boutique hotel glides between the 18th and 21st centuries. Amid the poetic disorder of Víziváros, the site has superb views of the Danube

New York Palace. *See p41.*

below and Castle Hill above. Urban at the front, it's baroque at the back, with the rear made up of four original 18th-century fishermen's houses, where the tastefully furnished rooms are graced with period fixtures and fittings – authentic down to the door handles – as well as arches and passageways. The huge rooms open on to the tiny romantic streets of Víziváros, which curve all the way up to the top of Castle Hill. The Danube-facing modern wing shows the abstract expressionist art of maverick New Yorker Donald Sultan. His minimalist work and postmodern rugs (thread and needle pattern in the rooms, domino pattern in the lobby and bar, buttons in the corridor), tableware and fountain design all lend a surreptitiously sweet touch. Each room features a decorative bird watching over the well-being of each guest. Those staying three floors up enjoy a castle vista as well as a riverside one. Übermodern with a medieval view – what could be better?
Services *Bar. Business centre. Concierge. Disabled: adapted room (1). Gym. Internet (rooms: high-speed; business centre: wireless). Parking (€13/day). Restaurant. Room service. TV (pay movies).*

Hilton Budapest Hotel

I.Hess András tér 1-3 (889 6600/fax 889 6644/www. hilton.com). Várbusz from M2 Moszkva tér/bus 16.
Rates €200-€430 double. **Credit** AmEx, DC, MC, V.
Map p245 B4 **②**
With spectacular views over the Danube and the old quarter, the Hilton is located in the heart of the romantic Castle District. One of the first of Budapest's high-end hotels, it's designed around a 17th-century façade (once part of a Jesuit cloister) and the remains of a 13th-century Gothic church, with a small, open-air concert hall between the two wings often used for summer opera performances. The medieval time travel more than compensates for the relative distance from the city centre. All rooms have undergone extensive refurbishment; the quieter ones have courtyard views. The foyer is now done out in sleek Canadian maple, with a new bar alongside and disabled access throughout.
Services *Bar. Business centre. Concierge. Disabled: adapted rooms (3). Gym. Internet (high-speed, wireless in all rooms). Parking (€28/day). Restaurants (2). Room service. TV (pay movies).*

Pest

Corinthia Grand Hotel Royal

VII.Erzsébet körút 43-49 (479 4000/fax 479 4333/ www.corinthiahotels.com). M1 Oktogon/tram 4, 6.
Rates €160-€380 double. **Credit** AmEx, DC, MC, V.
Map p246 G4 **③**
Faithfully reconstructed after a decade of neglect, the Royal, as it was christened when built for the 1896 millennial celebrations, is reborn. It was the Queen of the Boulevard, with a façade of cast-iron statues from Paris, a tropical garden, concert and banqueting halls, plush restaurants and cafés. Destroyed in the war, this vast warren of a hotel was twice reconstructed, to the contemporary tastes of the 1960s and 1980s, before being closed in the early 1990s. It was then used for DJ parties. Malta-based Corinthia Hotels dragged the Royal from the club culture of the late 20th century back into the quiet elegance of the late 19th; it was reopened in 2002. Modern twists embellish this majestic icon of Hungarian hospitality. An exquisite lobby features original fittings, set under a glassed-in triple atrium. The rooms combine historic grandeur with tasteful contemporary furniture – marble bathrooms, South African carpets, cherrywood headboards and modern artwork. The Grand Ballroom is beautifully restored and lined with portraits of Hungary's cultural giants. Five restaurants – two under glass atriums – include the French-influenced Brasserie

timeout.com

The hippest online guide to over 50
of the world's greatest cities

Royale and popular Bock Bistro. To top it off, in 2006 a tasteful and spacious spa opened downstairs, with a sizeable pool and relaxing areas. Breakfast is a completely indulgent piggery. One snag: more time and thought could have gone into the signposting – the corridors are vast and signs are few.

Services *Bars (2). Business centre. Concierge. Disabled: adapted rooms (2 junior suites). Gym. Internet (high-speed in all rooms; wireless in business centre). Parking (€20/day). Pool. Restaurants (3). Room service. Spa. TV (video, movies).*

Danubius Health Spa Resort Margitsziget

XIII.Margitsziget (889 4700/fax 889 4988/www. danubiusgroup.com/thermalhotel). Bus 26. **Rates** €180-€230 double. **Credit** AmEx, DC, MC, V. More modern than the Grand (*see p41*), with high-quality medical and spa services. *See p50* **Spa city**.

Services *Bars (2). Business centre. Concierge. Disabled: adapted rooms (4). Internet (high-speed shared terminals in business centre). Parking (€20 per day). Pool (indoor, outdoor, thermal). Restaurant. Room service. TV.*

Four Seasons Gresham Palace

V.Roosevelt tér 5-6 (268 6000/fax 268 5000/ www.fourseasons.com). M1 Vörösmarty tér/tram 2. **Rates** €280-€775 double. **Credit** AmEx, DC, MC, V. **Map** p246 D5 ④

This daddy of the deluxe, opened in 2004, still sets the standard for the five-stars. The keenest eye for architectural and service detail makes the glitzy Gresham a destination in itself – and there are surprising seasonal specials. Created by in art nouveau style by Zsigmond Quittner and the Vágó brothers in the early 1900s, the Gresham was opulence itself. Ruined in the war and left to fade, it was acquired by Canadian investment company Gresco, who raised $85 million to restore it. While 90% of the marble was found intact, the production details of the specially glazed Zsolnay tiles were pieced together from memories of the workers who had worked in the old Zsolnay factory. Modern design touches embellish an awesome lobby, and the natural light-flooded floors have a Central-European ambience. Danube-facing rooms come at a hefty price, while courtyard-facing rooms offer views of the building's stunning stained glass work and architecture. Nothing is claustrophobic, thanks to high ceilings and generous space. The spa on the fifth floor, tucked just under the roof, is a must.

Services *Bars (2). Business centre. Concierge. Disabled: adapted rooms (2). Gym. Internet (high-speed in rooms, wireless high-speed in meeting rooms). Parking (€40/day). Pool (1). Restaurants (2). Room service. Spa. TV (DVD in every room).*

Hotel Inter-Continental Budapest

V.Apáczai Csere János utca 12-14 (327 6333/fax 327 6357/www.intercontinental.com/icbudapest). M1 Vörösmarty tér/tram 2. **Rates** €265-€331 double; Danube view €40 surcharge. *Breakfast* €25. **Credit** AmEx, DC, MC, V. **Map** p249 D6 ⑤

The forerunner of the renovation rush, the Inter-Continental boasts newish rooms and one of the town's biggest conference facilities. Don't let the lugubrious brown façade discourage you: it hides a buzzing lobby with live music at the bar, and offers dramatic views from the Danube-facing rooms, well worth the surcharge, the angle beautifully integrating the Chain Bridge with the river and Castle District. Excellent service spoils guests, coupled with what the Inter-Continental calls 'icons': massage, jetlag recovery kit, instant money pack for tipping, and international newspapers.

Services *Bars. Business centre. Concierge. Disabled: adapted rooms (2). Gym. Internet (rooms: high-speed; business centre: wireless). Parking (€28/day). Pool. Restaurant. Room service. TV (pay movies).*

Kempinski Hotel Corvinus Budapest

V.Erzsébet tér 7-8 (429 3777/fax 429 4777/www. kempinski-budapest.com). M1, M2, M3 Deák tér. **Rates** €222-€439 double. *Breakfast* €29. **Credit** AmEx, DC, MC, V. **Map** p246 E5 ⑥

Built in 1992, the glass-laden Kempinski offers the biggest rooms in the very heart of Budapest. Madonna stayed here while filming *Evita*. The rooms come in 70 different shapes and some have views over a small courtyard. The quality of the decor is such that some of the smaller decorative statues were stolen even after being nailed to their stands. The spacious but somewhat cold lobby has a popular meeting point, as is the Kempi pub-restaurant, a good spot for TV sports. The Asian-inspired spa features a wide variety of massage treatments, some specially designed for couples.

Services *Bars (2). Business centre. Concierge. Disabled: adapted rooms (3). Gym. Internet (high-speed, dataport). Parking (€35/day). Pool. Restaurants (3). Room service. Sauna. Spa. TV (in-house movies).*

Marriott Hotel Budapest

V.Apáczai Csere János utca 4 (266 7000/fax 266 5000/www.marriotthotels.com/budhu). M1 Vörösmarty tér/tram 2. **Rates** from €200 double. *Breakfast* €25. **Credit** AmEx, DC, MC, V. **Map** p249 D6 ⑦

Celeb-spotting? The surprisingly low-cost Marriott is your patch. Brad Pitt, Robert Redford and Glenn Close are all recent guests at this burgundy and brass old-timer – almost all visiting film crews stay here. One of the late '60s designed Danube-side eyesore sisters, the Marriott found that guests weren't using the balconies and built them back into the rooms, boosting their size to a comfortable 30sq m (300sq ft). The facelift gave the façade a softer look, and the rooms overhaul brought in super-soft bedding and ergonomic work stations. All rooms have a river view. For all its comings and goings, the buzzing lobby is always welcoming and cosy. The upstairs gym is popular with expats.

Services *Bar. Business centre. Concierge. Disabled: adapted rooms (2). Gym. Internet (high-speed, wireless in public areas). Parking (€28/day). Restaurants (3). Room service. TV (video, movies).*

Spas and Secessionist architecture at the **Danubius Hotel Gellért**. *See p44.*

Le Méridien Budapest

V.Erzsébet tér 9-10 (429 5500/fax 429 5500/
www.lemeridien-budapest.com). M1, M2, M3
Deák tér. **Rates** from €239 double. *Breakfast* €25.
Credit AmEx, DC, MC, V. **Map** p246 E5 ❸
Morphed from a police headquarters in 2000, the
Méridien meticulously adopted clear millennial min-
imalism. The white austerity of the exterior is ornamented with wrought-iron balconies and statuettes,
while the rooms feature shades of beige and blue and
are adorned with high ceilings, French windows and
oriental rugs. The top-floor health club features a
pool bathed in natural light. Destination restaurant
Le Bourbon sparkles under a stained-glass dome.
Services *Bar. Business centre. Concierge. Disabled:*
adapted rooms (2 deluxe suites). Gym. Internet
(dataport, high-speed in deluxe rooms). Parking
(€36/day). Pool. Restaurants (2). Room service.
Spa. TV (pay movies).

New York Palace

VII.Erzsébet körút 9-11 (886 6111/fax 886 6199/
www.newyorkpalace.hu). M2 Blaha Lujza tér/tram
4, 6/bus 7. **Rates** €220-€800 double. *Breakfast* €25.
Credit AmEx, DC, MC, V. **Map** p247 G5 ❾
An icon meticulously renovated, this abused gem of
a building has finally received fair treatment in the
hands of Italian designers and the Boscolo's exper-
tise in luxury hoteliership. *See p48* **So good they**
built it twice. **Photos** *pp36-37.*
Services *Bar. Business centre. Concierge. Disabled:*
adapted rooms (2). Gym. Internet (high-speed
in rooms, wireless high-speed in meeting rooms).
Parking (€10/day). Pool (1). Restaurants (2).
Room service. Spa. TV.

Expensive

Buda

Lánchíd 19

I.Lánchíd utca 19 (488 7390/fax 212 9989/
www.lanchid19hotel.hu). Bus 16, 86, 105. **Rates**
€151-€191 double. *Breakfast* €15. **Credit** AmEx,
MC, V. **Map** p245 C5 ❿
The most splendid boutique hotel in town, bedecked
completely in Hungarian design, taking inspiration
from the Danube. *See p43* **Boutique Budapest**.
Services *Bar. Business centre. Conference facilities.*
Disabled: adapted rooms (2). Internet (dataport,
wireless. Parking (€16/day). Restaurant. TV.

UhU Villa

II.Keselyű út 1A (275 1002/fax 398 0571/www.uhu
villa.hu). Tram 56. **Rates** €150-€190 double. **Credit**
AmEx, DC, MC, V.
This excellent *panzió* is nestled among fir trees in
the quiet valley of Szalonka, a ten-minute tram ride
from Moszkva tér – it's the perfect getaway from
downtown bustle. A fin-de-siècle villa, the UhU is
done up in monarchical white and yellow, with
small but cosy rooms and a quaint charm pervad-
ing the common areas. A fine American breakfast

overlooking the lovely flower garden is the perfect
prelude to a short walk down the hill to the tram and
the heart of Budapest in relatively no time.
Services *Bar. Internet (dataport). Parking (free).*
Pool. TV.

Óbuda

Corinthia Aquincum Hotel

III.Árpád fejedelem útja 94 (436 4100/fax 436
4156/www.corinthiahotels.com). M2 Batthyány
tér/HÉV to Árpád-híd. **Rates** €140-€200.
Credit DC, MC, V.
The Aphrodite Spa and Wellness Centre salvages
this five-star aspirant of a red-brick relic from the
1980s, plopped in between old Buda's remains and
housing estates. Aquincum's leisurely attractions
spring (literally) from the nearby healing waters
of Margaret Island and the medicinal mud of Héviz.
See p50 **Spa city**.
Services *Bar. Business centre. Concierge. Disabled:*
adapted rooms (2). Gym. Internet (high-speed,
wireless). Parking (€16/day). Pool. Restaurant.
Room service. Spa. TV (in-house movies, video).

Pest

Andrássy Hotel

VI.Munkácsy Mihály utca 5-7 (462 2100/fax 462
2195/www.andrassyhotel.com). M1 Bajza utca.
Rates €135-€240 double. *Breakfast* €20. **Credit**
AmEx, DC, MC, V. **Map** p247 H2 ⓫
This yellow eyesore is the black sheep of embassy
central – the leafy land of imposing villas now housing diplomatic missions just off Heroes' Square – but
the Andrássy still offers five star-ish services in the
small luxury hotel category. The 69 modest bed-
rooms and three suites are graced with warm tones
of beige and blue, but reflect little of the lobby's
grandly serene and chic elegance. The Baraka
restaurant, which earned an excellent reputation
downtown, has recently been relocated to this hotel,
where it's a major plus. Rates here can vary wildly
according to season and availability.
Services *Bar. Concierge. Disabled: adapted room*
(1). Internet (wireless in public areas). Parking
(€16/day). Restaurant. Room service. TV (pay).

Boutique Hotel Cosmo

VI.Király utca 6 (413 7213/fax 413 7214/
www.hotelcosmo.hu). M1, M2, M3 Deák tér.
Rates €160-€280 double. **Credit** AmEx, DC,
MC, V. **Map** p246 E5 ⓬
Designer inspiration in the heart of happening
Király utca. *See p43* **Boutique Budapest**.
Services *Bar. Conference facilities. Disabled rooms*
(2). Gym. Internet (free wireless in rooms). Parking
(€20). Restaurant. Smoking rooms (25). TV.

Danubius Grand Hotel Margitsziget

XIII.Margitsziget (889 4782/fax 889 4939/www.
danubiusgroup.com/grandhotel). Bus 26. **Rates**
€137-€180 double. **Credit** AmEx, DC, MC, V.

Sister hotel of the Danubius Health Spa Resort Margitsziget (*see p39*) with old-world charm and superb facilities. *See p50* **Spa city**.
Services *Bar. Business centre. Concierge. Disabled: adapted rooms (4). Gym. Internet (high-speed shared terminals in business centre, wireless). Parking (€16/day). Pool (indoor, outdoor, thermal). Restaurant. Room service. Spa. TV (pay movies).*

Hilton Budapest Westend

VI.Váci út 1-3 (288 5500/fax 288 5588/www. hilton.com). M3 Nyugati pu./tram 4, 6. **Rates** €190 double. *Breakfast* €23. **Credit** AmEx, DC, MC, V. **Map** p246 F2 ⑬
Wedged in between shops and surrounded by office buildings, this business travel-focused Hilton is overshadowed by the lugubrious shopping mall project it is located in, ambitiously aiming at becoming the new downtown. Purpose-built and with a separate entrance, the hotel offers tastefully furnished, spacious rooms, a warm colour scheme with a stroke of yellow and purple, and a good diving board into the city – if you dodge the maddening mall.
Services *Bar. Business centre. Concierge. Disabled: adapted rooms (2). Gym. Internet (wireless). Parking (€16/day). Restaurants (2). Room service. TV (pay per view).*

K+K Hotel Opera

VI.Révay utca 24 (269 0222/fax 269 0230/www. kkhotels.com). M1 Bajcsy-Zsilinszky út/M1 Opera. **Rates** €170 double. **Credit** AmEx, DC, MC, V. **Map** p246 E4 ⑭
Around the corner from the Opera House and within easy reach of the theatre district, the location can't be beaten for cultural and dining options. The neighbourhood is also undergoing pedestrianisation. An ultra-modern interior radiates Austrian efficiency and calm ('Kaiserlich und Königlich', as the chain name regally suggests), while the rooms feature bright yellow walls and light wooden furniture – although don't expect much of a view for your money. Service is attentive and friendly, and there's a big buffet breakfast too. The underground parking is a real boon for this part of town.
Services *Bar. Concierge. Disabled: access. Gym. Internet (high-speed, shared terminal). Parking (€15/day). Room service. TV.*

Madách Starlight Suiten Hotel

VII.Madách tér 2 (801 6300/fax 801 6311/ www.starlighthotels.com). M1, M2, M3 Deák tér. **Rates** €183 double. **Credit** AmEx, MC, V. **Map** p246 E5 ⑮
Housed in a historic Bauhaus brick complex that dominates much of Deák tér, the brand new Madách suites and apartments occupy a quiet side wing overlooking a square at the front and a courtyard at the back in the very centre of the city. A heritage building, the interior also had to be restored to its original state – a serene, simple, elegant space. The 43 suites range from 40sq m (430sq ft) to 60sq m (650sq ft), each consisting of two spacious rooms, representing extremely good value for the kind of

traveller who likes to retreat to airy, private quiet after spending time around town. From the seventh floor, the Synagogue bursts into view.
Services *Bar. Disabled rooms (partial access). Gym. Internet (wireless). Parking (€16.50/day). Room service (breakfast only). TVs (2).*

Mérleg Starlight Suiten Hotel

V.Mérleg utca 6 (484 3700/fax 484 3711/ www.starlighthotels.com). Bus 16, 105. **Rates** €183 double. **Credit** AmEx, MC, V. **Map** p246 D5 ⑯
Like its sibling, the newly renovated and refurbished Mérleg Starlight wins hands down in terms of the location, room size and value ratio: tucked right behind the Gresham, it might not afford the precious view but you will have 40sq m (430sq ft) to 70sq m (750sq ft) in the centre of Budapest, just off the Danube on a quiet street, halfway between the commercial and government quarters. The suites feature the Starlight signature homy simplicity and pared-down amenities.
Services *Bar. Concierge. Disabled (room partially adapted). Internet (wireless). Parking (€16/day). Room service (from the bar only). Smoking rooms (21). TVs (2).*

Radisson SAS Béke Hotel Budapest

VI.Teréz körút 43 (889 3900/fax 889 3915/www. radissonsas.com). M3 Nyugati pu./tram 4, 6. **Rates** €155-€195 double. *Breakfast* €16. **Credit** AmEx, DC, MC, V. **Map** p246 F3 ⑰
While the Béke boldly oozes a Vienna-esque air on the outside, its recent refurbishment and business upgrade have dragged the interior into the standard light wood world of four-star hotels. Although the rooms have also lost the old Communist decor, the Béke ('Peace') has in truth been refurbished so many times, there's little to show for its eventful 80-year history. Built with all the trappings as the Hotel Britannia in 1912, the Béke also housed a famous jazz club in the 1950s. Footballer Ferenc Puskás was among the many Magyar personalities to live here for a while. These days non-guests come here for afternoon tea and gooey cakes at the old-world Zsolnay Café – and for guests, *béke* is best found in the quieter rooms away from busy ring-road traffic.
Services *Bars (2). Business centre. Concierge. Disabled: adapted room (1). Internet (high-speed, shared terminal, wireless). Parking (€22 per day). Pool (indoor). Restaurant. Room service. Sauna. TV.*

Zara

V.Só utca 6 (357 6170/fax 357 6171/www. zarahotels.com). M3 Kálvin tér/tram 2, 47, 49. **Rates** €155-€178 double. **Credit** AmEx, MC, V. **Map** p249 F7 ⑱
Recently opened downtown designer hotel near Szabadság Bridge, a meticulous exercise in understatement. *See p43* **Boutique Budapest**.
Services *Bar. Business centre. Concierge. Conference centre. Disabled room (1). Internet (high-speed, wireless). Laundry. Minibar. Parking (€18/day). Restaurant. Room service. Smoking rooms (12). TV.*

Boutique Budapest

Budapest's coming of age can be measured in the number of boutique hotels recently opened around the capital.

For design, **Lánchíd 19** (see p41) is king. This purpose-built construction wears a veil of accordion-like glass panes, their tiny decorative, hand-painted graphics chronicling the eco-system of the Danube. When closed, these panes morph into little waves. Set in riverside Víziváros, L19 glistens in the sun; the panes backlit, it shines kaleidoscopically at night. It's built on top of 14th-century Anjou-era remains of a watermill and water tower, integrated in the lower levels as if its chic modernity is growing organically out of the past. Staff uniforms are by up-and-coming local designers and cutlery is more award-winning Hungarian handiwork. A stone's throw from the Chain Bridge (Lánchíd), the Danube vista encompasses Margaret Island, the Buda Hills and the whole of Pest. The angle is enhanced by a tender curve in the river by the bridge, best enjoyed from the top-floor suites, from the terrace and most of the bathtubs.

Pioneering **Zara** (see p42; see photos), on a quiet street off Váci utca, is textbook boutique: clean, meticulous lines, the front reflecting the building opposite. A modest floral pattern recurs from reception through restaurant and bar, finding its way as wall decoration in the minimalist, light-filled, soundproofed and air-conditioned rooms. From no.603, you can peep at Szabadság Bridge. Zara's boutique sibling, **Avantgarde**, is due to open behind the Marriott.

The **Atrium Hotel** (see p44) is sited near two deluxe hotels on the Nagykörút, and is the core of its gentrification. Here 57 rooms comprise this renovated and superbly refurbished building whose overwhelming height heads towards the sky seen through the glass roof. This seven-storey wall is graced with an oversized pendulum, the second hand of a behemoth clock, sweeping above the bar and restaurant. The colour scheme and design of the comfortable rooms, all soundproofed and air-conditioned, follow the airy feel of the common areas. Amid light lime and plum, the lobby's aubergine touches strike against the flood of sunshine through the roof.

The opening of the **Boutique Hotel Cosmo** (see p41) adds a push to the revival of cute Király utca. It occupies a simple neo-Classical property near the main square of Deák tér, with floral prints perking up the serene architecture, brown and purple adding soothing touches to the rooms, 50 in all, including one suite. One parquet-floored storey is allergy-free.

Moderate

Buda

Danubius Hotel Gellért

*XI.Szent Gellért tér 1 (889 5500/fax 889 5505/www.
danubiusgroup.com/gellert). Tram 18, 19, 47, 49/
bus 7.* **Rates** €70-€240 double. **Credit** AmEx, DC,
MC, V. **Map** p249 E8 ⑲
This historic art nouveau gem overlooking the
Danube basks in luxurious illumination at night –
although many of its rooms are in urgent need of
refurbishment and not all have air-conditioning. The
amazing architecture, spa, outdoor pool and terrace
perched halfway up Gellért Hill compensate. The
baths and pools are being renovated in turn throughout 2007, so expect some closures and disruption.
See p50 **Spa city**. *Photos p40.*
Services *Bar. Business centre. Concierge. Internet
(wireless in business centre). Parking (€9/day). Pool
(indoor, outdoor). Restaurant. Room service. Spa.
TV (in-house movies).*

Hotel Victoria

*I.Bem rakpart 11 (457 8080/fax 457 8088/www.
victoria.hu). M2 Batthyány tér/tram 19/bus 60, 86.*
Rates €96-€123 double. **Credit** AmEx, DC, V.
Map p245 C4 ⑳
One of Budapest's first private hotels occupies a
townhouse below the castle, facing the Danube and
within easy reach of the main sights. The 27 rooms
are comfortable in a simple way, commanding a
view of the river, and the garden rooms offer nice
patios at no extra charge. Excellent value for the
location, size of rooms and services offered.
Services *Bar. Internet (high-speed, wireless).
Parking (€13/day). Room service. TV.*

Novotel Budapest Danube

*II.Bem rakpart 33-34 (458 4900/fax 458 4909/
www.accorhotels.com). M2 Batthyány tér/tram
19/bus 86.* **Rates** €98-€150 double; Danube view
€30 surcharge. *Breakfast* €17. **Credit** AmEx, MC, V.
Map p245 C3 ㉑
This new property right on the Buda bank, smack
across from the Parliament, features 175 rooms, 36
facing the river. They are bedecked in beige and burgundy, while the sign of the times eloquently surfaces in the common areas, giving them an edge over
older and dustier four-star peers. The gym and five
conference rooms encourage business trade.
Services *Bar. Concierge. Disabled access (3 rooms).
Gym. Internet (cable modem free in rooms, wireless
for charge throughout the hotel. Parking (€15).
Restaurant. Room service. TV.*

Petneházy Club Hotel

*II.Feketefej utca 2-4 (391 8010/fax 376 5738/
www.petnehazy-clubhotel.hu). Bus 63.* **Rates**
small bungalow from €104. *Breakfast* €7.
Credit AmEx, MC, V.
Doubling as a country club, this hotel is actually 45
private bungalows – four with disabled access –
with a central building housing the reception, pool

and restaurant. Every room has its own sauna, a
plus to this peaceful, albeit remote location. There
are loads of sports and leisure facilities here, including horse-riding next door (*see p200*), as well as
organised bus and boat excursions.
Services *Bar. Bicycles. Disabled: adapted bungalows
(4). Gym. Internet (shared terminal in lobby). Parking
(free). Pool (indoor, outdoor). Restaurants (2). Room
service. TV.*

Pest

Atrium Hotel

*VIII.Csokonai utca 14 (299 0777/fax 215 6090/
www.hotelatrium.hu). M2 Blaha Lujza tér/tram 4,
6/bus 7.* **Rates** €120-€180 double. **Credit** AmEx,
MC, V. **Map** p250 H5 ㉒
In an up-and-coming location, the inventive Atrium
Hotel is wedged between the new glam and residue
realism. *See p43* **Boutique Budapest**.
Services *Bar. Conference facilities. Disabled
rooms (2). Internet (free wireless). Parking (€17).
Restaurant. Smoking rooms (12). TV.*

Best Western Premier
Hotel Parlament

*V.Kálmán Imre utca 19 (374 6000/fax 374 0843/
www.bestwestern.com). M2 Kossuth tér/tram 2.*
Rates €115-€150 double. **Credit** AmEx, MC, V.
Map p246 E3 ㉓
Its laced façade recently renovated to its tender
glory, the Best Western Parlament is almost a
boutique hotel, its 65 rooms offering a stylish
foothold in the government quarters a stone's throw
from Parliament and the Danube. While the neighbourhood might come across as morose and insti-
tutionally grey, here within are minimalist art reds,
oranges and wood tones, and a splendid glass atrium, a comfort zone complete with spa services.
Services *Bar. Business centre. Concierge. Disabled:
adapted rooms (2). Gym. Internet. Room service
(breakfast only). Smoking rooms (25). TV.*

Danubius Health Spa Resort Helia

*XIII.Kárpát utca 62-64 (889 5800/fax 889 5801/
www.danubiusgroup.com/helia). M3 Dózsa György út,
then trolleybus 79.* **Rates** €140 double. **Credit**
AmEx, DC, MC, V. **Map** p246 E1 ㉔
This modern spa hotel has the cleanest and most
comprehensive facilities in town, surrounded by a
housing estate. *See p50* **Spa city**.
Services *Bar. Business centre. Concierge. Disabled:
adapted rooms (5). Gym. Internet (high-speed,
wireless). Parking. Pool. Restaurant. Room service.
Spa. TV (pay movies).*

Domina Inn Fiesta

*VI.Király utca 20 (328 3000/fax 266 6024/
www.dominohotels.com). M1, M2, M3 Deák tér.*
Rates €82-€120 double. **Credit** AmEx, MC, V.
Map p246 F5 ㉕
This four-star emerges from a neo-classicist block,
shedding period character to give way to a light,
modern hotspot with a Mediterranean touch. The

preserved façade hides 112 IKEA-esque rooms, spacious and sun-soaked on the higher floors. Ideally located on up-and-coming Király utca, the Domina Fiesta reflects the slow gentrification of the area between the city centre, the theatre district, and the nightlife of Liszt Ferenc tér. Superb access, in fact, to all the city spots that matter.

Services *Bar. Concierge. Conference rooms. Disabled: adapted rooms (4). Internet (wireless). Parking (nearby; €15/day). Restaurant. Room service. TV.*

Hotel Astoria

V.Kossuth Lajos utca 19-21 (889 6000/fax 889 6091/www.danubiusgroup.com/astoria). M2 Astoria/ tram 47, 49/bus 7. **Rates** €104-€189 double. **Credit** AmEx, DC, MC, V. **Map** p249 F6 ㉖

Opened in 1914 and lending its name to the busy junction on which it stands, the landmark Astoria was where the first Hungarian government was formed in 1918. The hotel was popular with Nazi officials in World War II, before housing the famous Pengő jazz club. It became the Soviet headquarters during the 1956 Uprising. The elegant chandeliered art nouveau coffee lounge and restaurant recall the atmosphere of pre-war Budapest. Windows are now soundproof, and the 43 rooms have been refurbished in Provençal style – nos.609 and 610 have views of the Synagogue. The last wave of refurbishment was completed in 2006.

Services *Bar. Business centre. Concierge. Disabled: access. Internet (wireless). Parking (€20/day). Restaurant. Room service. TV (pay).*

Hotel Erzsébet

V.Károlyi Mihály utca 11-15 (889 3700/fax 889 3701/www.danubiusgroup.com/erzsebet). M3 Ferenciek tere/tram 2/bus 7. **Rates** €98-€135 double. **Credit** AmEx, DC, MC, V. **Map** p249 E6 ㉗

The hotel's original was christened Erzsébet (Elizabeth) with Empress Sissi's permission, in her honour. Unfortunately, that building was demolished, with not so much as a ghost remaining in this modern construction. The good news is that the recent refurbishment ripped off the staple dark wood, replacing it with lighter shades and a fresher feel. The main draw is still the downtown location, and while the street is one-way and congested, the precious Károlyi kert a block away offers an oasis of calm. The higher rooms offer a view to Gellért Hill.

Services *Bar. Business centre. Internet (wireless). Parking (€13/day). TV.*

Hotel Pest

VI.Paulay Ede utca 31 (343 1198/fax 351 9164/ www.hotelpest.hu). M1 Opera. **Rates** €110-€130 double. **Credit** MC, V. **Map** p246 F4 ㉓

Set back on a quiet street parallel to Andrássy, near the Opera House, the theatre district and nightlife attractions, this unostentatious Pest bargain is a real boon. Behind the attractive façade (dating from 1790), all 25 rooms are (for the price) surprisingly spacious, with gleaming bathrooms and shiny new wooden fixtures. Some look out on an ivy-clad

Kulturinnov Hotel. See p47.

courtyard. Not all rooms are air-conditioned; some are parquet floored to ease allergy symptoms. An excellent deal for comfort and location.

Services *Bar. Internet. Parking (€9/day). TV.*

Novotel Budapest Centrum

VIII.Rákóczi út 43-45 (477 5400/fax 477 5454/ www.novotel-bud-centrum.hu). M2 Blaha Lujza tér/ tram 4, 6/bus 7. **Rates** €145 double. *Breakfast* €17. **Credit** AmEx, DC, MC, V. **Map** p247 H5 ㉙

Built as the Palace Hotel in 1911 and closed after 1989, this neglected Jugendstil treasure was at last restored in 2002, becoming a 227-room Novotel hotel. Unfortunately, the rooms reflect standard industry decor rather than period, but represent good value given that they're in the vicinity of the gentrifying Nagykörút. Rákóczi út views from the balconies can be Vienna-esque, but come with traffic noise; the Csokonai utca rooms are quieter and some are equipped with balconies.

Services *Bar. Disabled: adapted rooms (3). Gym. Internet (high-speed, wireless). Parking (€14/day). Restaurant. Room service. TV.*

Sissi Hotel

IX.Angyal utca 33 (215 0082/fax 216 6063/www. hotelsissi.hu). M3 Ferenc körút/tram 4, 6. **Rates** €100-€180 double. **Credit** AmEx, DC, MC, V. **Map** p250 G8 ㉚

Nestled in the up-and-coming IX District, Sissi opens a little gateway to the various neighbourhood regeneration projects in the area – from the busy barland of Ráday utca to the colourful residential revival of the hotel's surroundings. Smartly, no allusion is made to the simplicity of the 44 rooms by the terraced façade. The tacky influence of Habsburg namesake legend Sissi surfaces in pleasingly modest attempts at liberal antique decoration and the unassuming Sissi room.

Services *Bar. Concierge. Disabled: adapted room (1). Internet (high-speed, wireless). Parking (€10/day). TV (satellite).*

Budget

Buda

Ábel Panzió

XI.Ábel Jenő utca 9 (209 2537/fax 372 0299/www. abelpanzio.hu). Tram 61. **Rates** €75 double. **Credit** MC, V. **Map** p248 B8 ㉛

Probably the most beautiful *panzió* in Budapest, set in an ivy-covered 1920s' villa on a quiet side street, and fitted out with period furniture in the common areas. The ten air-conditioned rooms are all sunny, clean and have antique furniture, although those on the ground level are slightly bigger and come with bathtubs. There are no television sets in the rooms. Breakfast takes place around a pleasant common dining table overlooking a terrace and well-kept garden. This is a summer favourite, so be sure to reserve. Discounts are offered for cash payments.

Services *Bar. Parking (free).*

Hotel Charles

I.Hegyalja út 23 (212 9169/fax 202 2984/www. charleshotel.hu). Bus 8, 112. **Rates** €57-€100 double. **Credit** AmEx, DC, MC, V. **Map** p248 B7 ㉜

The old Charles Apartments have been elevated to hotel status. Sizes range between modest and the medium units upgraded to deluxe in 2006, new furniture and open-plan kitchens giving a spacious and modern feel. The rest are studios with a separate kitchen. Breakfast is included. Good location, but make sure you don't overlook noisy Hegyalja út.

Services *Business centre. Concierge. Internet (high-speed in business centre). Parking (€9/day). Restaurant. TV.*

Hotel Császár

II.Frankel Leó út 35 (336 2640/fax 336 2644/ www.csaszarhotel.hu). Tram 4, 6/bus 6, 86/HÉV Margit híd Budai hídfő. **Rates** €56-€105 double. **Credit** AmEx, MC, V. **Map** p245 C2 ㉝

Citadella Hotel. *See p49.*

of air-conditioning deter you – the old walls are thick enough to protect from the heat. A decent buffet breakfast is included in the rates. For the location, it's the best cheapie in town – and it's also the office of the Hungarian Culture Foundation. **Photos** *p45.*
Services *Bar. Conference facilities. Disabled: access. Internet (wireless). Parking (€12/day).*

Pest

City Hotel Pilvax
V.Pilvax köz 1-3 (266 7660/fax 317 6396/www.city hotels.hu). M3 Ferenciek tere/bus 7. **Rates** €80-€110 double. **Credit** AmEx, DC, MC, V. **Map** p249 E6 ⑮
Laden with history, the Pilvax café played host to the revolutionaries of 1848 – although its existence as a hotel only goes back ten years. The common areas pay some homage to the building's Biedermeier past, while the rooms are light and out-fitted by the usual three-star pastel cartel in furnishings of the day. Sister hotel the Mátyás (V.Március 15 tér 7-8, 338 4711, same website) has similar great rates and superb location.
Services *Bar. Internet. Parking (nearby; €25/day). Restaurant. TV.*

City Hotel Ring
XIII.Szent István körút 22 (340 5450/fax 340 4884/ www.taverna.hu/ring). M3 Nyugati pu./tram 4, 6. **Rates** €57-€79 double. **Credit** AmEx, DC, MC, V. **Map** p246 E3 ⑯
All 39 rooms in this hotel are air-conditioned and non-smoking – some offer free internet – and are within easy reach of Margaret Island and Nyugati train station. The rooms are slightly bigger than average at this price and decorated in standard pastel and light wood.
Services *Internet. Parking (nearby; €20/day). Minibar. TV.*

Hotel Benczúr
VI.Benczúr utca 35 (479 5650/fax 342 1558/www. hotelbenczur.hu). M1 Hősök tere. **Rates** €60-€99 double. **Credit** AmEx, MC, V. **Map** p247 H2 ⑰
Located in a concrete cube, the Benczúr's 153 rooms still manage a bucolic atmosphere, tucked away from the quiet street in a pristine garden. Some are air-conditioned, renovated to the three-star pastel and light wood standard, and represent great value in the diplomatic quarter off Andrássy út, near the Városliget. Its most famous guest was John Paul II. The hotel also has dental and hairdressing services on the premises.
Services *Bar. Conference facilities. Internet (wireless). Parking (€8/day). Restaurant. TV.*

Ibis Budapest Centrum
IX.Ráday utca 6 (456 4100/fax 456 4116/www.ibis-centrum.hu). M3 Kálvin tér/tram 47, 49. **Rates** €55-€150 double. **Breakfast** €8. **Credit** AmEx, DC, MC, V. **Map** p249 F7 ⑱
There's plenty of night-time entertainment around this plain and simple Ibis hotel, built in 1998. The 126 rooms are air-conditioned and soundproofed, all

Talk about excellent value. Hotel Császár's 34 rooms are housed in a former convent built in the 1850s, now beautifully renovated, with the air-conditioned rooms modern and mixing monastic simplicity with warmth and comfort. As the hotel shares walls with the Komjádi-Császár baths, you have access to all the pools, indoors as well as outdoors – the room rate includes one entrance per day. The adjacent hospital specialises in thermal water treatments, where you can arrange appointments separately. The location, too, is a winner: just off Margaret Island and the Pest side Bauhaus complex, it sits within easy reach of sights on both embankments.
Services *Internet (wireless). Parking on the street (or €6/day). TV.*

Hotel Villa Korda
II.Szikla utca 9 (325 9123/fax 325 9127/www. hotelvillakorda.com). Bus 29, 65. **Rates** €49 double. **No credit cards.**
The owners are an evergreen couple of former stage singers, and their hotel brings another era to life too. Yellow and white dominate the purpose-built villa, with rustic antique furniture testifying to a higher style. Gorgeous views can be enjoyed from this quiet spot in the rich heartland of the Buda hills: half the rooms have a city vista, the other half overlook the woods. Of the 21 rooms, ten have air-conditioning.
Services *Bar. Internet (wireless). Parking (€5/day). TV (cable).*

Kulturinnov Hotel
I.Szentháromság tér 6 (224 8102/fax 375 1886). Várbusz from M2 Moszkva tér/bus 16. **Rates** €80 double. **Credit** MC, V. **Map** p245 B4 ⑭
Sixteen big rooms in a Gothic palace built in 1904 make up this gem of a budget hotel. The entrance is across from Matthias Church, and while only three rooms have a street view (of the older wing of the Hilton; the rest overlook a courtyard), the bustle of the Castle District will compensate. Don't let the lack

So good they built it twice

The **New York Palace** (*see p41*) is another exquisitely renovated hotel whose opening harks back to Budapest's chequered history.

However magnificent, this mighty fin-de-siècle building originally served a prosaic purpose, as an office for the New York Life Insurance Company. Designed by Alajos Hauszmann, Flóris Korb and Kálmán Giergl, taking inspiration from Italian Renaissance and Baroque, it displayed the eclecticism and opulence of the day, with fountains and frescoes meshing in an orgy of Venetian glass, marble, velvet, brass and bronze, prompting comparisons with Ludwig II's Bavarian palaces. The building also housed the editorial offices of *Otthon Köre* and apartments on the higher floors.

Its fame was sealed with the opening in 1894 of the **New York Café** (*see p135*) downstairs, a meeting place for the leading literary and artistic figures of the day. Such was its status that playwright Ferenc Molnár is said to have thrown the keys into the Danube, so that the café would never close. After World War I, a change of management saw a restaurant opened in place of the billiards room, and a dress code introduced. The economic crisis and pending World War II forced its closure. The New York was used as storage space, not of memories but of sumptuous artefacts.

After 1945, the New York was transferred to state ownership, and first became a shop for sports accessories, then a travel agency. In 1954, it opened as a restaurant, Hungária. For locals it remained the New York, even if its gilded paraphernalia barely shone through the dark days of the era. In the 1990s, literary magazine *2000* held its editorial meetings here, trying to recapture the creative élan, but market forces proved mightier and the building was put up for sale. The Italian Boscolo group bought it in 2001.

Some 80 million euros later, the NYP has been carefully restored to its past glory, meticulous work polishing the faded gilt, adding more glint and inviting in the sunshine flooding the busy boulevard. Reconstruction took five years, twice as long as its construction a century or so earlier. Boscolo's project management company worked in tandem with the Hungarian state restoration agency, uncovering previously unknown art.

The relics of this lightly lavish and opulent landmark are augmented by contemporary Italian design handiwork: Boscolo's Maurizio Papiri and New York-based Ádám D Tihany added their own Italianate touches to the building's history, rather than simply offer a straightforward re-creation. Since the building's treasure remains its baroque café, the designers took that as gilded guidance to build a glass atrium over the courtyard. Around the otherwise simple courtyard building, they spread colourful marble. More updated baroque awaits in the rooms: silk and leather wallpaper, metallic drop curtains in the bathrooms, beige tones with splashes of reds and blues. In the suites, Murano glass chandeliers crown the living rooms.

The café has a more faithful relationship with its old look, keeping a finger on the cultural pulse with regular events – but it occupies a smaller space. Locals, eager to see the old legend reborn, were aghast at the modest modern design elements and the hefty prices. The café's red-trimmed tables irk domestic visitors as they come to terms with the fact that this café is no longer theirs but a foreign luxury hotel's. The restaurant, Mélyvíz ('Deep Water') is sunk below café level.

This is the last of Budapest's great five-star renovations. Signor Boscolo is said to have thrown away the keys – not in the Danube but in the Tyrrhenian Sea.

dressed in uniform green. Downstairs is a spacious bar area; bar and reception staff are friendly and efficient. Ideal downtown location too.

Services *Bar. Disabled: adapted rooms (4). Internet (wireless). Parking (€20 per day). TV.*

Inn-Side Hotel Kálvin Ház

IX.Gönczy Pál utca 6 (216 4365/fax 216 4161/ www.kalvinhouse.hu). M3 Kálvin tér/tram 47, 49. **Rates** €89 double. **Credit** AmEx, DC, MC, V. **Map** p249 F7 ⊛

Kálvin Ház harks back to the Budapest of the late 19th century. In the city centre end of the IX District, and at the gateway to Ráday utca's bars, the KH doesn't only attract with location; the rooms are all different, featuring parquet flooring and antique furniture, and buffet breakfast is included in the price. The location is also handy for the main market hall.

Services *Internet (wireless in rooms). Parking (€15/day). TV.*

Medosz Hotel

VI.Jókai tér 9 (374 3000/fax 332 4316/www.medosz hotel.hu). M1 Oktogon/tram 4, 6. **Rates** €60-€70 double. **Credit** MC, V. **Map** p246 F4 ⊛

Not the most luxurious hotel in the city centre, but one of the least expensive, and certainly one of the best located; and a slow but optimistic renovation of this former party workers' hostel is going on. Rooms are simple, stuffy and spartan, and beds can be lumpy. But being right next to Liszt Ferenc tér, transport hub Oktogon and the Opera House, you'll perhaps not mind the drabness.

Services *Bar. Conference facilities. Internet (wireless). TV.*

Panzió Leó

V.Kossuth Lajos utca 2A (266 9041/fax 266 9042/ www.leopanzio.hu). M3 Ferenciek tere/bus 7. **Rates** €76-€119 double. **Credit** MC, V. **Map** p249 E6 ⊛

Budget meets excellent location in this new hotel – as well as most of the city traffic. But the rooms are tastefully furnished, even if the interior lays on thick the blue, mahogany and yellow touches in an effort to recreate some of the building's Habsburg history and grandeur. It is a convenient option all the same, and the views over this main artery of downtown Budapest reward generously.

Services *Internet (wireless). TV.*

Youth hostels

The websites www.backpackers.hu, www.hungary hostels.hu and www.reservation.hu centralise the budget end of the industry online. There are agents offering a face-to-face booking service on the trains, and at Keleti station two information desks (343 0748, 303 9818, keleti@mellowmood.hu; open June-Aug 7am-10pm daily, Sept-May 7am-8pm daily) help you find a place in one of 15 hostels. Rates are about €10-€20 per person. International Youth Hostel cards are recognised and earn a ten per cent discount. There's no booking fee and you're entitled to free transport to the hostel you book.

Caterina Hostel

VI.Teréz körút 30, doorbell 48 (269 5990/www. caterinahostel). M1 Oktogon/tram 4, 6. **Rates** *per person* €13 triple; €10-€12 dorm bed; €13 apartment. **No credit cards. Map** p246 F3 ⊛

Once favoured by its location in an architectural gem, Caterina had to move house to a more modest but still historic building on a smaller, more intimate scale, but the family-run business also offers an apartment elsewhere in central Pest. The rooms are clean, accommodating from one to ten people, and you get free pick-up from wherever you arrive. Only the apartment has a separate bathroom.

Services *Internet. Kitchen. Laundry. TV (not in every room).*

Citadella Hotel

XI.Citadella sétány (466 5794/fax 386 0505/ www.citadella.hu). Bus 27. **Rates** €50 double; €11 dorm bed. *Breakfast* €5. **No credit cards. Map** p248 D7 ⊛

In a fortress built by the Habsburgs to intimidate locals, this no-frills hotel boasts spectacular views from the top of Gellért Hill over the Danube. Book in advance, as the 12 double and four-bed rooms go fast; there's also one 14-person dorm room. The site features the very touristy Citadella restaurant, beer terrace and dance club (*see p193*). **Photos** *pp46-47.*

Services *Bars (2). Café. Parking (free). Restaurant.*

Mellow Mood Central Hostel. *See p51.*

Spa city

was an essential stop for any visiting dignitary or touring member of high society. It was the closest Magyarország ever got to Monte Carlo.

Things are different now. The grande dame still has a wonderful façade and fabulous outdoor and indoor pools. But only a third of the rooms have been renovated since post-war reconstruction, with the rest left to time's devices, so room inspection before registration is the key to a stay here. Spa access is included in the room rate, with guests going down by a special lift; the extensive medical services are run by the Budapest Thermal Baths and Springs. (*See pp160-162* **Baths**.) The pools are currently being refurbished; some may be temporarily closed in 2007.

While the Gellért was resting on its laurels, a new generation of spa hotels was opening. On Margaret Island, the **Danubius Grand Hotel Margitsziget** (*see p41*) and its sister **Danubius Health Spa Resort Margitsziget** (*see p39* offer a range of spa facilities and supervised health services such as spine treatments and balneotherapy. Fully renovated in 2000, the Grand contains fin-de-siècle furniture; while the Thermal has standard decor, it can provide guests with more comprehensive medical services. A tunnel between the two gives indoor access to facilities in both.

The modern **Danubius Health Spa Resort Helia** (*see p44*) offers curative reflexology, along with hydromassage, electrotherapy, mud body wraps and rheumatic treatments. In Óbuda, the **Corinthia Aquincum Hotel** (*see p41*) is set in a thermal complex, making use of the healing waters of nearby Margaret Island and the medicinal mud of Hévíz.

Perhaps the most exquisite hotel spa, attached to the **Corinthia Grand Hotel Royal** (*see p37; see photos*), was commissioned

Budapest is a major spa destination. Few European capitals can provide a salubrious break of the quality offered by a handful of top-class hotels. Thanks to abundant curative thermal spring waters and a century-old tradition, ten per cent of visitors come purely for the good of their health.

The oldest and most famous of the genre, the **Danubius Hotel Gellért** (*see p44*), was built on the site of an old Turkish mud-bathing facility, pulled down to make way for the construction of Szabadság Bridge. An opulent spa hotel in art nouveau style opened in 1918 at the foot of the hill of the same name: Gellért. Overlooking the Danube, the hotel featured a dome-topped hall, music hall, marble-columned indoor swimming pool and labyrinth of thermal pools. In the rooms, the taps ran thermal and mineral waters as well as plain hot and cold. With the finest chef in the land, János Gundel, running a hotel restaurant of impeccable taste, the Gellért

by Vilmos Freund in the 1880s. A public facility, it served locals and later the adjacent hotel's guests with steam baths, treatment rooms and a cold water medical room. It closed in 1944. The Corinthia renovated and refurbished it to its original neo-Classical splendour, upgrading its spa services in the process. Treatments and beauty therapies pamper and spoil; massages, including volcanic stone and deep-tissue varieties, relax and rejuvenate. An exquisite pool under a stained-glass ceiling, a tropical rain shower, Niagara bathtubs, steam rooms and sauna cabins comprise the immaculate space.

In the absence of historical baths to convert, others created their own spa spaces. The **Four Seasons Hotel Gresham Palace** (see p39) decked out its light-soaked fifth floor with undulating wooden panels, and inserted a tiled pool, steam rooms and sauna. As well as aromatic massages and energising therapies, bathing treatments include the signature Gresham bath rich in Bükk minerals. In one package, you are scrubbed with fruit brandy, grape-seed oil and brown sugar, washed off with streams of hot and cold water, then given a full-body and milk-and-honey facial massage. A glass of Tokaj wine bids you farewell if you're not relaxed and radiant enough already.

The Asian-inspired spa at the **Kempinski Hotel Corvinus Budapest** (see p39) occupies almost 600sq m (6,500sq ft) of serenity in the city centre, and with a view too. Pool, controlled showers and water jets, Finnish and aromatic saunas and steam room apart, a catalogue of massage treatments (Hawaiian Lomi Lomi, Pantai Luar) take care of the body. Couples and twosomes receive massage treatment in the same room by two therapists, then can cap their joint adventure in a 'body and soul' shower, practically a private steam bath. Therapies devised around Ajaran products aim at purging the system of toxins, and conclude with a tea ceremony.

The **New York Palace** (see p41) lets Italian design fantasy run wild downstairs, where the spa emulates an ice cave lit in psychedelic blue. Post-natal massage, and Hammam and Moroccan water therapies stand out among the treatments.

Domino Hostel

V.Váci utca 77 (235 0492/www.dominohostel.com). M3 Kálvin tér/tram 2, 47, 49. **Rates** €20-€30 double; €10-€25 dorm bed. **No credit cards**. **Map** p249 E7 ⑭
It's hard to beat the location, on the south side of Váci utca. The clean dorm rooms have 146 beds, four, six or eight in each room, and four rooms have an en-suite bathroom. Entrance is at Havas utca 6.
Services *Bar/restaurant. Breakfast. Disabled access (1 room). Internet (high-speed). Lockers. TV.*

Hostel Marco Polo

VII.Nyár utca 6 (413 2555/fax 413 6058/www. marcopolohostel.com). M2 Blaha Lujza tér/tram 4, 6/bus 7. **Rates** €43-€50 single; €58-€72 double; €12-€18 dorm bed. **Breakfast** €2. **No credit cards**. **Map** p249 G5 ⑮
True to its name, Marco Polo ventures into new realms of hosteldom, matching budget facilities with hotel-like services. Clean and conveniently located, it has access to the barland of the VII District. Rooms for two, for four en-suite and dorms for 12.
Services *Bar. Garden. Internet (coin-operated). Kitchen. Reception (24hr). Restaurant. TV.*

Mellow Mood Central Hostel

V.Bécsi utca 2 (411 1310/fax 411 1494/www. mellowmoodhostel.com). M1 Vörösmarty tér/ M2, M3 Deák tér. **Rates** per person €23-€27 twin; €25-€31 triple; €11-€18 dorm bed. **No credit cards**. **Map** p249 E5 ⑯
Opened in 2004 and repainted in 2006, this smart, well run, four-floor, 160-bed former bank headquarters is as central as it gets. All air-conditioned, the bargain twin rooms have private facilities, while the dorm rooms accommodate from four to eight people. Reception is open 24 hours and the attic houses a popular bar and communal space. **Photo** p49.
Services *Bar. Disabled access. Internet (shared terminal). Kitchen. Reception (24hr). TV.*

Camping

Budapest has several campsites, the better ones in leafy Buda. Most are clean and well kept – some have a swimming pool. Prices vary from Ft2,500 to pitch a tent to Ft3,500 for caravans and Ft2,500 for bungalows. If you're planning on camping here in summer, book ahead. If you're planning to camp illegally, don't – parks and green spaces are regularly inspected for that very reason. **Tourinform** (see p234) can provide a list of available campsites; the following is the largest and open all year round.

Római Camping

III.Szentendre út 189 (388 7167/fax 250 0426/ www.romaicamping.hu). HÉV Római fürdő. **Rates** €4/€2.50 concessions. **No credit cards**.
There's room for more than 2,000 campers at this huge site on the main road to Szentendre. Bungalows are also available. Euros accepted.
Services *Parking. Pool (outdoor). Restaurant.*

The Labyrinth of the Buda Castle

The Labyrinth of the Buda Castle is one of the most exciting sights in Budapest.

The Labyrinth of the Buda Castle is situated in a depth of several storeys, under Buda Castle, which is part of the World Heritage. This 1200-meter long system of caves and cellars welcomes its visitors with historic walls and mysterious "exhibitions".

The Prehistoric Labyrinth: authentic copies of the most celebrated cave paintings of Europe.

The Historical Labyrinth: "millennial wanderings" in the entrails of the Hill, among symbolic figures and scenes of Hungarian and World History.

The Labyrinth of an Other-world: the fate of our civilisation as reflected in fossils of 40 million years.

Night-time Labyrinth: with an oil lamp among the shadows of history.

Sightseeing

Museum of Fine Arts. *See p95.*

Introduction

The Magyar metropolis is a messy, majestic masterpiece.

Panoramically divided by the Danube, the twin city of Budapest can lay claim to being the most beautiful capital in Europe. Of all the spots on the river's long course between the Black Forest and the Black Sea, Budapest is the one to make full aesthetic use of the river. It's necklaced by a series of pretty bridges, as if the Danube has been invented to lend the city its beauty.

The metropolis spread out on either bank is a city built on the economic boom of the late 19th century, Hungary's Golden Age. Most of the major sights and features – **Parliament**, the **Basilica**, the neo-medieval confectionery of **Castle Hill**, the attractions of **City Park**, the grandiose, municipal edifices of **Pest** – derive from Dual Monarchy dynamism.

The iconic **Chain Bridge**, built on the eve of the revolution that would eventually grant Hungarians the political and economic freedom to assemble their superb capital, was the first permanent span to connect **Buda** and Pest. Before 1848, each developed independently. Early settlers, rulers and royalty – Celtic, Roman, Magyar, Mongol and Turk – were

drawn to hilly Buda's controlling vantage over the river. Behind German-speaking Buda stood the rigid order of Vienna. The wide plain of Pest would remain unfettered until the onset of rapid urbanisation and the gradual cultural intervention of Hungarian after 1848. Beyond Pest lay the Byzantine chaos of the Balkans.

Once linked, Buda and Pest would be joined by the ancient village of **Óbuda**, in north Buda, to create the one city of Budapest in 1873.

Altitude and attitude still mark Buda from Pest, the one quiet, leafy and comfortable, the other busy, sprawling and smoggy. Wearing the scars of conflict, Holocaust and Uprising, this is a city of extraordinary architecture, some of it pleasingly tatty, some swishly renovated as the grand landmarks of the Golden Age are returned to their fin-de-siècle glory. Glance up while you stroll – any stretch of street might contain a fabulous façade, some faded and awaiting construction, others already restored.

Today's Budapest boasts two opera houses, 40 theatres, 60 museums, 90 galleries and countless cinemas. Entry to most costs little,

Budapest by district

District I
The Castle District and Vízíváros below, also incorporating the Tabán. See pp63-73.

District II
The other main district of Buda, stretching to the hilly outskirts. Dotted with remnants of the Turkish occupation. See pp74-75.

District III
Óbuda – the bygone village. See pp76-77.

District V
The shopping showcase of Pest, fringed by the Danube. The northern half, Lipótváros, is the city's business quarter, interspersed with grand Habsburg edifices. See pp78–86.

District VI
Terézváros, bordered by Nyugati station, Heroes' Square, Districts V and VII, with Andrássy út as its spine. Best for nightlife and cultural entertainment. See pp90–91.

District VII
Erzsébetváros, the Jewish quarter, bordered by Keleti station, Városliget, Districts VI and VIII, with quiet inner-city strolls and raucous bars. See pp95-97.

District VIII
Józsefváros, run down except for its western tip by the National Museum. See pp98-99.

District IX
Ferencváros, similar to Józsefváros but for the new riverside development between Petőfi and Lágymányosi bridges. See pp99-100.

District X
Distant district of Pest, bordered by Népliget. See p100.

District XI
Southern riverside district of Buda, featuring Gellért Hill and Hotel, and the thoroughfares to the leafy hills. See pp68–69.

Sightseeing

Parliament in Pest and the picturesque landscape of Buda, both accessible by tour bus.

The curse of the Combinos

The tramline along the Nagykörút through Pest is said to be the busiest in the world. Every two minutes, the nos.4 and 6 whizz to a central aisle on the busy ring road, disgorging and picking up scores of passengers. At rush hour, you feel there should be a small Japanese guy in a uniform pushing people in.

To bolster the fourth metro line and general improvements in public transport, the council decided to invest in a new fleet of trams. Sleek, fast and efficient, the German-built Siemens Combino Supra trams were meant to usher in a new era of mass transport when they were introduced in June 2006. The Supras, designed specifically for Budapest, are the longest trams in the world. Crowds gathered to watch the inaugural ride down the Nagykörút. It seemed that the little yellow rattle-trap Budapest trams with their quaint wooden seats and roll-down windows would finally join neon signs and Socialist statues on the heap of nostalgic victims to progress. For months, Budapesters bore the expense and inconvenience thinking that the prestigious new Combinos would be worth it.

But no. Soon after the first new trams hit the rails, problems began. Their doors stuck, some doors showed cracks. One Combino crossing Margaret Bridge tore down a power cable pole, stopping traffic.

The Combino is heavier than the old trams and some sections of the old track couldn't take the strain: the authorities had to rip them out and replace them. As more of these heavier trams rumbled over Margaret Bridge, it was found to be in urgent need of repair. Combinos ride low to the ground, so that passengers can gain easier access. But the low ride is achieved by having the wheel housings stick up into the body of the car, taking up valuable seating space.

As if these problems weren't enough, Budapest plunged into a summer heatwave in 2006, exposing another of the new Combinos' faults: it lacked air-conditioning, and its windows were permanently closed. Temperatures inside reached five degrees higher than the permitted EU maximum for transporting livestock.

The Combino was the Little Engine that Couldn't. The Mayor fumed. The head of the Budapest Transport Service (BKV) blamed Siemens. Political parties blamed each other. Siemens pointed out that the cars had been built to exacting specifications sent by Budapest, which – surprise, surprise – cut costs on air-conditioning. Yet, the interior design sacrifices even more scarce seating space to accommodate large wall mouldings – for the non-existent air-conditioning system. As a result there is less room to sit or stand on a Combino than on the old trams. The single seats are strangely elevated, so that your feet barely touch the floor.

At rush hour the Combinos can seem inhumanely packed, with little space to get to the door. And everybody lets you know what they think of the new trams. Hungarians unleash torrents of Ob-Ugric obscenity at the mere mention of Combino. During the riots that gripped Budapest in late 2006, the Combinos were kept off the tracks for fear that the mere sight of them would constitute an outright provocation. Police stopped one radical group that was hoping to rig a trap to derail a Combino in front of Parliament.

Today locals seems to have resigned themselves to living with the Combinos. The old trams are still around. The BKV hopes to have them off the tracks by 2008, but with the Combinos still full of surprises, nobody is saying goodbye to them quite yet.

and travel between each is easily achieved with a superb transport system of three – soon to be four – colour-coded metro lines, as well as buses, trams and trolleybuses. A taxi journey across town shouldn't cost more than Ft1,500. Even the furthest flung Roman ruins of Óbuda are no more than 20 minutes from Margaret Bridge by the fast suburban train, the HÉV.

Unlike Prague or Kraków, Budapest has no impenetrable old town of dark, narrow streets. Its main tourist treasures stand amid the rebuilt remains of what was Buda, the baroque city that emerged from lackadaisical Turkish occupation and the bitter conflict that ended it. Buda's remodelled **Royal Palace**, galleries, **Fishermen's Bastion** and the museums and churches of its Castle District can all be reached from the river by a two-minute funicular and covered in an afternoon.

For the grimy, grid-patterned districts of Pest, let a strong pair of shoes do the walking, and a strong eye wander on its detail. Signs, shopfronts, secret courtyards, so soon devoured by globalisation, preserve a pre-war past. Even as they go the way of most of the city's bright neon, the sounds and smells remain: a cello rehearsal, football in the yard, a barking dog following the wafts of stewing meat from kitchen windows. It seems as if someone has bottled up your childhood and tipped its contents gently out in front of you. Interspersed are snatches of Hungarian and its bizarre speech pattern, a sound made all the more alien by the warm familiarity of the tatty streets.

The city comprises 23 districts (*see p54* **Budapest by district**). The key areas of Buda are Districts I and II. Óbuda is District III. Pest is divided into its Habsburg quarters, linked by ring roads as part of 19th-century planning. Downtown is the **Belváros**, District V, the hub for shopping and business. Districts VI and VII, bisected by the main ring road, or **Nagykörút**, and the grand avenue of **Andrássy út**, brim with theatres, clubs, bars and cinemas. An average weekend's tourism will be beyond VI and VII, apart from the **Városliget** (City Park) at the northern edge of each.

In this chapter we take you around Budapest area by area, single out important sights and round up an assortment of other things to see and do. Places marked in **bold**, if not listed below, will be found with full listings in the appropriate chapters elsewhere in the book. Museums (www.museum.hu) range from those of national importance to the downright bizarre (*see p70* **Offbeat treasures**). Most open Tuesday to Sunday, 10am to 6pm, some closing earlier in winter. Ticket offices close an hour before the museum does. Tours in English are available where indicated.

Budapest Card

If you're sightseeing in a hurry, you should invest in a Budapest Card, available from main metro stations, tourist offices, travel agencies and some hotels. It allows free travel on public transport, admission to 55 key sights and museums, and discounts around town. A card for one adult plus one under-14 costs Ft6,450 for two days, Ft7,950 for three.

Tours

For sightseeing tours of the city along the river, *see p60* **Budapest by boat**.

Budapestbike.hu

18 Wesselényi utca (06 30 944 5533 mobile/www. budapestbike.hu). M1, M2, M3 Deák tér/tram 4, 6. **Open** 9am-10pm daily. *Tours* 10am daily. **Tickets** Ft5,000. **No credit cards. Map** p249 F5.
As well as a rent-a-bike service, this young firm based at the Szóda bar takes groups on cycle tours of the city, each showing a different aspect of daily life. There are tours of Budapest by sunset, plus a bar crawl by bike. The more adventurous can sign up for a four- or seven-day cycle around Balaton.

Budatours

VI.Andrássy út 2 (353 0558). M1 Bajcsy-Zsilinszky út. **Tours** *Sept-June* every hr 10.30am-3.30pm daily. *July, Aug* every hr 10.30am-5.30pm daily. **Tickets** Ft5,000. **No credit cards. Map** p246 E4.
Two-hour tours leave from outside the main office. Some buses in summer are open-top.

City-Circle Sightseeing

EUrama, c/o Hotel InterContinental, V.Apáczai Csere János utca 12-14 (327 6690/www.eurama.hu). **Tours** *Mar-Dec* 10am-5pm daily. *Jan, Feb* 10am-2pm daily. **Tickets** Ft4,500; Ft3,000 concessions; under-8s free. **No credit cards. Map** p249 D5.
Hop-on and hop-off bus tour around the sights, calling at convenient stops every half-hour. Tickets are valid for 24 hours. Live English commentary.

Ibusz

V.Ferenciek tere 10 (485 2700/www.ibusz.hu). **Tours** *City tours* 11am, 2pm daily. *Parliament* 10am, 11am daily. **Tickets** *City tours* Ft6,500; Ft3,000 concessions. *Parliament* Ft9,800. **Credit** MC, V. **Map** p249 E6.
Buses set off from Le Méridien hotel (*see p41*) on Erzsébet tér. Tours last three hours; Parliament visits four and a half. One under-12 allowed free.

Queenybus

XI.Törökbálinti út 28 (247 7159). **Tours** *City tours* 9am, 11am, 2.20pm daily. *Parliament* 9am Mon, Wed-Sun. **Tickets** *City tour* Ft6,000; Ft3,000 concessions. *Parliament* Ft8,500. **No credit cards.** Parliament tours set off from the Museum of Ethnography. City tours leave from the Basilica. One child under 12 allowed free.

The Danube & Bridges

The soul of the city.

The Danube river is integral to Budapest's history, economy and soul – as well as being a major contributor to the city's most beautiful scenery. Always present in the panorama from the Buda Hills, the Danube asserts itself even when out of sight. Stroll along one of the Pest streets leading down to the embankment and the light changes as you begin to approach the river, the result of refraction and sudden space.

After heavy rains or thaws upstream, the river can swell to twice its normal volume, flooding riverside roads. The worst flood in recent memory was in April 2006, but Budapest was ready. After the devastating deluge of 1838, flood-control measures were implemented and Pest's streets were redesigned to incorporate the concentric ringed boulevards in place today.

Even when the water is at normal height, the Danube isn't blue, but a dull, muddy brown. People might swim in the river north of the city, but by the time the Danube passes through Budapest it is heavily polluted – although old men seem to enjoy fishing here.

The river is at its narrowest in Budapest, which makes it easier to span, and all of the eight bridges (and one railway bridge) that carry traffic over the river are short enough to stroll across in a matter of minutes. Stopping in the middle of any bridge (*híd*) affords excellent views of the city.

The northernmost crossing, the Újpesti Train Bridge, carries only rail, pedestrian and bicycle traffic over the river. The next one along, **Árpád**, is the longest. It connects the districts of Óbuda and Újpest, and also passes over the northern tip of Margaret Island.

Car-free **Margaret Island** (Margitsziget), between Buda and Pest, is the city's main pleasure garden. The ruins of a 13th-century Dominican church and convent – former home of Princess Margit, after whom the island is named – can still be seen, by a UNESCO-protected water tower and exhibition space. After 19th-century landscaping work, and the extension of **Margaret Bridge** in 1901, a spa, hotel and sports facilities provided entertainment around 10,000 trees dotted about this pleasant downtown recreation area.

Little has changed since. There's now a jogging track around the island, several outdoor clubs and more contemporary spa hotels, the **Danubius Grand Hotel Margitsziget**

Chain Bridge.

(*see p42*) and the **Danubius Health Spa Resort Margitsziget** (*see p39*). Swimming pools include the **Hajós Alfréd Nemzeti Sportuszoda** and the **Palatinus** (for both, *see p200*). Other island attractions are a rose garden and modest petting zoo. Bikes and pedalos can be hired (but do bring a passport).

In theory, it's possible to get off in the middle of Árpád Bridge to access Margaret Island, but vehicle traffic is restricted. The best way to reach the island is from the fork in the middle of the Y-shaped, French-built Margaret Bridge (Margit-híd), which carries the körút over the Danube. A major tram stop lets you off to walk to the island. The southern side of the bridge at this spot has spectacular postcard views.

The next bridge down the Danube is the **Chain Bridge** (Lánchíd), constructed by anglophile Count István Széchenyi, whose foresight would create much of general civic benefit throughout the 19th century. Guarded

Budapest by boat

Floating down the Danube lets you see what you're supposed to see in Budapest, from the most striking point of view. The riverfront is the city's main stage, so it's also where the most important buildings and monuments are arranged. You can catch more major sights in a two-hour boat ride than you might with hours of pounding the streets.

There are several ways to do this, all setting off from, or calling at, the main terminal at Vigadó tér on the downtown Pest embankment. There are regular hour-long boat tours of Pest, pleasant enough but leaving first-time visitors feeling like they've just had an unsatisfying afternoon quickie. There are timetabled shuttles up the Danube Bend via Szentendre, carrying commuters to and from the city – workaday and low-key, but ideal if you've been up all night in the city's bars. BKV, the Budapest transport authority, also runs a local service between Pünkösfürdő north of the city and Boráros tér at the Pest foot of Petőfi Bridge, stopping at most bridges, Vigadó tér and either end of Margaret Island. Services run from May to September and timetables are posted at all stops. Fares are almost as cheap as a standard tram ticket.

But to do it in style, the dinner-dance option is the answer. At first it sounds a bit odd – but then the big passenger craft churns out into the black river, the synth and sax two-piece kicks into Strauss's *Blue Danube* and the receding sun backlights Budapest's melodramatic skyline. That's when you realise the trip will be pleasantly unreal. The **MAHART Passnave Sightseeing** dinner-dance boat leaves around 7.30pm. For a reasonable Ft5,990, you get a two-hour boat trip past most of the city's big sights, a buffet-style dinner and live music from the two-piece. It's a cash bar but reasonably priced. Dancing is permitted, though neither *Chattanooga Choo-Choo* nor *The Girl from Ipanema* seem to pack the floor. It doesn't matter – the band provides convivial background sound and oodles of atmosphere. Just grab a table on the open deck and effortlessly take in the town.

Leaving from Vigadó ter, in the heart of the tourist district, you stay toward the Pest side of the river, passing under the Chain Bridge, fronted by the **Gresham Palace** (*see p39*), whose gilded façade glints in the setting sun.

Across the river, the spotlights are already turned on for the sights of the Castle District, giving them a Disneyland glow. The next sight is **Parliament** (*see p86*), with its medieval-looking dome and spires. From this low vantage point, the structure looks monstrous, its height doubled by the reflection on the water. You pass **Margaret Island** and continue upriver in a less urban, more tree-lined stretch until somewhere next to wild-looking Óbuda Island, where the **Sziget** music festival (*see p159* **Budapest's biggest bash**) is held every August. By now dusk has set in. The boat heads back downriver along the Buda side, going far enough south to allow you an view of modern architectural oddities, the **National Theatre** (*see p202*) and the bizarrely lit **Palace of Arts** (*see p100*).

As soon as the boat sets off, dinner is served in the covered part of the top deck. It's a buffet-style affair, with steam trays full of stuffed cabbage, beef stew and other Magyar standards. Have your partner hold a good table while you fill your plates. Many restaurants in town would do better, but the food's not bad, there's plenty of it, and with a boat ride for the price, it's reasonable. The moving backdrop more than compensates for any lingering feeling of naffness.

MAHART and other companies also offer floating folk dances or operettas, though it seems a shame to let anything distract from the main act, the Danube at sunset. Other tours provide headphones for those who want to know exactly what they're floating past. **Legenda** offers many varieties. You'll see the city from a spectacular viewpoint that even the natives rarely enjoy. By the time you disembark, you're likely to feel a strong desire to get out into the city you've just sailed past.

Legenda

Pier 7, Vigadó tér (317 2203/www.legenda. hu). **Departures** *Summer* 10 times daily. Winter five times daily. **Admission** Ft3,800-Ft4,700; Ft2,900-Ft3,500 concessions.

MAHART Passnave Sightseeing Boat

Vigadó tér (484 4013/318 1223/www. mahartpassnave.hu). **Departures** *Apr-Sept* hourly 10am-9.30pm daily. *Oct-Mar* six times daily. **Admission** Ft2,990; Ft1,490 concessions. *With dinner* Ft5,990.

by stone lions and lit up like a bright necklace at night, Széchenyi's bridge is one of the city's great icons. Plans are afoot to pedestrianise it.

Just south is Vigadó tér, site of the MAHART terminal, with hourly sightseeing boats around Budapest and regular traffic up the Danube Bend (*see p60* **Budapest by boat**). This part of the Pest embankment is the Duna korzó, a stretch of five-star hotels and terrace cafés.

Further south is **Elizabeth Bridge** (Erzsébet-híd), a modern, prosaic suspension bridge that replaces the ornate single-span chain version built in 1903. This is the one you see when a TV newsbite refers to Budapest. All of Budapest's downtown bridges were blown up by retreating Nazis towards the end of the war; this was the last to be rebuilt, in the 1960s. **Szabadság Bridge**, linking the Kiskörút with Gellért tér, has an appealing

criss-cross of sturdy green girders, topped with golden-coloured mythical turul birds. Trams 47 and 49 rattle regularly over it.

Further south, on the lower stretch of the Nagykörút, is ordinary-looking **Petőfi Bridge**. Like **Lágymányosi** south of it, Petőfi is long, full of fast-moving traffic and less inviting to sightseers. On the Buda side are a clutch of popular outdoor nightspots.

The southernmost bridge for traffic, shiny Lágymányosi, is the city's newest, opened in 1995. Nearby on the Pest side is the riverside development of the **National Theatre** (*see p202*) and **Palace of Arts** (*see p100*). The high-tech, low-energy lighting overhead reflects the bright beams shooting up from pinpoint spotlights at road level.

Just ten metres south of Lágymányosi is the rail bridge that was once the only crossing here.

Parliament gives the riverbank gravitas, whichever way you look at it.

Buda

The city's most prestigious sights, surrounded by scenic hills.

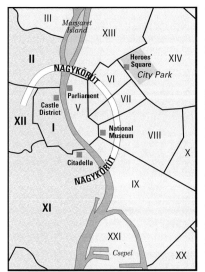

Quiet, garden neighbourhoods amid rolling hills make Buda a great place to live, and a pleasant place to visit. While it doesn't have the bars and nightlife of Pest, Buda does contain the city's biggest tourist attractions: the castle (or **Royal Palace**) and **Matthias Church**. Terrace restaurants, visible history, scenic riverside strolls and hikes in the hills are other reasons to pop over to this side of the Danube. Buda offers unforgettable views too, from the Castle District, **Citadella** and the **Buda Hills**.

Buda is named after the old Slavic word for the kind of huts that in the post-Roman era were dotted beneath the flat crag of today's Castle Hill on the western riverbank. After the first Mongol attack in the 1200s, residents moved up the hill. King Béla IV established cosmopolitan Buda as his capital by building a castle here later in the 13th century; he also founded a church at the same time, although it would not be completed for another 200 years, in Buda's golden age. Castle and church would be destroyed and rebuilt, many times, most recently during Buda's 31st siege in 1945.

Castle and Gellért Hills carve up central Buda into a patchwork of separate neighbourhoods. Below lie the old quarters of the **Tabán** and

the **Víziváros**. Behind them, the area loses its definition around the two main transport hubs this side of the river, seedy Moszkva tér and Móricz Zsigmond körtér. To the north and west, smart residential districts amble up into still higher hills – leafy, lined with villas and laced with hiking trails.

Castle District

Castle Hill (Várhegy) is the city's leading tourist attraction, and an afternoon here is a basic requirement for Budapest sightseers.

Aside from the obvious major landmarks – the Royal Palace complex, Matthias Church and the **Fishermen's Bastion** – the narrow streets and open squares that top this 60-metre hill also contain museums, from appealing oddities (*see p70* **Offbeat treasures**) to national institutions, such as the **Széchényi Library** and the **National Gallery**, as well as assorted churches, mansions and statues. Practically every building, as the ubiquitous stone plaques with their Hungarian-only inscriptions indicate, seems to have been declared a *műemlék* (historic monument).

The air of unreality is abetted by the quiet. You have to hold a permit, or stay at the Hilton Hotel, to bring a car into the Castle District. Because this UNESCO-protected area is neatly contained on the top of a hill, the tourists have their own playground, isolated from the rest of the city – though there still are real full-time residents in the old homes here. Tourists arrive by coach, by the regular diminutive Várbusz that pootles up from Moszkva tér, or by clip-clopping horse and carriage steered by traditionally costumed coachmen (for hire at Szentháromság tér). Alternatively, for a nominal fee, a public elevator leads here from Dózsa György tér by the stop below for the nos.5 or 78 buses or no.18 tram.

A more romantic way to ascend the hill is the *sikló* (**funicular**) that crawls up the side of Castle Hill in two minutes, offering a wonderful view of the Danube and Pest on the way up. Originally built in 1870 to provide cheap transport for clerks working in the Castle District – in the days when it was a hub of municipal offices and not museums – the first funicular was powered by a steam engine. It was restored and electrified in 1986.

Matthias Church. *See p68.*

Its lower entrance stands on Clark Ádám tér, named after the Scottish engineer who supervised the construction of the nearby Chain Bridge and then thwarted the Austrian army's attempt to destroy it shortly before its grand opening in 1849. Later, adjacent to it, Clark built the Tunnel (Alagút) running under Castle Hill. On this same square stands the **Zero Kilometre Stone**, the point from which all distances from the city are measured.

Above towers the flat, rocky promontory of Castle Hill, whose strategic setting above the Danube has seen it fought over for centuries. Evidence of the most recent attack on the castle, during the last desperate battles between the Nazis and Soviets, can be seen at Dísz tér, in the wrecked stump of the former Ministry of Defence, which is still bullet-pocked from the fighting in 1945. Buda Castle has been destroyed and rebuilt so many times that virtually nothing historically authentic remains.

Still, the past manages to peek through the reconstruction: baroque façades on Úri utca often include Gothic windows and doorframes; reconstructed merchants' houses can be found at Tárnok utca 14 and 16; and distinctive *sedilias*, seats for servants inside gateways, are to be seen at Országház utca 9 and 20 and Szentháromság utca 5 and 7.

The centrepiece of Castle Hill, though, is the huge **Royal Palace**, a post-war reconstruction of an architectural hotchpotch from the 18th, 19th and 20th centuries, with several wings and interconnecting courtyards. Under the reign of King Mátyás (1458-90), the Royal Palace reached its apogee. Mátyás' Renaissance-style court featured hot and cold running water and fountains that spouted wine. Partially wrecked during the Turkish siege of 1541, the area was completely laid waste when recaptured from the Turks in 1686. Empress Maria Theresa caused a new 203-room palace to be built in the late 18th century. This was badly damaged in the 1848-49 War of Independence, then rebuilt and expanded in neo-baroque style by Miklós Ybl and Alajos Hauszmann at the same time as Frigyes Schulek's reconstruction of Matthias Church and erection of Fishermen's Bastion at the end of the century.

Buda Castle was destroyed in World War II, and it took 30 years to return it to the simpler state you see today, a complex housing the **Hungarian National Gallery**, the **National Széchényi Library** and the **Budapest History Museum**.

The Hungarian National Gallery is a vast museum that attempts to chronicle Magyar art since the birth of the nation. Seeing all six permanent exhibits of paintings, sculptures, ecclesiastical art, medallions and graphics would require more than one visit. The two collections considered the most important are its 15th- and 16th-century winged altarpieces and its mid 19th- to early 20th-century art. Most of the work here derives from major European art movements of classicism, impressionism, Fauvism and art nouveau. There are depictions of Hungarian history by Viktor Madarász and lively sculptures of Hungarian peasants by Miklós Izsó. Mihály Munkácsy's paintings are considered a vital contribution to Hungarian art, especially his *Yawning Journeyman* (1868).

Also noteworthy are the many works of impressionist József Rippl-Rónai, Hungary's Whistler (he even painted his mother), and great early 20th-century painters such as the symbolists Lajos Gulácsy and János Vaszary, the mad, self-taught genius Tivadar Koszta Csontváry and the sad figure of István Farkas, a Jew murdered at the end of the war. For a small fee, a guide can take you round the Palatine Crypt under the museum, built in 1715 as part of the Habsburg palace reconstruction.

The seven-storey National Széchényi Library houses five million books, manuscripts, papers, newspapers and journals – anything, in fact, related to Hungary or published in Hungarian anywhere in the world. To browse or research, bring a passport and ask for English-speaking staff. The building is named after Count Ferenc Széchényi (father of 19th-century reformer István), who donated his library to the state in 1802. The institution has volumes (Corviniani) that belonged to King Mátyás, who owned one of the largest collections in Renaissance Europe. Sadly, these are rarely displayed.

The Budapest History Museum presents the city in an attractive historical light. Beginning with the earliest tribal settlements, artefacts, illustrations and excavation photos (all described in English) trace Budapest's development up to the present day. Displays focus on key symbols: Charles of Lothringen's Triumphal Arch to celebrate the defeat of the Ottomans; the Danube; the May Day 1919 red drapes, which represent the Socialist ideal; and contemporary urban sites, including József Finta's hotels and bank centres contrasted with Imre Makovecz's organic villas and yurt houses. A dark room is full of ghoulish Gothic statues unearthed at the castle, some even pre-dating King Mátyás.

Outside the palace, at Szent György tér, perches the Turul Statue, a huge mythical bird executed in bronze by Gyula Donáth in 1905. According to local legend, this protector of the Hungarian nation raped the grandmother of Árpád, conqueror of the Carpathian Basin, and sired the first dynasty of Hungarian kings. Later he flew with the invading tribes, carrying the sword of Attila the Hun;. Donáth

Medieval palace remains lurk in the **Budapest History Museum**. *See p67*.

has shown his turul grasping such a sword. In Siberian mythology, the eagle is the creator of the world, lord of the sun. Ancient Magyars believed they were descended from this god. By 1896, Austrian conquerors claimed their share of this Magyar blue blood. The turul myth, co-opted to serve this new master, was located here by the palace. The turul is a common motif on key fin-de-siècle Budapest structures, including the main gates of Parliament and Szabadság Bridge. These days it's used as a symbol by nationalist groups. See breathtaking views of Pest from the foot of the statue.

Strolling away from the palace towards Szentháromság tér, you'll pass the **Golden Eagle Pharmaceutical Museum** set in a 15th-century house, one of the oldest on Castle Hill. Exhibits include a reconstruction of an alchemist's laboratory and mummy powder from Transylvania, believed to cure epilepsy. On the parallel street of Úri utca, **Buda Castle Labyrinth** (Budavári Labirintus) is a ten-kilometre network of caves and man-made passageways, used as an air-raid shelter in the war. It now houses a quirky, tongue-in-cheek installation, put together by art students, that pokes fun at typical museum exhibitions. Also here is the appealingly antiquated **Telephone Museum** (*see p70* **Offbeat treasures**).

At the heart of the Castle District, Szentháromság tér (Holy Trinity Square) is dominated by the neo-Gothic mish-mash of Mátyás templom (Matthias Church), named after Good King Mátyás, who was twice married here. Parts of the structure date from the 13th century, but most was reconstructed in the 19th century. Converted into the Great Mosque by Buda's Turkish rulers in 1541, the building suffered terribly during the six-week siege in 1686, when Vienna took it back from Istanbul. Some 200 years later, architect Frigyes Schulek returned to the original 13th-century plan but added his own decorative details, such as the gargoyle-bedecked stone spire. The interior is brightly coloured, almost playful, as is the gingerbread house roofing. These are Zsolnay tiles, of frost-resistant pyrogranite, used by the leading architects of the late 1800s. On summer evenings, the church hosts classical concerts.

Harmonising his romanticised reconstruction of Matthias Church, Schulek built the crenellated Fishermen's Bastion (Halászbástya) next door. Guarded by a statue of St Stephen on horseback, this neo-Romanesque vantage point offers fantastic views of Pest. It has seven turrets, one for each of the original Hungarian tribes.

Less ostentatious sights abound. Where Úri utca and Szentháromság utca meet stands the equestrian statue of the hussar András Hadik, a favourite of Maria Theresa and later governor of Transylvania. Pre-exam engineering students still consider it good luck to rub the testicles of Hadik's horse. Around the corner, on Hess András tér – named after the man who printed

Built to transport clerks, restored to thrill tourists – the **Funicular**.

the first Hungarian book on the same square – is the Red Hedgehog House (Vörös Sünház), which dates back at least as far as 1390. Once apparently owned by a nobleman whose coat of arms was the hedgehog, it is now a private residence with several flats. Nearby is the **Ruszwurm** (*see p127*), the city's oldest pastry shop (*cukrászda*) and a tourist haven.

The Castle District's streets still follow medieval lines, and are protected by a series of gates. At the northern end, between the Vienna Gate (Bécsi kapu), the Memorial to the last Pasha of Buda and the Anjou Bastion, stands the **Museum of Military History** in a former 18th-century barracks, with displays on hand weapons and the street fighting of the 1956 Uprising. Across from it is the site of the Mária Magdolna templom (Church of St Mary Magdalene), where Magyar Christians worshipped when Matthias Church was used by Buda's German population. All but the tower and gate were pulled down after the destruction of World War II. Next to the Military Museum, a large neo-gothic building, with decorative roof tiles like those of Matthias Church, houses the National Archives.

Along the western ramparts is Tóth Árpád sétány, the promenade overlooking Vérmező, a pretty park, given its name, Blood Meadow, after a mass execution of Hungarian rebel leaders by the Habsburgs in 1795. The view, beautiful at sunset under the chestnut trees, extends westwards over the rolling Buda Hills.

Relatively tourist-free, this street is where the few citizens who actually live up here in the Castle District come to stroll.

Buda Castle Labyrinth

Budavári Labirintus
I.Úri utca 9 (212 0287 ext 34). Várbusz from M2 Moszkva tér/bus 16. **Open** 9.30am-7pm daily. **Admission** Ft1,100; Ft550 concessions. Call to arrange tours in English. **No credit cards**. **Map** p245 B4.

Budapest History Museum

Budapesti Történeti Múzeum
I.Buda Palace, Wing E (487 8871/www.btm.hu). Várbusz from M2 Moszkva tér/bus 16. **Open** *Nov-Feb* 10am-4pm Mon, Wed-Sun. *Mar-mid May, mid Sept-Oct* 10am-6pm Mon, Wed-Sun. *Mid May-mid Sept* 10am-6pm daily. **Admission** Ft1,100; Ft550 concessions. Call to arrange a guided tour in English. **No credit cards**. **Map** p248 C5. **Photo** *p66.*

Fishermen's Bastion

Halászbástya
I.Várhegy. Várbusz from M2 Moszkva tér/bus 16. **Open** 24hrs daily. **Admission** (9am-11pm daily) Ft330; Ft165 concessions. **No credit cards**. **Map** p245 B4.

Funicular

Sikló
I.Clark Ádám tér (201 9128). Tram 19/bus 16, 86, 105. **Open** 7.30am-10pm daily. Closed every other Mon 7.30am-3pm. **Admission** *Return* Ft1,300; Ft750 concessions. *Single* Ft700; Ft400 concessions. **Map** p248 C5.

Golden Eagle Pharmaceutical Museum

Arany Sas Patikamúzeum
*I.Tárnok utca 18 (375 9772). Várbusz from M2
Moszkva tér/bus 16.* **Open** *Nov-Feb* 10.30am-4pm
Tue-Sun. *Mar-Oct* 10.30am-6pm Tue-Sun.
Admission free. **No credit cards. Map** p245 B5.

Hungarian National Gallery

Magyar Nemzeti Galéria
*I.Buda Palace, Wings B, C, E (355 9975/375 5567/
www.mng.hu). Várbusz from M2 Moszkva tér/bus 16.*
Open 10am-6pm Tue-Sun. **Admission** free.
Temporary exhibitions Ft1,500; Ft800 concessions.
Guided tour in English (max 5 people) Ft3,200.
Credit MC, V. **Map** p248 C5.

Matthias Church

Mátyás templom
*I.Szentháromság tér 2 (355 5657/www.matyas-
templom.hu). Várbusz from M2 Moszkva tér/
bus 16.* **Open** 9am-5pm Mon-Fri; 9am-noon Sat;
1-5pm Sun. **Admission** *Church* free. *Treasury*
Ft650; Ft450 concessions. **No credit cards.**
Map p245 B4. **Photos** *p64*.

Museum of Military History

Hadtörténeti Múzeum
*I.Tóth Árpád sétány 40 (325 1600/325 1601/
www.militaria.hu). Várbusz from M2 Moszkva tér/
bus 16.* **Open** *Oct-Mar* 10am-4pm Tue-Sun. *Apr-Sept*
10am-6pm Tue-Sun. **Admission** free. Call a week
ahead for group guided tour in English, Ft3,000.
No credit cards. Map p245 B4.

Museum of Military History.

National Széchényi Library

Országos Széchényi Könyvtár
*I.Buda Palace, Wing F (224 3848/www.oszk.hu).
Várbusz from M2 Moszkva tér/bus 16.* **Open**
Exhibits 10am-6pm Tue-Sat. *Library* 10am-8pm
Tue-Fri; 10am-5pm Sat. Closed mid July-20 Aug.
Admission Ft1,000. Full passport required to enter
library. **No credit cards. Map** p248 C5.

Tabán & Gellért Hill

South of Castle Hill, a quiet, shady park
dominates the neighbourhood known as Tabán.
The area was once a disreputable quarter
inhabited by Serbs, Greeks and Gypsies, most
of whom made their living on the river – until
the Horthy government levelled it in the 1930s.

One of the sites that wasn't levelled, now
housing the Várkert Casino, was originally
used as a pumphouse that furnished water
for the Royal Palace. It was designed in neo-
Renaissance style by Miklós Ybl, who also
designed the building across the street, at
Ybl Miklós tér 6. A plaque notes that this
now-empty building was the place where
Adam Clark, the Scotsman who designed
the Chain Bridge, lived and died (in 1866).

Next door is the **Semmelweis Museum
of Medical History**, named after Dr Ignác
Semmelweis, the Hungarian advocate of sterile
surgical procedures who was born in the
building. Semmelweis became known as the
'mothers' saviour' because he realised that
doctors who'd just performed an autopsy
should wash their hands before delivering
babies. The museum shows his belongings as
well as a general medical exhibition. Another
room contains the 1786 Holy Ghost Pharmacy,
transported whole from Király utca.

A few steps away, toward Szarvas tér,
a simple, bronze bust honours József Antall,
Hungary's first democratically elected prime
minister, who took office in 1990 and died in
1993. Antall's tie swirls with motion, his brow is
furrowed in a tough, knowing look and his hair
seems more his own than it ever did in real life.

The **Platán Eszpresszó** (*see p127*) at
Döbrentei ter is a relaxing terrace bar with
a great Danube view. A little further south,
past Elizabeth Bridge, another terrace bar, the
summer-only Rudas Rómkert (Döbrentei tér 9,
344 3155) serves decent food, has good views of
the river and draws a young professional crowd
in the evening. The bar is on one side of the
Rudas baths (*see p162*).

The intimidating Gellért Hill is easy to climb
via a network of paths and steps that are cut
into the cliff and begin at the stairs below the
Gellért Statue, across from the entry to
Elizabeth Bridge. The short, steep hike to the

Moszkva tér – the graceless gateway to Buda. *See p73.*

Citadella may leave you panting, but you'll be rewarded with fine views on the way up, and a close-up look at the 11-metre (33-foot) sculpture of Bishop Gellért raising his cross towards Pest. The statue and the artificial waterfall underneath were created in 1904 to mark the country's first Christian martyr. Gellért, an Italian missionary, was caught up in a ninth-century pagan revolt against St Stephen's efforts to make Hungary Catholic. According to legend, the heathens put the bishop inside a barrel lined with spikes and rolled him down this hill into the Danube.

The imposing Citadella on the 230-metre summit was constructed by the Habsburgs to assert their authority after they put down Hungary's 1848-49 War of Independence. Its commanding view put the city within easy range should the Magyars choose to get uppity again. The Dual Monarchy meant that its guns were never fired – although the Hungarian army sets off a blaze of fireworks from the hilltop on St Stephen's Day every 20 August. The site now houses a **youth hostel** (*see p49*), restaurant and **nightclub** (*see p193*), plus an exhibition of the area's history since its settlement by the Celts.

Perched above it, and visible from points all around the city, is the 14-metre **Liberty Statue** (Felszabadulási Emlékmű), depicting Lady Liberty hoisting a palm frond over her head. The statue was built to mark liberation from Nazi rule by Soviet soldiers in 1945. The story goes that sculptor Zsigmond Kisfaludy-Stróbl was commissioned to create the statue as a memorial to the son of Admiral Horthy, but this is a myth.

The figure is a rare example of surviving Soviet statuary in Budapest; the bronze figures of Soviet soldiers at its base have been moved, like many monuments of that era, to the **Statue Park** (*see p70* **Offbeat treasures**).

If you go downhill from the Citadella in a southerly direction, heading towards Gellért tér, you'll pass the **Cave Church**, a somewhat spooky place of worship run by monks of the Hungarian Paulite order. Although the caves in this cliff were inhabited 4,000 years ago, the Cave Church was only dedicated in 1926 and expanded in 1931 by Count Gyula Zichy, archbishop of Kalocsa, who had helped re-establish the Hungarian Paulite order of monks. The monastery next door opened in 1934, and the monks resumed their work after an interval of 150 years. The Communist Party jailed the monks in the 1950s and the cave was boarded up for decades, reopening in August 1989.

At the Buda foot of Szabadság Bridge stands the four-star **Gellért Hotel** (*see p44*), an imposing art nouveau edifice with a complex of thermal baths and swimming pools behind. Even if you don't want to swim, soak or sleep here, it's worth poking your head through the entrance on Kelenhegyi út, just to observe the impressively ornate secessionist foyer. The café offers suitably elegant surroundings, and one of Buda's even better bars can be found round the corner on Budafoki út: **Libella** (*see p127*).

The fountain in front of the Gellért, built by the city in 2003 in a mix of ancient Magyar and art nouveau style, is covered by a criss-cross

Offbeat treasures

Agriculture Museum

Mezőgazdasági Múzeum
*XIV.Vajdahunyad Castle in Városliget
(363 5099).* **Map** p247 J2.
Housed in a beautiful baroque wing of
Vajdahunyad Castle, this museum dedicated
to rural Hungary has stuffed animals and
farm-related displays, including antique
ploughs and, for some reason, an aerosol
spray can labelled 'PIG SEX'.

Capital Sewerage Works Museum

Fővárosi Csatornázási Művek Múzeuma
II.Zsigmond tér 1-4 (335 4984).
Smelly building full of shiny black pumps.

Crime & Police History Museum

Bűnügyi és Rendőrség-történeti Múzeum
*VIII.Mosonyi utca 7 (477 2183/
www.policehistorymus.com).* **Map** p250 J5.
Various police uniforms and weapons from
Habsburg times to the present, with ghoulish
re-creations of murder scenes featuring
stuffed police dogs and life-sized dummies.

Ferenc Hopp Museum of Eastern Asiatic Arts

Keletázsiai Művészeti Múzeuma
*VI.Andrássy út 103 (322 8476/
www.hoppmuzeum.hu).*
Map p247 H3.
In five trips around the world, Ferenc Hopp
(1833-1919) amassed more than 4,000

pieces of Asian art, including Lamaist scroll
paintings, old Indian art influenced by ancient
Greece and artefacts from Mongolia.

Gizi Bajor Theatre Museum

Bajor Gizi Színészmúzeum
*XII.Stromfeld Aurél út 16 (356 4294/
www.oszmi.hu/bajorgiziszineszmuzeum.htm).*
This lovely fin-de-siècle villa and former home
of actress Gizi Bajor (1893-1951) houses an
exhibition devoted to the history of early
cinema and actors from the National Theatre.

György Ráth Museum

VI.Városligeti fasor 12 (342 3916).
Map p247 H3.
György Rath was an artist and Asian art
historian who collected snuff bottles, scroll
paintings, miniature shrines, samurai armour
and a finely carved lobster on a lacquer comb
from Japan. Detailed English texts, and a
regular series of temporary exhibitions.

Hungarian Museum of Electrotechnics

Magyar Elektrotechnikai Múzeum
VII.Kazinczy utca 21 (479 0469).
Map p249 F5.
Inside a 1930s transformer station, men
in white coats demonstrate things that
crackle and spark, including the world's first
electric motor, designed by a Hungarian
Benedictine monk.

Museum of Commerce & Catering

Kereskedelmi és Vendéglátói Múzeum
*V.Szent István tér 15 (375 6249/
www.mkvm.hu).* **Map** p246 E4.
Since moving from the Castle District to
central Pest, this wonderful museum has yet
to open its permanent collection of adverts
and shopfronts from the early 20th century.
Temporary exhibits include commercial
posters from 1885 to 1945 and a tribute to
restaurateur Károly Gundel. *See photos.*

Museum of Firefighting

Tűzoltó Múzeum
X.Martinovics tér 12 (261 3586).
The first motorised water pump, brought to
Hungary by Széchenyi's son Ödön in 1870,
plus the original motorised dry extinguisher
invented by Kornél Szilvay in 1928.

Statue Park

Szobor Park
*XXII.Balatoni út (424 7500/www.szobor
park.hu). Bus 3 from tram 47, 49, then
bus 50 to terminus.* **Open** 10am-dusk daily.
Admission Ft600. **No credit cards**.
In the early 1990s, when other post-
Communist capitals were melting down their
statues of Stalin, Marx and fellow travellers,
Budapest shifted their metal and stone
Socialist-Realist monuments, some 40 of
them, many several metres tall, to this park

in the middle of nowhere. Among the historic
figures in familiar poses is a rare likeness of
Béla Kun, leader of the short-lived pro-Soviet
government in 1919. There's decent English-
language information and great Commie-era
kitsch in the gift shop in which revolutionary
songs blast out from an old radio.

Telephone Museum

Telefónia Múzeum
I.Úri utca 49 (201 8188). **Map** p245 A4.
Old switchboards and telephones described
in wonderfully useless Hunglish. Hungary's
own pioneer Tivadar Puskás, a major
influence on Thomas Edison, invented the
telephone exchange.

Transport Museum

Közlekedési Múzeum
XIV.Városligeti körút 11 (273 3840).
Map p247 K2.
Antique right-hand drive cars, trams, a steam
train, model boats and hands-on exhibits are
complemented by a model train revved up
every hour to whip through a realistic
miniature Hungarian countryside.

Underground Railway Museum

Földalatti Múzeum
V.Deák tér metro station (235 0207).
Map p249 E5.
Original carriages from continental Europe's
first underground, built in 1896.

Millenáris Park. *See p74.*

stone arch. Water from the fountain flows through an intricate set of grooves to eight drains, each labelled for one of the city's baths.

Cave Church
Sziklatemplom
XI.Gellérthegy (385 1529). Tram 19, 47, 49/bus 7.
Open 9-10.30am, noon-4pm, 6.30-7.30pm daily.
Admission free. **Map** p249 E7.

Citadella
XI.Gellérthegy. Bus 27. **Map** p248 D7.

Gellért Statue
XI.Gellérthegy. Tram 18, 19/bus 7. **Map** p248 D6.

Liberty Statue
Felszabadulási Emlékmű
XI.Gellérthegy. Bus 27. **Map** p249 D7.

Semmelweis Museum of Medical History
Semmelweis Orvostörténeti Múzeum
I.Apród utca 1-3 (375 3533/www.semmelweis. museum.hu). Tram 18/bus 5, 86. **Open** 10.30am-5.30pm Tue-Sun. **Admission** free. *Temporary exhibitions* Ft500; Ft300 concessions. *Guided tour in English* Ft1,500. **No credit cards. Map** p248 C6.

The Víziváros

From the north-east side of the Castle District, the ancient streets of the Víziváros (Water Town) cascade down towards the Danube. This neighbourhood stretches along the river from Clark Ádám tér, by the Chain Bridge, to the foot of Margaret Bridge. One of Budapest's oldest districts, Víziváros centres around Fő utca, which was built in Roman times.

The tree-shaded walkway along the Danube here provides some of Budapest's more pleasant riverside strolls.

This quiet neighbourhood is lined with medieval houses, baroque churches and narrow streets. Georges Maurois' **Institut Français**, built in 1992 at Fő utca 17, is one of the city's few decent modern buildings. It enjoys a prominent waterfront location, used for a flashy Bastille Day fireworks display every 14 July. The institute, home to a French library and dozens of cultural events, is on a tiny square that connects Fő utca to Bem rakpart. The French Institute's ground-floor **Café Alexandre Dumas** (225 8417; open 8.30am-9pm Mon-Fri, 9am-2pm Sat) serves good drinks and nice baguette sandwiches, and its terrace has gorgeous views of Pest, across the river.

If you move away from the river and head north on Fő utca to the pretty square of Corvin tér, the Budai Vigadó and **Hungarian Heritage House**, a newly renovated neo-classical building decked in ostentatious statuary, is the home venue for the Hungarian State Folk Ensemble. It also lets visitors peruse, and buy copies of, a large collection of audio and video field recordings of Hungarian folk music and dances.

Back along the river is shady Szilágy Dezső tér, the site of a neo-Gothic Calvinist church. You can grab a meaty meal nearby at the **Carne di Hall** restaurant (*see p106*).

Batthyány tér is the area's centrepiece, a pedestrianised square that serves as a transport hub, where buses meet the southern terminal of the HÉV suburban rail line to Szentendre. Fringed by 18th- and 19th-century architecture – including a former market hall that now houses

Chairlift. *See p74.*

a supermarket – the square offers an excellent view of Parliament across the river. Perched on its southern side is the **Church of St Anne**, one of Hungary's finest baroque buildings. If you only visit one church in Budapest, this should be it. Construction began in 1740, to the plans of Jesuit Ignatius Pretelli. Máté Nepauer, one of the most prominent architects of Hungarian baroque, oversaw its completion in 1805. The façade is crowned by the eye-in-the-triangle symbol of the Trinity, while Faith, Hope and Charity loiter around the front door. The theatricality of the interior is typical of the style. Larger-than-life statues are frozen in performance on the High Altar, framed by black marble columns representing the Temple of Jerusalem. In the former presbytery next door is the atmospheric **Angelika** café (*see p127*), with an interior illuminated through the glow of stained-glass windows and a cool shaded terrace outside.

North along Fő utca, at Nos.70-72, is the Military Court of Justice, used as a prison and headquarters by both the Gestapo in the early 1940s and the secret police in the Stalinist 1950s. Here Imre Nagy and associates were tried in secret and condemned to death after the 1956 revolution. Just a block away is the **Király Baths** (*see p161*), a leftover from the Turkish days and, unlike the other Ottoman bathhouses, interesting to view from outside.

The street ends at Bem tér, with its statue of General Joseph Bem, the Polish general who led the Hungarian army in the War of Independence. His aide-de-camp was national poet Sándor Petőfi, whose verse is engraved on the pedestal. On 23 October 1956, this small square was the site of a massive student demonstration against Soviet rule, held in sympathy with political changes in Poland at the time. Thousands of angry workers also joined in. This would be the beginning of the Uprising that lasted a week and finished with Nagy's fateful trial.

Budai Vigadó & Hungarian Heritage House

I.Corvin tér 8 (225 6058/www.heritagehouse.hu). Tram 19/bus 86. **Open** *Collection* 10am-6pm Mon; 2-6pm Tue; 11am-7pm Fri. *Performances* vary. **Admission** free. Map p245 C4.

Church of St Anne

Szent Anna templom
I.Batthyány tér 8 (201 3404). M2 Batthyány tér/ tram 19. **Open** *Services* 6.45-9am, 4-7pm Mon-Sat; 7am-1pm, 6pm Sun & public holidays. **Admission** free. **Map** p245 C4.

Moszkva tér & Buda Hills

Moszkva tér, an ugly transport hub connecting the Buda Hills to the rest of town, bustles with a cross-section of Budapest characters. Buskers busk, itinerant workers wait for someone to hire them, Hungarians from the countryside sell flowers, fruit and lace – and the wealthy pass by on their way to garden homes.

The tacky Socialist-era design of the metro entrance and attached shops is complemented by the tacky capitalist-era design of the nearby **Mammut Center** mall (*see p141*) and **Millenáris** complex. The **Millenáris Park** and events centre, opened in 2001 on the site of the old Ganz foundry and electrical factory, are renovated industrial spaces hosting concerts and exhibitions on things Hungarian. Now it's also known as the Jovő Ház – the House of the Future.

The complex was established by the government to mark the millennium of the crowning of St Stephen, which explains the patriotic exhibitions and the design of the park. It's shaped like a microcosm of Hungary, with a pool intended to symbolise Lake Balaton, and a tiny cornfield and grape arbour symbolising the various agricultural regions. It's a good venue for jazz and world music and exhibitions by local artists. The park also has a playground, puppet shows and other children's events.

Amid the postmodern overkill, the area has small pockets of tradition, like the antique-style Auguszt Cukrászda at Fény utca 8. A family business since the 1870s, it serves some of the city's finest cakes and sticky pastries.

Down near the Buda foot of Margaret Bridge, you can walk up Mecset (mosque) utca, or climb the steep, cobbled medieval street of Gül Baba utca and come to the **Tomb of Gül Baba**. Gül Baba was a Turkish dervish saint, a personal companion of Sultan Süleyman the Magnificent and a member of the Bektashi order. His name means 'father of roses' and, according to legend, he introduced the flower to Budapest, thus giving the name Rózsadomb (Rose Hill) to the area. Inside the mausoleum, renovated by the Turkish government, are verses inscribed by Turkish traveller Evliya Tselebi in 1663. This is the northernmost active centre of pilgrimage for Bektashi Muslims. All around the hilltop mausoleum are fantastic views of the city.

The tomb is at the foot of Rózsadomb, for generations Budapest's ritziest residential area. It was said in Communist times that inhabitants of airy Rózsadomb had the same life expectancy as in Austria, while denizens of polluted Pest below had the life expectancy of Syria. It's a quiet area with few tourist attractions.

If you go along the side of Rózsadomb, past Moskva tér to a neighbourhood called Pasarét, which is served by the no.56 tram and the no.5 bus, there are several Bauhaus-style delights, including the Szent Antal Church and round bus station at Pasaréti tér, both designed by Gyula Rimanóczy. The **Matteo** restaurant (*p106*) is here too. A little further along, the Bauhaus estate of Napraforgó utca has 22 houses, each by a different architect, showing various interpretations of the modern movement.

Uphill from Pasaréti tér to the left is another Bauhaus-style structure, the **Imre Nagy Memorial House**, former home of the ill-fated prime minister during the 1956 revolution. It exhibits photos of Nagy and family and events from his day, along with his archives. Call ahead for a free tour.

Uphill and right from Pasaréti tér is the **Béla Bartók Memorial House**, the composer's former residence, now a concert venue (*see p183*) and museum. Artefacts from his travels around Transylvania are the highlights here, including a fob watch metronome.

The farther reaches of hilly Buda attract hikers. The sprawling forest of Budakeszierdő park starts at Normafa, the terminus of the red no.21 bus from Déli station. Trail signs for Budakeszi lead you on an easy, downhill, three-hour hike to the village of Budakeszi, from where you can catch a bus back to Moszkva tér. From Moszkva tér, the red no.22 bus goes to the Budakeszi game reserve (Vadaspark), which stretches past the city limits into a huge forest. Near the entrance there is a small zoo.

There's also a strange network of eccentric forest transport: a cog-wheel railway runs from Szilágyi Erzsébet fasor, opposite the Budapest Hotel, up to the summit of Széchenyi Hill. Walk across the park here to catch the narrow-gauge Children's Railway. This was once run by the Communist youth organisation. Its charming trains, open to the breeze and still manned by children, snake hourly through wooded patches of the Buda Hills, including 527-metre Jánoshegy, the city's tallest hill.

Another odd conveyance goes up Jánoshegy: from the terminus of the 158 bus from Moszkva tér, the chairlift (*libegő*) goes most of the way up the hill. It's a short, steep hike to the top, with a vast view from the Erzsébet lookout tower. On a clear day, you can almost see Slovakia.

You can also get tours of the Szemlőhegyi caves (II.Pusztaszeri út 35, 325 6001) and Pálvölgyi cave (II.Szépvölgyi út 162, 325 9505), burrowed beneath Buda's hills.

Béla Bartók Memorial House
Bartók Béla Emlékház
II.Csalán utca 29 (394 2110). Bus 5. **Open** 10am-5pm Tue-Sun. **Admission** Ft700; Ft400 concessions. **No credit cards. Photo** *p75*.

Millenáris Park
II.Fény utca 20-22 (336 4000/www.jovohaz.hu). M2 Moszkva tér/tram 4, 6. **Open** 10am-6pm daily. **Admission** free. *Concerts* vary. **No credit cards. Map** p245 A3. **Photo** *p72*.

Nagy Imre Memorial House
Nagy Imre Emlékház
II.Orsó utca 43 (392 5011/www.nagyimrealapit vany.hu). Bus 29. **Open** 2-6pm Tue, Thur. **Admission** free.

Tomb of Gül Baba
Gül Baba Türbéje
II.Mecset utca 14 (326 0062). Tram 4, 6. **Open** 10am-6pm daily. **Admission** Ft400; Ft200 concessions. **No credit cards. Map** p245 B2.

Béla Bartók Memorial House: home of Hungary's greatest modern composer. *See p74*.

Óbuda

Roman ruins, Op Art and fine restaurants.

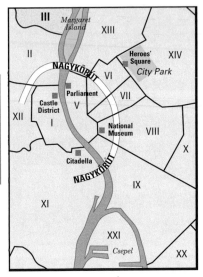

The oldest part of the city, Óbuda – Ancient Buda – was very much a separate entity until the unification of Budapest in 1873. Then a sleepy Danubian village of one-storey houses and cottages populated by Serb, German and Magyar fishermen and artisans, Óbuda still has the feel of a bygone era. Older residents still nuture strictly partisan sentiments. When cheering on the local football club, prosaically named III.Kerület, they are heard to shout 'Come On You District!'

Óbuda's green hills have been rediscovered as a prime patch of Budapest, bringing in expensive housing developments and a better class of bar and nightclub, particularly around the commercial hub of Kolosy tér. There's a good crop of restaurants up here, especially those specialising in traditional cookery, like the **Maligán** wine restaurant (*see p109*) and the locally beloved **Kéhli Vendéglö** (*see p109*). With easy access from town – regular suburban HÉV trains from Batthyány tér reach here in ten minutes – this is a prime spot for new office development.

The Romans established Aquincum, a town of some 4,000 people, in 35 BC, incorporating the surrounding region of Pannonia into the Empire in 14 BC. Little was known of their stay until archaeologists dug up its remains at the end of the 19th century. What can be seen today is mainly gathered at the **Aquincum Museum**. Its low walls composed of unearthed foundations, the venue is set in a large grassy area of scattered ruins, offset by a newly expanded museum. The highlight is a remarkable water-powered organ, the only one complete enough to be restored and played.

Hundreds of tombs have also been found in the grounds of the century-old **Óbuda Gas Factory**, a Ft4 billion site currently earmarked for development. Set between Aquincum and the Danube shore, facing Óbudai-sziget, the location is desirable but the hazardous waste in the soil might not be – the story looks set to dominate the headlines here for years.

Further Roman remains can be found nearby within the vast Flórián tér underpass, the so-called Baths Museum, unexciting ruins of Roman baths viewed from outside a glass enclosure. There's also a small amphitheatre by the HÉV station across the road, and parts of a military amphitheatre on the corner of III.Nagyszombat utca and Pacsirtamezö utca.

Óbuda's more recent past is evident at the quaint, cobblestoned square of Fő tér, where the Varósháza (Town Hall) and other buildings are stunningly restored. Here, you can get the feeling you've walked back into the early 1900s – though if you look up, you'll see the tops of grey, Communist-era housing blocks looming just beyond the square. At no.4 is the **Zsigmond Kun Folk Art Collection**. Kun was an ethnographer whose 18th-century lodging serves as a showcase for the items of 19th- and early 20th-century Hungarian art he brought together. Notable are ceramics from his hometown of Mezőtúr. In one corner of the square, Imre Varga's playful 1986 statue group *People Waiting* consists of a charming clutch of life-sized bronze figures holding umbrellas.

Right next to Fő tér is another square, Szentlélek tér, with a stately museum dedicated to the works of Viktor **Vasarely**, the Pécs-born modern artist credited with starting the Op Art Movement in the 1960s. Vasarely's patterns create optical illusions and 3D figures, some of which you've probably seen before even if you didn't know the name, and this collection, held in the two-storey wing of the old aristocratic home of the Zichy family, contains some 400 of Vasarely's works. This is one of the more worthwhile galleries in town.

From Fő tér, by the river a little bridge leads to the southern tip of Óbuda Island – at this end known as Hajógyári Sziget (Boat Factory Island). The old factories and boatyards are being colonised by nightlife venues and movie studios; there's even a golf range. One stop up on the HÉV, at Filatorigát, a footbridge leads to the northern end of Óbuda Island. For one week in August, the tree-shaded park is taken over by the massive **Sziget Music Festival** (*see p159* **Budapest's biggest bash**). For the rest of the year, most of the island is empty.

Equally secluded, away from the river up a quiet, wooded hill, is the **Kiscelli Museum**. This baroque Trinitarian monastery, built in 1745, now houses an important collection of Hungarian art from about 1880 to 1990. The works displayed upstairs include fin-de-siècle masters and paintings influenced by the impressionists, Pre-Raphaelites, cubists and surrealists. Among them are Rippl-Rónai's *My Parents After 40 Years of Marriage*, János Kmetty's cubist *City Park*, and works by Alajos Stróbl, Károly Ferenczy and Margit Anna. There are engravings of 18th- to 19th-century Budapest – you'll recognise the vantage point from what is now Petőfi bridgehead in Pest in an 1866 engraving by Antal Ligeti, showing the

newly built Chain Bridge, the church at Kálvin tér, Castle Hill, the Citadella and the twin domes of the new Dohány utca synagogue. The most atmospheric part of the complex is the ruined church, its bare brick walls left intact after Allied bombing and now transformed into a dim, ghostly gallery. Today it's used to stage operas, fashion shows and other performances.

Aquincum Museum

III.Szentendrei út 139 (250 1650/www.aquincum.hu). HÉV to Aquincum. **Open** *Oct, 15-30 Apr Ruins* 9am-5pm Tue-Sun. *Museum* 10am-5pm Tue-Sun. *May-Sept Ruins* 9am-6pm Tue-Sun. *Museum* 10am-6pm Tue-Sun. **Admission** Ft700; Ft300 concessions. Call for guided tour in English Ft3,000. **No credit cards.**

Kiscelli Museum

III.Kiscelli utca 108 (430 1076/www.btm.hu). Tram 17/bus 165. **Open** *Nov-Mar* 10am-4pm Tue-Sun. *Apr-Oct* 10am-6pm Tue-Sun. **Admission** Ft600; Ft300 concessions. **No credit cards.**

Vasarely Museum

III.Szentlélek tér 6 (250 1540). HÉV Árpad hid/tram 1/bus 6, 86, 106. **Open** *15 Mar-31 Oct* 10am-6pm Tue-Sun. *1 Nov-14 Mar* 10am-5pm Tue-Sun. **Admission** free. *Temporary exhibitions* Ft300. **No credit cards.**

Zsigmond Kun Folk Art Collection

III.Fő tér 4 (368 1138). HÉV to Árpád-hid. **Open** 10am-6pm Tue-Sun. **Admission** Ft300; Ft200 concessions. **No credit cards.**

Hidden for 2,000 years, these Roman remains are now on show the **Aquincum Museum**.

Pest

Downtown delights and national treasures.

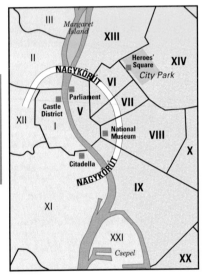

When a Hungarian says he's going to Budapest, he refers to it simply as *Pest*. Pest is where people work, shop and bar-hop. Most of all, Pest is where people live. At the turn of the 19th century, its population was 30,000. By the dawn of the 20th, it was more than ten times that, as block upon block of Districts VI, VII, VIII, IX and X were thrown up to accommodate factory workers, civil servants, shopkeepers and their families. Only Chicago grew faster. Away from fussy, German-speaking Buda, here blossomed a Magyar culture: 21 newspapers a day, drama, poetry, novels, all read and debated in any number of coffeehouses. Huge houses of culture were constructed, a State Opera House, a National Theatre and a Music Academy.

In this great urban expansion, previously disparate downtown districts became connected by three concentric ring roads. The main one, the Nagykörút, delineated the modest extent of the medieval settlements on the east bank of the Danube. Pest had been little more than a river village, its population 4,000 after the Turks had been driven out in the late 17th century.

By the late 1880s, the Nagykörút encircled a surprisingly compact area where the daily business of this burgeoning metropolis was being carried out: **Parliament**, the Stock Exchange, the **National Museum**, the **Opera House**, big international hotels, grandiose department stores and elegant coffeehouses.

A century later, Hungary's demise was never better epitomised than by the bullet-holed façades, scaffolding and sex bars seen on Pest's main streets. Private investment and municipal planning have spurred change. Parts of the inner city previously lost to choking traffic are now pedestrianised, and renovation has reached about half the façades. Fashionable, sleek terrace cafés sit incongruously next to shabby shopfronts. Significant islands of trendy nightlife thrive near the hubs of Kálvin tér and Oktogon. Post-EU property prices are rocketing for flats in central Pest districts.

The heart of Pest is District V, divided into the **Belváros** (Inner City) nearest the river and **Lipótváros** to the north. Both lie inside the Kiskörút, the first of the concentric ring roads radiating out from the centre.

Belváros (District V)

The Belváros is bounded north-south between the Chain Bridge and Szabadság Bridge, and west-east between the Danube and the sections of the Kiskörút (inner ring) known as Károly körút and Múzeum körút.

At its centre is Vörösmarty tér, named after the patriotic poet and Shakespeare scholar whose statue stands in the middle. One side of the square is a construction site, where work is nearing completion on a six-storey commercial and residential building. Opposite stands the former home of the **Luxus Áruház**, the last of the old-style department stores, being renovated for more modern retail tenants. The original building opened in 1911, done out in Viennese style. The other building on the square is an institution, the **Gerbeaud** coffeehouse (*see p129*), a temple to gooey cakes, whose apron of terrace tables adds continental class to the bland commerce nearby.

This is tourist central, with portrait painters and lace peddlars. Its apex, leading south from Vörösmarty tér, is pedestrianised Váci utca, a stretch of cafés and shops catering almost solely to foreigners. The only Hungarian voices you'll hear will be the ones serving. Many of the things on offer can be bought elsewhere for less.

Shop in fin-de-siècle style at the **Párisi udvar**. *See p81.*

The best of Pest

Best for architecture

The art nouveau façade of bright Zsolnay tiles and ornate detail of the **Museum of Applied Arts** (*p89*).

Best for art treasures

The Spanish collection at the **Fine Arts Museum** (*p93*) and the contemporary gems at the **Ludwig Museum** (*p100*).

Best for kids

The stuffed animals at the **Natural History Museum** (*p99*), the live ones at the **Zoo** (*p95*) and the quaint rides at the **Vidám Park** (*p95*).

Best for modern history

The torture chambers and eyewitness accounts at the **House of Terror Museum** (*p91*).

Best obscure attractions

The illuminated mummified right hand of **St Stephen** at the **Basilica** (*p85*); the small statue of 1919 hero Harry Hill by the **American Embassy** (*p84*) and the samurai armour on display at the **György Ráth Museum** (*p91*).

Best outdoor activities

Skating at the **Városliget** (*p93*), skateboarding around **Heroes' Square** (*p91*) and chess on **Klauzál tér** (*p95*).

Near the end of the showcase shopping district, at Kossuth Lajos utca, is the beautifully elaborate edifice of Henrik Schmahl's **Párisi udvar**, the Parisian Arcade, completed in 1913 and still functioning as a shopping arcade today. It began life as the Inner City Savings Bank, which is why bees, symbols of thrift, can be found throughout, a theme continued with the detail of the interior and Miksa Róth's arched glass ceiling.

Another noteworthy building here, towards Elizabeth Bridge, is the **Inner City Parish Church**. Founded in 1046 as the burial site of the martyred St Gellért, this is Pest's oldest building, though little of its original structure remains. It's an extraordinary mixture of styles – Gothic, Islamic, baroque and neo-classical – testifying to the city's turbulent history. The beauty of its interior is in the light and shadow of the Gothic vaulting and most of the older detail is in the sanctuary, around the altar. Behind the high altar you'll find Gothic *sedilias*

and a Turkish prayer alcove, still surprisingly intact from when the church was used as a mosque. The sunken remains of Emperor Diocletian's Roman outpost Contra Aquincum lie just north, with an accompanying display outlining the Imperial fortifications.

On Váci utca, south of Kossuth Lajos utca, is Ferenciek tere, named after the Franciscan church that stands near the University Library. Past this square, Váci utca is dotted with unusual collectors' shops – maps, stamps, small toys – and decked out in summer with café awnings covering pricy tourist traps. Bars abound, including the **Tandem** (*see p138*), just past Váci's southern end. The lively **Kafana** (*see p112*), a great Serbian restaurant and café, is on Molnár utca, between Váci and the river.

A brief detour off Váci, down Szerb utca, takes you to the compact, bright yellow Serbian Orthodox Church (Szerb Templom), enclosed in a garden courtyard that features old Orthodox gravestones embedded in the wall. A Serbian plaque in Cyrillic, with a pointing finger, shows the height of 1838 flood waters. Originally built in the 17th century, by Serbs who fled the Turkish occupation of their country (remodelled to its present state in the 1750s), it is now a hub for the community of Serbs who fled before or during the 1999 NATO bombing of *their* country. Inside the tall, narrow structure hides a treasure: a towering neo-Renaissance iconostasis at the altar, covered in a gallery of oil portraits, depicting major Orthodox saints.

Parallel to Váci utca is a riverside stroll called the Korzó, also packed with tourists and almost as busy as Váci. Architecturally uninspiring, the Korzó has sprouted a dozen terrace cafés, all with the stunning backdrop of Danube cityscape – and all with prices to match. Here on Saturday afternoons you'll find motley bands of stag weekenders loudly bragging of their Friday night.

At nearby Vigadó tér, the bustle usually includes zither-playing buskers, stalls selling folkloric souvenirs and the **Pesti Vigadó** concert hall (*see p184*), currently closed for renovation. This stretch of the Korzó is the city's main gay cruise, though you wouldn't notice if you weren't looking for it. Absurd hustlers prowl around the bushes. On the other side of the tram tracks stands the MAHART terminal, with sightseeing tours around Pest (*see p60* **Budapest by boat**) and boats going to Szentendre, then up the **Danube Bend** to Visegrád and Esztergom (*see pp208-209*).

The Korzó ends at the convergence of Március 15 tér, with its stubby Roman ruins, and Petőfi tér, with its statue of the national poet. A little further along the Belgrád rakpart towards Szabadság Bridge, are the gay/mixed

Capella club (*see p179*) and busy terrace restaurants like the **Taverna Dionysos** and **Takebayashi** (for both, *see p117*).

This stretch of the Pest embankment is also the setting for the no.2 tramline. Riding this route by the river is a fine way to see the city. When lit up and reflected in the Danube, the Chain Bridge and Castle above form one of the most magical urban landscapes in the world.

Inner City Parish Church
Belvárosi Plébiána templom
V.Március 15 tér (318 3108). M3 Ferenciek tere/ tram 2/bus 7, 15. **Open** 9am-5pm daily. *Sunday Mass* 8.30am, 10am, 6pm. **Map** p249 E6.

Párisi udvar
V.Ferenciek tere 10-11/Petőfi Sándor utca 2-8. M3 Ferenciek tere/bus 7. **Map** p249 E6. **Photos** *p79*.

Serbian Orthodox Church
Szerb Templom
V.Szerb utca 2-4 (337 2970/06 30 205 7179 mobile). M3 Kálvin tér/bus 15. **Open** 9am-6pm Mon-Fri. *Mass* 8am Mon-Fri; 10pm Sun. **Map** p249 F6.

Basilica of St Stephen. *See p85.*

Lipótváros (District V)

Budapest gets down to business in Lipótváros, the northern part of District V: blocky, late 19th-century streets and austere neo-classical architecture provide a contrast to the smaller, twisty thoroughfares and baroque or secessionist whimsy that mark much of downtown Budapest. The neighbourhood maintains the grid pattern that was imposed on it by the Új Épület, the massive Habsburg barracks that once stood at what is now Szabadság tér. The barracks, where leaders of the nascent Hungarian nation were imprisoned and executed in 1849, were the base for Vienna's control over the city. Today, this is still the centre for business and bureaucracy.

The need to feed the business lunch crowd and downtown tourists has also made this a centre for diverse restaurants: there's French cuisine at **Lou Lou** (*see p113*), sushi at **Tom-George Restaurant & Café** (*see p117*), Asian dumplings at **Momotaro Ramen** (*see p113*), Indian at the **Kashmir Indian Restaurant** (*see p112*), Mexican at the **Iguana** (*see p112*), fancy Italian at the **Páva** (*see p115*) and creative Hungarian-continental at **Café Kör** (*see p110*). It gets quieter in the evening, though there's a cluster of terrace bars on Szent István tér behind the Basilica.

The **Basilica of St Stephen** points its façade down Zrinyi utca, towards the river. Budapest's largest church, it was designed in 1845 by József Hild, but only consecrated in 1905. Construction was so disrupted by wars and the deaths of its two major architects that one wonders if God actually wanted it built at all. The original dome collapsed in an 1868 storm. Miklós Ybl, the new architect, had the entire building demolished and rebuilt the original neo-classical edifice in the heavy neo-renaissance style favoured by the Viennese Court. It was devastated by Allied bombing and restored in the 1980s. The ceiling is pleasantly bright, with colourful frescoes of saints in gilt trim. The main attraction is the mummified right hand of St Stephen, known as the 'Sacred Right', housed in its own side chapel. The gruesome relic is preserved in an ornate glass and lead trinket box that's shaped like Matthias Church. The hand lights up if you drop a coin in a slot next to the box. On 20 August, **St Stephen's Day**, the hand is marched around the square in a religious procession.

Near the opposite end of Zrinyi utca, towards the river on Roosevelt tér, the more architecturally appealing **Four Seasons Gresham Palace** hotel (*see p39*) offers an example of Hungarian-Secessionist style on a grand scale (*see p82* **Strolling the**

Strolling the Secession

Among this city's magnificently eclectic mix of architecture, perhaps no style is more purely Budapest than the Secessionist movement, the local interpretation of art nouveau.

Much of the cultural dynamism of newly independent fin-de-siècle Budapest was born of a rejection of the staid Habsburg status quo and a search for Hungarian roots.

Musically, this meant Béla Bartók delving into Transylvania for ancient folk harmonies. Architecturally it meant Secessionist, using bright motifs from mainly Transylvanian folk art, coloured ceramics and sinuous curves. In many ways, the movement was the product of the eccentric mind of Ödön Lechner (1845-1914). Neglected throughout the 20th century, he now enjoys recognition as a peculiar genius, comparable as Budapest's version of Barcelona's Antonio Gaudí.

A pleasant walk downtown takes you past eight fine examples of Secessionist architecture. Allow yourself two hours, as you'll encounter some worthwhile distractions also suggested here.

Start with the landmark **Four Seasons Gresham Palace** hotel ➊ (see p39), facing the Chain Bridge. Built in 1906 for the London-based Gresham Life Assurance Company, it was splendidly restored as a luxury hotel just before its 100th birthday. Original architect Zsigmond Quittner employed the best artisans of the day, who decorated the exterior with statues and gilt and the sumptuous lobby with peacock gates, gilt Zsolnay tiles and a glass atrium. The hotel's bar, restaurant and café also give a flavour of the architectural style.

Stroll through Szabadsag tér to Vidor Emil's whimsically asymmetrical **Bedő ház** ➋ (1903) at Honvéd utca 3. The organic curving lines and flowery façade mirror the art nouveau style of Vidor's Belgian counterparts.

Two streets away, Lechner's **Former Royal Post Office Savings Bank** ➌ (1899-1901; see p86), his crowning achievement, is uniquely Hungarian. The exterior's orderly form is disguised by a brightly coloured façade of glazed brick and a freewheeling riot of line and pattern on the roof. The building's function is acknowledged by beehives, symbols of thrift, at the corners, with bees crawling towards them. Other decorative elements on the roof derive from Hungarian folklore and mythology. Told that

these were difficult to view from the street, Lechner answered: 'The birds will see them'. Today housing the Hungarian National Treasury, it is closed to the public but you can peek through the front door and catch a glimpse of the luscious lobby.

Lechner's visionary student Béla Lajta (1873-1920) probably did most to point Hungarian architecture towards its post-war future. Lajta's masterwork, a watershed in Hungarian architecture, is visible from Andrássy, opposite the Opera House. Gold-decked angels atop the **Új Színház** ➍ (1908-09; see p90) peer down Dalszínház utca from their perch on Paulay Ede utca. Get close to see the bright blue tile sign and monkeys guarding ornate doors. The Új Színház ('New Theatre') combines the playfulness of fin-de-siècle architecture, the lean aesthetic of modernism and elements typical of art deco, a style that did not catch on until the 1920s. Nearby, you'll find coffee and cakes in a grand setting at the **Művész** ➎ (p133), and fine dining at **Callas** ➏ (p119).

Down Székely Mihály and Kazinczy, you come to Béla and Sándor Löeffler's clean-lined, off-kilter **Orthodox Synagogue** ➐ (1913), bending with the street.

Across Rákóczi út, left, then right, at Vas utca 11, Lajta again predicts art deco in his wonderful **Trade School** ➑, with a sheer exterior featuring six second-floor owls and ornate folk-art doors. Slip discreetly inside during school hours and check the beautiful interior, especially the staircase on the right.

The second left leads to Gutenberg tér 4, László and József Vágo's luxury **Gutenberg-otthon** ➒ (1905-1907), with its wavy façade, bold sign and colourful details. Lechner was among its luminary tenants. There's good food, drink and atmosphere at the nearby **Csiga** bar ➓ (p136), just over the Nagykörút at the back of Rákóczi tér.

Walk a few blocks south along József körút, or take the 4 or 6 tram two stops, to the corner of Üllői út, where you can't miss Lechner's first major Secessionist work, the eye-catching **Museum of Applied Arts** ⓫ (1893-96; see p89). Lechner deployed an array of Moorish and Indian designs – along with patterns from Hungarian folk culture. The explosion of colour at the tiled entranceway attests to Lechner's

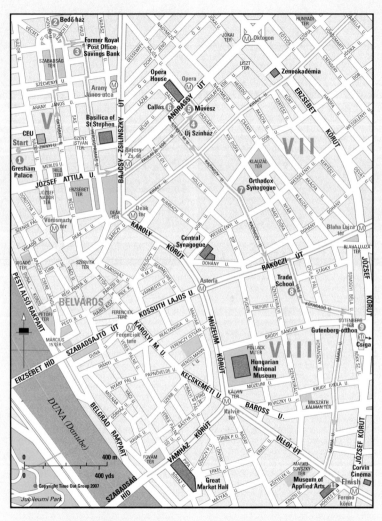

cooperation with the Zsolnay ceramics factory in Pécs, now being renovated in line with the city's status as European Capital of Culture for 2010 (*see p216* **Jeux Sans Frontières**).

Inside, floral motifs, some of which were whitewashed in the 1970s, can still be seen in the archways and arcades. Past the lobby,

you'll see a multi-storey interior courtyard, capped by a stunning stained-glass skylight. The abundant natural light owes its freedom to another daring architectural move, the decision to erect the building on a steel frame. At that time, no other museum in Europe had been designed in such a way.

Secession). This is revamped Budapest at its finest, the five-star hotel opened here in 2004 echoing fin-de-siècle glory while keeping pace with the new. Statues of Deák and Széchenyi stand among the trees on the square outside. Between the Gresham and the Basilica, on Nádor utca, stretches a complex of post-Communist institutions founded by Magyar billionaire philanthropist George Soros. The anchor is the Central European University, whose students use nearby English-language bookstore **Bestsellers** (*see p141*).

North from here is Szabadság tér (Freedom Square), laid out during Hungary's brief flirtation with imperialism and conceived as the hub of the Habsburg-era economy. The square has recently been fixed up, providing an oasis of green downtown, but it is still dominated by the Dual Monarchy's central bank (now the National Bank at no.9) and the Stock and Commodity Exchange (now the headquarters of Magyar Televízió at no.17). Completed in 1899, and meant to symbolise power and prosperity, the massive exchange building has a distorted perspective and exaggerated scale. In the 1920s, Szabadság tér was the site of a Hungarian flag flown at half-mast over a mound of soil from territories lost at Trianon (*see p19* **The terrible treaty**). After World War II, the Soviets erected a large white obelisk to mark their dead, right on top of the sacred mound.

The obelisk still stands here, topped by a Communist star that was vandalised during the demonstrations in late 2006 (*see pp29-31* **Hungarian Identity**) and surrounded by a wide pedestrian barrier. This is one of the few remaining Soviet-era monuments that hasn't been moved out to the Statue Park (*see p70* **Offbeat treasures**). Diagonally across the block, down Aulich utca, on the corner of Báthory utca and Hold utca, an Eternal Flame commemorates Count Lajos Batthyány, the prime minister of the 1848 provisional government, executed by firing squad here on 6 October 1849.

The American Embassy, also guarded by pedestrian barriers, stands at no.12. Nearby there's a small statue of US General Harry Hill Bandholtz, part of the peacekeeping force in 1919. He saved the treasures of the National Museum from rampaging Romanian soldiers by locking the doors with the only official-looking items he had to hand: censorship seals. Seeing the American eagle, the Romanians backed off.

The brightest spot in this sombre, officious quarter is Ödön Lechner's startlingly ornate and colourful **Former Royal Post Office Savings Bank**, now the Hungarian National Treasury (*see p82* **Strolling the Secession**). It's closed to the public, but you can get a feel for Lechner's finest work by peeking into the lusciously designed lobby.

Parliament. *See p86.*

Between Szabadság tér and Kossuth Lajos tér, on Vértanúk tere, Tamás Varga's statue of Imre Nagy, tragic hero of the 1956 Uprising, stands at the crest of a small, symbolic bridge, looking towards **Parliament** and away from the Soviet obelisk. Parliament defines Kossuth Lajos tér. Built, like the rest of Lipótváros, at a time when Hungary was getting a taste of empire, it was the largest parliament building in the world when it opened in 1902. Its 691 rooms have never been fully utilised, and governing Hungary today takes up only 12 per cent of the space.

Designed by Imre Steindl, the building is beautifully sited: the prominence of its position on the curve of the Danube defines the city and exploits the elegance of the river's sweep. The building itself, however, is an exercise in establishment kitsch. Guided tours (*see p58*) pass the numbered cigar holders outside the Upper House, where members left their Havanas during debates. The Sacred Crown in the Cupola Hall was a gift from the Pope to St Stephen in 1000 AD to mark Hungary's formation as a Christian state. It was moved here from the National Museum a few years ago, despite protests about the symbolic fusing of church and state.

The **Museum of Ethnography**'s position opposite Parliament says much about how seriously Hungarians take their folk traditions. Displays of Hungarian village and farm life, folk art and customs are accompanied by English labels. Originally constructed by Alajos Hauszmann of **New York Palace Hotel** fame (*see p88*) to serve as the Supreme Court, this monumental, gilt-columned edifice with ceiling frescoes by Károly Lotz is anything but folky. Worthwhile temporary exhibitions take place upstairs, plus occasional folk music concerts.

Equally, the setting and size of the adjacent Agriculture Ministry attests to its importance in a country where agriculture was once the leading export. Under the arcade surrounding the ministry, busts commemorate pioneers in husbandry and, near the Báthory utca corner, iron marbles indicate where 1956 bullet holes peppered the façade. As a plaque notes, this is the memorial to 'Bloody Thursday', 25 October 1956, when thousands marching on Parliament were caught in a crossfire between Soviet tanks and Hungarian Secret Police.

Along Balassi Bálint utca to the north, the venerable Szalai Cukrászda at no.7 serves coffees, pastries and snacks. Falk Miska utca, running parallel a block away from the river, is a street of art galleries and antique shops such as the **Pintér Antik Diszkont** (*see p152*).

Basilica of St Stephen

Szent István Bazilika
V.Szent István tér 33 (317 2859). M3 Arany János utca. **Open** 9am-5pm Mon-Fri; 9am-1pm Sat; 1-5pm

Sun. *Treasury Oct-Mar* 10am-4pm daily.
Apr-Sept 9am-5pm daily. *Tower* 10am-4.30pm daily.
Admission *Treasury* Ft250; Ft150 concessions.
Tower Ft500; Ft400 concessions. **No credit cards.**
Map p246 E4. **Photo** *p81*.

Former Royal Post Office Savings Bank
Postatakarékpénztár
V.Hold utca 4, entrance from Szabadság tér 8 (428 2600 ext 1532). M3 Arany János utca. **Map** p246 E4.

Museum of Ethnography
Néprajzi Múzeum
V.Kossuth Lajos tér 12 (473 2442/www.neprajz.hu).
M2 Kossuth tér/tram 2. **Open** 10am-6pm Tue-Sun.
Admission free. *Exhibitions* Ft800; Ft400
concessions. Call for tour in English. **No credit cards.** **Map** p246 D3.

Parliament
Országház
V.Kossuth Lajos tér (441 4415). M2 Kossuth Lajos
tér/tram 2. **Open** *Tours in English 10am, noon,*
2pm daily. **Admission** *EU citizens* free; *Non-EU.*
citizens Ft2,520; Ft1,200 concessions. **No credit
cards.** **Map** p246 D3. **Photos** *pp85-86*.

Vígszínház Comedy Theatre.
See p89.

Kiskörút

The southern half of Kiskörút, the inner ring
road, follows the line of the old city walls –
extant portions of which can be seen in Bástya
utca behind Vámház körút and also a few yards
down Ferenczy István utca off Múzeum körút.

It begins at Fővám tér. On the south side of
the small square are the Budapest University of
Economic Science and the **Great Market Hall**
(Nagy Vásárcsarnok; *see p148*). The university
was once the Main Customs Office, and an
underground canal used to run from the river,
taking barges through the customs house and
into the market. Opened in 1897, the three-
storey hall was a spectacular shopping mall
in its day, but fell apart under Communism.
It was restored and reopened in 1994, with a
new Zsolnay tile roof.

Vámház körút leads up to Kálvin tér, named
after the ugly Calvinist church on the square's
south side. Other parts of the square were
recently fenced off for construction to connect
the new M4 metro line to the existing M3 metro
station here, and the square is likely to stay this
way at least through 2008.

This busy intersection is where the Kiskörút
meets the main roads of Baross utca, Üllői út
and bar-lined Ráday utca. This pedestrianised
street, strewn with terraces, is where a bunch
of similar, spiffy but soulless venues cater to a
transient crowd. Worthwhile eateries include
Costes (no.4, 219 0696) and the **Pata Negra**
(*see p124*), near Kálvin tér. For drinks, try
Jaffa (*see p136*), a funky DJ bar, halfway down
Ráday; the recently opened **Café Eckermann**
(*see p136*) offers WiFi facilities and a menu
boasting several vegetarian options towards
the far end of the street.

Múzeum körút is named after the National
Museum. Built to Mihály Pollack's neo-classical
design between 1837 and 1847, it was then so
far out of town that cattle once wandered in.
This was where poet Sándor Petőfi read his
'National Song' on 15 March 1848, the start of
the revolt against Habsburg domination. The
exhibitions cover Hungary from its foundation
to the 20th century, the latter section including
selections of contemporary propaganda, retro
suites of furniture and shop window displays.

On the next corner, the century-old **Múzeum**
restaurant (*see p124*) offers fine Magyar cuisine
in elegant surroundings. It was opened soon
after the landmark it was named after. Nearby,
the **Múzeum Cukrászda** (*see p192*) serves
cakes, coffees and harder stuff to busy tables
until sunrise. Over the road are the **Központi
Antikvárium** (*see p142*) and other second-
hand booksellers. Múzeum körút ends at
Astoria (*see p45*), where the grand but faded

1912 hotel dominates the intersection to which it has lent its name. The Astoria's **Mirror Café & Restaurant** (*see p110*) serves fusion cuisine and Hungarian cakes in a luxurious, imperial setting.

After Astoria, Károly körút continues to Deák tér, passing the enormous **Central Synagogue** that guards the entrance to District VII (*see p96* **Walking Jewish Budapest**). Deák tér is where all three metro lines intersect; you'll find the **Underground Railway Museum** (*see p70* **Offbeat treasures**) by the ticket office.

Above ground at Deák tér there is heavy vehicle traffic in front of a cobble stone park surrounded by temporary stone and wood fencing. Plans call for making this the beginning of a mostly pedestrianised zone that stretches into District VII.

Across from this square is a modern, heavily sculpted park in one half of Erzsébet tér. Despite the attempt at greenery, the most pleasant spot here is probably the stone-floored terrace below ground level, in front of the **Gödör klub** (*see p188*), which fills up on summer nights with free concerts. Beyond a covered walkway, all that remains of the central bus station that once stood here is the old half of Erzsébet tér and its tall trees, offering shade and rest in the heart of town.

Great Market Hall

Nagy Vásárcsarnok
IX.Fővám tér (217 6067). Tram 2, 47, 49. **Open** 7am-6pm Mon-Fri; 7am-1pm Sat. **Map** p249 F7.

National Museum

Nemzeti Múzeum
VIII.Múzeum körút 14-16 (338 2122/www.hnm.hu). M3 Kálvin tér/M2 Astoria/tram 47, 49. **Open** *Winter* 10am-5pm Tue-Sun. *Summer* 10am-6pm Tue-Sun. **Admission** free. *Exhibitions* Ft1,000; Ft500 concessions. Guided tour in English (call ahead) Ft2,000 per person. **No credit cards**. **Map** p249 F6.

Nagykörút

At exactly 4,114 metres, the Nagykörút, or big ring road, is the longest thoroughfare in the city, running from Petőfi Bridge in the south to Margaret Bridge in the north, and bisecting Districts IX, VIII, VII, VI and XIII. Running its length are trams nos.4 and 6 (*see p56* **The Curse of the Combinos**), said to be the busiest in the world, starting in Buda and ending up on the same side at Moszkva tér. A busy commercial boulevard built, like much of 19th-century Pest, in eclectic style, the Nagykörút is where the everyday business of downtown Budapest takes place. Locals refer to it as simply the '*körút*'.

Most sections carry the name of a Habsburg. The first stretch, between Petőfi Bridge and Üllői út, is Ferenc körút. At Üllői út is Ödön Lechner's extraordinary, bright **Museum of Applied Arts** (*see p82* **Strolling the Secession**), decorated in ornate detail using Zsolnay tiles and first opened for the 1896 Millennial Exhibition. A statue of the architect sits outside this building, a masterful example of Lechner's efforts to create a Hungarian style. It was created to showcase Hungarian art objects and furnishings, which had already won global acclaim. It has a permanent exhibition of furniture and objets d'art from around Europe, with detailed explanations in English.

Just across this intersection is the site of the old Kilián barracks, and next to that, on the other side of Üllői út, is the **Corvin**, now a multi-screen cinema (*see p170*). During the 1956 Uprising, the soldiers in the Kilián barracks were among the first to join the insurgents. Soldiers and rebels, a number of them children, took over the Corvin for tactical reasons: the semi-enclosed theatre offered a

Budapest Puppet Theatre. *See p91.*

protected location from which to attack tanks advancing down the Nagykörút. A statue of a boy with a rifle by the cinema commemorates the rebels who died here. Work has begun on gentrifying the seedy area behind the Corvin, with a pedestrianised walkway, to be lined with offices and retail space.

Gentrification has also begun north of here, along József körút, where the ring road passes through District VIII. Twee new street lights line recently pedestrianised sections of Baross utca. Prostitutes are less visible after a 1999 law chased most of the business into mafia-controlled brothels. The most insalubrious patch used to be Rákóczi tér – a dusty square with a decorative old food market hall at the back – but the popular **Csiga** bar (*see p136*) has breathed new life into the area. The park in the square has been closed with plywood boarding, surrounding construction of an M4 metro station that should last through 2008.

Diagonally across the körút, down Krúdy Gyula utca, are a handful of other nightlife options, such as the **Darshan Café** and, facing it, **Darshan Udvar** (for both, *see p136*).

At Blaha Lujza tér, Népszínház utca runs away south-east towards **Kerepesi Cemetery** (*see p99*). Rákóczi út cuts across the körút, heading south to Astoria and north to Keleti station, its façade distinct from this vantage point. At this busy square, the Corvin department store, topped by **Corvintető** (*see p194*), an open-air club with dancing inside, is an ugly, windowless mass amid a sea of pavement and parking spaces. Catty-cornered across the street, the restored **New York Palace** hotel (*see p41*), with its **New York Café** (*see p135*), provides a marvellous contrast. Built in 1894 by Alajos Hauszmann, this handsome venue was *the* meeting place for writers, artists, directors and Hollywood moguls. Its post-war demise was reversed with a recent renovation that returned it to its original splendour. Just behind it is a little piece of local lore: the kitsch Kulacs restaurant at Osvát utca 11, where a marble plaque marks the writing of the song 'Gloomy Sunday' here by sometime regular Rezső Seress. Back on the körút, the five-star **Corinthia Grand Hotel Royal** (*see p37*) is another restored beauty, home to the **Bock Bisztro** (*see p122*).

Oktogon, where the körút crosses broad Andrássy út, is the grandest intersection and is, naturally, octagonal. But the shape did not always dictate the name: in Communist days this was 7 November Square; under Horthy it was named after Mussolini. Wonderfully, this major intersection still bears the classic

Home of Hungary's most famous composer – the **Franz Liszt Museum**. See p91.

concentric neon Tótó-Lottó sign of yesteryear. The M1 metro passes below ground on its way to Heroes' Square and Városliget (City Park).

Teréz körút features the **Művész** (*see p168*), a good arthouse cinema, and the respectable **Radisson SAS Béke Hotel Budapest** (*see p42*). It finishes at the Nagykörút's most magnificent landmark: Nyugati train station. Built by the Eiffel company of Paris in 1877, it's a pale blue palace of iron and glass. The panes in front allow you to see inside the station, making arriving and departing trains part of the city's streetlife. The mirror-glass frontage of the shopping centre opposite is oddly forbidding, despite attempts to enliven the place with concerts in the square. The metro underpass is a hangout for the hopeless and the homeless – this is as heavy as street action gets.

There's more shopping to be had at the sprawling **Westend City Center** mall (*see p141*), the biggest in the region, set directly behind Nyugati and connected to the station via passageways lined with hawkers. The multiplex in this otherwise inconspicuous mall is often the most convenient place at which to find mainstream movies. Views of Nyugati from the körút are spoilt by the unsightly road bridge carrying traffic over Nyugati tér towards the restored Lehel tér produce market.

After Nyugati, Szent István körút, the only section of the ring road not named after a Habsburg, has a busier feel. **Okay Italia**'s two restaurants (*see p113*) are popular, and the **Trocadero** (*see p195*) is Budapest's main Latin dance club. Here the körút divides Lipótváros from Újlipótváros, once a middle-class Jewish district, lively by day, with shops, busy streetlife and peaceful Szent István Park pleasantly opening out on to the river.

The centrepiece of the last stretch of körút is the stubbily baroque **Vígszínház Comedy Theatre** (*see p202*). Constructed in 1896 and renovated in 1995, it has staged performances by Budapest's top musical dramatists of the 20th century, such as Albert Szirmay, who worked with Gershwin in New York.

Szent István körút ends at Jászai Mari tér, terminus of the no.2 tram. Here traffic sweeps on to Margaret Bridge, which pedestrians can cross to reach the beautiful wooded park of **Margaret Island** (*see p59*).

Museum of Applied Arts

Iparművészeti Múzeum
IX.Üllői út 33-37 (456 5100/www.museum.hu/
budapest/iparmuveszeti). M3 Ferenc körút/tram 4,
6. **Open** 10am-6pm Tue-Sun. **Admission** Ft1,900;
Ft250 concessions. *Tour in English* Ft2,500/5 people.
No credit cards. **Map** p249 G7.

Shock tactics old and new at the **House of Terror Museum**. *See p91.*

Andrássy út & District VI

Andrássy út, a 2.5-kilometre boulevard built between 1872 and 1885, with the continent's first electric underground railway running underneath, is the spine of District VI. The development of the street, and many of the monuments along it, was part of the build-up for the country's 1896 millennium celebration. Intended as Budapest's answer to the Champs-Elysées, it even ends with its own version of the Arc de Triomphe: **Heroes' Square** monument in front of the **Városliget**, City Park.

The first half of Andrássy, between Bajcsy-Zsilinszky út and Oktogon, is thinner than the last half, with taller trees, making this stretch nicely shady. This is the liveliest part of the boulevard, now lined with trendy terraced cafés and restaurants, such as upmarket **Goa** (see p121) and **Callas** (see p119). The venerable **Művész** coffeehouse (see p133) is an elegant landmark that was in place long before.

The most important building, though, is Miklós Ybl's neo-renaissance **Opera House** (see p186), built in 1884 to mark the Magyar Millennium. Its cultural importance has always been linked to Magyar national identity. Ybl supervised every detail, including the Masonic allusions of the smiling sphinxes. The interior features seven kilograms of gold and 260 bulbs in an enormous chandelier.

Opposite the opera is the former Dreschler Café, co-designed by Ödön Lechner, before he got heavily into Secessionist style, as an apartment block in 1883. Plans are afoot to restore it as a hotel. Round the corner down Dalszínház utca is one of the most striking examples of the work of one of Lechner's protégés, Béla Lajta. His extraordinary 1910 Parisiana nightclub, now the **Új Színház** (see p204), was restored to its full art nouveau splendour in 1998. Its symmetrical geometric design features nine ceramic angels with gold inlaid wings, which carry turquoise mosaic plaques. The polished granite of its façade is punctuated by grey monkeys. See p82 **Strolling the Secession**.

Nagymező utca is known as Budapest's Broadway. Renovated theatre houses like the **Thália** (see p202) and the Operett Színház (no.17, 312 4866) are complemented by key nightspots such as the **Piaf** (see p192), an after-hours hangout for an older arty set; younger bohos gather at cafés like the lesbian-friendly **Café Eklektika** (see p131) and **Mai Manó** (see p131), the coffeehouse of the city's main photography gallery (see p173), once the studio of court photographer Manó Mai. Actors, artists and photographers would mingle around this elegant quarter in the early

20th century, many later to flee to Vienna or Paris, then New York or Hollywood as the political climate grew colder. Others met at the nearby the Café Japan, now the **Írók Boltja** (Writers' Bookshop; see p141), still a centre for literary events and a decent spot at which to find photographic histories of Budapest.

All this sits within a triangle of activity – bounded by Andrássy, Bajcsy-Zsilinszky út and Teréz körút – featuring ever more bars and restaurants down traffic-free zones. The heart of it is Hajós utca, leading from the Opera, with establishments such as **Chagall** (see p131) and **Balettcipő** (see p131). Here too are the late-opening **Noiret** (see p192) and **Picasso Point** (see p133) as well as the **Café Bouchon** wine restaurant (see p119) and the **Marquis de Salade** (see p121), with central Asian food.

There's an even heavier concentration of terrace bars and restaurants lining nearby pedestrianised Liszt Ferenc tér, with its permanent bustle beneath colourful awnings from Andrássy up to the **Zeneakadémia** (see p184). Only two blocks long – with a doleful statue of poet Endre Ady at one end and an effusive one of Franz Liszt at the other – the square throngs with life on summer evenings as customers pack pavement tables at the dozen major café-restaurants. Venues include **Incognito** (see p131), **Menza** (see p120) and the **Barokko Club & Lounge** (see p131). On the other side of Andrássy, Jókai tér also contains bars, including the excellent **Kiadó kocsma** (see p131), which serves decent food.

Past Oktogon, the boulevard gets broader and noticeably brighter, as the tall shady trees are replaced by younger, smaller ones. From here you can make out the Archangel Gabriel atop his column at Heroes' Square.

Such a sight would have been a dreadful one to anyone being dragged up here by men in overcoats in the early 1950s, for here at no.60 were the headquarters of the ÁVO, the Secret Police. A few years earlier, the right-wing Arrow Cross Party used it as a place in which to torture Jews and political opponents before and during the war; the ÁVO simply took over the premises. Shut down after the changes of 1989, the once-unassuming façade is now easy to spot due to the huge stencil sticking out from its roof, where the word 'TERROR' in mirror-reverse creates a shadow on the façade. Now the **House of Terror Museum**, this award-winning four-floor exhibition memorialises the cruelties committed during the Holocaust and those that followed under the Soviet occupation of Hungary. Critics have complained that the museum, opened in 2002 under the ruling right-wing FIDESZ party, focuses more on the events of 1956 as a dig at the Communist roots of today's Socialist Party. Politics aside, the museum is a sobering reflection on past inhumanities. Downstairs are prison cells, interrogation rooms and torture devices, many of which were used by both Fascists and Communists. There are video interviews with survivors from the 1956 Uprising, press clippings, documentation and samples of propaganda. The nearby **Lukács** café (*see p131*) at No.70, now a bright spot for coffee and cakes, was once an old ÁVO haunt.

Around the corner on Vörösmarty utca is the **Franz Liszt Museum**, in the composer's former home. Over the road at Andrássy no.69 is the neo-renaissance College of Fine Arts, once an exhibition hall, today accommodating the **Budapest Puppet Theatre** (*see p163*), designated by a large neon sign showing a crude outline of a doll.

Kodály körönd is Andrássy's *rond point* and was clearly once very splendid. Renovation is beginning on the palatial townhouses here. The composer Zoltán Kodály used to live in the turreted nos.87-89, his old flat now serving as the **Kodály Memorial Museum**.

The final stretch of Andrássy út feels wider than the rest of it, occupied by fine terrace restaurants – **Premier** (*see p120*), **Baraka** (*see p118*) and **Kogart** (*see p120*) – and villas set back from the road. The Kogart houses a large private **gallery** (*see p176*) that shows contemporary Hungarian works. There are also two nearby collections of Asian arts: **Ferenc Hopp** and the **György Ráth** (for both, *see p70* **Offbeat treasures**). This is the diplomatic quarter, with shiny plaques, bright flags and

imposing gates. The nearby streets of Benczúr utca and Városligeti fasor are quiet and shady, lined with Secessionist buildings. See whimsical villas designed by Emil Vidor at nos.23, 24, 33 and 45, all completed between 1902 and 1911. Other Secessionist gems are at Városligeti fasor nos.42, 44 and 47.

Franz Liszt Museum

Liszt Ferenc Múzeum
VI.Vörösmarty utca 35 (322 9804 ext 16). M1 Vörösmarty utca. **Open** 10am-6pm Mon-Fri; 9am-5pm Sat. **Admission** Ft500; Ft250 concessions. **No credit cards. Map** p246 G3. **Photos** *p88*.

House of Terror Museum

Terror Háza Múzeum
VI.Andrássy út 60 (374 2600/www.terrorhaza.hu). M1 Vörösmarty utca. **Open** 10am-6pm Tue-Fri; 10am-7.30pm Sat, Sun. **Admission** Ft1,500; Ft750 concessions. *Tour in English* Ft4,000. **No credit cards. Map** p246 G3. **Photos** *p89*.

Kodály Memorial Museum & Archive

Kodály Emlékmúzeum és Archívum
VI.Kodály körönd 1 (352 7106). M1 Kodály körönd. **Open** 10am-4pm Wed; 10am-6pm Thur-Sat; 10am-2pm Sun. **Admission** Ft230. **No credit cards. Map** p247 G3.

Hősök tere & Városliget

A proud symbol of confident 19th-century nationalism, Heroes' Square (Hősök tere) is a monumental celebration of mythic Magyardom. Completed for the 1896 Magyar Millennium that celebrated the anniversary of Hungarian

Hősök tere.

Sightseeing

60 minute Masters

Budapest is full of fine art, but if time is short and you want to see the best the city has to offer, you could limit your choice to the Spanish Old Masters Collection at the **Museum of Fine Arts** (see p95) in Heroes' Square. With nearly 100 paintings, it is one of the largest collections outside Spain.

When you enter the lobby of the museum, take the stairs to the right going up to the first floor. The first exhibition room on the right is the one you're looking for. This tour can take from 60 to 90 minutes depending on how long you like to ponder the paintings.

In seven rooms, including one cabinet, the collection represents five centuries of Spanish art from the 15th to the 19th centuries. The Church and the Monarchy were the two dominant patrons of Spanish art then, as is evident in the scenes portrayed.

Starting in chronological order, the first two rooms exhibit medieval panels, which originally formed parts of altarpieces. The piece by 'The Budapest Master', located on the left and made up of five panels, is from an unknown Castilian painter. It was not customary at the time for artists to sign their works, as all glory was to God and the Church. Note the many figures and details, including pained expressions. The purpose of such altarpieces was to inspire faith and educate the illiterate masses.

The most important works in the next room are the five autograph and two workshop paintings by El Greco, in mannerist style,

expressive and characterised by elongated figures, strong colours and distortions of perspective and scale. The *Penitent Magdalene* depicts the saint with ointment, her typical artistic attribute, and other symbols of contemplation.

The fourth room in the progression (which has Roman numeral VI above the door) presents works by the Spanish Baroque followers of Caravaggio, who used light and shadow to heighten the tension and emotion in the paintings, and by the naturalist Seville school. Note José de Ribera's *Martyrdom of St Andrew*, with its depiction of the saint's last chance to choose pagan idolatry over Christian beliefs before imminent crucifixion. His tense body and the title make clear the path he took. Seville at this time was a centre for religious orders and the biggest patron for painters. An early work here by Francisco de Zurbarán, the *St Andrew*, is a simple, powerful composition in the style of quietism, designed to inspire devotion and contemplation. Next to it is a work by an outstanding artist of the Golden Age of Spanish painting, Diego Velázquez. Mainly a court painter, his very early *Tavern Scene* is an example of the Bodegón genre, depicting everyday subjects with elements of still life.

The little room off this one contains works by court painters. The *Portrait of the Infanta Margarita* by Juan Bautista Martínez del Mazo, Velázquez's son-in-law, shows a girl in a dress not designed for getting through doorways easily. This is a copy of a painting by his father-in-law, now in Vienna, and was typical of portraits of young royals that were often sent to their betrothed, in her case, her uncle, Leopold I. Also here is the *Portrait of Infante Don Balthaser Carlos* by Alonso Cano, the 'Spanish Michelangelo'. It depicts the heir to the throne, who died in a hunting accident at the age of 16.

The room numbered IV above the door has more religious paintings, including two works by the renowned Bartholomé Estéban Murillo, who was so popular in his time that a law was passed to stop his paintings from leaving Spain. *The Christ Child Distributes Bread to the Pilgrims* was commissioned for the refectory of a retired priests' home in Seville. Murillo also influenced Zurbarán's later style, which changed to a softer, rather more sentimental approach, seen here in *The Virgin Immaculate*. This was painted in accordance with Pacheco's prescribed iconography of the *Immaculate Conception*, which insisted that Mary be an innocent young girl, with specific clothes, posture and hair colour.

The final room of the collection (number III) is worth the journey alone: five works by Francisco de Goya, said to be the last of the Old Masters and the first of the Modernists. He was a great portraitist, revealing subjects as he saw them, in realistic style. Compare his portrait of the Minister of Justice (*José Antonio, Marqués de Caballero*) to the wife of his friend, *Señora Ceán Bermúdez*, and you soon see which subject he preferred. The *Knife Grinder* and *Water Carrier* were painted during the War of Independence in Spain, depicting the workers who supported the troops by bringing them water and sharpening their weapons. These are the people Goya considered the heroes of the struggle. Usually full stature was reserved for royalty, but Goya honours a proud water carrier with a head-to-toe likeness.

This floor also houses the impressive Italian gallery, with Titian, Raphael and others. In the other permanent collections, you can find works by Cézanne, the Impressionists, Rodin, Dürer, Brueghel and Delacroix – to name but a few.

tribes arriving in the Carpathian Basin, it's flanked by the **Műcsarnok** gallery (*see p173*) and the **Museum of Fine Arts**, and centred on the Archangel Gabriel, perched on top of a 36-metre column and staring down Andrássy út. Posed around the pair of colonnades are statues of Hungarian kings and national heroes, from St Stephen to Lajos Kossuth. Now often crowded with teenage skateboarders, Heroes' Square has witnessed key events in modern Hungarian history – most significantly the ceremony for the reburial of 1956 leader Imre Nagy in June 1989. This marked the communal call for democracy in Hungary.

While the **Hungarian National Gallery** (*see p68*) is the nation's most prestigious venue for local artists, Hungary's major European collection is here in the Museum of Fine Arts. It has a magnificent collection of Spanish Masters, an excellent Venetian collection, a Dürer, several Brueghels, a beautiful work attributed to Raphael and some Leonardos. The museum hosts important temporary exhibitions in the grand halls leading from the entrance. *See left* **60 minute Masters**. Facing it across Heroes' Square is the Műcsarnok, which hosts rotating exhibitions and jazz concerts. Behind it, in a cobblestone lot called Felvonulasi tér (Parade Square) are two conspicuous modern memorials that have drawn jeers for being overpriced and unattractive. The giant disk stood on its side has an hour glass with 50,000 kilograms of sand that is supposed to run out annually on 1 May, the day in 2004 when Hungary joined the European Union. Unfortunately, the clock malfunctions frequently, and the local government is trying to sell it to any interested collector. The grouping of steel girders, which give the impression of progressively growing closer together and eventually solidifying into a big metal triangle, marks the 1956 Uprising. The memorial was unveiled on 23 October 2006, the 50th anniversary of the start of the Uprising, in the place where a statue of Stalin was torn down during 1956 riots. Designed by the i-Ypszilon team, who won a government tender, the monument has been derided as unattractive and symbolically obscure.

Hősök tere is essentially the front gate to the City Park (Városliget), Budapest's main area for leisure. Laid out by French designer Nebbion, its amenities include a boating lake and **ice rink** (*see p198*), the **Széchenyi baths** (*see p162*), the **Zoo** (*see p166*), the **Vidám** (Amusement) **Park** (*see p165*), the **Transport Museum** (*see p70* **Offbeat treasures**) and **Petőfi Csarnok** concert hall (*see p186*), with its weekend flea market. The setting for the 1896 Magyar Millennium celebrations, the area has a theme-park feel that survives in

Sightseeing

Zoo. *See p95.*

the Disneyfied Vadjahunyad Castle, a structure that incorporates replica pieces of famous Hungarian castles from throughout history. The castle's Transylvanian tower looms over the summer boating lake, and the baroque-style wing is home to the antiquated **Agriculture Museum** (*see p70* **Offbeat treasures**). Open-air concerts also take place here in summer.

The Vidám Park's beautiful merry-go-round is a protected landmark, but many of the other older rides in this amusement park have been replaced. Amid the dodgem cars and looping rollercoasters, one defiantly Hungarian ride dating back to 1912 is bizarrely fascinating: the János Vitéz Barlangvasút, a cave railway with cutesy dioramas from Sándor Petőfi's children's poem 'Kukorica Jancsi', recited over speakers as you ride through. There's a toddlers' park next door. The zoo, opened in 1911, was designed with buildings that placed every animal in an architectural surrounding characteristic of its place of origin. This included Neuschloss-Knüsli's extraordinary Elephant House, the faux-Moorish Africa House complex and the Main Gate. The Palm House, built by the Eiffel company, is a beautiful indoor tropical garden where exotic birds fly free in various halls, each with creatures indigenous to jungle regions. The Palm House's leafy café is ideal for a break.

Gundel (*see p122*), the most prestigious restaurant in town, is next door to the zoo. Opened in 1894 as the Wampetics, it was taken over in 1910 by top chef Károly Gundel, who transformed local cuisine by bringing in French influences. Gundel's adjoining branch, the Bagolyvár (*see p122*), serves equally fine food at more affordable prices.

Museum of Fine Arts

Szépművészeti Múzeum
XIV.Hősök tere (363 2675). M1 Hősök tere. **Open** 10am-5.30pm Tue-Sun. **Admission** free. *Exhibitions* Ft3,000; Ft500 concessions. *Tours in English* Ft5,000. **No credit cards. Map** p247 H2.

Vidám Park

XIV.Állatkerti körút 14-16 (363 2660/www.vidam park.hu). M1 Széchenyi fürdő. **Open** 11am-7pm Mon-Fri; 10am-8pm Sat, Sun. **Admission** *Day pass* Ft3,100-Ft3,500; Ft2,100-Ft2,500 concessions; free children under 100cm. **Credit** MC, V. **Map** p247 J1.

Zoo

Állatkert
XIV.Állatkerti út 6-12 (273 4900). M1 Széchenyi fürdő. **Open** *Winter* 9am-3.30pm daily. *Summer* 9am-6pm Mon-Fri; 9am-7pm Sat, Sun. **Admission** Ft1,700; Ft1,200 concessions. **No credit cards. Map** p247 J1. **Photos** *p94.*

District VII

District VII, Erzsébetváros, lies between Király utca and Rákóczi út, fanning out from the Kiskörút to the Városliget. This is Budapest's Jewish quarter. From 1944 to 1945, part of it became 'the Ghetto' when Arrow Cross Fascists walled off the area and herded the Jewish community inside. The junction near the Central Synagogue was one of two entrances. *See p96* **Walking Jewish Budapest**.

Dominating the estuary of Dohány utca into the Kiskörút, the Central Synagogue is simply enormous. Seating 3,000, it is too big to heat and has never been used in winter. The structure was designed by Lajos Förster and completed in 1859, and it is the second largest synagogue in the world after New York's

Temple Emmanuel. Newly cleaned brickwork glows in blue, yellow and red, the heraldic colours of Budapest. Interlaced eight-pointed stars in the brick detailing, continued in the stained glass and mosaic flooring inside, are a symbol of regeneration. The divisions of its central space are based on the cabalistic Tree of Life, giving it a similar floor plan to a Gothic cathedral; the ceiling entwines Stars of David outlined in gold leaf. A small **Jewish Museum** in one wing displays 18th- to 19th-century ritual objects from the region. The objects are arranged in three rooms according to function: Sabbath, holidays and life-cycle ceremonies. The fourth room covers the Hungarian Holocaust. One photo shows corpses piled up in front of this same building after a massacre by the Arrow Cross. Though the museum was established in 1931, at a time when Hungarian Jews were feeling reasonably secure, many more objects were donated after their owners were murdered. The exhibits here are well documented in English.

Behind the Central Synagogue, the back streets of District VII are dark, narrow, tatty and full of odd detail. It's not as picturesque as Prague's Jewish quarter, but although 700,000 Hungarian Jews died in the Holocaust, enough survived to mean that District VII is still a living community. You can hear Yiddish on Kazinczy utca or eat a kosher pastry at the Fröhlich Cukrászda on Dob utca 22. The Orthodox complex, including the non-kosher Carmel Pince restaurant (Dob utca 31, 322 1834), is centred around the corner of Dob and Kazinczy, dominated by the 1910 synagogue whose façade gracefully negotiates the curve of the street. The Rumbach Sebestyén utca synagogue, a nearby Moorish structure by Otto Wagner, can only be seen from the outside.

The community has survived both an exodus of younger, wealthier Jews into less noisy and congested districts, and post-war attempts by the Communist government to homogenise the area: flats emptied by the Holocaust were given to workers brought into Budapest to rebuild the city after the war. Many of these were Gypsies, and District VII is now also a Gypsy quarter – especially beyond the Nagykörút, an area of repair shops and dingy bars. It's worth a quick detour into this neighbourhood to see the sumptuous façade of Armin Hegedűs' 1906 primary school at Dob utca 85.

The heart of the Jewish quarter is Klauzál tér, with a playground and park, where old men play chess and cards in summer. Fresh food stalls spill out on to the square from the main covered market on Saturdays. Next to it, the cheap lunchtime **Kádár Étkezde** (*see p122*) serves great, home-style Magyar cuisine.

Király utca, recently a workaday street of shops selling second-hand appliances, is going upmarket. The pavement has been widened, drawing in boutiques, galleries, chic clothing shops, and restaurants like **Noir et l'Or** (*see p123*) and veggie-friendly **Püré Bár** (*see p123*).

Between Király utca 15 and Dob utca 16 is the Gozsdu udvar, an intriguing series of interlinked courtyards that make a semi-covered pedestrian pathway with a hidden feel. Built in 1904, it has been under renovation, in a development respecting the original design and including luxury apartments, spaces for outdoor cafés and shops. The reopening is planned for the summer of 2007.

This is a fine neighbourhood for drinking, thanks to a string of wantonly bohemian bars and alternative nightspots. The **Ellátó** (*p134*),

Walking Jewish Budapest

On Friday nights, after Sabbath services, Hasidic men wearing fur-brimmed *streiml* hats chat animatedly on Nagydiófa utca. On Saturday afternoons, boys with *yarmulkes* and curly *payes* and girls in long, billowy dresses play in the park on Klauzál tér.

No, it's not like in 1900, when Budapest's 170,000 Jews comprised a quarter of the city's population. But it's still evidence of a way of life that could not be wiped out by the Holocaust or Communist policies encouraging assimilation. Budapest's Jewish community today is 80,000-strong and the largest in the Central Europe region.

A leisurely stroll, centred around District VII, can take you through the past and present of Jewish Budapest. Everything described here is just a few streets apart, with the exception of the **Holocaust Memorial Centre** (*see p100*) in District IX, which is three stops away from nearby Deák tér by metro. You can cover the route in an hour, but in two hours you can also head to Ferenc körút metro station and the Holocaust centre.

The natural starting point is the vast **Central Synagogue ❶** (*see above*) on the corner of Károly körút and Dohány utca. It was built in 1859 and is still the second-largest synagogue in the world. The adjacent **Jewish Museum ❷** (*see above*) has a collection of ritual objects and a moving depiction of the Hungarian Holocaust.

This is the very tip of District VII, also known as Erzsébetváros, established as the Jewish quarter in the 18th century, when Jews were still forbidden to live within the city walls. By the 1830s, Jews began to play an important economic and political role, and they supported the 1848 Hungarian uprising against the Habsburgs. Under the relative independence of 1867, the new leadership rewarded them with legal equality, a provision that attracted Jews from Russia and southern Poland. Urbane and entrepreneurial, their commercial prowess saw Budapest become the largest financial centre east of Vienna before the end of the century.

The huge Central Synagogue was a symbol of the importance Jews had in Budapest. Behind it is the small **Heroes' Temple ❸**: built in 1931, based on a design by László Vágó and Ferenc Faragó, it was dedicated to Jewish soldiers killed in World War I.

After World War I, rising anti-Semitism under Horthy's right-wing government made many prominent Jews flee Hungary. Although deportations did not begin until 1945, by 1944 the Fascist Arrow Cross Party had begun to herd 70,000 Jews into a walled-off ghetto in the Jewish quarter. In all, some 700,000 Hungarian Jews were murdered in the Holocaust.

Connecting Heroes' Temple and the Central Synagogue, a simple concrete arching colonnade encloses the Garden of Remembrance, a mass grave for Jews massacred by fellow Hungarians in 1945, with a collection of retrieved Jewish headstones. Imre Varga's poignant weeping willow memorial to those murdered in concentration camps is visible from Wesselényi utca, at the corner of Rumbach Sebestyén utca. The family names of the victims are delicately inscribed on its leaves.

A couple of hundred metres away, at VII.Rumbach Sebestyén utca 11, is a **synagogue ❹** designed by Ottó Wagner and built in 1872 for Jews put off by the less traditional design of the Central Synagogue. It's no longer in use, but the pink and yellow Moorish-style façade is impressive.

Down Dob utca, across from no.11, you'll find a **statue ❺** of an angel swooping down the side of a building to help a fallen victim. The statue honours Swiss diplomat Carl Lutz, who issued passports to many Hungarian Jews during the Holocaust.

After the war, secular Communist leaders encouraged Jews to assimilate. District VII became less Jewish, as homes emptied by the **6tus** (*see p135*), the **Szimpla/Dupla** (*see p136*), the **Sark** (*see p135*) and the **Szóda** (*see p195*) are all intriguing places to start or end the evening, while the **Kuplung** (*see p194*) and the **Fészek Klub** (*see p191* and *p194* **Party under the stars**) provide variety in after-hours revelry, the latter a classic old artists' club offering nice summer dining (*see p122*) by day in a picturesque inner courtyard.

Central Synagogue/ Jewish Museum

Nagy Zsinagóga és Zsidó Múzeum
VII.Dohány utca 2 (344 5409). M2 Astoria/tram 47, 49. **Open** *Synagogue* 10am-3pm Mon-Fri, Sun. *Museum* 10am-5pm Mon-Thur; 10am-2pm Fri, Sun. *Heroes' Temple prayer* 6pm Fri; 9am Sat. **Admission** *for both* Ft1,400; Ft400 concessions. **No credit cards. Map** p249 F5. **Photos** *p99*.

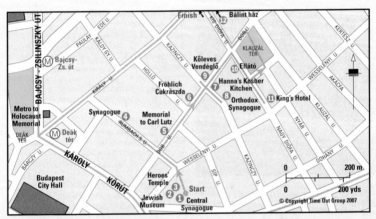

the Holocaust were filled with non-Jewish workers, brought from the countryside to rebuild Budapest. But Jews did not disappear from Erzsébetváros. A few steps from the Lutz statue is a kosher coffee and cake shop that was founded in 1953 and has become an institution: the **Fröhlich Cukrászda** ⑥ (VII.Dob utca 22, no phone, www.frohlich.hu; open 9am-8pm Mon-Thur, 7.30am-dusk Fri, 10am-4pm Sun). Here you can find *flódni*, a traditional Jewish dessert of poppy seeds, ground walnuts and apple custard.

Today's 3,000-member Orthodox community is centred around the small complex straddling the corner of Dob and Kazinczy, just down from the Fröhlich. In the front of VII.Dob utca 35, the kosher butcher sells a goose *kolbász* sausage tasty enough to convert the most confirmed pork eater. In the courtyard is **Hanna's Kosher Kitchen** ⑦ (342 1072; open 11.30am-4pm daily). You can cut through this passageway to reach the **Orthodox Synagogue** ⑧ at VII.Kazinczy utca 21. Designed by Béla and Sándor Löffler in 1913, the building has a façade angled to

fit the twisty street. Across Dob utca, the **Kőleves Vendéglő** ⑨ (*see p123*) is a café-restaurant with a friendly young clientele.

If you continue down Dob utca, you'll get to Klauzál tér, the heart and main square of the Jewish quarter. Here, the **Ellátó** ⑩ (see p134) is a lively place for a drink or meal. For true kosher, visit the **Salaman Restaurant** of the glatt kosher **King's Hotel** ⑪ (VII.Nagy Diófa utca 25-27, 352 7675, www.kosher hotel.hu) just off Klauzál tér.

If you're staying on, you can take in an event at the **Bálint Zsidó Közösségi Ház** ⑫ (VI.Révay utca 16, 311 9214, www.jcc.hu), a convivial ten-minute walk from Klauzál tér. The local Jewish community centre, this venue hosts shows, exhibitions, yoga classes, children's activities, poker nights and more. Round the corner at Deák tér, you can also take the M3 metro to Ferenc körút to reach the Holocaust Memorial Centre, a heart-wrenching exhibition about the concerted effort to wipe out Hungary's Jews.

The life back in Erzsébetváros is a glorious testament to the failure of that effort.

Király utca. See p96.

District VIII

Busy Rákóczi út divides District VII from grimier District VIII. Although synonymous with crime, the area is a safe, if shabby, place to walk around. And it's not all low-life. Bounded by Üllői út and Rákóczi, the urban pie-slice of Józsefváros, as District VIII is also known, has its point at the **National Museum** (*see p87*) on the Kiskörút. In Pollack Mihály tér behind, former mansions rub shoulders with the Socialist-style Magyar Rádió headquarters, scene of bloodletting during the 1956 Uprising.

The section of the District VIII beyond the Nagykörút is vast and unpredictable. On and around Népszinház utca there are many fine buildings, such as Béla Lajta's 1912 Harsányi House at no.19, and Emil Vidor's 1906 Dreher apartment block with its huge mosaic. Nearby Köztársaság tér boasts the Erkel Színház hall currently undergoing renovation. Népszinház utca leads to **Kerepesi Cemetery**, where politicians, artists and industrialists give a comprehensive overview of Hungarian society of the last century or more. Monumentally planned, it's a fine place for a stroll and features some grand memorials. Wide, leafy avenues direct you towards strategic mausoleums: novelist Mór Jókai and arch-compromiser Ferenc Deák, bourgeois revolutionary Lajos Kossuth and Count Lajos Batthyány. Nearby, music-hall chanteuse Lujza Blaha is tucked up in a four-poster bed, serenaded by adoring cherubs. Poet Attila József, thrown out of the Communist Party but rehabilitated in the 1950s, was buried here 20 years after his suicide.

Over Kerepesi's wall stands the main railway station, **Keleti**. Built as part of the great rail expansion of the 1800s, Keleti was the hub of an imperial network that kept its minorities dependent: all lines went via Pest. There is still no direct link from Zagreb to Vienna.

The heart of Józsefváros is the poor area south of Népszinház utca, centred on Mátyás tér. Courtyards buzz with a ragged, almost medieval life. The nearby **Roma Parliament** is headquarters for political activism on behalf of Roma (Gypsies), and an arts centre, with plays in the Romanes language and exhibitions by Roma artists. Hungary is home to a half million Roma. While most Budapest Roma are more assimilated, the Oláh or Vlach Roma, concentrated outside the capital, keep their tongue and traditions. Public opinion of Roma is low. Recently, international pressure has encouraged local efforts to reverse the worst discriminatory practices. Roma culture is deservedly receiving more attention, and bands like **Romano Drom** (*see p190* **Romano's road**) offer some of Budapest's best live shows.

You can shop cheaply at the Novák flea market, behind Keleti on Versény utca, and the sprawling Józsefvárosi piac, deeper into District VIII, with cut-price clothing and knockoffs. Many merchants there are Chinese, and if the city ever acquires a Chinatown it will be in Józsefváros. *See p148* **Flea market finds**.

Near the furthest reaches of District VIII is a complex containing the Botanical Gardens, the Orczy kert sport park and the child-friendly **Natural History Museum**. The main entrance shows the skeleton of a massive fin whale, while in the free permanent exhibition are stuffed animals and dioramas of the past and current wildlife of the Carpathian Basin.

Kerepesi Cemetery
VIII.Fiumei út 14 (323 5100). M2 Keleti pu./tram 23, 24, 28. **Open** *7am-8pm daily.* **Admission** *free.* **Map** *p250 F4.* **Photos** *p100.*

Natural History Museum
Magyar Természettudományi Múzeum
VIII.Ludovika tér 2-6 (210 1085/www.nhmus.hu). M3 Klinikák/M3 Nagyvárad tér. **Open** *10am-6pm Mon, Wed-Sun.* **Admission** *free. Exhibitions* Ft1,300; Ft800 concessions. *Guided tours in English* Ft8,000 up to 20 people. **No credit cards.** **Map** *p250 F6.*

Roma Parliament
VIII.Tavaszmező 6 (210 4798). Tram 4, 6. **Open** *9am-5pm Mon-Fri.* **Admission** *varies.* **Map** *p250 E5.*

District IX

District IX, known as **Ferencváros**, is a working-class neighbourhood, home to the football club of the same name (*see p196*). This once shabby district is undergoing a renaissance, with the pedestrianised bar strip of Ráday utca spreading across the Nagykörút to traffic-free Tompa utca. Nearby, the **Trafó** (*see p176 and p204*), a multi-function arts venue in an old transformer building, offers top-notch dance, theatre and music, with occasional art exhibitions. Downstairs is a great club (*see p195*), drawing the best local and visiting DJs.

One street from the Trafó, on Páva utca, is the new **Holocaust Memorial Center**, one of only a few such institutions built with state money. The memorial's stark, jagged façade was incorporated into an older synagogue. The main exhibition downstairs is a simple, moving display of reproductions from a photo record of day-to-day events in Auschwitz. Black-and-white videos of Jewish life before and during the war show at either end of the extended series of photographs. The rooms containing them are pitch dark, allowing visitors the privacy to weep.

Central Synagogue. *See p97.*

A few streets away, at Dandár utca 5, is the Dandár baths, a lesser known Turkish bath with the same mineral content as the water in the fancier Gellért in Buda. A couple of doors down, the **Unicum Museum**, attached to the plant where this national drink is produced, offers a history of the dark digestive (*see p132* **Black death in a bottle**).

Nearby is the riverside arts complex, with the modern, dubiously designed **National Theatre** (*see p202*) and Palace of Arts in a patch of green. It's an interesting location for a culture and entertainment centre, a bit far from downtown, but with fabulous views of this previously unsung stretch of the Danube.

In front of the Palace of Arts are a hedge maze and a small lookout tower for children's pleasure. Adults can enjoy the prestigious new venue for classical music, the **National Concert Hall** (*see p184*) and the **Ludwig Museum** (*see p173*), the city's main showcase for modern and contemporary art. One floor showcases Hungarian works, including a handful of installations that illustrate the local love for the absurd and sometimes pretentious. The Ludwig's upper floor includes big names, Picasso, Warhol, Lichtenstein and Haring, as well as interesting regional works, many with anti-Communist sentiments.

Just east of Ferencváros stretches industrial District X, most notable for **Új köztemető Cemetery**, final resting place of Imre Nagy, the prime minister who defied the Soviets in 1956. He's in Plot 301, along with 260 others executed for the Uprising, in the farthest corner to the right of the entrance.

Holocaust Memorial Center

Holokauszt Emlékközpont
IX.Páva utca 39 (455 3333/216 6557/www.hdke.hu).
M3 Ferenc körút. **Open** 10am-6pm Tue-Sun.
Admission Ft1,000. **Map** p250 H8.

Ludwig Museum

Ludwig Múzeum Budapest
Palace of Arts, IX.Komor Marcell utca 1 (555 3444/
www.ludwigmuseum.hu). HÉV to Lágymányosi-híd/
tram 2. **Open** 10am-8pm Tue-Sun. **Admission**
Ft1,200; Ft600 concessions. *Tours in English (call*
ahead) Ft5,000. **No credit cards. Map** p250 inset.

Új köztemető Cemetery

X.Kozma utca 8-10 (433 7300). Tram 28, 37. **Open**
Aug-Apr 7.30am-5pm daily. *May-July* 7am-8pm daily.

Unicum Museum

IX.Soroksári út 26 (entrance on Dandár utca)
(476 2383/www.zwackunicum.hu). Tram 2.
Open 10am-5pm Mon-Fri. **Admission** *with tasting*
Ft1,500. *Without tasting* Ft850. **No credit cards.**
Map p250 G9.

Monumental resting place of Hungary's greatest figures – **Kerepesi Cemetery**. *See p99.*

Csepel

An island of stoic Socialism in a sea of stormy history.

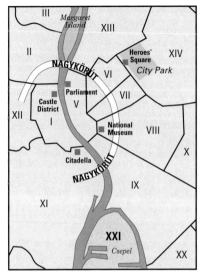

To see how the city looked in 1965, head down on the HÉV train from Boráros tér near Petőfi Bridge to **Csepel** island, District XXI. Close to the riverside developments of the IX District in south Pest, Csepel has been largely ignored since 1989. But this is soon due to change.

Csepel is both the name of the 47-kilometre long island lounging before Pestszenterzsébet and Budafok on each bank, and the name of the northern tip, lined with Socialist blocks and with a vast, mainly empty, factory complex at its centre. Csepel 'town', home to 85,000 souls, only occupies a tenth of the territory. This was the chunk annexed to Budapest in 1950. The remaining area, first settled in Roman times, then by Serbs and Germans in the 17th century, is undeveloped, disturbed only by fishermen.

The business end was transformed in the 1880s by the enterprising Manfréd Weiss, who built a canning factory there. Come 1914, he was responsible for the most modern armaments production in the entire Austro-Hungarian empire and a workforce of some 30,000 employees. After 1918, Weiss' factory made household appliances, agricultural machinery and cars. Schwinn Csepel bicycles are still a well-known brand.

Meanwhile 'Red Csepel' gained a reputation for bolshy politics. Strikes were commonplace – there was even a march for peace in 1917. The Weiss family lost the factory during World War II, but the workers' solidarity lived on. In 1944, Csepel staged one of the few successful acts of mass resistance against the Nazis.

This was fertile ground for the incoming Communists. The 520,000sq m works were rebuilt to create the great Socialist experiment: schools, sports grounds, nurseries and hospitals were set up alongside the factories; lanes were given names such as 'Sewing Machine Factory Street' and 'Coloured Metal Street'. This was the original workers' paradise, where happy labourers could produce, live and die, all without needing to leave the island. Yet by the Uprising of 1956, this workers' council was one of the longest to hold out against the Soviets.

Take the HÉV to focal Szent Imre tér, and you'll be at the big gate announcing entry into the Csepel Művek (Csepel Works), now a light industrial complex that is a shadow of its former self. Amid the clutch of printers, machine shops and assorted bits of commerce that have colonised the abandoned factories, there are still many old structures that have been unused since 1989. Peek in the window of one of these padlocked, empty factories for a ghostly sight: the machinery, furniture and often even the flooring are gone, leaving vast spaces, lit only by the sunlight coming through the broken windows in the corrugated roof.

The abundance of neighbourless space has made Csepel a magnet for rock bands, who can practise unmolested at top volume. Here and there, young men in black amble amid the murk with their instrument cases, as big 18-wheelers roar past, loaded with cement, lumber or bricks.

Several of the abandoned buildings in the Csepel Works have been turned into workers' hotels, with signs advertising a *munkaszálló* with beds for as little as Ft900 a night.

This should soon change. In 2006, Spanish real estate companies Sedesa and Fadesa Inmobiliaria announced the building of 15,000 flats and a conference centre. International developers Sirius are putting up a geothermal apartment complex, while another consortium has won the tender to rebuild the port.

Csepel's story is told at the downtown **Local History Museum** (Szent Imre tér 3, 278 0710).

Sightseeing

ARANY-EKSZER

Eat, Drink, Shop

Features

Párisi udvar.

Restaurants

In with modern cuisine and out with stodge as the dining scene goes global.

The most notable of all the rapid developments here over the last 20 years has been on the plate. Even in the late 1990s, the old approach was the norm: heavy, meaty fare served in large quantities with a side order of grimace. Now the situation has flip-flopped as menus shed calories, and global cooking brings more exotic ingredients into the local cuisine. Fewer places specialise in old-style Hungarian cookery. These days it's even hard to find real goulash (see p118 **In search of good goulash**).

There are more quality restaurants that can now be considered international than Hungarian. At the high end, these categories (although we use them in this chapter) are blurred and the ensuing competition has done much to increase quality among all restaurants, including Hungarian ones. Global influences have been the shot in the arm that Hungarian cuisine needed: places like **Café Kör**, **Callas** and **Cyrano** are incorporating different degrees of local and international cuisine and inventing the future of Hungarian food.

Other fashionable new restaurants that specialise in continental or fusion cooking are hiring a separate sushi chef to double their menus. There has also been a rapid growth in Indian venues and high-quality Italian restaurants are now among the best in town.

Another recent phenomenon has been the swift rise in the quality and availability of wines, particularly Hungarian ones. At least half-a-dozen establishments specialise in wine, with an encyclopedic selection offered by a savvy staff happy to suggest samples to taste (see p111 **In vino qualitas**).

HUNGARIAN CUISINE

Much of what is considered the best in Hungarian cuisine was developed a century ago, when Joseph Maréchal, József Dobos and János and Károly Gundel introduced a strong French influence into Budapest's kitchens.

Much of that invention and variety was later buried in four decades of post-war blandness. What you find at a typical neighbourhood restaurant today is meaty and hearty. The cooking method is often frying in lard or simmering in a stew, techniques that add flavour and cholesterol. Paprika is ubiquitous – but that doesn't mean the food is especially spicy. With a few exceptions, the paprika tends to be sweet and fragrant rather than hot. It comes into its own in dishes like *csirke paprikás* (chicken paprika), simmered in onions and paprika; *töltött káposzta* (stuffed cabbage); or *pörkölt*, often thought of as Hungarian goulash, for which meat and onions are stewed together in a fat flavoured with paprika.

For Hungarians, goulash (*gulyás*) is a hearty beef soup named after the people who used to eat it (*gulyás* means 'herdsman'). Other popular soups include *Jókai bableves*, bean soup with chunks of smoked ham and sausages, and *halászlé*, fish soup in which fatty carp is mercifully drowned in hot paprika. Carp (*ponty*) is what many Hungarians think of when they

❶ Purple numbers given in this chapter correspond to the location of each venue on the street maps. See pp245-250.

The best Restaurants

For carnivores
Carne di Hall (see p106); **China Lan Zhou** (see p124); **Kafana** (see p112); **Pampas Argentine Steakhouse** (see p115).

For contemporary Hungarian
Arcade Bistro (see p106); **Café Kör** (see p110); **Segal** (see p117).

For fish and seafood
Arany Kaviar (see p107); **Goa** (see p121); **Óceán** (see p117); **Régi Sipos Halászkert** (see p109); **Takebayashi** (see p117).

For hearty Hungarian
Alföldi Vendéglő (see p110); **Bagolyvár** (see p122); **Kádár Étkezde** (see p122); **Kéhli Vendéglő** (see p109); **Múzeum** (see p124).

For vegetarians
Marquis de Salade (see p121).

For wine
Bock Bisztró (see p122); **Borbírósag** (see p124); **Maligán Borétterem** (see p109); **Taverna Pomo D'Oro** (see p117).

think fish, but this landlocked cuisine also includes trout and *fogas*, a tasty fish unique to Lake Balaton, often translated as pike-perch.

An older Western infusion into Hungarian cookery is *Bécsi szelet* (Wiener schnitzel), which has inspired several spin-offs. Pork, chicken, turkey and fish are also fried in breadcrumbs, preparation referred to as *rántott*. Like much Hungarian cookery, which has peasant roots, these dishes have a high fat content. Equally rich is goose liver, *libamáj*, served cold as an appetiser or used in a hot stew with peppers, tomatoes and onions, done in paprika sauce.

Traditional restaurants are likely to offer sweet fillings for pancakes, *palacsinta*. Another classic dessert is *Somlói galuska*, rum-soaked sponge cake topped with chocolate sauce, nuts, raisins and whipped cream. In summer, look out for cold fruit soups, in particular the sour cherry variety, *hideg meggyleves*.

Most menus have an English translation *(see p114* **What's on the menu?**), and staff in most downtown restaurants have a good grasp of service-industry English. You'll find eating out in Budapest is generally more affordable than in most European capitals, although this price gap is narrowing. Some places now add a service charge to the bill, while in others it's customary to round up an approximate ten per cent tip to the nearest hundred forints. Our reviews attempt to give an idea of the costs of restaurants using the following scale, based on the average cost of starter plus main course. Be aware, however, that many places can charge a fortune for even an average bottle of wine.

€ – up to Ft4,000
€€ – Ft4,000-Ft6,000
€€€ – Ft6,000-Ft8,000
€€€€ – above Ft8,000

Buda

Víziváros

Hungarian

Carne di Hall

I.Bem rakpart 20 (201 8137/www.carnedihall.com). *M2 Batthyány tér/tram 19.* **Open** 11.30am-midnight daily. **Average** €€. **Credit** AmEx, MC, V. **Map** p245 C4 ❶

The name is a pun meant to emphasise the importance of meat in this attractive cellar restaurant on the Buda riverside. The more casual sister of the chic Lou Lou *(see p113)*, this was once the premier steak house in town, but they've trimmed their steak menu down to four types, and Pampas *(see p115)* may have stolen their crown. Still, the house special steak,

a whole kilo of beef fillet for Ft16,000, is impressive. The venison fillet and the decadently rich goose liver are other standouts. There's a list of top Hungarian wines, along with French and Italian.

International

Új Lan Zhou

II.Fő utca 71 (201 9247/www.lanzhou.hu). M2 Batthyány tér. **Open** 11am-11pm daily. **Average** €€. **Credit** AmEx, MC, V. **Map** p245 C4 ❷

Budapest's best Chinese restaurant in District VIII *(see p124)* recently opened this upmarket sister on the Buda side. While the two establishments share many dishes, some of the fare in the new location is a little fancier. Its prices are also slightly higher, topping off with the 'lobster cooked in three ways' for Ft28,900/kg. But most meals here are generally reasonably priced – and excellent. While several styles of Chinese food are featured, the main cuisine is from Yang-Zhou, which often calls for slow simmering in meat stock and soy sauce, a technique that makes food juicier. The generous meat portions are tender, and the 'five-flavour duck' melts in the mouth. Deservedly busy, so book at weekends.

Moszkva tér & the Buda Hills

Hungarian

Arcade Bistro

XII.Kiss János altábornagy utca 38 (225 1969). *Tram 59, 61/bus 105.* **Open** noon-4pm, 6pm-midnight Mon-Sat. **Average** €€. **Credit** MC, V.

The more formal sister of Pest's Café Kör *(see p110)* provides satisfying nouvelle-style presentations of Hungarian and international cuisine. Variety is ensured with a dozen daily specials – often the more interesting choices. A changing list of about 20 Hungarian wines is expertly drawn up and all can be bought by the glass. The floor-to-ceiling fountain, enclosed in a wide glass tube, lends panache to the tasteful modern interior. In summer, a grill goes out front, on the romantic terrace that overlooks a quiet, secluded junction. Having earned a good reputation, Arcade sometimes shows signs of complacency, but it's still a fine meal here nonetheless.

Matteo

II.Pasaréti út 100 (392 7531/www.matteo.hu). Tram 56/bus 5. **Open** noon-midnight daily. **Average** €€€. **Credit** MC, V.

This gem in distant Buda serves fine Mediterranean and Hungarian cuisine within a curved 1937 Bauhaus bus station complex at Pasaréti tér. The restaurant's glass-walled dining room is also in Bauhaus style, with glowing yellow columns illuminating an appealing mix of stained wood, tile and chrome, laid out in soft, modernist lines. Next to it is a peaceful sunken terrace. The menu is almost too large, but the kitchen seems up to it. There's a broad range of tapas, like veal carpaccio and quail's eggs with truffle and caviar. Mains include good sea fish, updated Hungarian dishes and Med-style meat and fowl. The service is commendable, and jovial chef Péter Buday frequently mingles with guests.

Vadrózsa

II.Pentelei Molnár utca 15 (326 5817). Bus 11, 91. **Open** noon-3pm, 7pm-midnight daily. **Average** €€€€. **Credit** AmEx, DC, MC, V.
Atop ritzy Rózsadomb, this restaurant in a sumptuous villa and garden provides a luxurious meal. Guests are offered a tray of raw fish, viands and other delicacies, and can make suggestions if they don't see what they want on the menu. The kitchen is known for its fine preparations of steak, pheasant and venison. If you're willing to shell out, you'll eat well – but you're also paying for the location.

International

Les Amis Vendéglő

II.Rómer Flóris utca 12 (438 4595). Tram 4, 6/ bus 91. **Open** noon-11pm Mon-Sat. **Average** €€€. **Credit** MC, V. **Map** p245 B2 ❸
On a steep Buda side street near Margaret Bridge, this restaurant has seven tables in a cosy red room below street level. One charming, busy waiter, and a skilled team in the kitchen, serve French bistrostyle cuisine with local influences. The extensive menu offers a wide range of meat, poultry and fish,

including steak with Dijon mustard and black pepper sauce, a superb duck breast with sour cherries, and a lobster thermidor that weighs in at Ft10,900. Though popular, the place has recently been subject to sporadic closings, so check before heading out.

Arany Kaviar

I.Ostrom utca 19 (201 6737/225 7370/06 30 954 2600 mobile/www.aranykaviar.hu). M2 Moszkva tér/ tram 4, 6. **Open** noon-11.30pm daily. **Average** €€€. **Credit** AmEx, DC, MC, V. **Map** p245 A3 ❹
This 20-year-old family-run restaurant with lavish imperial decor offers fine Russian food, prepared by Russo-Magyar chef Sasha, who trained at top hotels in the Motherland. The sturgeon is fantastic and they offer great prices on Beluga or Sevruga caviar. If money's no object, splash out for a sampling menu, the fanciest of which is seven courses for a hefty Ft32,000, including wines. It starts with black Beluga caviar and a shot of vodka – there are ten varieties. The impressive wine list has good Hungarian choices from the Budapest Wine Society around the corner, as well as international ones.

Nusantara

XI.Városmajor utca 88 (201 1478/06 30 474 3167 mobile/www.nusantara.hu). Tram 56. **Open** noon-3pm, 6-11pm Tue-Fri; noon-11pm Sat, Sun. **Average** €€. **Credit** MC, V.
The only Indonesian restaurant in town is a stellar representative that merits the trip to Buda beyond Moszkva tér. The Indonesian kitchen staff prepare a wide range of dishes with so much flavour that it

Nusantara.

Kafana. *See p112.*

seemed necessary to confirm they do not use MSG, just great combinations of spices. Dishes like barbecued skewers of chicken, pork and beef with peanut sauce, and fried red snapper with turmeric sauce, are brimming with varied tastes. Teak wood and loose cloth dress up a calm dark interior. There's no smoking inside, but that doesn't matter in warmer months, as the roof-top terrace with a park view provides superior seating. Warm, attentive service and a moderate selection of good local wines.

Óbuda

Hungarian

Kéhli Vendéglő

III.Mókus utca 22 (250 4241/www.kehli.hu). Bus 86/ HÉV to Tímár utca. **Open** noon-midnight daily. **Average** €€. **Credit** AmEx, MC, V.

When fin-de-siècle novelist and gastronome Gyula Krúdy made this place his favoured spot for a meal, he earned himself a plaque on the wall and helped stoke the legend of the Kéhli, which serves great Hungarian food that some locals swear is the best. The beautiful old structure is divided into several rooms, the most popular being the music room, where the Gypsy band plays. Book ahead if you want that one, or settle for the lovely terrace; avoid the cellar rooms if possible. There are many traditional meals. One speciality is a rich bone marrow soup: first drink the soup, then scrape out the marrow and spread it on toast with garlic. The portions are mountainous and the prices low.

Kisbuda Gyöngye

III.Kenyeres utca 34 (368 6402). Tram 17. **Open** noon-11pm Mon-Sat. **Average** €€€. **Credit** AmEx, DC, MC, V.

The 'Pearl of Kisbuda', set at one spot or another in Óbuda since the 1970s, has a high reputation as a must-visit Hungarian restaurant. The fare here is pretty standard, with classics like goose liver and indigenous Balaton *fogas*, but interesting specials can pop up. It's certainly a fine place at which to sample goulash, and there are some great wines too. The staff are completely charming, and you will be made to feel at home. Certainly not a bad way to get an education in the local cuisine.

Maligán Borétterem

III.Lajos utca 38 (240 9010/www.maligan.hu). Bus 6, 60, 86/HÉV to Szépvölgyi út. **Open** noon-11pm Mon-Sat. **Average** €€. **Credit** AmEx, MC, V.

Hungarian vintages are showcased in this cellar restaurant, which serves good versions of the kind of hearty local cuisine that soaks up wine well. The knowledgeable waiter will guide you through a handmarked list of hundreds of bottles, including a selection of about 20 types that are available by the glass. Sample your way around the regions of Hungary while you enjoy imaginative Magyar

cuisine, like tomato soup with crayfish; satisfying roast baby chicken; a rich, fatty duck breast; and pork from mangalica, a local pig. While the cuisine may be updates on mum's old recipes, it's close enough to draw a lot of locals, so book at weekends. *See p111* **In vino qualitas.**

Régi Sipos Halászkert

III.Lajos utca 46 (250 8082/www.regisipos.hu). Tram 17/bus 6, 86/HÉV to Szépvölgyi út. **Open** noon-11pm daily. **Average** €€. **Credit** AmEx, DC, MC, V.

This is a stellar example of a restaurant that specialises in both traditional Hungarian food and fish. When it moved from nearby to this bright location with a pretty garden a few years ago, regulars questioned whether it was still the best in this unusual genre. They certainly will make Budapest's best *halászlé* (fisherman's soup), which contains boned fillets – as well as roe and offal, the real benchmarks of quality preparation. The fish theme kicks off with starters like caviar or fish crackling, but there's more to the menu. You can't go wrong with the Hungarian classics like veal *paprikás* or the steaks, which are usually cooked to well-done. Excellent desserts include the local *túró gombóc* (warm curd cheese dumplings with sour cream).

International

Mennyei Ízek

III.Pacsirtamező utca 13 (388 6430/06 30 992 1945 mobile). Bus 86. **Open** noon-10pm daily. **Average** €. **No credit cards.**

A favourite in Óbuda, this simple, family-run place is the best Korean restaurant in Budapest. They also have a complete Chinese menu, but you can get that elsewhere; the flavours of Korea are the reason to come here. Meats can be grilled at your table. Try the delicious *bulgogi*, a beef fillet marinated with mashed kiwi fruit, which tenderises the meat and causes it to caramelise as it is grilled. Aside from meat, there's also killer Korean broiled fish and a full complement of home-style kimchi – the spicy, garlicky fermented cabbage pickle that is Korea's national dish. There is also a range of kimchi-style dishes made from fresh vegetables that have yet to see pickle sauce. Everything here is reasonably priced and delivery is available.

Okuyama Sushi

III.Kolosy tér 5-6 (250 8256). Bus 6, 60, 86. **Open** 1-10pm Tue-Sun. **Average** €€€. **No credit cards.**

Japanese regulars come here for Chef Okuyama's Osaka-style sushi, like the orange-mottled shrimp, glazed with a greenish translucent fish aspic, pressed delicately into a rectangular form and cut into squares. Sashimi and other types of sushi are also available, and there are decent, inexpensive cooked mackerel and herring dishes. Set in the cellar of a shopping complex, it's hard to find; there's only a sign in Japanese above the building entrance. Head straight to the back and down the stairs to the left.

Eat, Drink, Shop

Pest

Belváros & Lipótváros

Hungarian

Alföldi Vendéglő

*V.Kecskeméti utca 4 (267 0224). M3 Kálvin tér/
tram 47, 49.* **Open** 11am-11pm daily. **Average** €.
Credit AmEx, MC, V. **Map** p249 F6 ➎
Here you can look forward to traditional, meaty
Hungarian food in an inexpensive place that brings
rural atmosphere to the centre of town with slow service, low-frills decor and rustic cuisine. The Alföldi
makes a stand-out goulash soup, and the *Hortobágyi
palacsinta*, a meat-stuffed pancake with creamy
paprika sauce, is as delicious as anyone's. Deep-fried
white fish and chicken paprika are two other well-
handled high-cholesterol standards. Exotic specials
can include pickled veal lung with breadcrumb
dumplings. The recommended *Kolozsvári töltött
káposzta* consists of stuffed cabbage rolls with
sausage, bacon and a pork chop served alongside.
Wash it all down with sweetish brown beer.

Astoria Mirror Café & Restaurant

*V.Kossuth Lajos utca 19-21 (889 6022/889 6000).
M2 Astoria/tram 47, 49/bus 7.* **Open** 7am-10.30pm
daily. **Average** €€. **Credit** AmEx, DC, MC, V. **Map**
p249 F6 ➏
The empire lives on in the Astoria Hotel's lush
Habsburg-era dining room, with marble columns,
dark wood walls, gilt-framed mirrors and red velvet
seating. Always a wonderful place for a revitalising
coffee downtown, the Astoria Café has recently been
renamed and enhanced with a more ambitious menu
– though their claim of producing fusion cuisine may
be somewhat exaggerated. The kitchen can handle
the Hungarian standards, like chicken paprika, veal
stew and Balaton pike-perch, *fogas*, as well as international dishes like New York steak, saddle of lamb
with mint and, more adventurously, spicy duck
cooked in a wok. Lighter fare, like a tapas sampler
and decent sandwiches, suit anyone who's here as
much for the ambience as the sustenance.

Café Kör

V.Sas utca 17 (311 0053). M3 Arany János utca.
Open 10am-10pm Mon-Sat. **Average** €€.
No credit cards. Map p246 E5 ➐
Still one of the more recommendable restaurants in
town, Café Kör applies a creative gourmet touch to
Hungarian classics in a comfortable, bistro-like
atmosphere more reminiscent of Vienna or Berlin
than Budapest. There's a bar, with a fine selection
of local wines, and some small café tables, as well as
a more formal dining space. The refreshingly simple Hungarian international menu is complemented
by daily specials, and all dishes generally range
from good to memorable. Service can be slow, but is
generally friendly and knowledgeable. This is one

of the few places in Hungary to offer a truly first-
class steak; its limited vegetarian options include
excellent grilled goat's cheese. It's a splendid spot
for a downtown breakfast, served until 11.30am, but
do book ahead for dinner.

Onyx

*V.Vörösmarty tér 7 (429 9023/www.gerbeaud.hu).
M1 Vörösmarty tér, M2, M3 Deák tér/tram 2.* **Open**
noon-3pm, 6-10pm daily. **Average** €€€. **Credit**
AmEx, MC, V. **Map** p249 E5 ➑
In the upstairs of the famous Gerbeaud coffeehouse
(*see p129*), this lavish, marble-clad dining room provides a fine dining experience of Hungarian cuisine
with the occasional twist, as well as upscale international dishes. The formal interior and nice outdoor
seating are impressive, even in this commercial part
of town. The tendency to treat everyone as a moneyed tourist can be off-putting, especially the elaborate and expensive recommendations from the staff.

International

Le Bourbon

*Le Méridien Budapest, V.Deák Ferenc utca 16-18
(429 5500). M1, M2, M3 Deák tér.* **Open** 6.30am-
10.30pm daily. **Average** €€€. **Credit** AmEx, DC,
MC, V. **Map** p249 E5 ➒
The outstanding restaurant at Le Méridien Budapest
(*see p41*) serves some of the city's finest French food,
both classic and contemporary. Young chef Laurent
Vandenmeele is in charge of a seasonally changing
menu, while pastry chef Alain Lagrange creates
breathtaking desserts. Whatever the time of year,
the offerings usually include fresh or hot oysters,
duck confit and exquisite fish dishes. The cheese
trolley, featuring France's best, is worth consider-
ing. The hushed, elegant wood-panelled interior features classic-looking striped seating, the occasional
antique and a gorgeous behemoth of a flower
arrangement. There are brunch spreads on Sundays.

Creol Caribbean Restaurant & Bar

*V.Roosevelt tér 7-8 (302 7909/www.creolbar.hu).
M1 Vörösmarty tér/tram 2.* **Open** 6pm-1am Wed-Sat.
Average €€. **Credit** AmEx, MC, V. **Map** p246 D5 ➓
Dinner and dancing combine at this restaurant and
club, where Latin DJs and bands mix with Caribbean
cuisines and ingredients rare to Budapest. Many
main dishes come with rice and the house's special
beans, plus a medley of spices and fruits and served
in a chocolate cup that mixes in deliciously. The
seafood here is also good. The decor is over the top,
with ornately engraved columns, glowing red curtains and an atmospherically lit tunnel leading to the
toilet. The massive bar shaped like a grand piano
screams cocktail, and able staff oblige with reasonably priced, professionally prepared concoctions.

Cyrano

V.Kristóf tér 7-8 (226 3096). M1, M2, M3 Deák tér.
Open 10am-midnight daily. **Average** €€€. **Credit**
AmEx, MC, V. **Map** p249 E5 ⓫

Eat, Drink, Shop

In vino qualitas

For millennia, Hungary has had what it takes to make great wines – but when Socialist planners managed the wineries, the main product was plonk. Since privatisation, a new crop of serious vintners has been cultivating the best grapes and using modern production techniques. Their labour was bearing fruit by the new millennium, and Hungary now produces a range of world-class wines – with the reds of Villány leading the way.

The warmer southern region of Villány and Siklós, smack against the southern border with Croatia, has come to the fore in the development of subtler red wines based on the pinot noir and cabernet grapes. International attention has focused on the innovations – such as barrique ripening – made by the **Gere**, **Vylyan** and **Bock** labels. Attila Gere produces **Kopár Cuvée**, a mix of cabernet sauvignon, merlot and cabernet franc which is so highly regarded that the entire stock is available only by subscription, mostly to upmarket restaurants who charge top-shelf prices for it. Villány is also famous for its **Kékoportó**, which had to change its name to keep the EU labelling minions happy.

In the Transdanubian region, rich volcanic soils produce exquisite white wines. The Badacsony region along Lake Balaton is famous for its **Hárslevelű** and **Szürkebarat** wines, which were often semi-sweet until vinters such as **Huba Szeremley** began the painstaking work of reviving the original pinot gris varieties into an astounding rebirth of the variety as a subtle dry wine. The nearby Somló region produces a unique, green-tinted **Juhfark**, while the vast vineyards of the more prosaic **Olaszrizling** varieties are a common sight along Lake Balaton's northern coast. **Cserszegi fűszeres** is a sweetish new variety that cross traditional Gewürztraminer with **Irsai Oliver** grapes.

The Carpathian mountain range shields its southern slopes from strong northern winds. The northeast **Tokaj** region, for example, is famed for its sweet dessert wines, the most famous being the luxuriously sweet **aszú**. It acquires its unique flavour by mixing regular grapes with late-season aszú grapes, which are left on the vine until they rot and turn raisiny. You can taste the raisin flavour in the wine. Tokaj is rated by the number of *puttonyos* ('baskets') of aszú grapes that are mixed in with each batch, six being the

sweetest and most expensive. Top producers include **Szepsy István**, **Hétfürtös** and **Tokajicum**, alongside the privatised state vineyards of **Oremeus** and **Disznókő**.

Sampling Hungary's best over a leisurely meal in a local restaurant can be a rewarding experience. You order several courses and have one or two different glasses with each course. Alongside the growth in good wines, there has been a boom in fine restaurants focused on wine. These places will usually have a stock of several hundred types of wine, and will offer at least a dozen by the glass. Waiters in a wine restaurant know their stock and can make recommendations.

Popular examples include the **Maligán Borétterem** (*see p109*), the pretty **Borbíróság** (*see p124*) or the 1894 Food & Wine Cellar at Budapest's most famous restaurant, **Gundel** (*see p122*). The **Bock Bisztro** (*see p122*) is operated by Villány wine producer József Bock as a way to promote his wines. In **Klassz** (*see p119*), on Andrássy, the cuisine is more continental, with Hungarian influences, while at the **Café Bouchon** (*see p119*) the food is French-Hungarian – but the wines at both are mainly Hungarian. At the **Taverna Pomo D'oro** (*see p117*), the food and most of the hundreds of wines on offer are Italian, but you can also sample Hungarian there as well.

Eat, Drink, Shop

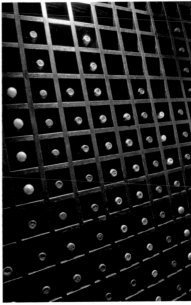

Fusion cuisine and fine Hungarian wines at **Baraka**. *See p118.*

An excellent choice in tourist central, Cyrano and its two shaded terraces are just off Váci utca. The cuisine is Mediterranean with Hungarian offerings: dishes such as king prawns with garlic and chilli, potato purée with pesto and Japanese ginger mingle comfortably on the same menu with veal paprika or a fine goulash; separate lunch and dinner menus change frequently. Staff are refreshingly human in a part of town where diners are seen as one-time guests, though things can take time when the place is packed. The wild, contemporary interior incorporates rococo touches and features a sassy black feather boa chandelier.

Iguana

V.Zoltán utca 16 (301 0215). M2 Kossuth tér. **Open** 11.30am-11.30pm daily. **Average** €€. **Credit** AmEx, MC, V. **Map** p246 D4 ⓬
Homesick Americans flock to Budapest's only real Tex-Mex beanery in a tall dining room, cheerfully decorated with vintage Mexican movie posters. There's panoramic seating in the large gallery and a terrace overlooking Szabadság tér. The cuisine would not take the blue riband in Tijuana, but the standard burritos, fajitas, quesadillas and tacos are hard to find elsewhere in town. Non-Mexican fare includes chorizo and a passable Cuban sandwich – pork on a toasted baguette. Burgers and BLTs get wolfed up at lunchtimes. Pitchers of sangria are popular, but the margaritas seem meagre now that the rest of Budapest has worked out how to make them.

Kafana

V.Sörház utca 4 (266 2274/06 20 320 5772 mobile/ www.kafana.hu). M3 Ferenciek tere/tram 2. **Open** 10am-midnight Mon-Fri; 2pm-midnight Sat, Sun. **Average** €. **No credit cards. Map** p249 E7 ⓭
Chef Nenad Andjelić left Novi Sad for Budapest, and ended up in charge of the deservedly popular kitchen at the Castro Bisztró (*see p134*). He now presides over a feast of meat, grilled Balkan-style, in a lively restaurant with a high ceiling and a long gallery. Along with some of the best steaks in town, this is also the place for Serbian-style mixtures of lamb, pork and beef, in the form of *pljeskavica*, *ćevapčići* and *vesalica*. Hearty portions of meat, made using the less fatty method of grilling, provide a break from deep-fried or stewed Hungarian preparations. The place is a meeting point for the local Serb community, other foreigners and Hungarians, and the bar fills with an animated *sljivović*-swilling crew at weekends and on Serb holidays. **Photos** *p108.*

Kashmir Indian Restaurant

V.Arany János utca 13 (354 1806/www.kashmir etterem.hu). M3 Arany János utca. **Open** 11am-11pm Mon-Fri; 6-11pm Sat, Sun. **Average** €. **Credit** MC, V. **Map** p246 D4 ⓮
After successes in town, Allen Diwan, a master of the tandoori oven, opened his own restaurant in a high-ceilinged space with tall windows and a gallery. You can't go wrong with any of the tandoori options, like the bright red chicken tikka or the seekh

A wine for all seasons at the **Café Bouchon**. *See p119.*

kebab. Other cooking styles, including masala and vindaloo, are well represented. Spices are toned down for local tastes – the keema curry is delicious, but has less of a bite than you might expect. The most popular item is the wallet-pleasing, business buffet lunch at Ft1,990, with two meat dishes, two vegetarian, bread, rice and dessert.

Lou Lou

V. Vigyázó Ferenc utca 4 (312 4505). M3 Arany János utca/tram 2. **Open** noon-3pm, 7-11pm Mon-Fri; 7-11pm Sat. **Average** €€€€. **Credit** AmEx, MC, V. **Map** p246 D4 ⓯

One of Budapest's best restaurants has expanded its floor space and replaced its antique decor with something modern. It has also upgraded its already high-quality kitchen, which produces superior French and Italian flavours with the odd Hungarian-inspired dish. After years of reasonable prices, Lou Lou now charges high rates for small nouvelle-sized portions of spectacular food; this place is more about tastes than tanking up. The ginger-marinated fillet steak, boiled in guinea-hen soup, can stand up to any steak in town, and the truffled rice is superb. You can span the flavour spectrum with an eight-course tasting menu at Ft14,900 or Ft21,500 with wine.

Momotaro Ramen

V. Széchenyi utca 16 (269 3802). M2 Kossuth tér/ tram 2. **Open** 11am-10pm daily. **Average** €. **No credit cards. Map** p246 D4 ⓰

The titular ramen noodle soups are just one reason to come to this superb low-key restaurant, serving simple Japanese and Chinese food near Szabadság tér. Another reason is the dumplings, fried or pre-pared in a bamboo steamer, which are probably the best in Budapest. They also do dim sum and great sesame chicken toasts. For a veggie ramen, ask for it to be cooked without a meat broth. You may be asked to share a long table with your neighbours during the busy lunch hour. The clientele is generally made up of cosmopolitan regulars who know the menu, so if you see something tasty, don't be bashful about asking what it is.

Okay Italia

XIII. Szent István körút 20 (349 2291/www.okay italia.hu). M3 Nyugati pu./tram 4, 6. **Open** 10am-11pm Mon-Fri; noon-11pm Sat, Sun. **Average** €€. **Credit** DC, MC, V. **Map** p246 E2 ⓱

One of the first restaurants to offer genuine Italian food in Budapest, Okay Italia is still among the most consistent. Inexpensive and satisfying fare is served by waitresses in tiny skirts at two sister locations a couple of hundred metres apart. Okay's pizzas are perfect, with a crispy thin crust and generous top-pings, and the pasta and salads are made from fresh, authentic ingredients. The two spots have slightly different menus with more northern food (including an fine cordon bleu) at this main branch, and the one by Nyugati station serving up more southerly fare. The atmosphere at both is casual, comfortable and

Eat, Drink, Shop

What's on the menu?

Useful phrases

Are these seats taken? *Ezek a helyek foglaltak?*
Bon appétit! *Jó étvágyat!*
Do you have...? *Van...?*
I'm a vegetarian. *Vegetáriánus vagyok.*
I'd like a table for two. *Két fő részére kérek egy asztalt.*
I'd like the menu, please. *Kérem az étlapot.*
I didn't order this. *Nem ezt rendeltem.*
Thank you. *Köszönöm.*
The bill, please. *Számlát kérek!*

Basics (*Alapok*)

Ashtray *Hamutartó*
Bill *Számla*
Bread *Kenyér*
Cup *Csésze*
Fork *Villa*
Glass *Pohár*
Knife *Kés*
Milk *Tej*
Napkin *Szalvéta*
Oil *Olaj*
Pepper *Bors*
Plate *Tanyér*
Salt *Só*
Spoon *Kanál*
Sugar *Cukor*
Teaspoon *Kiskanál*
Vinegar *Ecet*
Water *Víz*

Meats (*Húsok*)

Bárány Lamb
Bográcsgulyás Thick goulash soup
Borjú Veal
Comb Leg
Jókai bableves Bean soup with pork knuckle
Kacsa Duck
Liba Goose
Máj Liver
Marha Beef
Mell Breast
Nyúl Rabbit
Pulyka Turkey
Sonka Ham
Szarvas Venison

Fish/Seafood (*Hal/Tengeri gyülmölcs*)

Halfilé roston Grilled fillet of fish
Harcsa Catfish
Homár Lobster
Kagyló Shellfish, mussels
Lazac Salmon
Pisztráng Trout
Ponty Carp
Rák Crab, prawn
Tonhal Tuna

Accompaniments (*Köretek*)

Burgonya (or *Krumpli*) Potatoes
Galuska Noodles
Hasábburgonya Chips
Rizs Rice
Tészta Pasta

Salads (*Savanyúság*)

Cékla Beetroot
Fejes saláta Lettuce salad
Paradicsom Tomato
Uborka Cucumber

Vegetables (*Zöldség*)

Gomba Mushrooms
Karfiol Cauliflower
Kukorica Sweetcorn
Lencse Lentils
Paprika Pepper
Sárgarépa Carrot
Spárga Asparagus (white/*fehér*, green/*zöld*)
Spenót Spinach
Zöldbab Green beans
Zöldborsó Peas

Fruit/Nuts (*Gyümölcs/Dió*)

Alma Apple
Cseresznye Cherry
Dió Nut, walnut
Dinnye Melon
Eper Strawberry
Gesztenye Chestnut
Málna Raspberry
Narancs Orange
Őszibarack Peach
Sárgabarack Apricot
Szilva Plum

Drinks (*Italok*)

Ásványvíz Mineral water
Bor Wine
Édes bor Sweet wine
Fehér bor White wine
Kávé Coffee
Narancslé Orange juice
Pálinka Fruit brandy
Pezsgő Sparkling wine
Sör Beer
Száraz bor Dry wine
Vörös bor Red wine

loud in lunch hour. You can usually drop in without a booking, and they do deliver. Officially this is in Újlipótváros, as it's on the XIII District side of the Nagykörút – but it's less than ten minutes' walk from Parliament.

Other locations: XIII.Nyugati tér 6 (332 6960).

Pampas Argentine Steakhouse

V.Vámház körút 6 (411 1750/www.steak.hu). M3 Kálvin tér/tram 47, 49. **Open** noon-12.30am daily. **Average** €€€. **Credit** MC, V. **Map** p249 F7 ⑱

While more restaurants in Budapest are providing great steak, there are only a handful of dedicated steakhouses: and this one, serving aged Argentine Angus, is arguably the best. Tenderloin, filet mignon, New York strip-style sirloin and other cuts of top-quality meat are prepared by a kitchen that understands rare means red. All steaks here are offered in three sizes, ranging from just under a half pound to a pound, so you won't leave hungry. The prices are competitive, with the majority of one-pound steaks costing around Ft5,000 and the most expensive, the tenderloin, weighing in at Ft7,340. Other carnivorous offerings here include a crown roast of pork ribs and saddle of New Zealand lamb baked on lava stone.

Papageno

V.Semmelweiss utca 19 (485 0161/06 20 934 6680 mobile). M2 Astoria/bus 7. Open 6.30pm-midnight Mon-Sat. **Average** €€€. **Credit** MC, V. **Map** p249 F6 ⑲

Under the new management of Zsolt Szondi, the worldly Papageno now has the hallmarks of a man fluent in style. He hand-painted the walls with distressed Jugendstil patterns, and bathed this intimate space, ten tables in all, in chic pink backlighting. Even a simple dish like the quail consommé comes in an unassuming but powerful arrangement of galantine, roughly chopped carrots, vegetables and an egg on top. The global fare features Bahia shrimps with spaghetti neri, New Zealand lamb, Japanese tuna with sweet fennel and purple onion chutney, or goose liver on fruit bread, all reflecting a more open-minded approach to culinary pleasures. In summer, a terrace operates in the adjacent lot. With the gilded youth of Budapest filing in fast, phone reservations are recommended.

Papaya Japan Café

V.Képíró utca 9 (266 7899). M3 Kálvin tér/tram 47, 49. **Open** noon-11.30pm daily. **Average** €€€. **Credit** MC, V. **Map** p249 F6 ⑳

After turning the Fuji restaurant in Rózsadomb into the darling of Budapest's Japanese community, chef Jin recently moved closer to the action to preside over what he calls an 'eccentrically shaped' round brick cellar in downtown Pest. Here, Jin jumps from the sushi bar to the tempura bar, whipping up orders before your very eyes – just try to follow the deft moves of his flying knife. Sushi, sashimi and tempura are the mainstays, and the light, fresh preparations can compete with any in town. Tell Jin the

basic type of food or ingredients you're after and let him go to work. The Hungarian service is sweet and deferential, and the karaoke room in the back fires up at weekends.

Páva

Four Seasons Gresham Palace, V.Roosevelt tér 5-6 (268 5100). M1 Vörösmarty tér/tram 2. **Open** 6-10.30pm Mon-Sat. **Average** €€€€. **Credit** AmEx, DC, MC, V. **Map** p246 D5 ㉑

Two years after opening, the fine-dining arm of the five-star Gresham Palace hotel (*see p39*) is still the gold standard for Budapest restaurants. The Italian menu, featuring the best local ingredients, changes frequently, as does the cherry-picked list of two dozen Hungarian and Italian wines available by the glass. The welcoming servers can guide you through the wine list and the menu, which consists of a limited number of well-made appetisers, soups, pastas, risottos, and seafood, meat and vegetarian courses. You can order half measures or make a full meal out of the exquisite pastas, like squid ink spaghetti with clams or home-made seafood ravioli with basil and tomato fondue. For something more substantial, there's a rich beef tenderloin and goose liver with truffles and potato cake in a red wine reduction; but leave room for the decadent desserts, such as the mousse or tiramisu. The Gresham's softly lit, grand art-deco interior offers diners an eye-level view of the Chain Bridge. **Photos** *p119*.

Pomo D'Oro

V.Arany János utca 9 (302 6473/www.pomodoro budapest.com). **Open** 11am-midnight Mon-Fri; noon-midnight Sat, Sun. **Average** €€. **Credit** AmEx, MC, V. **Map** p246 D4 ㉒

This popular Italian in the quieter business quarter downtown offers fine dining in a lively atmosphere. The cavernous split-level space is packed at lunchtime and can fill up with football lovers on certain evenings – you won't get an unreserved table if there's a key game on. The whole thing is kept afloat nicely by swift, friendly, efficient waiters. The food? Extremely pleasurable and certainly plentiful – the titular tomato is put to fine use in the traditional Tuscan soup or in the fresh blue mussels in spicy sauce starter. Octopus, prawn tails and calamari all get a regular look-in as opener, but leave room for grilled steak, fish or game mains. Excellent Italian and Hungarian wines are chosen by sister restaurant, the Taverna Pomo D'Oro (*see p117*).

Salaam Bombay

V.Mérleg utca 6 (411 1252/www.salaambombay.hu). M1, M2, M3 Deák tér/tram 2. **Open** noon-3pm, 6-11pm daily. **Average** €€. **Credit** MC, V. **Map** p246 D5 ㉓

This relaxed Indian restaurant near Roosevelt tér, in a chic, modern space with a split-level floor and a photo mural of Bombay Bay, concentrates on curries and sizzlers. Examples of the former include pepper chicken madras and lamb vindaloo; the latter chicken tikka masala and tandoori chicken.

Eat, Drink, Shop

The classy **Callas** – contemporary cuisine with Opera House opulence. *See p119.*

There are also vegetarian dishes and a warming mulligatawny soup. The spices are relatively mild, the way locals seem to prefer it, but there's a broad range of substantial flavours that will leave your mouth pleasantly buzzing. You can accompany your dish with a refreshing mango lassi or any one of a dozen reasonably mixed tropical cocktails.

Segal

V.Magyar utca 12-14 (328 0774). M2 Astoria/ tram 47, 49/bus 7. **Open** 6pm-midnight Mon-Sat. **Average** €€€. **Credit** AmEx, DC, MC, V. **Map** p249 F6 ㉔
While fusion cuisine has created confusion in many Budapest kitchens, Segal is a happy exception. Fine ingredients from around the world are blended masterfully in interesting dishes like calamari sautéed in pistachio, cilantro pesto with fresh mango, or duck breast in a sauce of red wine and chocolate. When Baraka (see p118) moved to Andrássy, its chef, Victor Segal, stayed in the old location and opened his own place. He's always popping out of the kitchen to chat with the customers about the day's specials, built around seasonal ingredients. The cocktails are well mixed, and the wine list includes top-quality Hungarian varieties, with some fancy bottles running up to Ft20,000. There's one efficient waiter allocated to the half-dozen tables here, adding to the feeling that you're being pampered throughout the meal.

Takebayashi

V.Belgrád rakpart 18 (318 1144/www.bambusz liget.hu). Tram 2. **Open** 11.30am-11pm Mon-Fri; noon-11pm Sat, Sun. **Average** €€. **Credit** AmEx, MC, V. **Map** p249 E7 ㉕
This proven, standard sushi place with a terrace on the Pest bank is run by a non-Japanese chef, trained in Vienna, but who knows his stuff. Friendly staff guide you through the menu with seafood, vegetarian and roll-your-own sushi options from a huge list of raw ingredients – it's not often you see sea urchin (Ft990) or red snapper (Ft490) on a sushi menu in these parts. Sashimi offerings include decent salmon roe and tuna, and there's tempura as well. Set menus give a good range of tastes. Not the best sushi in town but reasonably priced and reliable.

Taverna Dionysos

V.Belgrád rakpart 6 (318 1222). Tram 2. **Open** noon-midnight daily. **Average** €€. **Credit** AmEx, MC, V. **Map** p249 E7 ㉖
Satisfying Greek cuisine and a great view of the Citadella and Castle Hill from the Pest bank ensure that the terrace of this whitewash-and-blue restaurant is packed most summer evenings. The inside, a two-level sprawl of long tables, also fills up, keeping waiters scurrying in peak hours. The fare is acceptable versions of Aegean standards: the huge mixed fish and seafood platters will feed a hungry couple well, as will the barbecued meat ones. Vegetarians are well catered for and they can make a meal out of the many starters. Book for the terrace.

Taverna Pomo D'Oro

V.Széchenyi utca 14 (312 1405/www.taverna pomodoro.com). M3 Arany János utca/tram 2. **Open** 6-11.30pm Mon-Sat. **Average** €€. **Credit** MC, V. **Map** p246 D4 ㉗
The owners of the Pomo D'Oro (see p115) took over this high-ceilinged cellar with warm brick walls, and hired sommelier Christian Forlani to open what he calls 'a wine bar with a different kind of Italian cuisine from our sister restaurant'. The wine is hand-picked from Italy, and the cuisine is superb. Starting with the best fresh ingredients – seafood and veal flown in from Italy or lamb from New Zealand – chef Ricardo Pinna makes hearty but subtly flavoured meals such as hefty tenderloin in a delicately belly-warming grappa sauce. Watch the board for specials, like tagliatelle vongole, which comes with a heaped bowl of shellfish to spread on to saucy pasta. The genial Forlani travels Italy to bring back tantalising bottles, priced about the same as local vintages. He'll happily discuss the several hundred wines on the seasonally changing list. Half-a-dozen recommended wines are available by the glass.

Tom-George Restaurant & Café

V.Október 6 utca 8 (266 3525). M1, M2, M3 Deák tér. **Open** noon-midnight daily. **Average** €€€. **Credit** AmEx, DC, MC, V. **Map** p246 E4 ㉘
The flavours of Asia and Hungary dominate, but most cuisines are in the mix at this big slick eatery that draws diners from the Central European University. A good sushi chef adds another level to the menu, and hearty steaks are a crowd pleaser. Tom-George is good, but not always as good as it thinks it is: the service can be complacent, some of the dishes sound better than they taste, and the dramatic nouvelle presentations can seem overdone. These slights aside, it's a still a classy place for a meal, and if you pick carefully, you can eat well. Bold modern decor is complemented by a large terrace.

Seafood

Óceán

V.Petőfi tér 3 (266 1826/www.oceanbargrill.com). M1 Vörösmarty tér/M3 Ferenciek tere/tram 2. **Open** noon-midnight daily. **Average** €€€. **Credit** AmEx, MC, V. **Map** p249 D6 ㉙
This stellar restaurant, serving fresh fish flown in daily, would be impressive anywhere, but is all the more so in a landlocked country where most of the seafood is frozen and most of the locals aren't too interested. Foreigners go to Óceán for extensive saltwater offerings including octopus, lobster and molluscs, and sea fish such as sole, sea bream and bass. The fresh flesh is handled with care, and you can watch as they grill your selection. The kitchen, visible behind a glass wall in this large, well-lit location, uses a deft hand with spices, to let delicate fish flavours shine. Desserts are distinguished by their subtle flavours. Óceán is managed by Norwegian importers who operate a fish shop next door.

Eat, Drink, Shop

In search of good goulash

Goulash is the first dish that you associate with Hungary. But if you've had something called 'goulash' abroad, odds are it was what Hungarians refer to as *pörkölt*, which is a hearty beef stew. *Gulyás*, often called *gulyásleves* ('goulash soup'), is a soup, much more watery than *pörkölt*, but still very rich.

Gulyás means herdsman. It was the food of the cattle herdsmen of the great Hungarian plains, cooked in a vat known as a *bogrács* (which can still be purchased at any garden shop), using fresh beef and ingredients that could be stored in their primitive straw cowboy huts: dried paprika, onions and potatoes. Paprika only became widespread in Hungarian cuisine in the late 1700s, and the adoption of *gulyás* as a national food symbol

only began in the 1860s, during the upsurge in national pride following the 1867 Ausgleich with Habsburg Austria.

A good *gulyás* is a huge bowl of paprika-flavoured soup (often served in a miniature *bogrács*) filled with hunks of beef, potatoes, perhaps a hint of cumin seed or marjoram, and in some places, small fresh egg dumplings called *csipetke* ('little pinches' of dough). It's a hearty, warming soup, with just a bit of a bite. The spicing in a *gulyás* is not hot enough to make your mouth sizzle, but will probably leave a pleasant warm feeling at the back of your throat. It's real comfort food, great in the winter, and although it is just a soup, a big, hearty *gulyás* can suffice as an entire meal.

Sampling *gulyás* is easy enough in Hungary. Any traditional restaurant is likely to list *gulyás* in the soups section of the menu. Finding the best *gulyás* is more of a personal quest and everyone has a favourite.

The **Bagolyvár** (*see p122*) specialises in home-style Hungarian soups, and is a logical place to look for top *gulyás*; you may also do well at this restaurant's upmarket sister, the famous **Gundel** (*see p122*). At the other end of the scale, the homely **Kádár Étkezde** (*see p122; see photo*) offers the kind of *gulyás* that a Magyar mum would be proud to make – if Magyar mums made *gulyás* any more. Another low-frills, high-quality local, the **Alföldi Vendéglő** (*see p110*), serves its own version of *gulyás*, the way they make it in Alföld, on the Hungarian plain. The **Püré Bár** (*see p123*) breaks with tradition by making mashed potatoes the main course, and the chef here has no compunction about taking a different approach to *gulyás*, by making it with deer meat. This kind of culinary experimentation would probably never fly at the **Múzeum** (*see p124*), a venerable bastion of traditional Magyar cuisine with a serious approach to the national soup.

Andrássy út & District VI

Hungarian

Baraka

Andrássy Hotel, VI.Andrássy út 111 (483 1355/ www.barakarestaurant.hu). M1 Bajza utca.
Open 11.45am-3.30pm, 6.30-11.30pm daily.
Average €€€. **Credit** AmEx, DC, MC, V.
Map p247 H2 ㉚

The creative team of Leora and David Seboek, who ran Baraka successfully for several years in District V, took over a bigger location at the Hotel Andrássy and continue their tradition of exposing Budapest to well-handled fusion cooking. They remade the Andrássy's big dining area in dramatic black and silver and hired a new chef, Shani Prusman, who does a splendid job of blending flavours in dishes like ceviche of shrimp with mango, avocado and coriander, or beef tenderloin with truffled potatoes and sake-miso sauce. It's generally worth the high price, though a few fusion combinations are so delicately seasoned that no flavour dominates. A good Hungarian wine list and a beautifully decorated terrace, with a view of this lovely, quiet stretch of Andrássy út, complete the picture. **Photos** *p112.*

Café Bouchon
VI.Zichy Jenő utca 33 (353 4094). M1 Oktogon/M3 Nyugati pu./tram 4, 6. **Open** 9am-11pm Mon-Sat. **Average** €€€. **No credit cards. Map** p246 F4 **③①**
Friendly, enthusiastic manager Lajos Tisza makes sure the atmosphere in this bistro is lively and laid back. But he keeps the kitchen and servers on their toes, which is what makes this place a favourite of local gourmands. Check the big daily specials board for local classics, like *fogas*, a Balaton fish handled better here than in many restaurants, or a dish of layered potatoes, *kolbász* sausage, hard-boiled eggs and light cheese. Well-chosen Hungarian vintages, described lovingly on the long wine list, come by the glass, and the able waiters will help you pick something different for each course. **Photos** *p113.*

Callas
VI.Andrássy út 20 (354 0954). M1 Opera. **Open** 8am-midnight Mon-Fri; 10am-midnight Sat, Sun. **Average** €€. **Credit** MC, V. **Map** p246 F4 **③②**
With its grand, arching interior and huge terrace by the Opera House, this place could probably make a good income as a tourist trap. Thankfully, the owners had loftier plans. Located in the opulent old opera ticket office, the Callas is a sprawling establishment supplying recommendable meals, fine cocktails and

a lively atmosphere at reasonable prices. The cuisine is a mix of Hungarian and continental dishes, served traditionally or in interesting fusion combinations, along with – oddly – sushi, prepared by one of Budapest's master Japanese chefs. The kitchen handles this range well, whether it's the comforting Hungarian-style duck with onion-and-pepper sauce, the bold lasagne with rabbit, or the tasty tuna sashimi. The service here is pretty slick, even bordering on smug, but the staff generally move with reasonable speed. **Photos** *p116.*

Klassz
VI.Andrássy út 41 (no phone). M1 Opera. **Open** 11.30am-11pm Mon-Sat; 11.30am-6pm Sun. **Average** €€. **Credit** AmEx, MC, V. **Map** p246 F4 **③③**
It's hard to spot the sign, and they don't give out a phone number or take bookings, but this brightly decorated wine restaurant on a busy section of Andrássy is always packed. Although it's owned by the local Wine Society, Klassz by no means neglects the food. Manager Roland Radványi, who used to work with Menza (*see p120*), can be seen carefully overseeing things. Courteous, well informed servers help you peruse a frequently changing wine list, with 30 Hungarian labels available by the glass. The continental and Hungarian menu also alternates. Light, delicious dishes, like duck liver with apple purée and Tokaj wine sauce or roasted leg of lamb with Chinese cabbage and spinach, put much of the competition to shame. If you show up around 8pm, expect to wait for a table, but it will be worth it.

Páva. See p115.

Il **Terzo Cerchio**. See p124.

Kogart

VI.Andrássy út 112 (354 3839/www.kogart.hu). M1 Bajza utca. **Open** 10am-midnight daily. **Average** €€. **Credit** AmEx, DC, MC, V. **Map** p247 H2 ③④

The ground floor of this art gallery in a restored villa in the diplomatic quarter provides a grand setting for a restaurant offering Med and Magyar cuisine. The lavishly decorated, wood-panelled downstairs dining room is an attractive space with rotating exhibitions, though the quiet terrace off Andrássy is probably the superior place to sit. A grill goes out on the terrace in summer, expanding the menu. Dependable pasta and fish are light alternatives, but meat-eaters are well tended to, with steak, veal, lamb and venison. Live jazz performances take place on Wednesday and Thursday evenings.

Menza

VI.Liszt Ferenc tér 2 (413 1482). M1 Oktogon/tram 4, 6. **Open** 10am-midnight daily. **Average** €€. **Credit** AmEx, MC, V. **Map** p246 F4 ③⑤

Still the locals' favourite bar-restaurant on Liszt Ferenc tér, this retro spot done up to resemble a 1970s cafeteria pays homage to classic Hungarian cookery with standards and creative updates of the cuisine. A recent change of chef has beefed up the meaty home-style offerings, but there are still a few decidedly non-Magyar dishes, like duck breast with mango and blueberries and salmon in hollandaise sauce. Offbeat Hungarian specials include *lángos* (fried dough) dressed up with chicken-breast stuffing. Watch the weekly changing menu for any other

Magyar medleys. The location means that prices are competitive and the cocktail menu extensive, as is the one for the affordable wines. **Photos** *p123*.

Premier

VI.Andrássy út 101 (342 1768/www.premier-restaurant.hu). M1 Bajza utca. **Open** *Apr-Oct* 11am-11pm daily. *Nov-Mar* 11am-11pm Mon-Sat. **Average** €€. **Credit** AmEx, DC, MC, V. **Map** p247 G3 ③⑥

The small premium you pay for the location and old school service is more than worthwhile. There's an art-deco themed cellar, but the terrace on tree-lined Andrássy is the main draw. The food is also interesting, with good Hungarian offerings augmented by enough international ones to please most palates. Even vegetarians can find substantial dishes, like asparagus salad with cherry tomatoes and smoked quail egg, the hearty 'fitness salad', and a superior rendition of *főzelék*, a vegetable purée. Carnivores can enjoy goose liver with fruits or a recommendable wild boar, baked in pastry. The fish selection includes Balaton *fogas* and local carp soup.

International

Arigato

VI.Ó utca 3 (353 3549). M3 Arany János utca. **Open** noon-3pm, 5-11pm Mon-Sat. **Average** €€. **Credit** AmEx, DC, MC, V. **Map** p246 E4 ③⑦

This unpretentious family restaurant is where Japanese residents go for home cooking. The sushi can stand with the best in town, but this is also a good place to try the rest of what Japanese cuisine has to offer. Tonkatsu-don (rice topped with fried pork, egg and caramelised onions) is good, as are the simple noodle dishes. Watch for specials like curried rice or noodles – or ask chef Kaoru Uehara and his wife Tomoko for that day's suggestions.

Chez Daniel

VI.Sziv utca 32 (302 4039). M1 Kodály körönd.
Open noon-3pm, 7-11pm daily. **Average** €€€.
Credit AmEx, DC, MC, V. **Map** p247 G3 ③
Lovingly operated by skilful owner and chef Daniel Labrosse, this restaurant can offer the best French meal in town, and certainly the most original. Daniel appreciates the importance of good ingredients. He has his own truffle supplier and makes the best goose liver terrine in town, his menu heavily influenced by what's good at the market. Don't bother with the menu; it's the illegible specials board you're after – or better yet, ask Daniel. The duck parmentier, buttery, silky-smooth mashed potatoes studded with duck confit, is a perennial pleaser, as is the veal chop in mustard sauce, and monkfish with butter and capers. The hidden courtyard terrace is stunning. Service is knowledgeable but shambolic and table reservations are recommended in the evenings.

Fausto's Étterem

VI.Székely Mihály utca 2 (06 30 589 1813 mobile/ www.fausto.hu). M1 Opera. **Open** noon-3pm, 7-11pm Mon-Fri; 6-11pm Sat. **Average** €€€€.
Credit AmEx, MC, V. **Map** p246 F5 ③
Long considered one of Budapest's best restaurants, the relocated Fausto's now has more competition than it used to, but it's still a contender. The food is gourmet-quality Italian, served nouvelle style. Whether it's loin of rabbit with lobster or own-made tagliatelle with boar-and-rosemary flavoured lentil cream, every dish is an experience. The wine list includes 45 Italian choices, arranged by region, and an equal number of the better Hungarian vintages. The decor is clean and modern, though the big rosy lampshades don't bear up to close scrutiny. An army of servers, almost disconcerting for those accustomed to old-style Budapest waiters, attends to the ten tables. The expert kitchen is also amply staffed. Owner Fausto Di Vora tours the dining room to greet guests and chat with the moneyed, foreign regulars.

Goa

VI.Andrássy út 8 (302 2570). M1 Bajcsy-Zsilinszky út. **Open** noon-midnight daily. **Average** €€€.
Credit AmEx, MC V. **Map** p246 E4 ④
The well-travelled American chef here fuses the flavours of the world to turn this big, tastefully modern space on Andrássy into a deservedly popular venue. Europe and the Americas are represented by great paella and Argentine steak, and there are some good North African offerings as well as Hungarian-style veal paprika. Perhaps the bulk of the dishes come from the Far East, with several wok recipes and a selection of sushi. The kitchen is up to most challenges posed by the menu, even with seafood,

often a risk in Hungary. A broad range of pastas and hearty salads, like duck with capers, make it easy to put together a light meal. Daily specials feature popular bargain lunches.

Marquis de Salade

VI.Hajós utca 43 (302 4086). M3 Arany János utca. **Open** noon-midnight daily. **Average** €€.
No credit cards. Map p246 E4 ④
Budapest's first salad bar is a haven for veggies, and purveyor of dishes from across the former USSR. English-speaking staff guide you through the big menu – Azeri and Georgian lamb soups and stews are among the best items. Most of the seating is in cellar rooms lined with carpeting and low seating.

Millennium da Pippo

VI.Andrássy út 76 (374 0880). M1 Vörösmarty utca. **Open** noon-midnight daily. **Average** €€. **Credit** MC, V. **Map** p246 G3 ④
A Juventus supporter took over this cheery, white-tiled corner restaurant, put some tables outside and started serving pizzas and pasta the way they make them back home. The own-made pasta and softly flavourful garlic bread show attention to detail; the pizza crusts are thin and crispy, topped with just the right amount of tomato sauce and molten cheese. There's also a good wine list, substantial meals like veal marsala or branzino, and a pasta of the day for lunch. The atmosphere is relaxed, and often lively, and staff gab in Italian to animated regulars.

Ristorante Krizia

VI.Mozsár utca 12 (331 8711/www.ristorante krizia.hu). M1 Oktogon/M1 Opera/tram 4, 6.
Open noon-3pm, 6.30-11pm Mon-Sat. **Average** €€€. **Credit** AmEx, MC, V. **Map** p246 F4 ④
In a cellar on a side street near Liszt Ferenc tér hides an under-appreciated, upscale Italian restaurant that rates with the best in town. Chef and owner Graziano Cattaneo dishes simple, creative touches, such as paper-thin prosciutto, beef tenderloin steak with ewe's milk cheese and truffle, or a sublime scallop appetiser with rocket and balsamic vinegar. The chef is usually on hand, and you can ask him to recommend something off-menu. It's a relaxing space, in a tall, airy, split-level cellar filled with natural light. A dozen wines from the huge list of Hungarian and Italian vintages are available by the glass.

Taj Mahal

VI.Szondi utca 40 (301 0447/www.tajmahal.hu). M3 Nyugati pu./tram 4, 6. **Open** noon-11pm Tue-Sun. **Average** €. **Credit** AmEx, MC, V.
Map p246 F3 ④
This Indian on a side street near Nyugati station doesn't hold back on spices. It is also the only place in town to offer south Indian breads and fermented rice batter pancakes, including enormous uttappams wrapped around a vegetarian filling and served with sambar vegetable sauce. The menu spans all the Indian regions and cooking styles, with a nice range of spicy Goan dishes. They also deliver, unusual for good restaurants in Budapest.

Eat, Drink, Shop

Hungarian

Bagolyvár

XIV.Állatkerti út 2 (468 3110/www.bagolyvar.com).
M1 Hösök tere. **Open** noon-11pm daily. **Average**
€€. **Credit** AmEx, DC, MC, V. **Map** p247 H1 ⑮
Gundel's more affordable sister establishment, in a
mock Transylvanian castle attached to the main
restaurant, provides simpler, more homely meals
with a menu that varies daily. Big, hearty soups are
a speciality, and this can be a good spot to try a local
goulash. All the staff are women, because owner
George Lang reckons they're the best home cooks.
A tasty roulade of fresh breads, served with various
spreads, is part of the starter. The secluded terrace,
shaded in summer, gets odd noises from the nearby
zoo. The service and quality has been slipping of
late, but it's still a good meal at a reasonable price
in a cosy setting.

Gundel

XIV.Állatkerti út 2 (468 4040/www.gundel.hu). M1
Hösök tere. **Open** noon-2.30pm, 6.30pm-midnight
Mon-Sat; 11.30am-2pm Sun (brunch only). **Average**
€€€€. **Credit** AmEx, DC, MC, V. **Map** p247 H1 ⑯
The city's most famous restaurant is still one of the
best and priciest. Opened in 1894 as the Wampetics,
it was taken over in 1910 by top chef Károly Gundel.
His restaurant helped create modern Hungarian cuisine by incorporating French influences, and he
invented many now standard dishes, such as Gundel
pancakes. After years of neglect, Gundel was
acquired by restaurant impresario George Lang (of
the Café des Artistes in New York) and Ronald
Lauder (son of Estée), and given an expensive
makeover with the aim of recreating the glory days.
It's a huge place, set in an art nouveau mansion by
the zoo, with a ballroom, garden and terrace, and
several private dining rooms, as well as the large
main room hung with paintings by Hungarian masters. Tables are laid with Zsolnay porcelain and ster-
ling silver, and the Gypsy band is slick. The menu
is, not surprisingly, a little old-fashioned; starters
and desserts almost outshine the main courses.
These include fine versions of Hungarian standards
and Magyar versions of international dishes, such
as the Tournedos Franz Liszt, made with local goose
liver. Chef Kálmán Kalla produces lighter versions
of Hungarian favourites, like chicken paprika, to
please modern palates. A long and authoritative list
of Hungarian wines is rounded off with excellent
sweet Tokaj from the restaurant's own vineyard.
Service is smooth and formal, and men must wear a
jacket and tie for dinner. The Sunday brunch is a
more relaxed and affordable way to enjoy this landmark. You can also go downstairs, where Gundel's
more casual 1894 Food & Wine Cellar allows you to
sample from about 100 Hungarian wines by the
glass. The cellar's food is less expensive and less
sophisticated, but still excellent.

Hungarian

Bock Bisztro

Corinthia Grand Hotel Royal, VII.Erzsébet körút
43-49 (321 0340/www.bockbisztro.hu). M1 Oktogon/
tram 4, 6. **Open** noon-midnight Mon-Sat. **Average**
€€€. **Credit** DC, MC, V. **Map** p246 G4 ⑰
Vintner József Bock, whose Villány winery makes
excellent reds, showcases a variety of Hungarian
labels in this wine restaurant that's inside the five-
star Corinthia Grand Royal but has a separate street
entrance. Classy renditions of rich Hungarian food,
like roast pork, veal paprika or fillet of chicken
breast with goose liver compote provide a base for
your tasting. The intelligent and efficient waiters
will guide you through a list that includes about 20
wines from Bock's own label, 40 reds and whites
from other labels and ten Tokaj dessert wines. Some
20 are available by the glass. They also sell bottles
to go. Booking is advisable.

Fészek

VII.Kertész utca 36 (322 6043). Tram 4, 6. **Open**
noon-2am daily. **Average** €. **No credit cards.**
Map p246 G4 ⑱
In 1903, a former cloister with a stunning garden in
the heart of Budapest was converted into the artists'
club. Some time after the war, the artists' association hired out the garden and an adjacent ballroom
to a restaurant where overworked waiters served
traditional Hungarian food from an encyclopedic
menu. Now new management installed in 2007 has
shortened the choice, straying from the traditional,
for example by adding tuna steak alongside the veal
paprika. And the waiters are still overworked. But
there's no rush. The garden, now obscured from the
sun by massive chestnut trees that were seedlings
in 1903, is a magical space that becomes a lively
outdoor nightspot on summer evenings (*see p194*
Party under the stars). The recently spruced up
baroque-style interior, watched over by plaster
nudes, is pretty impressive too.

Kádár Étkezde

VII.Klauzál tér 10 (321 3622). M1 Opera/tram 4,
6. **Open** 11.30am-3.30pm Tue-Sat. **Average** €.
No credit cards. Map p246 F5 ⑲
This charming no-frills restaurant offers Hungarian
home-style cooking in the heart of the old Jewish
quarter. Autographed photographs and caricatures
of Hungarian showbiz stars adorn the walls and
each table has its own (dangerously high-powered)
soda siphon. Share a table with a stranger and check
for daily specials, like *libacomb* (goose leg), served
with red cabbage and mashed potatoes, or the fabulous Jewish dish *sólet*, made of smoked goose breast
and baked beans. This is also a fine place for *főzelék*,
puréed vegetables with a fried egg on top. The most
authentic Hungarian food you can muster without
having a Magyar mum.

Kőleves Vendéglő

*VII.Kazinczy utca 35/Dob utca 26 (322 1011/www.
koleves.com). M1, M2, M3 Deák tér.* **Open** 11am-
midnight daily. **Average** €. **Credit** AmEx, MC, V.
Map p246 F5 ⑤

This bright, funky spot in District VII's bar vortex
attracts an alternative crowd who come for simple,
lightened-up Hungarian cookery with global and
veggie options. The dinner-themed decor features a
chandelier made of wine glasses, plates embedded
in the bar counter and a lamp made of forks. The so-
called stir-fry vegetables are sautéed in olive oil, but
they taste great. Appropriately for a restaurant in
the former ghetto, they offer decent renditions of a
couple of traditional Jewish-Hungarian dishes: *sólet*,
made from goose and beans and served at the weekend; and a soft *flódni* pastry of walnut apple and
poppy seeds. Occasional live jazz performances are
staged downstairs.

Püré Bár

VII.Király utca 41 (322 5526). M1 Opera. **Open**
8am-midnight daily. **Average** €. **No credit cards.**
Map p246 F4 ⑤

Püré means purée, as in mashed potatoes, which are
the speciality at this quirky little place in a nicely
restored art nouveau storefront on increasingly gentrifying Király utca. The signature dish is whipped
up with carrots, basil, pepper and onion in more than
a dozen varieties. You can get a sampler plate with
three types of mash if you prefer. The potatoes can

also be a side to more standard Hungarian fare, like
a venison goulash or other meaty specials, but most
of the offerings here are lighter. *Főzelék*, a Hungarian
dish of puréed vegetables and flour, goes nicely with
mash on the side, as do the flavourful sandwiches
of smoked salmon or grilled vegetables. Service is
casual but generally efficient.

International

Noir et l'Or Kávézó és Étterem

*VII.Király utca 17 (413 0236/www.noiretlor.hu).
M1, M2, M3 Deák tér/M1 Opera.* **Open** 8am-
midnight daily. **Average** €€. **Credit** AmEx,
MC, V. **Map** p246 F4 ⑤

This fastidiously chic restaurant adds a touch of
class to up-and-coming Király utca. Inside, along
with tasteful modern black, gold and white decor –
and a strange, airport-like wide screen displaying
images of raw ingredients – the restaurant offers
food that you probably won't find anywhere else in
Hungary. The cuisine is from French colonies in
Africa and the Caribbean, as well as the French
Mediterranean coast, which means good seafood,
including a superb Côte d'Azur fish platter for two.
You can have any meat or fish grilled and served
with one of the house sauces. Attentive servers
check several times to see how your meal is going.
It can feel like presentation trumps substance, but
overall it's a pretty good meal.

Eat, Drink, Shop

Cafeteria chic, contemporary cuisine and competitive prices at **Menza**. *See p120.*

Osteria Fausto's

VII.Dohány utca 5 (269 6806/www.fausto.hu). M2 Astoria. **Open** noon-11pm Mon-Sat. **Average** €€. **Credit** AmEx, MC, V. **Map** p249 F5 ⑬

The casual sister restaurant of one of the best places in town, Fausto's Étterem (*see p121*), this is the spot to find quality Italian dishes at decent prices. The mains menu consists of seven varieties of pasta (Ft1,500-Ft2,200) and three each of meat and fish. Turkey breast with ham and mashed potato in marsala sauce is filling and affordable at Ft2,400, but you can also make a meal out of the hearty pastas, like pappardelle with deer ragout, the house ravioli and linguine with king prawns and zucchini. The friendly waiter will help you with the wine list, which includes about 40 Italian and Hungarian choices. Everything takes place in a dark-wood dining room, below a gallery that receives cheery natural light at lunchtime.

Il Terzo Cerchio

VII.Dohány utca 40 (354 0788). M2 Astoria. **Open** noon-11.30pm daily. **Average** €€€. **Credit** MC, V. **Map** p249 G5 ⑭

This favourite of Budapest's Italian community has moved to a fancier location, and slightly raised its prices to draw a bigger crowd without losing its loyal following – or its great food. The walls and high arched ceiling are made of cosy brick, as is the hulking oven, staffed by an Italian team who produce what may be Budapest's best pizzas. The extensive menu also features superb own-made pastas, great wood-grilled steaks and seafood such as grilled branzino. There are 80 choices of Italian and Hungarian wines, with a few sold by the glass. The cellar, with its TV showing Rai Uno, is often booked by regulars for a big Serie A game. A good bet for an excellent night out. **Photos** *p120*.

Districts VIII & IX

Hungarian

Borbíróság

IX.Csarnok tér 5 (219 0902/www.borbirosag.com). M3 Kálvin tér/tram 47, 49. **Open** noon-midnight Mon-Sat. **Average** €€. **Credit** AmEx, MC, V. **Map** p249 F7 ⑮

The 'Wine Court', a warm brick restaurant behind the Great Market Hall, provides a casual, affordable way to sample superior Hungarian wines by the glass or bottle. The food is belly-lining Hungarian standards, all prepared well. The house appetiser of sausage, goose cracklings and goose liver pâté or the goulash may be all you need to soak up the grape. If that's not enough, try the tenderloin Hungarian style or smoked ham knuckle with cabbage. The price per bottle averages Ft5,000; for the full experience, order by the glass, from 60 vintages divided by region and maker, and let the coded menu and the clued-up waiter help you choose something for before, during and after dinner.

Múzeum

VIII.Múzeum körút 12 (267 0375). M3 Kálvin tér/tram 47, 49. **Open** noon-11.30pm Mon-Sat. **Average** €€€. **Credit** MC, V. **Map** p249 F6 ⑯

Tasty and representative Hungarian cuisine has been served in this popular, elegant setting by the National Museum since 1885. High ceilings, tiled walls and tall windows provide plenty of light, and well-spaced tables embellish the fin-de-siècle ambience. The menu is extensive, with a big difference in price from one dish to another: you can easily spend a fortune or dine reasonably cheaply. Hungarian and a number of international dishes are carefully prepared and served in big portions, but presentation occasionally wins out over culinary good taste. Smooth service and the pleasant surroundings keep this old place buzzing; if you only have time for one Magyar meal, this is a decent choice. It's also a good spot for late dining, with a nightcap awaiting if required at the busy, 24-hour Múzeum Cukrászda (*see p192*) next door.

International

China Lan Zhou

VIII.Luther utca 1B (314 1080). M2 Blaha Lujza tér/tram 4, 6. **Open** noon-10.30pm daily. **Average** €. **No credit cards.** **Map** p250 H5 ⑰

On a narrow side street near the beginning of dowdy District VIII, this unpretentious eaterie serves what may be the best Chinese food in town, with the only real competition coming from its sister restaurant, Új Lan Zhou (*see p106*) in Buda. The menu here is alarmingly large but repeated visits have yet to turn up any duds. The kitchen employs the potential of livestock to the utmost in dishes like spicy tripe, duck heart and tongue salad. Vegetarians and seafood lovers also have lots of choices, including some simple but superb salads such as a sublime concoction of quick-blanched potato shreds simply seasoned with a few drops of sesame oil.

Pata Negra

IX.Kálvin tér 8 (215 5616). M3 Kálvin tér. **Open** 10.30am-midnight Mon-Fri; noon-midnight Sat, Sun. **Average** €. **No credit cards.** **Map** p249 F7 ⑱

Budapest's only tapas bar that approaches authenticity does an impressive job of recreating the food and atmosphere of Spain, making this one of the best places to eat at before diving into the bar-heavy neighbourhood of Ráday utca. Just as you might expect in Spain, the waiters are overworked and the music is too loud. Amid cheery tiled walls of white, blue and red, there's a big dog-leg bar with glass cases displaying the treats on offer. The menu includes 40 tapas, several varieties of snacky montadito sandwiches, and larger lamb, pork or beef cuts. But tapas is the way to go here: good chorizo, great flavoured meatballs and fine seafood. The wine list includes several Spanish reds by the glass or bottle, and they'll also make a sangria. All in all, ideal preparation for a bar crawl round the corner.

Cafés & Bars

A barfly's paradise goes upmarket.

Paris, Texas. *See p138.*

Budapest has always thrived on an all-hours, anything-goes bar culture that reaches from gutter to glitz. In tandem with the city's dining choices, the bar scene has been transformed in the last five years. Slick, professional venues with classy (English-speaking) service, a cosmopolitan atmosphere and contemporary decor and drinks have come to the fore. It's easier to find a good cocktail in this town than ever before. Even the most basic of snacks is well presented, and nearly every venue can turn out a decent salad and main dish. Vegetarian options abound. Restaurants are being given a run for their money.

New places like the **Ellátó** and the recently moved **Café Eklektika** and **Castro Bisztró** attract an exciting crowd that's out to party. The swell of decent bars in District VII and, to a growing extent, in District VI create the potential for several nights of bar crawling. These are supplemented by a healthy selection of late options (*see pp191-195* **Nightlife**).

Fancy terrace cafés, long established on Liszt Ferenc tér and the Kálvin tér end of Ráday utca, are now spread over pedestrianised sections of Hajós utca, Baross utca and Mikszáth Kálmán tér. Liszt Ferenc tér still offers the best and

easiest bar stroll; Ráday's bars (**Jaffa** and **Eckermann** excepted) are blander and close earlier. The prime spot of the Pest embankment is also lined with bar-table umbrellas – but sadly they belong to overpriced tourist traps.

Away from the side-by-side terraces, a random outdoor courtyard ('garden') bar scene thrives in Districts VII and VIII (*see p194* **Party under the stars**) and beats Liszt Ferenc tér hands down. It's hit and miss – but hit lucky and it's fun all the way.

DRINKS AND VENUES

Most places have at least two draught beers, one domestic, one Czech, Belgian or German, often with a wheat one on offer too. Wines (mainly domestic, with some Spanish and Italian) are listed according to year and origin, and the fad for cocktails means that care is now taken over the hiring of bar staff. It's no longer enough to don a short skirt or hair gel, flash

> ❶ Pink numbers given in this chapter correspond to the location of each café on the street maps. *See pp245-250.*

a fake smile and let a top 40 station do the talking. Ten years ago you couldn't get a proper cappuccino. Now it's *carajillos*, lattes and macchiatos. Some spots do breakfast, many host DJs or care about the music on offer.

The price for all this, of course, is the price. You can still get drunk for a fiver, but you'll be slumming it with cash-strapped locals. Radical improvement has polarised bar culture. Do-it-all designer establishments have closed many a local. The *borozó*, the basement bar selling *bor* (wine), and *söröző*, the beer hall selling *sör* ('shur', beer) are going the way of another dying breed, the *presszó*, a tacky, neon-lit café from the 1960s; the **Bambi** is the best example.

Wine, white (*fehér*) or red (*vörös*), dry (*száraz*) or sweet (*édes*), is measured by the decilitre. Two dl (*két deci*) is a medium measure, three (*három*) a hefty one. A spritzer is a *fröccs*. Decent local brands abound. Spirits include Unicum (*see p132* **Black death in a bottle**) and fruit brandy, *pálinka,* plum (*szilvapálinka*) and pear (*körtepálinka*) being the most common. Beer is sold by the half-litre, *korsó,* or smaller glass, *pohár.* An average bar will charge about Ft500 a *korsó*.

The *kávéház,* proffering *kávé* (coffee), is still going strong. Coffee arrived in Hungary with the Ottomans, and coffeehouses were a feature in Budapest long before they appeared in Paris or Vienna. They reached their heyday with the Dual Monarchy – in 1900 there were 600,

a breeding ground for burgeoning Magyar culture. A list of regulars at the Café Japan, now the Írók Boltja bookstore (*see p141*), reads like a who's who of early 20th-century Hungarian culture. Writers and filmmakers mingled with Hollywood moguls at the **New York Café**, only now renovated a century later. Many of today's finest cafés (eg the **Gerlóczy**) model themselves on their fin-de-siècle forebears. Coffeehouses are not only the domain of caffeine and cultural discussion – gooey cakes are another speciality. The most elegant and colourful creations are found at a *cukrászda*, a pâtisserie-café hybrid, the **Ruszwurm** being the most prominent example.

Age-old custom dictates that clinking beer glasses is still not done – although a hearty shout of '*Egészsegedre!*' (*Ege-sheged-re*, or 'To your health!') is always welcome.

Buda

Castle District

Miró Café

I.Úri utca 30 (201 5573). Várbusz from M2 Moszkva tér/bus 16. **Open** 9am-midnight daily. **No credit cards. Map** p245 B4 ❶
Although set in the tourist-swamped Castle District, the Miró has resisted the temptation towards the phonily historic. Decor and furniture have been designed in the shapes and colours of the artist

Casual but visually striking – the **MU Színház**. *See p127.*

himself. The green metal chairs are surprisingly comfortable; extraordinary sofas and hatstands impel you to pause and admire. The staff is accustomed to fleeting visits from tourists, so service ranges from indifferent to occasionally somewhat snarly. Still, there's a fine selection of cakes and snacks, a small summer terrace, and real alternatives are otherwise few in the Castle District. Order a full dinner, though, and you could be here till the next invasion of Buda.

Ruszwurm Cukrászda

I.Szentháromság utca 7 (375 5284). Várbusz from M2 Moszkva tér/bus 16. **Open** 10am-7pm daily. **No credit cards.** Map p245 B4 **②**
Founded in 1827, Hungary's oldest *cukrászda* (café-cum-pastry shop) has a warm interior that retains some of the 1840s Empire-style cherrywood fittings. Its history and Castle District location guarantee its popularity with tourists, and the handful of tables, inside and along the pavement, are often full. The kitchen produces masterful pastries, freshly made ice-cream and quite delicious *pogácsa* scones. Damn fine espresso too.

Tabán, Gellért Hill & south Buda

Libella

XI.Budafoki út 7 (209 4761). Tram 18, 47, 49. **Open** 8am-1am Mon-Fri; noon-1am Sat, Sun. **No credit cards.** Map p249 E8 **③**
Amicable drinkers frequent this unpretentious café-bar around the corner from Gellért tér. Afternoons, it's perfect for a quiet beer, a newspaper and perhaps the best *meleg szendvics* (toastie) in town. Towards evening, it fills with check-shirted engineering students from the nearby college lashing back the VBKs (red wine and cola). A TV goes up for any football match worth watching on a terrestrial channel, there's good, cold HB and Dreher Bock on tap, occasionally deadly *házi pálinka* and, the pièce de résistance, fantastic pickled eggs. An alternative crowd gathers to compare weekends on Sunday afternoons.

MU Színház

XI.Kőrösy József utca 17 (06 70 294 4986 mobile). Tram 4. **Open** 3pm-midnight daily. **No credit cards.** Map p249 D9 **④**
Oran MacCuirc, the hospitable Dubliner behind the groundbreaking and artily alternative Csiga (*see p136*) and 6tus (*see p135*), took over the big lobby area and rear garden of the MU Színház dance theatre to create another idiosyncratic party space with a great vibe and a mixed crowd of young dancers, students and locals. Inside is casual but visually striking, with a quiet side room for chatting and a separate gallery that gets taken over by DJs or concerts at weekends. **Photo** *p126.*

Platán Eszpresszó

I.Döbrentei tér 2 (06 30 665 7094 mobile). Tram 18/bus 5, 7. **Open** 11am-11pm daily. **No credit cards.** Map p248 D6 **⑤**

A mixed crowd of alternative slackers, tourists and locals watches the Danube pass from this terrace on the Buda riverbank in a scenic neighbourhood that is severely underutilised as a drinking venue. Set near the flyover of Elizabeth Bridge, all is shaded under a lovely old plane tree (*platán*) that gives the place its name. An efficient service and affordable drinks add to the attraction.

Víziváros

Angelika

I.Batthyány tér 7 (201 0668). M2 Batthyány tér. **Open** 9am-midnight Mon-Sat; 9am-11pm Sun. **No credit cards.** Map p245 C3 **⑥**
Located in the former crypt of St Anne's Church on the south side of Batthyány tér, this refined café attracts Buda ladies who gossip. Of a late September afternoon, when the sun's streaming through the stained-glass windows, it's an atmospheric spot for coffee and cakes. The terrace affords a fine view of Parliament across the river.

The best Bars

For downmarket drinks
Grinzingi (*see p129*); **Hat-három (6:3) Borozó** (*see p136*).

For fin-de-siècle grandeur
Centrál Kávéház (*see p128*); **New York Café** (*see p135*).

For musical accompaniment
Filter Klub (*see p135*); **Kiadó kocsma** (*see p131*); **Rock Café** (*see p138*); **Sark** (*see p135*); **6tus** (*see p135*).

For quality cuisine
Ba Bar (*see p134*); **Café Eklektika** (*see p131*; **Ellató** (*see p134*); **Gerlóczy Kávéház** (*see p129*).

For retro chic
Jaffa (*see p136*); **Lánchíd Söröző** (*see p128*); **Melypont** (*see p129*).

For riverside views
Gresham Café (*see p129*); **Platán Eszpresszó** (*see p127*).

For sticky cakes
Gerbeaud (*see p129*); **Gresham Café** (*see p129*); **Lukács** (*see p131*); **Ruszwurm Cukrászda** (*see p127*).

For upmarket cocktails
Gresham Bar (*see p129*); **Negro** (*see p129*); **Oscar Café** (*see p128*).

Eat, Drink, Shop

Bambi Presszó

II.Frankel Leó út 2-4 (212 3171). Bus 60, 86. **Open**
7am-10pm Mon-Fri; 9am-9pm Sat, Sun. **No credit
cards. Map** p245 C2 **7**
The classic example of the Communist-era *presszó*,
the Bambi is where time has stood still. Ancient plastic ferns and the background noise of dominoes
being slapped on to mosaic-topped tables by unsmil-
ing locals complement designer touches since 1965.
The service is nostagically pokey, but the beer's cold
and the omelettes rock. There's even a view (just) of
the Danube from the summer terrace – and the low
prices are in a similar time warp.

Belgian Brasserie

*I.Bem rakpart 12 (201 5082). M2 Batthyány tér/
tram 19/bus 86.* **Open** noon-midnight daily. **Credit**
AmEx, MC, V. **Map** p245 C4 **8**
Although a reasonable restaurant in its own right,
the raison d'être for this fine if slightly pricey establishment is its extensive beer menu. The best
Belgium has to offer – Kriek, Chimay, Hoegaarden
and many more – can be enjoyed on the riverside
terrace, a sad rarity in Buda. The two-room interior,
too, is done out in reasonable taste, with publicity
posters from way back when.

Lánchíd Söröző

I.Fő utca 4 (214 3144). Tram 19/bus 86.
Open 10am-midnight daily. **No credit cards.**
Map p245 C5 **9**
Comfortable neighbourhood bar of agreeably retro
character within a modest, wooden cabin. Mini bill-
boards for lost Hungarian film classics complement
accordions, old radios, 1960s fashion magazines,
artistic black-and-white shots of Budapest and red-
checked tablecloths. Beneath a gig-postered ceiling
are pictures of the genial owner beside BB King and
John Mayall; ask him gently and he'll regale you
with the rueful tale of the unsuccessful autograph
pursuit of Carlos Santana down Váci utca. Draught
Dreher and local toasties (*meleg szendvics*) preserve
the retro theme; a shelf of bourbons may complement a Stones rockumentary on TV. A couple of
tables dot the narrow strip of pavement on summer
evenings, convivial after the traffic fumes from the
nearby Clark Ádám tér roundabout have subsided.

Moszkva tér

Oscar Café

*II.Ostrom utca 14 (212 8017). M2 Moszkva tér/tram
4, 6.* **Open** *Winter* 5pm-2am Mon-Thur, Sun; 5pm-
4am Thur-Sat. *Summer* 6pm-2am Mon-Wed; 6pm-
4am Thur-Sat. **No credit cards. Map** p245 A3 **10**
Buda's young professionals mingle enthusiastically
in this dark, cinematically themed pub a short hop
from Moszkva tér. For all the stills and star portraits
from Hungary and Hollywood, the main feature is
the irresistibly long bar counter – as opposed to the
silly 'Nam corner decked out in camouflage nets. The
well-heeled regulars enjoy an upgraded selection of
cocktails, one of the best in town.

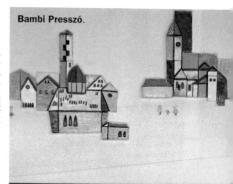

Bambi Presszó.

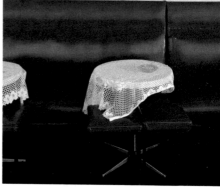

Pest

Belváros & Lipótváros

Beckett's

*V.Bajcsy-Zsilinszky út 72 (311 1033). M3 Nyugati
pu./tram 4, 6.* **Open** noon-1am Mon-Thur, Sun;
noon-2am Fri-Sat. **Credit** AmEx, DC, MC, V.
Map p246 E3 **11**
Main expats' hangout offering pricey pub food and
Sky Sports. Given the beer prices too, some even nip
out at half-time for a more affordable jar nearby.

Centrál Kávéház

*V.Károly Mihály utca 9 (235 0599). M3 Ferenciek
tere/bus 7.* **Open** 7am-midnight daily. **Credit**
AmEx, DC, MC, V. **Map** p249 E6 **12**
This beautifully restored Golden Age landmark
recreates a time when the Centrál was one of the
standouts among hundreds of coffeehouses, a gathering place for intellectuals. Delicious cakes, well
priced coffees and stronger drinks, plus warming
coffee cocktails, help fuel conversation. Full meals
are also available. As if replacing the free sheets of
writing paper common to coffeehouses a century
ago, there's an internet facility downstairs.

Gerbeaud

V.Vörösmarty tér 7 (429 9000). M1 Vörösmarty tér/ tram 2. **Open** 9am-9pm daily. **Credit** AmEx, DC, MC, V. **Map** p249 D5 **⑬**

This elegant institution, founded in 1870 and still radiating fin-de-siècle opulence, anchors pedestrianised Vörösmarty tér in the heart of the tourist district. As soon as the weather is anywhere near clement, Gerbeaud fills a big chunk of this square with umbrella-shaded tables that provide a good view of the daytime downtown bustle. The prices, aimed at the tourist trade, are higher than elsewhere, but the cakes are of superior pedigree – founder Émil Gerbeaud invented the cognac cherry here.

Gerlóczy Kávéház

V.Gerlóczy utca 1 (235 0953/www.gerloczy.hu). M2 Astoria/tram 47, 49/bus 7. **Open** 7am-11pm Mon-Fri; 8am-11pm Sat, Sun. **Credit** AmEx, MC, V. **Map** p249 E5 **⑭**

The best breakfast in town is found at this exquisitely restored traditional coffeeshop on a hidden, leafy, downtown square. More substantial meals are also available, including seafood risotto, steaks and lamb chops – but regulars best enjoy a long, late, leisurely breakfast on the terrace overlooking Kamermayer Károly tér, leaves drifting on to scribbled manuscripts. Among the lighter choices are parma ham finely woven around breadsticks, and salads drizzled with balsamic vinegar. The interior is equally beautiful, its big mirror reflecting the snappy but unhurried bustle of the smart waitstaff. This is Budapest at its best, combining the style of the early 1900s with the savvy of 21st-century European integration. **Photos** *p130.*

Gresham Bar

Four Seasons Gresham Palace Hotel, V.Roosevelt tér 5-6 (268 5100). M1 Vörösmarty tér. **Open** 11am-2am daily. **Credit** AmEx, DC, MC, V. **Map** p246 D5 **⑮**

The best (and priciest) cocktails in town are served with finesse at the bar of the Gresham Palace hotel, accessed through the grand lobby, within earshot of a gentle piano tinkle from the indoor terrace. 'Good evening,' is offered in English as you pull up a little square chair or round-backed bar stool in the two-space, low-lit bar. Just as you're feasting on the range of cocktails on offer – and frowning at the range of prices (Ft3,000-Ft4,000) demanded for them – you're presented with bowls of marinated olives, salted nuts and puff pastries. At that point it seems churlish to baulk at the amount charged for a coolly mixed Cosmopolitan (Absolut and fresh lime) or blood-red Moulin Rouge (Stolichnaya, champagne, raspberry juice). Scottish smoked salmon and caviar blinis and Asian flavoured tuna tartar with Melba toast provide sustenance – although the free snacks keep coming.

Gresham Café

Four Seasons Gresham Palace Hotel, V.Roosevelt tér 5-6 (268 5100). M1 Vörösmarty tér. **Open** 6.30am-10pm Mon-Wed; 6.30am-10.30pm Thur-Sat; 7am-10pm Sun. **Credit** AmEx, DC, MC, V. **Map** p246 D5 **⑯**

It's no surprise that the café of Budapest's finest luxury hotel is an upmarket gem, done out in the same art-deco fashion as the superbly restored surroundings. The prime feature, apart from the view of the Chain Bridge from the picture windows, is the cakes. The Páva restaurant (*see p115*) has master chef Simone Cerea, the bar (*see above*) is staffed by accomplished cocktail-makers and the café has one hell of a pastry chef. This artist creates inventive, colourful combinations which change with the seasons, chocolate browns and pistachio greens topping all kinds of crèmes and crunchy crusts. The full range of coffees are sourced from Jamaica, Costa Rica and elsewhere, while the sorbets, ice-creams and milk shakes maintain the overall high standard.

Grinzingi

V.Veres Pálné utca 10 (317 4624). M3 Ferenciek tere/bus 7. **Open** *Borozó* 9am-1am Mon-Sat; 3-11pm Sun. *Cellar* 1pm-1am Mon-Sat. **No credit cards.** **Map** p249 E6 **⑰**

Large, dark-wood establishment on a downtown corner, the Grinzingi is probably Budapest's best *borozó* or wine bar. Upstairs, big street-level windows and marble-topped tables screwed to the floor form a horseshoe around the large bar, where passers-by, dedicated locals and the odd tourist neck *fröccs* (spritzers) and bottled lager. Downstairs is cramped, smoky and rammed with students counting out their last forints for a glass of wine. Cheap though it is, the wine has at least seen grapes and won't give you that awful chemical hangover that can follow a night's drinking in many a less reputable *borozó*.

Melypont

V.Magyar utca 23 (06 30 812 4064 mobile). M2 Astoria/M3 Kálvin tér. **Open** 6pm-1am Mon, Tue; 6pm-2am Wed-Sat; 6pm-midnight Sun. **No credit cards.** **Map** p249 F6 **⑱**

A downtown cellar, furnished like a typical Hungarian home in the 1970s, becomes a big house party thanks to sociable regulars born a decade later. They lounge amid the fish-scale patterned wallpaper, their chatter resonating around the bulky shelving unit cluttered with a period console stereo and sundry trinkets. A house special is beer with a shot of raspberry syrup but they also have a decent selection of liquor. The music is decent alternative rock, much of it Hungarian.

Negro

V.Szent István tér 11 (302 0136). M1 Bajcsy-Zsilinszky út/M3 Arany János utca. **Open** 8am-1am Mon-Thur, Sun; 8am-2.30am Fri, Sat. **Credit** AmEx, DC, MC, V. **Map** p246 E4 **⑲**

The cocktail bar that set the standard in 2005 still creates a buzz on a pretty paved square behind the Basilica. A thick drinks directory categorised by spirit type offers affordable standards to an upscale clientele served by a sexy, black-uniformed staff. English is the lingua franca on the busy terrace for Negro's stellar breakfast. Free nuts and titular cough sweets on the bar counter are a nice touch.

Eat, Drink, Shop

Reinventing Budapest's classic coffeehouse culture – the **Gerlóczy Kávéház**. *See p129*.

Andrássy út & District VI

Balletcipő

*VI.Hajós utca 14 (269 3114). M1 Opera/M3 Arany
János utca.* **Open** 10am-midnight Mon-Fri; noon-
midnight Sat; noon-11pm Sun. **No credit cards.**
Map p246 E4 ⓴

This old local near the Opera House got spiffed up
with the rest of Hajós utca and the 'Ballet Shoes' is
now a chic, dark-wood continental café, with picture
windows and scrubbed floorboards. Only the dinky
pink ballet shoes hanging in the window remain. A
white wine from northern Hungary or a Villányi red
might accompany a tapas-like offering or a recommended version of the Philly cheese steak sandwich
with thinly sliced meat and caramelised onions.

Barokko Club & Lounge

*VI.Liszt Ferenc tér 5 (322 0700/www.barokko.hu).
M1 Oktogon.* **Open** 11am-1am Mon, Tue, Sun; 11am-
2am Wed-Sat. **No credit cards.** **Map** p246 F4 ㉑

A new option on Liszt Ferenc ter with a summer terrace, a slick interior and a downstairs dance club.
The food includes attractive tapas platters and the
impressive list of cocktails ranges from frozen margaritas to zombies. DJs take over the club after 9pm
or you can drift to the nearby bars of District VII.

Café Eklektika

*VI.Nagymező utca 30 (266 1226/www.eklektika.hu).
M1 Opera/M1 Oktogon.* **Open** 10am-midnight
Mon-Fri; noon-midnight Sat, Sun. **No credit cards.**
Map p246 F4 ㉒

This lesbian-friendly bar (*see p180*) in the heart of
town, with high ceilings, a split-level floor and modern decor, attracts a mixed alternative crowd with a
good buzz and upgraded food. A fine place for an
afternoon libation or getting the night started.

The Caledonia

*VI.Mozsár utca 9 (311 7611/www.caledonia.hu).
M1 Oktogon/tram 4, 6.* **Open** 11am-midnight Mon-
Thur, Sun; 11am-1am Fri-Sat. **Credit** AmEx, MC, V.
Map p246 F4 ㉓

Opened in 2006, this authentic, Scot-themed pub
offers 42 types of whisky (ten-year Ardbeg, 18-year
Talisker), Belhaven Best on tap, heart-attack break-
fasts, Sunday roasts, Scotch broth and haggis. Most
of all, the Caledonia doesn't feel like forint flytrap
for footie-centric expats – though there are plenty of
sports on TV, a dartboard and burgeoning golf club.

Chagall

*VI.Hajós utca 27 (302 4614). M1 Opera/M3 Arany
János utca.* **Open** 8am-midnight Mon-Fri; 9am-
midnight Sat, Sun. **Credit** MC, V. **Map** p246 E4 ㉔

This slick-looking café, tastefully decorated with
Chagall prints, pastel walls and Russian memorabilia, generates a nice buzz. A capable kitchen produces big salads and fancier mains, like medallions
of mangalica pork with asparagus, duck liver and
trout. There's wheat beer on tap and two dozen regular cocktails, mixed to a decent standard.

Incognito

*VI.Liszt Ferenc tér 3 (342 1471). M1 Oktogon/tram
4, 6.* **Open** noon-midnight Mon-Wed; noon-1am
Thur; noon-2am Fri; 2pm-2am Sat; 2pm-midnight
Sun. **No credit cards. Map** p246 F4 ㉕

The first and perhaps the best of the designer cafés
lining Liszt Ferenc tér, the jazz-themed Incognito
still exudes good taste. Done out in dark wood, the
interior features framed covers of classic jazz and
soul albums. Coffees include fiery *carajillos*, a suc-
cint shot list (Prérifarkas, Ft850) complements an
extensive cocktail one, Pilsner Urquell comes on
draught, wines feature Balatonboglár and they even
sell Rizla papers. Not as cool as it thinks it is – but
above average for the neighbourhood.

Kiadó kocsma

VI.Jókai tér 3 (331 1955). M1 Oktogon/tram 4, 6.
Credit MC, V. **Map** p246 F4 ㉖

When managers András Kelemen and Viktor
Schanz left the old Castro, they brought their popular staff with them, guaranteeing a good atmosphere
and a sizeable buzz of sociable young customers.
This two-storey venue is the result, a modern, funky-
looking street-level bar complemented by a traditional pub-style cellar, complete with private booths.
It can be hard to find a free table most nights. The
varied selection of music is supplemented by DJs,
and the menu features respectable bar food. A wiser
drinker would bypass the bland terraces of Liszt
Ferenc tér and cross Andrássy út for here.

Lukács

VI.Andrássy út 70 (302 8747). M1 Vörösmarty utca.
Open 9am-8pm Mon-Fri; 10am-8pm Sat, Sun. **Credit**
AmEx, MC, V. **Map** p246 G3 ㉗

This historically infamous *kávéház* is now part of
the main office for CIB Bank – but for a dark decade
it was a meeting place for the secret police, the dread-
ed ÁVO, whose headquarters were nearby at no.60,
today the Terror Museum. Lukács' present-day stab
at elegance is spoiled by the correct impression that
you're walking into a bank. Sit by the window and
relive the café's more palatable, earlier days echoed
by the tea-time piano player, friendly waitresses in
frilly uniforms and gooey cakes on display.

Mai Manó Kávézó

*VI.Nagymező utca 20 (269 5642/http://maimano
kavezo.hu). M1 Opera/M1 Oktogon.* **Open** 10am-1am
daily. **No credit cards. Map** p246 F4 ㉘

The best choice on Budapest's Broadway, attached
to the photo gallery (*see p173*) of the same name, the
Mai Manó is intimate and suitably arty. Red ban-
quettes line walls dotted with smoky photos and
touches of faux Klimt. Staropramen and dark
Borostyán comprise the draught options, with quality local wines by In Vino Veritas; there's a lengthy
choice of coffees. Pies (Ft450) come in meat or fruit
varieties, although most of the gossipy twentysomethings prefer nicotine. Should it all be a little
too smoky for comfort, tables are set outside.

Eat, Drink, Shop

Black death in a bottle

First-time visitors to Hungary usually try all the well known tipples during their first days here: Tokaj wine, pear brandy, whatever the waiter recommends. An unchaperoned visit to any local bar, however, is when you cross the Rubicon. Late at night, the locals get friendly and invite you to try their favourite local drink. The bartender smiles knowingly as he pours a dark brown syrup into the shot glass. All eyes are upon you as you raise the glass for the first sip. First a burning sensation hits the throat and tickles your nose. The burn lasts all the way down the gullet to your belly. Followed immediately by the taste. The crowd looks on appreciatively as you reel from the assault. You fight for breath. 'GACK! What is this stuff?'

That stuff is Zwack Unicum, Hungary's bitter answer to anything else calling itself a digestif. Except nobody actually uses it as a digestif unless a midnight session is on doctor's orders. If ever the term 'herbal bitters' ever needed to be defined, Unicum would be the shining example. Dark and syrupy, a delicate balance of sweet and very, very bitter, with a bouquet hovering between herb garden and nuclear waste dump, the flavour of Unicum is literally indescribable. Think 'essence of hospital corridor in a glass'

and you will be closer than the rather hopeful 'something not as sweet as Jägermeister' that first had you flimflammed.

And Hungarians love it with a passion that – like so many Magyar passions – is hard to explain to foreigners. At least at first.

Like Guinness and Marmite, Unicum's dark mystery has been enhanced by decades of intelligent advertising. Sold in its unique bottle shaped like an anarchist's bomb, Unicum had its publicity material designed by Sándor Bortnyk, a leading figure of the avant-garde art movement, in 1915. The iconic posters, such as the one of the drowning man, can still be seen in many bars today.

Of course, it gets you drunk. But there is more. Unicum, like absinthe, tequila and Siberian black-market miner's vodka, embodies a mythology of spectacular para-alcoholic effects. Unicum isn't famous because it gets you drunk. Unicum affects the Hungarian psyche as the catalyst that causes the meek, local post-Habsburg Euro-persona to explode into the whip-cracking, moustache-twirling, wild Magyar of the steppes. Mousy intellectuals become swaggering poets and tongue-tied foreigners suddenly find them selves fluently conversing in agglutinative *magyarul* after only a couple of shots.

Unicum ups the ante for the night's revelry. Although, like most brandies, it has an alcohol content of 40 per cent, Unicum's secret mix of herbs has a reputation for sending the evening more than a little bit over the top. Once you acquire the taste, beware. One shot of Unicum makes the evening glow a bit warmer, two shots make anything possible... even desirable.

You don't want to know what happens after three.

Everybody has tales of behaving strangely while intoxicated, but Hungarians have a special category of 'what am I doing in the dry-out house again?' stories. These are the ones in which people wake up astonished to find themselves married to their local librarian, enrolled in the French Foreign legion or wandering naked with a newly shaved head in some suburb of Bratislava. Thank goodness Budapest has no 24-hour tattoo parlours. Yet.

And then, once realisation sinks in, there's the morning after, Unicum-style. 'Hangover' doesn't do it justice. The human body is but a frail match for Unicum. The only thing that's going to help is – more Unicum.

And so it grows on you. Perhaps it is because Unicum is so strange, so divisive, so self-defining. Unicum is the one bar drink that cuts across class and economic divisions – everyone drinks it. The Ft400 plastic jigger of Unicum that you have with your coffee at a suburban bus station *büfé* is the same Zwack that New York's prestigious Four Seasons Restaurant offers to bankers celebrating hostile takeovers at $35 a shot. You'll see it in bars all over Italy, a reminder of the immediate post-war era when the Zwacks had to smuggle the secret recipe out of Hungary and start producing the drink again overseas.

The official legend, dating back to 1790, is that the name Unicum celebrates the day when the Moravian-born József Zwack offered his newly invented concoction to Kaiser Joseph II of Austria. It seems the Habsburg Emperor took a sip, screwed up his face, shuddered, then pronounced of this curiosity: 'Das is ein Unikum!' Das ist ein understatement.

Művész

VI.Andrássy út 29 (352 1337). M1 Opera.
Open 9am-midnight daily. **No credit cards**.
Map p246 F4 ㉙
This landmark site is probably the most famous of the city's old-style coffeehouses, across from the Opera House. The interior exudes antique elegance and the small enclosed terrace is a fantastic place to watch Andrássy breeze past. However, reputation and location seem to have bewitched the new management. Prices are steep and, instead of creating an atmosphere, the somewhat sullen staff is better suited for handling one-off visits from tourists. The selection of cakes and light snacks could also be improved. Always busy, nonetheless.

Picasso Point

VI.Hajós utca 31 (312 1727/www.picassopoint.hu).
M1 Opera/M3 Arany János utca. **Open** 6pm-midnight Tue-Thur; 6pm-2am Fri, Sat. **No credit cards**. **Map** p246 E4 ㉚
The big bar that was the hottest spot in town way back when is now a laid-back café with large windows that let in an early evening light while sheltering a cosy atmosphere. Downstairs is a cellar dance floor, where DJs sometimes spin pop and disco classics and major football matches show on the maxi screen. Upstairs houses a standard restaurant. There's a respectable list of cocktails and many a fancy coffee, including the house iced variety.

Pótkulcs

*VI.Csengery utca 65B (269 1050). M3 Nyugati pu./
tram 4, 6.* **Open** 5pm-1.30am Mon-Wed; 5pm-2.30am Thur-Sun. **No credit cards**. **Map** p246 F3 ㉛
The Spare Key is accesssed through a discreet metal door, behind which a large, secluded courtyard fills with tables in summer. Beyond, within an L-shaped interior, changing exhibitions enliven the attractive brick walls of this former workshop. Popular with students, backpackers and younger expats, the Pótkulcs has acceptable pub food, occasional DJs, recitals and plays, and cheapish booze.

Sirály

VI.Király utca 50 (06 20 957 2291 mobile). M1 Opera/tram 4, 6. **Open** 8am-midnight Mon-Fri; 10am-midnight Sat, Sun. **No credit cards**.
Map p246 F4 ㉜
A fantastic three-storey space in the heart of the party district has been caught up in legal limbo since opening in 2007, and may close down, move or stay where it is. The Seagull merits a mention because it's such a hot destination. It opened as a non-profit cultural centre hosting exhibitions and readings. They didn't charge for drinks, but took 'donations' instead. The venue was soon embraced by a young, arty crowd, who packed the cellar, with its big, old wooden bar counter and large floor space. The ground floor and upstairs, reached through a big open stairwell, are scattered with chairs, taken up by chatty regulars, sipping coffee or harder stuff throughout the day. **Photos** *p134*.

Eat, Drink, Shop

District VII

Ba Bar

*VII.Huszár utca 7 (06 20 919 7979 mobile/www.
babar.hu). M2 Keleti pu./bus 7.* **Open** 11.30am-1am
Mon-Thur; 11.30am-2.30am Fri, Sat. **Credit** MC, V.
Map p247 H5 ⓼

One of the better of the lounge cafés, thanks to its
superior, well presented Med-Hungarian fare, sleek
decor and side terrace facing the Buddhist School,
whose members mingle with the cosmopolitan
crowd here. Set on a corner of a pedestrianised street
near Keleti station, Ba Bar offers four menus, the
Latin-dominated cocktail one with nearly 70 varieties, Havana Club used in the mojitos, Myer's rum
in the Planter's Punch. Some 20 well chosen
Hungarian wines include a Gere Attila Villányi
cabernet sauvignon barrique and a Nyakas pince
Budai sauvignon blanc. A slim tapas menu complements the main food options, also scaled down to
three dozen thoughtfully conceived dishes. Oven-
baked broccoli ragù with cheddar and olives is the
standout of the vegetarian ones; fish gets a good
look-in too. Once the kitchen closes at 11.30pm,
regulars seeking intimacy drift towards a side room
of bean bags and candlelight.

Castro Bisztró

*VII.Madách Imre tér 3 (215 0184). M1, M2, M3
Deák tér.* **Open** 11am-midnight Mon-Thur; 11am-
2am Fri; noon-2am Sat; 2pm-midnight Sun. **No
credit cards. Map** p249 E5 ⓽

Success proved a burden for the sublime Castro.
After single-handedly turning Ráday utca into a bar
hub, this beloved hotspot lost its lease because the
buzz it had created drove up local rents. This new
location in eminently central Madach tér continues
to be popular, though the old management is gone,
as are some of the big-name musicians and hard-core
partygoers. Still, the food is decent, the atmosphere
casual and the crowd lively.

Champs Sports Pub

*VII.Dohány utca 20 (413 1655/www.champs.hu).
M2 Astoria/tram 47, 49/bus 7.* **Open** noon-2am
daily. **Credit** AmEx, DC, MC, V. **Map** p249 F5 ⓽

Sport, beer, bar food and underdressed waitresses –
what more could a lad wish for? A big brick cellar
with 35 TVs and two giant screens shows most
major sporting events and a lot of minor ones. In the
evening, occasional dance or music performances,
often featuring your server, provide entertainment
between matches. Even if you don't need a dancing
barmaid, the reasonable prices for draught
Guinness, Pilsner Urquell and Kilkenny make this
a fair choice at which to catch the game.

Ellátó

*VII.Klauzál tér 2 (no phone). M1 Opera/tram 4,
6/bus 7.* **Open** noon-1am Mon-Thur; noon-4am Fri;
5pm-4am Sat; 5pm-1am Sun. **No credit cards.
Map** p246 F5 ⓽

Crazily popular as soon as it opened, this spacious,
attractively designed venue with picture windows
overlooking Klauzál tér continues to be a bustling

A great three-storey space in the heart of Budapest's party vortex – the **Sirály**. *See p133.*

nightlife hub. Loveable staff work the busy, main bar and small side one, while a creative kitchen, presided over by chef Siniša Prole, offers a hearty mix of Serb, French, Hungarian and Asian specials, depending on who's working. A great place at which to start a District VII bar crawl, though it can be hard to leave. The closing hours are theoretical and depend on how much fun the staff are having. In summer, the scene shifts to sister bar, the outdoor Fészek kert (see p194 **Party under the stars**).

Filter Klub

VII.Almássy utca 1 (06 30 921 4212 mobile). M2 Blaha Lujza tér/tram 4, 6. **Open** 7pm-4am Mon-Sat. **No credit cards. Map** p247 H5 **37**
A rare punk rock bar, smack in the middle of town, has gigs through the week and attitude all the time. A new generation of enthusiastic, if insufficiently disaffected young Magyars come here to share camaraderie and a love of speed guitar. Sassy, efficient bar staff offer a professional touch.

New York Café

VII.Erzsébet körút 9-11 (886 6167/www.newyork palace.hu). M2 Blaha Lujza tér/tram 4, 6. **Open** 10am-midnight daily. **Credit** AmEx, MC, V. **Map** p247 G5 **38**
Steeped in local legend, the New York Café was renovated in opulent style and reopened in 2006 as part of the five-star hotel of the same name (see p48 **So good they built it twice**). The original building, the offices of the New York Life Insurance Company, also contained a café on its ground floor. Unveiled on 23 October 1894, lined with statues and ornaments, it quickly became the hangout for Budapest's literati, its tables morphing into editorial offices. Playwright Ferenc Molnár is said to have stolen the keys and thrown them into the Danube to make sure that the café would always stay open. The address developed such gravitas that according to urban myth, letters meant for New York City were delivered here. The café stored its own supply of ink in the cellar to give to writers along with paper. With works written, drawn and composed under its roof, its regulars also included Mihály Kertész, later Michael Curtis of *Casablanca* fame, and Sándor Korda, aka Alexander Korda, the film producer. The landmark literary magazine, *Nyugat*, set up shop here. After World War I, a restaurant was installed in place of the billiards room and a dress code introduced. The post-war era saw the venue sadly decline before being taken over by the Boscolo hotel group in 2001. The café manages a faithful relationship with its past, hosting literary and arts evenings – but it occupies a smaller space. Hefty prices and modest modern design touches, like the red-trimmed tables, have irked locals – although few tourists will care about this. The service here could be improved – competition is now fierce amid the high-end coffeehouses. Still, given a such rich history, it would seem churlish not to welcome back the New York into the fold after more than a century of grief and grandeur. **Photos** *p137.*

Sark

VII.Klauzál tér 14 (328 0753). Tram 4, 6. **Open** *Oct-May* noon-3am Mon-Fri; 4pm-3am Sat, Sun. *June-Sept* noon-1am Mon-Fri; 4pm-1am Sat, Sun. **No credit cards. Map** p246 F5 **39**
One of the first big bars to enliven District VII, the Sark is a key stop on any bar crawl through the neighbourhood, but you can easily find yourself spending the whole night here. Street level is an airy bar room with a modest gallery decorated with larger-than-life mug shots. The cellar contains a stage area/dance floor hosting concerts and DJs, as well as its own bar.

6tus (Sixtus)

VII.Nagy Diófa utca 26-28 (413 6722). M2 Blaha Lujza tér/bus 7. **Open** 5pm-2am Mon-Fri; 8pm-2am Sat. **No credit cards. Map** p246 F5 **40**
Gabi and Mariann conduct a superb service at the ever libertine Sistine Chapel, the pokey, smoky, dangerously fun bar in the depths of District VII. Helped by well chosen music, anywhere from Curtis Mayfield to Iggy and the Stooges, the 6tus has been a mainstay of the expat alternative scene since the mid 1990s. Now Magyar run, expertly so, it attracts a more diverse, international crowd with the same kernel of regulars. Standard beers, good wines and a killer Cocaine cocktail comprise the liquid arsenal that also attracts staff from other bars who have their own night out here. Everyone's happy to join the regulars dancing on the bar counter whenever the mood suits. The back room is for chatting.

All bar crawls start here – the **Ellátó**.

Eat, Drink, Shop

Szimpla/Dupla

VII.Kertész utca 48 (342 8991). Tram 4, 6. **Open** 10am-midnight Mon-Fri; noon-2am Sat; noon-midnight Sun. **No credit cards. Map** p246 G4 ⑩

This funky, alternative café-bar was the first venture by the people who created the hugely successful Szimplakert (*see p195*), and it still retains its original fun vibe. The Szimpla ('Single') is linked to a cheap eaterie, the Dupla ('Double'), by way of a large, smoky cellar bar. Both places conform to a pretty basic formula: fire-sale furniture, squeaky floorboards, cheap fare and decent music. The seating in Szimpla's gallery is great, but you have to walk down to the bar for service. All term-time, Szimpla is rammed on Fridays with students, backpackers and musicians here for the live jazz sessions. In summer, the crowd hits the Szimplakert.

Districts VIII & IX

Café Eckermann

IX.Ráday utca 58 (786 0795). Tram 4, 6. **Open** 8am-11pm Mon-Sat; 10am-10pm Sun. **No credit cards. Map** p249 G8 ⑫

On the ground floor of the Goethe Institute, this friendly café comprises outdoor seating out front, a small, atmospheric courtyard in the back, and a comfortable, modern interior in between. Fancy coffee variations attract a mixed, studenty crowd, as does daytime WiFi. Good food with meat-free options.

Csiga

VIII.Vásár utca 2 (210 0885). Tram 4, 6. **Open** *Winter* 11am-1am Mon-Sat; 4pm-1am Sun. *Summer* 11am-1am Mon-Sat. **No credit cards. Map** p250 H6 ⑬

On a corner of the slightly seedy, former red-light drag of Rákóczi tér, this brightly decorated bar of tall ceilings, picture windows, cheerful lampshades and yellow-orange walls decked in art is a mainstay of the alternative set. Bar DJs pick the platters and there's a good buzz most evenings. A creative kitchen, stocked by the market hall next door, offers quality fare – and still cheap. Watch for specials like swordfish steak or Moroccan-style lamb. The small bar area and rear gallery seating foster intimacy – the long tables in the main room encourage communal socialising in a relaxed setting.

Darshan Udvar

VIII.Krúdy Gyula utca 8 (266 5541/www.darshan.hu). M3 Kálvin tér/tram 4, 6. **Open** 11am-midnight daily. **No credit cards. Map** p249 G6 ⑭

This huge, popular, studenty pub sparked the bar revival of Krúdy Gyula utca and adjoining Mikszáth Kálmán tér. The bar, with a beautiful roof terrace open in summer, forms the centrepiece for a mock Mongolian courtyard containing two other bars, a Buddhist bookshop and the Indigo CD outlet. There's a menu of daily specials, plus a soundtrack of world music, reggae, jazz, dub and ambient. Across the street, the Gaudí-esque Darshan Café (no.7, 266 7797) is the better daytime option.

Frank Zappa Café

VIII.Mikszáth Kálmán tér 2 (06 20 972 1711 mobile). M3 Kálvin tér. **Open** 11am-1am Mon-Thur; 11am-4am Fri; 6pm-4am Sat; 6pm-1am Sun. **No credit cards. Map** p249 G6 ⑮

The Tilos az Á, a landmark underground music club from the early 1990s, still haunts these former premises thanks to the 15-year-old mural of New York City's East Side. The rest has been given over to stylised images of Zappa, practically deified in Hungary. A young crowd populates the umbrella-covered terrace filling pedestrianised Mikszáth Kálmán tér in summer and creates a party vibe sizzling from Szabó Ervin tér to the Nagykörút.

Hat-három (6:3) Borozó

IX.Lónyay utca 62 (217 0748). Tram 2, 4, 6. **Open** 7am-10pm Mon-Thur; 7am-midnight Fri, Sat; 9am-7pm Sun. **No credit cards. Map** p249 G8 ⑯

This intimate wooden sit-down wine bar is a temple to the greatest victory in the history of Hungarian football, the 6-3 (*hat-három*) trouncing of former masters England at their own temple of Wembley stadium in 1953. Key to the victory was the deep-lying centre-forward Nándor Hidegkuti, who used to own this bar. Three framed sepia photographs decorate the walls, the best one showing a gaggle of celebrating Magyars running away laughing from a recently filled English net. You can order the usual array of wines, beers and hard spirits to celebrate the victory – watch the team's modern-day counterparts give a textbook, televised display of what's wrong with the local game today. *Photos p138.*

Jaffa

IX.Ráday utca 39 (219 5285). M3 Ferenc körút/ tram 4, 6. **Open** 10am-1am Mon-Thur; 10am-2am Fri; noon-2am Sat; 2pm-midnight Sun. **No credit cards. Map** p249 G7 ⑰

The best of the Ráday venues, this great DJ bar does so many things right. The retro is well sourced, with adverts for wallpaper glue, squares of carpet on the wall, a German clock calendar and a Carillon jukebox – not to mention the round-cornered, formica-topped tables. The music is also expertly conceived, from the nearby Deep record store, and there's a retro clothing store next door. Ten well chosen Hungarian wines complement draught Zlatý Bazant beer. The menu includes several vegetarian options, although the house special ('Ráday kedvence') is a slab of pork slathered in turkey liver, pea and mushroom ragù. What matters most, though, is the ambience, young and vibrant, encouraged by bar staff as sweet as the titular fruit. Not to be missed.

No Name Söröző

IX.Tompa utca 8 (218 9383). Tram 4, 6. **Open** 7am-midnight Mon-Fri; 8am-midnight Sat, Sun. **No credit cards. Map** p250 G8 ⑱

Small, friendly neighbourhood place on pedestrianised Tompa has pictures of the taxi-driver regulars on its dark red walls, discounts for students and

New York Café. *See p135.*

loads of character, a contrast to the slick places lining Ráday across the körút. A dark, old-style bar area encourages you to stay for one more, as do the terrace chairs in summer. A delightful staff is fully appreciated by the chatty young local crowd that keeps the place busy. Pastries served for breakfast.

Paris, Texas
IX.Ráday utca 22 (218 0570). M3 Kálvin tér/tram 47, 49. **Open** *noon-3am daily.* **No credit cards.** **Map** p249 F7 ❹
One of the older and more characterful bars on Ráday, this one is dolled up with period portrait photos, not unlike an Amsterdam brown café. Upstairs is a relaxed bar area, downstairs is for pool and occasional live music. There are tables outside in summer, but the emphasis is mainly inside – hence the more generous opening hours than elsewhere on the strip. Pizza and pasta can be ordered from the partner restaurant next door. **Photo** *p125.*

Prága Kávéház és Teázó
VIII.Baross utca 8 (486 1937). M3 Kálvin tér/tram 47, 49. **Open** *7am-10pm Mon-Fri; 9am-10pm Sat.* **No credit cards.** **Map** p249 F7 ❺⓪
A fun-loving, gossipy crowd of students and twentysomethings pack this hangout at the end of the pedestrianised bar strip that begins on Krúdy Gyula utca. The space is doubled by a busy terrace in summer. Music, from top 40 to cutting-edge electronica, depends on the whims of the staff.

Rock Café
VIII.Krúdy Gyula utca 17 (06 70 334 8176 mobile). Tram 4, 6. **Open** *noon-2am Mon-Sat.* **No credit cards.** **Map** p249 G6 ❺①
In the student-heavy bustle of bars along Krúdy Gyula utca, the Rock Café, a cellar bar with several rooms, provides a rocking oasis for drinkers older than 25. In a town where electronica dominates, this is one of the few places where you'll hear REM, Neil Young or the Ramones, as well as something more contemporary and alternative. The big booths are comfortable and the small stage in the back hosts bands at weekends. Standard bar food menu too.

Tandem Café
IX.Pipa utca 6 (218 9319/www.tandemcafe.hu). M3 Kálvin tér/tram 47, 49. **Open** *9am-1am Mon-Thur; 9am-2am Fri; 4pm-2am Sat.* **No credit cards.** **Map** p249 F7 ❺②
In the premises of the much lamented Ötödik Bejáró, so called because it was the Fifth Entrance to Budapest's main market hall across the street, the Tandem has been quick to capitalise on its legacy. Old-style dark-wood furnishings and a fancy floor mosaic dress up a friendly café, frequented by young, alternative regulars. During the day students from the School of Economics next door gab and take advantage of the WiFi. After dark, the downstairs opens up for live music in the classically appointed cellar bar area. Szőke Mátyás wines and draught Leffe and Hoegaarden help things along.

Hungarian football history in all its sepia glory at the **Hat-három Borozó**. *See p136.*

Shops & Services

Out with cheap charm, in with quality local design and big-hitting global names.

Prices creep high here and the shelves are not exactly weighed down by the selection you find in the West; Budapest can afford only so many shops. The good news is the interesting local choice, particularly in hand-made applied arts, fresh in its naivety and originality. The future for young craftsmen and artists is looking brighter. Although their output seems to consist only of individual commissions, their exposure is growing. Small and medium-sized flagship shops have popped up alongside Hungarian design showcase **Magma**, aligning local talent with commercial demand. A lack of access to mass production keeps things authentic. The government has even set up a public body to support local design: **Design Terminal**.

The inching towards challenge and change is exciting. New alternative fashion brands crop up, while couturier **Katti Zoób** has liaised with heirloom porcelain-maker **Zsolnay** to create stunning jewellery. Interior designers have shown strength and imagination – **Lánchíd 19** (*see p41*), a new boutique hotel, commissioned Hungarian designers to supply its uniforms as well as curios. Frequent fairs set up shop (or rather tents and stalls) at various central locations, recreating an old market spirit and providing space for smaller artisan outlets to sell clever knick-knacks, folksy memorabilia, antiques, porcelain, Magyar mode and smart arts and crafts. Real antique trade continues on **Falk Miksa utca**, with **Ecseri piac** (*see p148* **Flea market finds**) offering antiquities as well as genuine junk.

The main shopping strip of Váci utca still appears busy, but many side-street stores are empty, their owners priced out of the market. Nearby **Deák Ferenc utca** is now Fashion Street after developer Immobilia and leasing partner Cushman & Wakefield nominated a heritage stretch as a style strip, dragging shoppers back to the Belváros. Established tenants Hugo Boss, Max Mara and shoe store **La Boutique** now stand alongside Puma, Benetton and Mexx. If Orco's plans to build a department store on Vörösmarty tér come to fruition, downtown will have never looked so attractive for the modern-day shopper.

Andrássy út brims with luxury brands, with lower rents than around Váci utca. Sitting comfortably on Budapest's best boulevard, Zegna and Louis Vuitton are hoped to attract

Fashionable **Deák Ferenc utca**.

other global heavyweights. Big brand stores stock a fragment of their parent collections, and for longer, because the local clientele can't afford to keep up with the change of seasons at Zara speed. Even at the luxury end, locals will shop for bits and bobs rather than a full collection of sizes, models and colours.

The days of cheap charm are gone. Prices for the same services may vary but are converging steadily. Certain services such as a private beauty treatment or massage will cost less than in the West, but good dry-cleaning tends to be shamelessly expensive. The price of local wine compares to expensive imports. In general, services mainly catering to foreigners will charge Western prices, while what average locals can afford should be cheap for the visitor.

TIPS, TIMES AND TAX

Most assistants speak English and a fledgling service mentality has surfaced from the knee-jerk urge to earn a tip. Standard opening hours are 10am-5pm or 6pm on weekdays and 10am-1pm on Saturdays. In touristy areas, shopping

Eat, Drink, Shop

Aqua-tick. *See p144.*

malls and outlets, stores stay open later as well as on Sundays. For basic necessities at all hours, there's a non-stop in every locality.

Since EU accession, EU citizens can no longer claw back VAT refunds on goods. Non-EU visitors can reclaim the VAT on purchases over Ft45,000 in one shop in one day, provided they don't qualify as a commercial quantity. Not all shops participate in the refund scheme, nor are they bound to return the full VAT; the amount you can reclaim varies from store to store, up to 15 per cent. Those that do fill a form for you, to be stamped at your point of departure. There is a Global Refund counter at IBUSZ (V.Ferenciek tere 10, 485 2700; open 9am-5pm Mon-Fri). The **Hungarian Customs Office** (XIV.Hungária körút 112-114, 470 4119) also has details. For complaints, see the **Consumer Protection Authority** (VIII.József körút 6, 459 4800).

General

Malls

Budagyöngye
II.Szilágyi Erzsébet fasor 121 (275 0839/www. budagyongye.com). M2 Moszkva tér, then bus 22/ tram 56. **Open** 9am-7pm Mon-Fri; 10am-3pm Sat; 10am-1.30pm Sun.
Buda's most functional mall deters with a chaos of smaller stores, but attracts with its comprehensive services catering to its better-heeled customers. Good fresh fish and imported cheese and vegetables.

Mammut
II.Lövőház utca 2-6 (345 8020). M2 Moszkva tér/ tram 4, 6. **Open** 10am-9pm Mon-Sat; 10am-6pm Sun. **Map** p245 A3.
Two massive wings make up the Mammut mall, the newer one with Benetton and Mango, the older with dozens of smaller shops. There's a huge food store, Smatch, in the basement. Adjacent is the Fény utca market for fresh produce.

MOM Park
XII.Alkotás utca 53 (487 5500). Tram 61. **Open** 10am-8pm Mon-Sat; 10am-6pm Sun. **Map** p248 A6.
This most recent of malls contains Goa for exotic interior design, Jacadi for kiddie couture, a seafood specialist and Match, stocking imported vegetables such as sweet potatoes, fennel and baby zucchinis, much to locals' bemusement.

Rózsakert
II.Gábor Áron utca 74-78 (391 5998/www.rozsa kert.hu). Bus 11, 91. **Open** 10am-8pm Mon-Fri; 10am-7pm Sat; 10am-4pm Sun. **Credit** AmEx, MC, V.
Rózsakert attracts the Rózsadomb rich. The vegetable stand is fabulous, the health clinic an expat favourite and the Thai massage parlour always full.

Westend City Center
VI.Váci út 1-3 (238 7777/www.westend.hu). M3 Nyugati pu./tram 4, 6. **Open** 10am-9pm Mon-Sat; 10am-6pm Sun. **Map** p246 F2.
This huge mall is the city's busiest and most comprehensive – everyone in retail and services is here.

Specialist

Books & magazines

English-language

Bestsellers
V.Október 6 utca 11 (312 1295). M3 Arany János utca. **Open** 9am-6.30pm Mon-Fri; 10am-5pm Sat; 10am-4pm Sun. **Credit** AmEx, DC, MC, V. **Map** p246 E4.
Budapest expats' favourite bookstore offers the city's best selection of foreign literature.

Treehugger Dan's Bookstore & Café
VI.Csengery utca 48 (322 0774/www.treehugger.hu). M1 Oktogon. **Open** 10am-7pm Mon-Fri; 10am-5pm Sat; 10am-4pm Sun. **No credit cards.** **Map** p246 G3.
Environmentally conscious to the nth degree, Dan Swartz's new establishment sells second-hand and remaindered English-language books, hosts readings, launches and craft exhibitions, and offers fairtrade coffee to sip while you're reading.

General

Alexandra Könyvesház
VII.Károly körút 3C (479 7070/www.alexandra.hu). M2 Astoria. **Open** 10am-10pm Mon-Sun. **Credit** MC, V. **Map** p249 F6.
Alexandra has created its own wine shop, also offering a good selection of books on Hungary in English, and 360-degree calendars showing the sights.
Other locations: VI.Nyugati tér 7 (428 7070); VI.Andrássy út 35 (413 6670).

Inmedio – A Világsajtó Háza
V.Városház utca 3-5 (317 1311). M3 Ferenciek tere/bus 7. **Open** 7am-7pm Mon-Fri; 7am-4pm Sat; 8am-noon Sun. **Credit** AmEx, DC, MC, V. **Map** p249 E5.
Part of Hungaropress, these shops carry 2,000 international titles and foreign-language books.
Other locations: V.Kálvin tér 3 (266 9730).

Írók Boltja
VI.Andrássy út 45 (322 1645). M1 Oktogon/tram 4, 6. **Open** Sept-June 10am-6pm Mon-Fri; 10am-1pm Sat. July, Aug 10am-6pm Mon-Fri. **Credit** AmEx, MC, V. **Map** p246 F4.
Hungarians in English translation are available here, with a huge photo album selection. An intellectual atmosphere is fostered by a coffee corner.

Eat, Drink, Shop

Second-hand & antiquarian

Központi Antikvárium

V.Múzeum körút 13-15 (317 3514). M2 Astoria/ tram 47, 49. **Open** 10am-6.30pm Mon-Fri; 10am-2pm Sat. **Credit** AmEx, MC, V. **Map** p249 F6.
Spacious collectors' shop, especially good for old books, maps and engravings. Also second-hand books in various obscure foreign languages.

Children

Fashion

Benetton Zerododici

V.Váci utca 42 (266 4287). M3 Ferenciek tere/bus 7. **Open** 10am-7pm Mon-Sat; 10am-5pm Sun. **Credit** AmEx, MC, V. **Map** p249 E6.
True to form, the Italian wizard of the uniformed multi-culti brings a no-nonsense collection of infant gear to Benetton's Central European store.

Sonia & Oliver

V.Régi posta utca 11 (318 2515). M1 Vörösmarty tér/M2, M3 Deák tér. **Open** 10am-6pm Mon-Fri; 10am-2pm Sat. **Credit** MC, V. **Map** p249 E6.
Haute outfitting for fashionable children by a mixture of Baby Dior, Moschino Junior and the like.

Zara

V.Váci utca 6/Kristóf tér 2 (327 0210). M1, M2, M3 Deák tér. **Open** 10am-8pm Mon-Fri; 10am-6pm Sat; 10am-5pm Sun. **Credit** AmEx, MC, V. **Map** p249 E6.
The Spanish star brand took over the old premises of the Benetton megastore in this most central location. Kiddy chic with a twist Latin of style.

Toys

Autó Modell Szalon

XIII.Victor Hugo utca 24B (270 2850/www.auto modellszalon.hu). M3 Lehél tér. **Open** 10am-7.30pm Mon-Fri; 10am-2pm Sat. **No credit cards**. **Map** p246 E1.
A collectors' paradise, AMS showcases mini models from all over the world, delicate little structures easily broken in the hands of children.

Babaház

IX.Ráday utca 14 (213 8295). M3 Kálvin tér/tram 47, 49/bus 15. **Open** noon-8pm Mon-Sat. **No credit cards**. **Map** p249 F7.
Pretty dolls from the pre-Barbie era fill this workshop and store where owner Ilona Kovács creates her masterpieces. Careful, though – the limbs are real porcelain and the manes real hair.

Babaklinika

V.Múzeum körút 5 (267 2445). M2 Astoria/bus 7. **Open** 9.30am-5pm Mon-Fri; 9.30am-noon Sat. **No credit cards**. **Map** p249 F6.
A clinic where broken dolls have their limbs screwed back on. Dolly wear and folksy dollies also sold.

Fakopáncs Fajátékbolt

VIII.Baross utca 46 (337 0992). Tram 4, 6. **Open** 10am-6pm Mon-Fri; 9am-1pm Sat. **No credit cards**. **Map** p250 G6.
Fabulous wooden trains, board games, traditional Christmas decorations, garden tools and looms.

Gondolkodó Játékbolt

II.Fény utca 10 (316 4082/www.nimbusz.hu). M2 Moszkva tér/tram 4, 6. **Open** noon-6pm Mon; 10am-6pm Tue-Fri; 10am-1pm Sat. **No credit cards**. **Map** p245 A3.
Gondolkodó stocks games that require brainpower, deftness or skill. Hungarian Rubik's inventions, chess games, puzzles and wooden building blocks and toys grace the shelves.

Játékszerek anno

VI.Teréz körút 54 (302 6234/www.kelle.hu). Tram 4, 6. **Open** 10am-6pm Mon-Fri; 10am-1pm Sat. **No credit cards**. **Map** p246 F3.
Original and copies of old toys amaze and enchant here; the shop also organises monthly exhibitions with themes like US paper toys or carnival masks.

Electronics & photography

General

Saturn

Mammut mall, II.Lövőház utca 2-4 (336 3200/ www.fukar.hu). M2 Moszkva tér/tram 4, 6. **Open** 10am-9pm Mon-Sat; 10am-8pm Sun. **Credit** AmEx, MC, V. **Map** p245 A3.
Saturn is a newcomer to the cut-throat local electronics market. Its ad campaign appeals to all misers (*'fukar'*) – hence the website address. Located in the Mammut mall, its endless aisles display a comprehensive array of gadgets.

Specialist

AT Design

II.Erőd utca 16 (201 1843). Tram 4, 6. **Open** 11am-5pm Mon-Fri. **No credit cards**. **Map** p245 B3.
Don't let the laid-back atmophere deter you: the staff here are professional in their computer repair and fair in their pricing.

Photo Hall

V.Váci utca 7 (318 3005). M1, M2, M3 Deák tér. **Open** 10am-6pm Mon-Fri; 9am-1pm Sat. **Credit** MC, V. **Map** p249 E6.
Besides film development, cameras and accessories, this store scans paper photographs or film.

Soós Kereskedés

V.József Attila utca 22 (317 2341). M1, M2, M3 Deák tér. **Open** 9am-5pm Mon-Fri; 10am-1pm Sat. **Credit** MC, V. **Map** p249 D6.
Rows of old cameras beckon you in. Once inside, walk to the back counter and side room for more cameras, enlargers and a film-processing service.

Eat, Drink, Shop

Fashion

Designer

Anda Emilia
V.Galamb utca 4 (06 30 933 9746 mobile). M3 Ferenciek tere/bus 7. **Open** 11am-6pm Mon-Fri; 11am-2pm Sat. **Credit** MC, V. **Map** p249 E6.
One of the most revered and inventive couturiers in the industry, Anda designs soft, cerebral and structural women's collections. Accessories to die for.

Artista
VIII.Puskin utca 19, 2nd floor (328 0290). M2 Astoria/tram 47, 49/bus 7. **Open** by appointment. **No credit cards. Map** p249 F6.

The label stands for six quirky designers on the cutting edge. The collections reflect colouful moods and inspirations, cut from lavish fabrics.

Bál Szalon
V.Dorottya utca 11 (266 4602). M1 Vörösmarty tér/tram 2. **Open** 10am-7pm Mon-Sat; 10am-4pm Sun. **Credit** MC, V. **Map** p246 D5.
In case of ball-wear emergency, this hidden showcase of fashion fantasists and fanatics is your saviour – various haute couture collections proffer red carpet material for any event that requires a splash.

Christina Designer Shop
V.Semmelweis utca 8 (266 8009). M2 Astoria/tram 47, 49/bus 7. **Open** 10am-6pm Mon-Fri; 10am-1pm Sat. **Credit** AmEx, DC, MC, V. **Map** p249 F6.

Tailor to the stars

Every time **Györgyi Vidák** puts on a show, all Hungary's leading stage stars happen to be available at the same time. It's a busy night elsewhere in town for stand-ins.

The idea to use actors and actresses instead of models arose when Vidák, winner of an Emmy for costume design for *the Josephine Baker Story*, was still a full-time costume designer for Hungarian television. 'If you do a show,' one actress said, 'I'd be happy to model for you.' The free market soon curtailed TV film production and the new rich fuelled demand for haute couture. High fashion is theatre. Who better suited to show it off to maximum effect than thespians?

Almost every year since 1995, Vidák has liased with agents and theatres. Hand-picking her models, she designs collections with certain people in mind. 'They're all different, and the clothes are just not interchangeable', proclaims Vidák, flying in the face of the usual catwalk logic, in which clone-like waifs allow the outfit to hang well. Vidák channels the performers' own energy and aura to bring out the best in the clothes, as if to say that the dress alone won't do. This in turn raises the bar: you have to breathe life into your attire, you have to perform. The dress itself provides its wearer with a role.

While stars such as Dorottya Udvaros and Enikő Eszenyi always participate, every collection has its special appearances. In the past, Vidák has managed to secure local legend Mari Törőcsik, whose fragile, unassuming walk down the runway brought a tear to the eye.

The show over, the dresses return to their atelier. They are available for purchase as well as rental, complete with alterations. Bespoke orders are also welcome so long as you're ready to act it all out.

Dressy
VI.Ó utca 23 (311 8654/269 1174/ www.vidakgyorgyi.hu). M1 Opera. **Open** by appointment 7am-4pm Mon-Thur; 7am-1pm Fri. **Credit** MC, V. **Map** p246 E4.

Vasseva. *See p145.*

This formerly two-branch boutique has been reduced to one of them, showcasing its diaphanous sleepwear and luxurious bathrobes all the more. It also does must-have beachwear like wraps and bags, all made in-house.

Eclectick

V.Irányi utca 20 (266 3341). M3 Ferenciek tere/bus 7. **Open** 10am-7pm Mon-Fri; 11am-4pm Sat. **Credit** MC, V. **Map** p249 E6.
Fashion of another kind, Edina Farkas's Eclectick represents Hungarian designers who do trendy against the grain, in small series: between five and ten of each model. Also available are Aquanauta, PUCC, Xthismo and a slew of local alternatives. Look out also for its equally fashionable branch a couple of doors down, Aqua-tick, at V.Zrinyi utca 12 (302 3277). **Photos** *p140.*

Fidji Couture

V.Haris köz 5 (318 2565). M3 Ferenciek tere/bus 7. **Open** 10am-7pm Mon-Fri; 10am-5pm Sat. **Credit** AmEx, DC, MC, V. **Map** p249 E6.
Ostentatious outrage for women, somewhat sombre suits for men, plus colourful must-have accessories.

Hampe Katalin

V.Váci utca 8 (318 9741). M1 Vörösmarty tér/tram 2. **Open** 10am-6pm Mon-Fri; 10am-1pm Sat. **Credit** AmEx, MC, V. **Map** p249 E5.
Katalin Hampe adapts historical Hungarian wear to today's standards and comfort. A small selection of original folklore is also on sale.

Katti Zoób

V.Szent Istán körút 17 (312 1865/www.kattizoob.hu). M3 Nyugati pu./tram 4, 6. **Open** 10am-7pm Mon-Sat; 10am-4pm Sun. **Credit** MC, V. **Map** p246 E3.
Arguably the most business-oriented line, Zoób's design ranges from luxurious couture showpieces to her own 'biznisz luk', a Donna Karan-esque take on women's suits and essentials. Clothing also made to order from Zoób's magnificent fabrics. The most acclaimed of Budapest's modern designers.

Látomás

VII.Dohány utca 20 (266 5052/www.latomas.hu). M2 Astoria/tram 47, 49. **Open** 11am-7pm Mon-Fri; 11am-4pm Sat. **Credit** MC, V. **Map** p249 F5.
Over 30 Hungarian designers hang their work here, mostly clothes and accessories, while in the gallery second-hand items and shoes fill the shelves.

Lilu

V.Régi posta utca 2 (235 0061). M1 Vörösmarty tér/ M2, M3 Deák tér. **Open** 10am-6pm Mon-Fri; 11am-3pm Sat. **Credit** AmEx, MC, V. **Map** p249 E6.
Among the upmarket menswear specialists focusing on suits, this shop went straight for male sex appeal and tease wear. Lines Bray Steve Alan, Ice B and the black label of John Richmond reign supreme.

Luan by Lucia

VI.Bajcsy-Zsilinszky út 62 (331 6675). M3 Arany János utca. **Open** *call for appointment* 9am-5pm Mon-Fri. **No credit cards**. **Map** p246 E4.
Lucia S Hegyi's work screams bespoke tailoring. Her lavish fabrics are a sartorial expression of the client's personality, elegant and haut bourgeois.

Manier

V.Nyáry Pál utca 4 (483 1140/www.manier.hu). M3 Ferenciek tere/bus 7. **Open** by appointment. **Credit** AmEx, MC, V. **Map** p249 E6.
Hardly street-smart, more theatrical couture, Anikó Németh creates eccentric women's gear to order in the atelier or to buy off the peg in the store. Fine copper and silver clothing items and stunning accessories by Timea Balák.
Other locations: V.Váci utca 68 (411 0852).

Náray Tamas

V.Károlyi Mihály utca 12 (266 2473). M3 Ferenciek tere/bus 7. **Open** 10am-8pm Mon-Fri; 10am-2pm Sat. **Credit** AmEx, MC, V. **Map** p249 E6.
Náray dresses women caught in a Nina Ricci time warp – the collection is status design with a good selection of matching accessories. The elegant store is now double its original size.

Orlando

V.Zoltán utca 11 (311 8242). M2 Kossuth tér/tram 2.
Open *appointment advised* 10am-6pm Mon-Fri;
10am-1pm Sat. **No credit cards. Map** p246 D4.
Successful fashion-design graduates Éva Halász and
Ágota Nagy are the creative team behind Orlando,
churning out their ready-to-wear, haute and wedding collections for over ten years. Thanks to their
personal service, the designs cross over into made-
to-measure territory, with a high-street edge. Shoes
and men's suits also available.

Poster Urban Outfit

*V.Múzeum körút 7 (266 0673). M2 Astoria/tram 47,
49/bus 7.* **Open** 10am-7pm Mon-Fri; 10am-3pm Sat.
Credit MC, V. **Map** p249 F6.
Somewhere between Asian trash and vintage junk
lies the creative genius of Roland Suyehola and
Melinda Sipos, who design and produce custom-
made get-ups in a cacophony of colour and at prices
few others can beat. Look out for their particularly
smart, sequin-trimmed, hand-decorated cotton tops.
The shop is Bangkok-sourced cheap and chic accessories are also available. Set inside the courtyard.

Retrock Deluxe

*V.Henszlmann Imre utca 1 (06 30 556 2814 mobile/
www.retrock.com). M3 Ferenciek tere/bus 7.* **Open**
10.30am-7.30pm Mon-Fri; 10.30am-3.30pm Sat. **No
credit cards. Map** p249 F6.
Up-and-coming Hungarian labels Use Unused,
Nanushka, Tamara Barnoff and Je Suis Belle offer
their limited-edition series.
Other locations: V.Ferenczy István utca 28 (06 30
678 8430 mobile).

Vasseva

VI.Paulay Ede utca 67 (342 8159). M1 Opera.
Open noon-8pm Mon-Fri. **No credit cards.**
Map p246 D3.
Éva Vass' minimalist store proffers her casual,
clever design in clothing, bedding and accessories.
The signature stuffed bunnies are a joy. **Photo** *p144.*

General

Barna Szabóság

*V.Vitkovics Mihály utca 12 (266 9410). M3
Ferenciek tere/bus 7.* **Open** 3-5pm Tue-Fri;
9-11am Sat. **No credit cards. Map** p249 E5.
Quintessentially Hungarian suits are the exquisite
product of this specialist tailor's shop. The outfits
are delicately hand-stitched in minute detail.

Brioni

*V.Roosevelt tér 5-6, entrance on Mérleg utca (411
9000). Tram 2/bus 105.* **Open** 11am-8pm Mon-Fri;
11am-4pm Sat. **Credit** AmEx, MC, V. **Map** p246 D5.
The most expensive men's shop in town, Brioni
offers hand-stitched suits in luxurious Italian fabrics and exotic leathers, such as python. The collections take a head-to-toe approach: from underwear,
socks and shoes to overcoats, you can cultivate a
totally Italian look – even signature shoe trees.

Ferdinand Max

*III.Bécsi út 88-92 (387 1499/www.szabosag.hu).
Tram 17.* **Open** 10am-6pm Mon-Fri. **Credit** MC, V.
Ferdinand Max comes to your house to take mea-
surements, a truly personal service. Great quality
apart, distinguishing details and expert advice complete the picture.

Ingkészítő

*VI.Nagymező utca 7 (267 4756/www.ingkeszito.hu).
M1 Opera.* **Open** 10am-2pm, 3-6pm Mon-Fri. **No
credit cards. Map** p246 F4.
Ms Schreiner's thriving small business has seen and
survived history, and her tiny corner shop is still
making the most exquisite shirts to order.

Merino-Szivárvány

*V.Petőfi Sándor utca 18 (318 7332). M1, M2, M3
Deák tér.* **Open** 10am-6pm Mon-Fri; 9.30am-1.30pm
Sat. **Credit** AmEx, MC, V. **Map** p249 E6.
Founded in the late 1800s and preserving the feel of
a dry goods store, Merino-Szivárvány has fine lace,
velvet silks and woollens stacked up on wide shelves
lining wood-panelled walls.

Pelote

VI.Andrássy út 15 (411 1615). M1 Opera. **Open**
10am-7pm Mon-Wed, Fri, Sat; 10am-8pm Thur.
Credit MC, V. **Map** p246 F4.
One of several menswear boutiques on this stretch
of Andrássy, Pelote specialises in made-to-measure
shirts, shoes and suits, and accessories for the high
flyer. The salon opposite does bespoke service.
Other locations: VI.Andrássy út 12 (472 7450).

Tangó Classic

*V.Váci utca 8 (267 6647/www.tangoclassic.hu).
M1 Vörösmarty tér/M2, M3 Deák tér.* **Open** 10am-
5.30pm Mon-Fri; 10am-1pm Sat. **Credit** AmEx, DC,
MC, V. **Map** p249 E5.
If you need something chic in a day, quick couture
is at hand at Tangó Classic, which integrates antique
fabrics into new designs – the style is very pre-war.

Used & vintage

Ciánkáli

*XI.Repülőtéri út 6 8/D building (06 30 456 7018
mobile/www.majomketrec.hu). Tram 41.* **Open**
10am-5.30pm Mon-Thur. **Credit** MC, V.
Ciánkáli stocks the best collection of vintage clothes
in Budapest. The old central location had to close
down but this depot has it all. Expect loads of polyester, shoes, suits, jewellery, theatre and leather jackets from the threshold of schlock.

Iguana

*VIII.Krúdy Gyula utca 9 (317 1627). M3 Kálvin tér/
tram 4, 6.* **Open** 10am-9pm Mon-Fri; 10am-2pm Sat.
No credit cards. Map p249 G6.
Scores of funky duds from the 1960s and 1970s, and
even some accessories: sunglasses, Indian jewellery,
belts, bags and the like.
Other locations: IX.Tompa utca 1 (215 3475).

Eat, Drink, Shop

Fashion accessories & services

Hats & gloves

Ékes Kesztyű
V.Régi posta utca 14 (266 0986). M3 Ferenciek tere.
Open 10am-6pm Mon-Fri; 10am-1pm Sat. **Credit** AmEx, DC, MC, V. **Map** p249 E6.
A family-run and nonchalantly operated artisan store since 1883, Ékes makes gloves in various leathers, including boarskin, by hand.

Fazekas Valéria Művészi Kalapszalon
V.Váci utca 50 (337 5320). M3 Ferenciek tere.
Open 10am-6pm Mon-Fri; 10am-4pm Sat. **No credit cards. Map** p249 E6.
Hats of avant-garde style, in shapes and fabrics that stretch the imagination.
Other locations: V.Belgrád rakpart 16 (337 0327).

Violetta Kalapszalon
V.Régi posta utca 7-9 (266 0421). M1 Vörösmarty tér/M2, M3 Deák tér/tram 2. **Open** *Winter* 10am-6pm Mon-Fri. *Summer* noon-6pm Mon-Fri; Sat by appointment. **No credit cards. Map** p249 E6.
For the head held high, hand-made hats are stocked in all styles, fabrics and colours. Violetta also offers repairs and dry-cleaning.

Jewellery

Bartha
V.Károly körút 22 (317 6234). M2 Astoria. **Open** 10am-6pm Mon-Fri. **Credit** MC, V. **Map** p249 F5.
This courtyard shop designs and produces original gold and silver jewellery, mostly in art deco style.

Gallwitz Pipes & Pearls
V.Régi posta utca 7-9 (318 5139). M1 Vörösmarty tér/M2, M3 Deák tér/tram 2. **Open** 10am-6pm Mon-Fri; 10am-2pm Sat. **No credit cards. Map** p249 E6.
Founded in 1880, Gallwitz's tradition lives on with pipes and accessories, pearls and jewellery, walking sticks, even mah-jong, introduced to Hungary by the shop between the wars. Repairs also.

Glamour Boutique
VI.Andrássy út 20 (302 8209/www.glamour boutique.hu). M1 Opera. **Open** 10am-7pm Mon-Fri; 10am-6pm Sat. **Credit** MC, V. **Map** p246 F4.
Push aside the usual accessories suspect like ck and Kenzo, and head for Hungarian mode messiah Katti Zoób and Zsolnay jewellery. Chunky but fragile porcelain neck pieces feature rich and tender ornamentation with design signatures.

M Frey Wille
V.Régi posta utca 19 (318 7665). M1 Vörösmarty tér/ M2, M3 Deák tér. **Open** 10am-6pm Mon-Fri; 10am-noon Sat. **Credit** AmEx, DC, MC, V. **Map** p249 E6.

Gustav Klimt and ancient Egypt are the inspirational sources behind this Austrian collection of fine jewellery and accessories in enamelled gold.

Ómama Bizsuja
V.Szent István körút 1 (312 6812). Tram 2, 4, 6.
Open 10am-6pm Mon-Fri; 10am-1pm Sat. **No credit cards. Map** p246 D2.
A treasure trove of nifty antique bijoux – display cases of rhinestones, beads of all sorts, semi-precious stones and silverwork – all at extremely reasonable prices. This location also features vintage clothes.
Other locations: II.Frankel Leó utca 7 (315 0807).

Lingerie & underwear

Glamour Accessories
VI.Nagymező utca 6 (321 5161). M1 Opera. **Open** 11am-7pm Mon-Fri; 11am-2pm Sat. **No credit cards. Map** p246 F4.
Naughty undies by Pussy Deluxe and Vive Maria perk up under attire for both sexes. Also sold are party-wear accessories such as masks and boas.

Luggage

Laoni
VI.Klauzál tér 1 (322 7481/www.laoni.hu). Tram 4, 6. **Open** 9.30am-6pm Mon-Fri. **Credit** MC, V. **Map** p246 F5.
Ilona Ács' artistic vision dominates in this quiet corner shop full of high-quality leather wallets, handbags and accessories, hand-made on the premises.

Louis Vuitton
VI.Andrássy út 24 (373 0487). M1 Opera. **Open** 11am-8pm Mon-Fri; 11am-5pm Sat. **Credit** AmEx, DC, MC, V. **Map** p246 F4.
LV's big arrival in 2006 brought monogrammed bags and briefcases for men and women to Budapest. Splash out on the Damier check, a splendidly understated black briefcase or leather accessories from wallets to bracelets. **Photo** *p147.*

Real System Kft-Menedzser Shop
V.Ferenciek tere 74 (338 3370). M3 Ferenciek tere/tram 47, 49/bus 7. **Open** 10am-8pm Mon-Fri; 10am-6pm Sat, Sun. **Credit** AmEx, MC, V. **Map** p249 E6.
Stocks a selection of Montblanc pens, Lacoste bags and the best range of Samsonite in town.
Other locations: Westend City Center, VI.Váci út 1-3 (238 7706).

Shoes

La Boutique
VI.Andrássy út 16 (302 5646). M1 Opera. **Open** 10am-7pm Mon- Sat; 10am-4pm Sun. **Credit** AmEx, DC, MC, V. **Map** p246 F4.
One of the best collections of foreign designer styles, such as Dolce & Gabbana. Strong men's selection.
Other locations: V.Deák Ferenc utca 16-18 (266 7585).

Luxury on Budapest's Champs-Elysées – **Louis Vuitton**. *See p146.*

Cipőkészítő Kkt

IX.Vámház körút 7 (218 7893). M3 Kálvin tér/tram 47, 49. **Open** 10am-6pm Mon-Fri; 10am-1.30pm Sat. **No credit cards. Map** p249 F7.
Simple shoes and sandals all hand-made by this local cobbler. A relaunched legend, Alföldi Cipő, is also sold here, with Alföldi slippers for men and women enjoying cult status.

Havalda Leather

VI.Hajós utca 23 (312 9120/www.havalda.hu). M1 Opera. **Open** 11am-7pm Mon-Fri. **No credit cards. Map** p246 F4.
The bulk here is tailor-made leather goodies, such as belts for the fashion- and leather-conscious. Pet necessities also sold, bespoke collars studded with Swarowski crystals for glam cats and dandy dogs.

Humanic

V.Váci utca 26 (266 3536). M3 Ferenciek tere/bus 7. **Open** 10am-6.30pm Mon-Fri; 10am-5pm Sat, Sun. **Credit** AmEx, MC, V. **Map** p249 E6.
The improved Humanic chain has emerged from the mass market as a trendy, affordable and convenient alternative to the more expensive boutiques..

Kukor & Réti Manufaktúra

V.Aranykéz utca 1 (266 0526/www.budapest-shoes. hu). M3 Ferenciek tere/bus 7. **Open** 10am-6pm Mon-Fri; 10am-2pm Sat. **Credit** MC, V. **Map** p249 E6.
Top-quality Hungarian hand-made shoes stitched to perfection in a variety of styles and soles for men. Stingray stands out as the most glamorous choice.

Tisza Cipő

VII.Károly körút 1 (266 3055). M2 Astoria/tram 47, 49/bus 7. **Open** 10am-7pm Mon-Fri; 9am-1pm Sat. **Credit** AmEx, MC, V. **Map** p249 F6.
The Communist answer to adidas, newly hip after being salvaged. The shoes come in funky colours, and there is an accessories range. Socialist nostalgia does not get any better.

Vass

V.Haris köz 2 (318 2375). M3 Ferenciek tere/bus 7. **Open** 10am-6pm Mon-Fri; 10am-2pm Sat. **Credit** AmEx, DC, MC, V. **Map** p249 E6.
The Manolo Blahnik of Budapest makes fine men's shoes in excellent quality leather, as well as custom-made to order. The prices here are comparable to designer labels. Limited women's collection too. Off-the-rack items are also available.

Food & drink

For more information on local wine producers, *see p111* **In vino qualitas.**

Drinks

Budapest Wine Society

I.Batthyány utca 59 (212 2569/www.bortarsasag.hu). M2 Moszkva tér/tram 4, 6. **Open** 10am-8pm Mon-Fri; 10am-6pm Sat. **Credit** AmEx, MC, V. **Map** p245 A3.
More than 600 of the best domestic wines, presided over by knowledgeable staff. Free Saturday tastings 2-5pm. Imported wines are also available.
Other locations: V.Szent István tér 3 (328 0341).

In Vino Veritas

VII.Dohány utca 58-62 (341 3174/341 0646). M2 Astoria/tram 47, 49/bus 7. **Open** 9am-8pm Mon-Fri; 10am-6pm Sat. **Credit** MC, V. **Map** p249 F5.
Excellent overview of local vintners' output. The selection is top quality, the staff eager to help.

Magyar Pálinka Háza

VIII.Rákóczi út 17 (338 4219). M2 Blaha Lujza tér/ bus 7. **Open** 9am-7pm Mon-Sat. **Credit** MC, V. **Map** p249 G5.
Excellent selection of top-class Hungarian fruit brandies in a bewildering variety of flavours, all tastefully wrapped to make the perfect gift.

Eat, Drink, Shop

Flea market finds

Flea markets are the perfect way to dispose of excess forints and treat your friends to a real taste of the Carpathian Basin, the black hole into which Europe's unwanted and unusable gifts have drifted. What's one man's junk is another's piece of history, and Budapest provides rich pickings for the curious traveller.

The **Novák piac** (VII.Dózsa György út 1-3; open 7am-4pm daily), a lesser known but conveniently centrally located market, is active early in the mornings. A lot of the junk from here shows up as pricier antiques a few hours later at the better known Petőfi Csarnok and Ecseri markets (for both, *see below*). Although open until 4pm, most stalls will have packed up by 1pm. It's a ten-minute walk past the railway sidings up Versény utca from Keleti station – markets as good as this have to be located in no-man's-land.

The Novák is about junk: cheap, shabby and perhaps purloined. The motor scooters for sale still carry their Belgian and Polish number plates. Dozens of tables offer cheap used mobiles if you need a disposable one. If you want a bike for a week, buy a one here and then resell it when you leave. But buried amid the debris are real treasures. If you die alone and unloved in Budapest, the Novák is where all your earthly stuff goes on sale.

The wooden stalls offer mountains of Communist-era lava lamps, complete works of Lenin, souvenirs from a 1964 tour of the Bulgarian Riviera or medals awarded to Workers' Brigades. Stock up on old-fashioned tin wind-up helicopters, still fresh in their East German boxes. Transylvanian Gypsies wander the aisles hawking tablecloths and kitchen cutlery. Smart scroungers should keep an eye out for Zsolnay ceramics from the art-deco era. Collector's items can still go for a song.

Another Sunday adventure hidden in the nether regions of Pest is the **Józsefvárosi piac** (VIII.Kőbányai út 21-23; open 6am-6pm daily) – known by all as the Chinese Market. Tram no.28 from Blaha Lujza tér will get you there. Municipal laws don't really apply here – a former minister runs the entire market zone as a private fiefdom. Thousands of Chinese immigrants have refashioned this old factory storage zone into a credible copy of a Beijing suburban market. The goods are mostly cheap underwear, fishing tackle, rip-off copies of name-brand trainers, and plush blankets that sport giant teddies with logos such as 'Happy Lucky Happy Bears!'

Another reason to visit are the food stalls hidden in back of the warehouses: real Chinese lunch plates and noodle shops unlike anything you see downtown – and

Zwack Shop

IX.Soroksári út 26 (476 2383/www.zwack unicum.hu). Bus 23, 54. **Open** 9am-6pm Mon-Fri. AmEx, MC, V. **Map** p249 G9.
Hungary's pre-eminent booze bandwagon's flagship shop stocks all of its products from fine wines to *pálinka* but at the core of the brand remains the legendary herbal bitter, Zwack Unicum. Entrance is on Dandár utca. *See p132* **Black death in a bottle**.

Markets

Biopiac

XII.Csörsz utca 18 (214 7005/www.biokultura.org). Bus 8, 112/tram 61. **Open** 6.30am-noon Sat. **No credit cards. Map** p248 A6.
With the atmosphere of an old, open-air market, the Biopiac is easy to find – just follow the wicker baskets, as there's no plastic allowed. Only controlled, certified organic farms may trade here, and they offer the widest selection of greens and organically farmed meat, as well as wines and honey. Small kitchens provide snacks and meals prepared with organic ingredients, such as goulash. **Photos** *p150*.

Hold utcai vásárcsarnok

V.Hold utca 13 (332 3976). M2 Kossuth tér/ M3 Arany János utca. **Open** 6.30am-6pm Mon-Fri; 6.30am-2pm Sat. **No credit cards. Map** p246 E3.
This gem of a food hall features lines of fresh farm produce and food counters. **Photo** *p153*.

Nagyvásárcsarnok

IX.Vámház körút 1-3 (366 3300). Tram 2, 47, 49. **Open** 6am-5pm Mon; 6am-6pm Tue-Fri; 6am-2pm Sat. **Map** p249 F7.
This popular food hall, renovated more than a decade ago to its original turn-of-the-century glory, is in a prime spot at one end of Váci utca. From the entrance, the stalls on the right-hand side are more expensive than those on the left. There are organised shopping expeditions and cooking classes.

Specialist

Bio-ABC

V.Múzeum körút 19 (317 3043). M2 Astoria/tram 47, 49/bus 7. **Open** 10am-7pm Mon-Fri; 10am-2pm Sat. **Credit** MC, V. **Map** p249 F6.

uniformly cheap. You'll find hand-pulled
noodles and Beijing-style *shiu-jao* dumplings.
Ask for a plate of rice and start pointing at
the entrées on the steam tables – as much
as can be piled on costs Ft500. The best
stalls are the Vietnamese and northern
Chinese ones in the back of the main market,
behind the middle entrance.

The mother of all flea markets is **Ecseri**
(XIX.Nagykörösi út 156; open 8am-2pm Mon-
Fri, 7am-4pm Sat; *pictured*). Take bus no.54
from Boráros tér until you get to what looks
like the end of the world – that's where
everyone else will get off. The main market is
a warren of antique dealers' shacks serving
big buyers from the West; on Saturday the
open areas fill with weekend vendors
spreading their wares on blankets and card
tables. There are treasures to be found, but
they are buried beneath the piles of Soviet-
era cameras, East German toy cars, pottery,
folk costumes, furniture and broken violins.

There's also weekend flea market at **Petőfi
Csarnok** (XIV.Zichy Mihály út, 251 2485;
open 7am-2pm Sat, Sun) in the City Park.
Junk outnumbers antiques but this is where
you can find that wind-up Chinese Barbie to
complete your collection, a set of old Polish
Polaroid nudie pictures, Russian officers'
pocket watches or prog rock 8-tracks.

Soy milk and sausages, carrot juice, organic produce, wholegrains, natural cosmetics, herbal teas, oils, medicinal herbs and jars of Marmite.

Culinaris

VI.Hunyadi tér 3 (341 7001). M1 Vörösmarty utca.
Open noon-7pm Mon; 9am-7pm Tue-Sat. **Credit**
AmEx, MC, V. **Map** p246 G3.
Grocers on a mission to bring global delights to land-locked Hungary – fresh veg, spices and preserves.

Dóczy Delicatessen

*I.Országház utca 16 (212 3761).Várbusz from M2
Moszkva tér.* **Open** 9am-6pm Mon-Fri; 10am-6pm
Sat, Sun. **Credit** MC, V. **Map** p245 B4.
Magyar gastronomic gifts to take home: *pálinka*,
Unicum, goose liver pâté, salami and Tokaj wine.

Pick

*V.Kossuth Lajos tér 9 (331 7783). M2 Kossuth tér/
tram 2.* **Open** 6am-7pm Mon-Fri. **No credit cards**.
Map p246 D4.
Trademark Pick Salami's cold cuts, salami and
meats fill this store-buffet. Many products are pack-aged to keep for longer and to transport easily.

T Nagy Tamás

V.Gerlóczy utca 3 (317 4268). M1, M2, M3 Deák tér.
Open 9am-6pm Mon-Fri; 9am-1pm Sat. **Credit** MC,
V. **Map** p249 D5.
Bigger supermarkets in Budapest now stock a num-ber of imported cheeses, but this central store
remains by far the best, with over 100 types avail-able. The branch round the corner specialises in cold
cuts, salamis, terrines and ham.
Other locations: V.Vitkovics Mihály utca 3-5
(06 20 443 5012 mobile).

Gifts & souvenirs

Art supplies & stationery

Hobby Művész

*3rd floor, Mammut mall, II.Lövőház utca 2-6
(345 8050). M2 Moszkva tér/tram 4, 6.* **Open**
10am-9pm Mon-Fri; 10am-6pm Sat, Sun. **Credit**
AmEx, DC, MC, V. **Map** p245 A3.
Aisle after aisle, the shelves here are packed with
creative equipment, from needle-point and knitting
to tie-dyeing and painting.

Intérieur Studio

*V.Vitkovics Mihály utca 6 (266 1666). M2 Astoria/
tram 47, 49.* **Open** 10am-6pm Mon-Fri; 10am-1pm
Sat. **No credit cards**. **Map** p249 D5.
Hand-made paper goods, fancy gift trimmings, dried
flowers and local handicrafts compose the attractive
stock of this tiny shop. Bath oils, hand-dipped candles and pretty baskets fill the rest of the space.

Ceramics, glass & pottery

Herend Porcelain

*VI.Andrássy út 16 (374 0006/www.herend.com).
M1 Opera.* **Open** 10am-6pm Mon-Fri; 10am-2pm
Sat. **Credit** AmEx, DC, MC, V. **Map** p246 F4.
Herend has been producing Hungary's finest
hand-painted porcelain since 1826; Queen Victoria
picked out its delicate bird and butterfly pattern to
put on her own table.
Other locations: V.József Nádor tér 11 (317 2622);
XIV.Szentháromság utca 5 (225 1050).

Hollóházi Porcelán

*VII.Rákóczi út 32 (413 1463). M2 Blaha Lujza tér/
bus 7.* **Open** 10am-6pm Mon-Fri; 10am-1pm Sat.
Credit AmEx, DC, MC, V. **Map** p247 G5.
Established in 1777, this porcelain manufacturer has
followed tastes and demand. Traditional patterns
range from folklore to more bourgeois florals.

Zsolnay Porcelain

*II.Margit körút 24 (336 0984/http://zsolnay.com).
Tram 4, 6/bus 11.* **Open** 10am-6pm Mon-Fri.
Credit MC, V. **Map** p245 B2.
Established in 1853, Zsolnay's free-flowing designs
are as bright as the iconic mosaic roof tiles you see
on Matthias Church and the Applied Arts Museum,
and all over the Four Seasons-operated Gresham
Palace. Bold, more contemporary new patterns are
a recent feature; in a maverick move, Zsolnay also
has a range of accessories in partnership with fashion chief Katti Zoób.
Other locations: Budagyöngye, II.Szilágyi
Erzsébet fasor 121 (275 0839 ex 271).

Flowers

Fleurt

*VI.Andrássy út 31 (321 8122/www.fleurt.hu).
M1 Opera.* **Open** 9am-8pm Mon-Sat. **Credit** MC, V.
Map p246 F4.
Of the many flower stalls and shops, Fleurt makes
a conversation piece out of of a bouquet: try a hori-
zontally arranged bunch for a centrepiece.

Folklore

Váci utca flogs the folklore theme to death:
embroidery, leather accessories and pottery.
Stands on Deák Ferenc utca, Vörösmarty tér
and the Vigadó tér embankment sell all of the
above, plus leather goods and fur.

Biopiac. *See p148.*

Folkart Centrum

V.Váci utca 58 (318 4697). M3 Ferenciek tere/bus 7.
Open 10am-7pm daily. **Credit** AmEx, DC, MC, V.
Map p249 E6.
The best bet for folk items on Váci; hundreds of local
artists sell their wares here. Wooden knick-knacks,
embroidery and clothing, plus rugs and pottery.

Magyar Régiségek Boltja

*V.Váci utca 23 (06 30 274 5850 mobile). M1
Vörösmarty tér.* **Open** 11am-7pm Mon-Fri; 10am-
5pm Sat. **No credit cards. Map** p249 E6.
Folkloric collectors' items from Hungary and ethnic
Magyar communities abroad.

Majolika

V.Váci utca 46 (266 3165). M3 Ferenciek tere/bus 7.
Open 10am-7pm Mon-Sat. **Credit** AmEx, DC, MC,
V. **Map** p249 E6.
This store showcases simple folklore-inspired pot-
tery – good value and functional in a colourful way.

Health & beauty

Complementary medicine

Béres Egészségtár

VI.Bajcsy köz 1 (311 0009). M3 Arany János utca.
Open 9am-7pm Mon-Fri; 9am-1pm Sat. **Credit**
AmEx, DC, MC, V. **Map** p246 E4.
Hungary's first alternative treatment specialist and
the product range he created is the focus here, starting with Béres drops to boost immunity. Natural
beauty products, oils and teas also available.

Hairdressers & barbers

Hairclub & Bazaar

VI.Paulay Ede utca 55 (321 0590). M1 Opera.
Open 9am-10pm Mon-Fri; 9am-2pm Sat. **Credit**
AmEx, MC, V. **Map** p246 F4.
Just off Andrássy út, in a stylishly minimalist snip-
ping suite, you can get your hair sorted under an
imposing chandelier. Fashion shop downstairs.

Hajas

V.Erzsébet tér 2 (485 0170). M1, M2, M3 Deák tér.
Open 7am-7pm Mon; 7am-9pm Tue-Fri; 7am-3pm
Sat. **Credit** MC, V. **Map** p249 E5.
Hungarian veteran star stylist operates this suc-
cessful business for the local upper classes. Wella
hair products are also available.

Opticians

Libál

*V.Veres Pálné utca 7 (337 9690). M3 Ferenciek tere/
bus 7.* **Open** 11am-5.30pm Mon-Fri; 11am-1pm Sat.
No credit cards. Map p249 E6.
This family business goes back a long way. The
grand selection of frames is a relief after the logo-
laden ones of the large chains.

Shops

Drogerie Markt

*V.Károly körút 26 (317 6741/www.dm-drogerie
markt.hu). M1, M2, M3 Deák tér.* **Open** 8am-7pm
Mon-Fri; 8am-2pm Sat. **Credit** AmEx, MC, V.
Map p249 E5.
All essential and mainstream cosmetics, perfumes,
shampoos, toiletries, washing powders and various
house-cleaning products, plus organic foodstuffs.
More than 60 branches across Budapest.

Ilcsi Néni

*V.Apáczai Csere János utca 5 (267 0343/www.ilcsi.
com). M1 Vörösmarty tér/tram 2.* **Open** 7am-7pm
Mon-Fri; 9am-1pm Sat. **No credit cards.**
Map p249 D5.
Hungary's own preservative-free fruit, vegetable
and herbal beauty product range, managed by Ms
Molnár and son Ferenc since 1958, has a considerable local following. Their products are only available via beauty salons around town, such as the one
given here – the website has all other locations.

Lush

*V.Szent István körút 1 (472 0530/www.lush.hu).
Tram 2, 4, 6.* **Open** 10am-7pm Mon-Fri; 10am-
6.30pm Sat; 11am-6.30pm Sun. **Credit** AmEx,
MC, V. **Map** p246 D2.
Offers an enticing range of natural, organic beauty
products at its two main branches.
Other locations: MOM Park, II.Alkotás utca 53
(201 5937).

Spas & salons

Estée Lauder

*V.Váci utca 12 (266 7829). M1 Vörösmarty tér/
M2, M3 Deák tér.* **Open** 10am-6pm Mon-Sat.
Credit AmEx, DC, MC, V. **Map** p249 E5.
Hungarian-born Estée Lauder's business occupies a
boutique here and provides beauty treatments by
appointment in the back of the exclusive salon.

Fekete Tulipán

*VI.Révay utca 14 (302 5577/www.feketetulipan.hu).
M1 Opera.* **Open** 2-8pm Mon; 10am-8pm Tue-Fri;
10am-4pm Sat. **Credit** AmEx, MC, V. **Map** p246 F4.
Set behind an oriental entrance, this men's beauty
parlour plucks, pops, peels, pulls and pampers for
cleaner skin, more radiant complexion and balanced
aura. Treatments use state-of-the-art equipment
combining infra-red and hydro therapies in what is
claimed to be a feng-shui spa experience.

Lancôme

*V.Váci utca 14 (486 1760). M1 Vörösmarty tér/
M2, M3 Deák tér.* **Open** 8am-8pm Mon-Fri; 10am-
2pm Sat; and by appointment. **Credit** AmEx, DC,
MC, V. **Map** p249 E5.
Full-feature pampering treats for the face or body.
Lancôme's own products are also available in this
stylish downtown location.

House & home

Antiques

Antik Emma
XIII.Pozsonyi út 59 (06 30 970 7455 mobile).
Trolleybus 76, 79. **Open** by appointment. **No**
credit cards. Map p246 D2.
Full of antique fabrics and complete with design
services, Antik Emma also stocks Ildikó Fáczány's
clothes, inspired by old lace and silk. Bedding too.

BÁV
V.Ferenciek tere 10 (318 3733/www.bav.hu). M3
Ferenciek tere/bus 7. **Open** 10am-6pm Mon-Fri; 9am-
2pm Sat. **Credit** AmEx, DC, MC, V. **Map** p249 E6.
These state-run pawn shops buy and sell everything
from quality antiques to used fridges and can be
recognised by a maroon-and-white Venus de Milo
sign. This refurbished central location flogs a range
of random treasures, from paintings to jewellery.
Other locations: V.Szent István körút 3 (473 0666).

Ernst Galéria
V.Irányi utca 27 (266 4016/266 4017/www.ernst
galeria.hu). M3 Ferenciek tere. **Open** 10am-7pm
Mon-Fri; 10am-2pm Sat. **Credit** AmEx, MC, V.
Map p249 E6.
An elegant shop of antique and vintage gems, from
furniture to ornaments. It has a world class pre-war
film poster collection, from an era when Hungarian
graphic artists reigned supreme in the industry;
Ernst is also a specialist in ceramics from the 1930s.

Játékudvar
IX.Ferenc körút 10 (215 6864/www.jatekudvar.hu).
Tram 4, 6. **Open** 10am-6pm Mon-Fri. **No credit**
cards. Map p249 G8.
A shop for collectors of model trains, toy soldiers,
dolls, pictures, postcards, mini books and the like.

Judaica Gallery
VII.Wesselényi utca 13 (267 8502/www..judaica.hu).
M2 Astoria/tram 47, 49/bus 7. **Open** 10am-6pm
Mon-Thur; 10am-2pm Fri. Closed Jewish hols.
Credit AmEx, MC, V. **Map** p249 F5
Articles related to Hungarian Jewish culture: old
prayer books, illustrations by local Jewish artists
and village pottery with Hebrew sayings and
Haggadahs. Also stocks a good selection of books
in English on Jewish themes.

Moró Antik
V.Falk Miksa utca 13 (311 0814/www.moroantik.hu).
M2 Kossuth tér. **Open** 10am-6pm Mon-Fri; 10am-
1pm Sat. **Credit** MC, V. **Map** p246 D3.
A shop in which the past is celebrated, Moró deals
in antique weapons, walking sticks and canes, and
Eastern etchings and statues.

Pintér Antik Diszkont
V.Falk Miksa utca 10 (311 3030/www.pinter
antik.hu). Tram 2, 4, 6. **Open** 10am-6pm Mon-Fri;
10am-2pm Sat. **Credit** MC, V. **Map** p246 D2.

In a former World War II bomb shelter, 1,800sq m
of floor space stocks antique furniture and crystal
chandeliers by Bohemia Salon. The Pintér Szonja
Gallery specialises in contemporary Hungarian
painting and sculpture, and there's also a coffee shop
– a relief after winding through the maze of rooms.

Auctions

BÁV
V.Bécsi utca 1-3 (317 2548/www.bav.hu). M3
Ferenciek tere/tram 2/bus 7. **Open** 10am-6pm Mon-
Fri; 9am-1pm Sat. **Credit** AmEx, DC, MC, V. **Map**
p249 E6.
The largest, state-owned network of vintage goods
in a newly refurbished auction space. For auction
schedules, call the central office at IX.Lónyau utca
30-32 (325 2600) or check the website.

Dunaparti Aukciósház és Galéria
V.Váci utca 36 (266 8374/www.auctiongallery.hu).
M3 Ferenciek tere/tram 2/bus 7. **Open** 10am-6pm
Mon-Fri; 10am-4pm Sat. **Credit** AmEx, DC, MC, V.
Map p246 E6.
Right downtown, the Dunaparti can come across as
chaotic, but is a collector's delight. In high season
there are auctions every Monday; twice a year it
holds a bigger auction over several days.
Other locations: V.Szabadság tér 1 (428 0028).

Kieselbach Galéria
V.Szent István körút 5 (269 3148/269 3149/www.
kieselbach.hu). Tram 2, 4, 6. **Open** 10am-6pm Mon-
Fri; 10am-1pm Sat. **Credit** AmEx, DC, MC, V.
Map p246 D2.
The city's most successful auction house, Kieselbach
holds three auctions yearly of about 200 select art-
works, mostly Hungarian of the 1850-1950 period.

Nagyházi Galéria
V.Balaton utca 8 (475 6000/www.nagyhazi.hu).
Tram 2, 4, 6. **Open** 10am-6pm Mon-Fri; 10am-2pm
Sat. **Credit** AmEx, DC, MC, V. **Map** p246 D2.
One of the city's biggest auction houses holds a
dozen auctions a year. Collections comprise antique
furniture, folk art, silver, jewellery and paintings.
Exhibitions can affect opening hours.

Virág Judit Gallery
V.Falk Miksa utca 30 (312 2071/www.mu-terem.hu).
Tram 2, 4, 6. **Open** 10am-6pm Mon-Fri; 10am-1pm
Sat. **Credit** MC, V. **Map** p246 D2.
An array of 19th- and 20th-century paintings makes
up the best of this frequently changing stock, with
a particularly strong collection of antique art-deco
Zsolnay porcelain. Auctions three times a year.

Flea markets

See p148 **Flea market finds**. For bric-a-brac,
try **Antik Bazár** (VII.Klauzál utca 1, 322 8848,
www.antik-bazar.hu) and **Nosztálgia Bazár**
(VII.Dohány utca 7, 342 0655).

General

Brinkus Design

VI.Paulay Ede utca 56 (321 2138/www.brinkus design.com). M1 Oktogon. **Open** 2-8pm Mon-Sat. **No credit cards. Map** p246 F4.

Kata Brinkus' degree is in textile design, and whatever she can do with fabric, she will. Curtains, bags and accessories, along with macramé statues.

Forma

V.Ferenciek tere 4 (266 5053/www.forma.co.hu). M3 Ferenciek tere/bus 7. **Open** 11am-7pm Mon-Fri; 11am-4pm Sat. **Credit** MC, V. **Map** p249 E6.

This modern shop brings together varied yet complementary decorative elements, imported and Hungarian, from vinyl stickers to perk up your wall to home accessories such as lamps.

Gepetto

XIII.Katona József utca 15 (270 0107/www. gepetto.hu). M3 Nyugati pu./tram 4, 6. **Open** 10am-6pm Mon-Fri. **No credit cards. Map** p246 E2.

Four Hungarian designers here have earned accolades with their lamp systems and inventive accessories such as an electrostatic high-end sound system. Smaller items – eggcups made of spoons, for example – are also available.

Hephaistos Háza/Bazaar

V.Molnár utca 27 (266 1550). M3 Ferenciek tere/ bus 7. **Open** 11am-6pm Mon-Fri; 10am-2pm Sat. **Credit** MC, V. **Map** p249 E6.

Eszter Gál's light designs defy the weight and austerity of wrought iron. She creates everything from beds to candelabras; all made to order.

Holló Folkart Gallery

V.Vitkovics Mihály utca 12 (317 8103). M2 Astoria/ tram 47, 49/bus 7. **Open** 10am-6pm Mon-Fri; 10am-2pm Sat. **No credit cards. Map** p249 E5.

László Holló's authentically traditional folk ornaments are matched in naive and simple beauty with original work from the countryside. Figurine cork screws and painted pepper mills make perfect souvenirs, but there are chunkier pieces of furniture too.

Kátay

VI.Teréz körút 28 (374 0380). M1 Oktogon/tram 4, 6. **Open** 9.30am-6.30pm Mon-Fri; 9.30am-2pm Sat. **Credit** MC, V. **Map** p246 F3.

Excellent shop for things to put in the kitchen, fix up the bathroom, tidy the garden and set the table. For other locations in town, call 311 0116.

Magma

V.Petőfi Sándor utca 11 (235 0277/235 0278). M3 Ferenciek tere/bus 7. **Open** 10am-7pm Mon-Fri; 10am-3pm Sat. **Credit** MC, V. **Map** p249 E6.

Sells local handiwork by a collective of talented artisans, breaking the mould set by the folksy merchants on nearby Váci utca. Look out for ceramics and woodwork, sliver and plastic jewellery, handmade and embroidered pillows or funky bags, to name but some of the unending display of creative accessories and furniture that broadly falls under applied arts. Unique and highly recommended.

Maota

VI.Hajós utca 26A (06 20 824 8710 mobile/ www.maota.com). M1 Opera. **Open** *Jan-May, Sept-Nov* 11am-7pm Wed-Fri; 11am-5pm Sat, Sun. *June-Aug, Dec* 11am-7pm Mon-Fri; 10am-5pm Sat. **No credit cards. Map** p246 F4.

A gem of a food hall right by Parliament – the **Hold utcai vásárcsarnok.** *See p148.*

Eat, Drink, Shop

High-quality artefacts by Hungarian artists that range from exorbitantly to modestly priced. The shop is knownfor putting an emphasis on sourcing work by local disabled artists.

Originart

IX.Ráday utca 20 (215 3763/www.originart.hu). *M3 Kálvin tér.* **Open** 10am-8pm Mon-Sat. **Credit** AmEx, MC, V. **Map** p249 F7.
Items that make you smile: figurines, ceramics and glazed gatemarkers, all authentic handiwork.
Other locations: V.Arany János utca 18 (302 2162).

Vasedény 1,000 Aprócikk

V.Bajcsy-Zsilinszky út 62-64 (312 7635). *M3 Arany János utca.* **Open** 9am-6pm Mon-Fri; 9am-1pm Sat. **Credit** MC, V. **Map** p249 E4.
If you melt the gasket in your espresso-maker, this is where to get a new one, as well as 999 other household gadgets and spare parts.

Music & entertainment

CDs & records

Akt.Records Aktuellmusik

V.Múzeum körút 7 (266 3080). *M2 Astoria/tram 47, 49/bus 7.* **Open** noon-7pm Mon-Fri; 10am-1pm Sat. **No credit cards.** **Map** p249 F6.
Small shop bursting with the alternative sounds of jazz and electronica. Loads of vinyl and DJ gear.

Concerto Records

VII.Dob utca 33 (268 9631). *Tram 4, 6.* **Open** noon-7pm Mon-Fri; noon-4pm Sun. **Credit** AmEx, DC, MC, V. **Map** p246 G4.
A charming shop stocking an impressive collection of new and second-hand classical on vinyl and CD.

Fonó Budai Zeneház

XI.Sztregova utca 3 (206 5300). *Tram 47.* **Open** 5-10pm Wed-Fri; 10am-7pm Sat. **No credit cards.**
Provides a fine selection of local folk, jazz and world music and details of concert at the same venue.

Indie-Go

VIII.Krúdy Gyula utca 7 (486 2927). *Tram 4, 6.* **Open** 11am-8pm Mon-Fri; 11am-4pm Sat. **No credit cards.** **Map** p249 G6.
Breakbeat, trip hop, hip hop and loads of indie CDs.

Rózsavölgyi Zeneműbolt

V.Szervita tér 5 (318 3500/www.rozsavolgyi.hu). *M1, M2, M3 Deák tér.* **Open** 9.30am-7pm Mon-Fri; 10am-5pm Sat. **Credit** AmEx, DC, MC, V. **Map** p249 E5.
An institution, with a fine selection of classical, ballet, opera and sheet music. F olk and pop downstairs.

Wave

VI.Révay utca 4 (331 0718). *M3 Arany János utca.* **Open** 11am-7pm Mon-Fri; 11am-3pm Sat. **No credit cards.** **Map** p246 E4.
Run by young music lovers, this store specialises in the underground scene and world music.

Sport & fitness

Magyar Focisták Boltja

V.Váci utca 23 (06 30 274 5850 mobile). *M1 Vörösmarty tér/M2, M3 Deák tér.* **Open** 10am-7pm Mon-Fri; 10am-5pm Sat; noon-5pm Sun. **Credit** MC, V. **Map** p249 E6.
This small courtyard store is announced by a window full of football pictures from the black-and-white era. *The* place to find rare football badges, shirts and scarfs from across Eastern Europe.

Tickets

Broadway Jegyiroda

VII.Károly körút 9 (352 7142/www.ticketportal.hu). *M1, M2, M3 Deák tér.* **Open** 10am-6pm Mon-Fri. **Credit** MC, V. **Map** p249 D5.
Tickets for all events.

Concert & Media

IX.Üllői utca 11-13 (455 9000/www.jegyelado.hu). *M3 Kálvin tér.* **Open** 10am-6pm Mon-Fri. **Credit** AmEx, MC, V. **Map** p249 F7.
Tickets for various events. Service also available in most Libri bookshops.
Other locations: VI.Jókai tér 9 (374 3026).

Ticket Express

VI.Andrássy út 18 (312 000/www.tex.hu). *M1 Opera.* **Open** 9am-5pm Mon-Fri. **Credit** MC, V. **Map** p246 F4.
Tickets for all events in town. Delivery too.

Travellers' needs

Move One

VII.Rákóczi út 70-72 (266 0181/www.moveone relo.com). Bus 7. **Open** 8.30am-5pm Mon-Fri. **Credit** AmEx, MC. V. **Map** p247 H5.
Among several relocation and expat services, Move One does shipping all over the world.

Vista

VI.Andrássy út 1 (452 3636/www.vista.hu). *M1 Bajcsy-Zsilinszky/M2, M3 Deák tér.* **Open** 9am-6.30pm Mon-Fri; 10am-2.30pm Sat. **Credit** AmEx, DC, MC, V. **Map** p246 E5.
The largest private travel agency in town has a separate adjoining location to cater to tourists.
Other locations: MOM Park, XII.Alkotás utca 53 (201 4546).

Laundry & dry-cleaning

Home Laundry

V.Galamb utca 9 (266 7694). *M1, M2, M3 Deák tér.* **Open** 8am-7.30pm Mon-Fri; 9am-1pm Sat. **No credit cards.** **Map** p249 E5.
Very good cleaning services in a pair of locations make this an expat fave. Home pick-up and delivery also available (200 5305).
Other locations: XI.Németvölgyi út 53B (214 2902).

Arts & Entertainment

Features

Vidám Park. *See p165.*

Festivals & Events

Twelve months of rite, ritual and cultural celebration.

Hungarians are big on festivals and tradition. The biggest event of the year is the **Sziget** festival, a week-long celebration of rock, world and electronic music, film, theatre and scores of side events, on an otherwise empty island in the Danube (*see p159* **Budapest's biggest bash**). Aficionados of highbrow culture are well catered for with the **Spring** and **Autumn Festivals**. The biggest sporting event in the calendar is the **Grand Prix**, held in August. For ticket information, *see p197*.

National holidays have been marred since 2006 by demonstrations by right-wing protesters (*see p24*). Minor skirmishes still might occur on historic days in the Hungarian calendar: 23 October, **Remembrance Day**, and 15 March, **Revolution Day**. If they break out, they will be isolated to small areas in town.

Christmas is a stay-at-home family affair – only bars and restaurants in major hotels stay open, while the rest of the city shuts down completely for two days by noon on Christmas Eve. **New Year** is a street party, with big crowds gathered in the main squares.

PUBLIC HOLIDAYS

New Year's Day (1 Jan); **Revolution Day** (15 Mar); **Easter Sunday**; **Easter Monday**; **Labour Day** (1 May); **Whit Monday**; **St Stephen's Day** (20 Aug); **Remembrance Day** (23 Oct); **Christmas** (25, 26 Dec).

Spring

The **Budapest Spring Festival** ushers in modest counterparts nationwide and signals the official start of the tourist season.

Revolution Day

Public holiday. **Date** 15 Mar.
Revolution Day commemorates poet Sándor Petőfi reciting his *Nemzeti Dal* ('National Song') on the steps of Budapest's National Museum in 1848, an event commonly held to have launched the national revolution. Gatherings at Petőfi's statue were illegal until 1990. Current mayor Gábor Demszky received a serious biffing by police for going to the statue back in his dissident days. Now he stands with an ironic smile on his face in the official ceremony with prominent politicians outside the National Museum. The city gets decked out in red, white and green. Street protests marred the 2007 version – it may be less of same in 2008. **Photo** *p157.*

Budapest Spring Festival

Tickets & information: Budapesti Fesztiválközpont, V.Egyetem tér 5 (486 3311/www.fesztivalvaros.hu). **M3** *Kálvin tér.* **Open** *Box office* 10am-5pm Mon-Fri. **Date** 2wks end Mar/early Apr.
The most prestigious event in the arts calendar. A smattering of internationally renowned talent from the world of classical music – and local orchestras and classical music stars – provide a fortnight of concerts. It's also a showcase for art and drama. Book early for big-name shows.

Easter Monday

Public holiday.
The most drunken occasion in a calendar soaked with them, Easter Monday is when the menfolk go door to door indulging in the pagan rite of *locsolkodás* – spraying women with cheap perfume and getting a large *pálinka* brandy in return.

Labour Day

Public holiday. **Date** 1 May.
No longer a forced wave at medal-festooned leaders along Dózsa György út, May Day still brings people out for entertainment in the city's parks. Open-air May Day (*Majális*) events from pre-Communist days are organised in village squares, a more recent tradition being the rock festival at the open-air stage in the Tabán in Buda. EU accession is also marked with flag-waving and fireworks the night before.

Summer

As the temperature climbs into the 30s, locals leave the city to the tourists and go to Balaton. Doing business in Budapest after 10am on a Friday is unfeasible. In August, everyone heads up the Danube to Óbuda Island for the **Sziget** festival (*see p159* **Budapest's biggest bash**).

World Music Day

Date nearest weekend to 21 June.
Although a French invention, Hungary takes World Music Day to heart. Nearly every town of any size has some kind of concert, usually in the main hall or square. In Budapest, leading venues open their doors to jazz, folk and rock musicians and stages are set up for an eclectic array of international talent in open spaces such as Városliget, Népliget and Klauzál tér.

Budapesti Búcsú

Information: Budapesti Fesztiválközpont, V.Egyetem tér 5 (486 3311/www.fesztivalvaros.hu). **M3** *Kálvin tér.* **Open** 10am-5pm Mon-Fri. **Date** last weekend in June.

Arts & Entertainment

A decade and a half after the event, Budapest still celebrates the withdrawal of Soviet troops from Hungary. Open-air music and theatre events are organised in main squares and parks.

Bridge Festival

Information: Budapesti Fesztiválközpont, V.Egyetem tér 5 (486 3311/www.fesztivalvaros.hu). M3 Kálvin tér. **Open** 10am-5pm Mon-Fri. **Date** end June.
The Chain Bridge is closed for a day and its arrival in 1849 marked with fireworks and boat processions.

Bastille Day

Institut Français, I.Fő utca 17 (489 4200/www. franciaintezet.hu). M2 Batthyány tér/bus 86.
Map p245 C4. **Date** 14 July.
This free open-air ball between the Danube and the French Institute celebrates Bastille Day by inviting leading accordion players from France, laying out a decent spread of French wines and snacks (though don't expect to get anywhere near them), and setting off loads of fireworks. Always attracts a big crowd.

Sziget

Óbudai-sziget, Május 9 park (372 0650/www. sziget.hu). HÉV Filatorigát/night bus 906, 913, 956. **Admission** *Day pass* Ft8,000. *Weekly pass* Ft30,000. *Weekly pass including tent pitch* Ft37,000. **Credit** AmEx, MC, V. **Date** 1wk Aug.
Bringing thousands of music fans from all over Europe, the Sziget ('Island') festival is a week-long open-air party on an island in the Danube. *See p159* **Budapest's biggest bash**.

Budafest

Information: VIP-Arts, VI.Hajós utca 13-15 (302 4290/opera 353 0170/www.viparts.hu). M1 Opera. **Date** July-mid Aug. (Tickets sold from end June.) **Map** p246 F4.
Budafest is a series of top-flight performances at a time when lesser classical music talent is wasted on busloads of Austrian tourists. Prices for the Opera House events are high, but so is the quality of acts.

Hungarian Formula One Grand Prix

Hungaroring, Mogyoród. Information: Ostermann Formula-1, V.Apáczai Csere János utca 11 (266 2040) or Hungaroring (06 28 444 444/www. hungaroring.hu). **Open** 8am-4pm Mon-Thur; 8am-2pm Fri. **Date** Aug.
The biggest event in the sporting calendar sees the town fill up with Formula One fans, creating trade for hotels, restaurants and sex clubs. The course is at Mogyoród, 20km from town on the M3 motorway.

St Stephen's Day

Public holiday. **Date** 20 Aug.
Hungarians celebrate their founding father in style. The right hand of St Stephen, inside a reliquary, is taken in a strange religious procession in front of the Basilica. Around town, cruise boats and river-view restaurants are booked up weeks in advance to get the best look at the huge fireworks display set off from Gellért Hill at 9pm. Downtown streets are packed with all generations of Hungarians waving the red, white and green.

Budapest Parade

Information: Sziget Csoport Kulturális Egyesület (www.sziget.hu). **Date** end Aug.
This event tries to ape Berlin's Love Parade, though it's somewhat smaller and tamer. Still, it's a fun party as crowds estimated at close to 100,000 line Andrássy út to watch a parade of floats carrying DJs and dancers, before it ends its route near Hősök tere by the City Park, where DJs keep spinning and outdoor dancing continues until 10pm. Most clubs then host special after-parties.

Jewish Summer Festival

Information: Budapesti Zsidó Kulturális Központ, VII.Síp utca 12 (343 0420/www.jewishfestival.hu). **Date** 1wk end Aug.
A week of Jewish theatre, art and concerts around town. The musical performances include classical, jazz and klezmer.

Revolution Day. See p156.

Autumn

Autumn sees Budapest emptying of tourists. Cultural life starts up again, and bars, clubs and concert halls reopen their doors to locals.

Budapest Wine Festival

Magyar Szőlő és Borkultúra Alapítvány (203 8507/ www.winefestival.hu). **Date** 2wks Sept.

Hungary's leading wine producers descend on Budapest to woo major buyers, with concerts in the Castle District and folk dancing in Vörösmarty tér.

Budapest Autumn Festival

Tickets & information: Budapesti Fesztiválközpont, V.Egyetem tér 5 (486 3311/www.fesztivalvaros.hu). M3 Kálvin tér. **Open** *Box office* 10am-5pm Mon-Fri. **Date** late Sept/Oct.

The leading annual contemporary arts festival, focusing on cinema, fine arts, dance and theatre.

Budapest Music Weeks

Tickets & information: Budapest Filharmónia, VI.Jókai utca 6 (302 4961/www.deltasoft.hu/filharm). M1 Oktogon/tram 4, 6. **Date** 2wks Sept/early Oct.

The opening of the classical season, kicking off with a major concert as near to the anniversary of Bartók's death (25 Sept) as possible.

Music of Our Time

Information: Budapest Filharmónia, VI.Jókai utca 6 (302 4961/www.filharmoniabp.hu). M1 Oktogon/ tram 4, 6. **Date** 10 days late Sept/early Oct.

Top-notch classical musicians play works by Hungary's leading contemporary composers, many written especially for this ten-day event.

Remembrance Day

Public holiday. **Date** 23 Oct.

The anniversary of the 1956 Uprising is a national day of mourning, and an excuse for right-wing groups to gain media attention, particularly after the riots of 2006. Wreath-laying ceremonies take place at plot 301 of Uj köz Cemetery, where 1956 leader Imre Nagy was secretly buried after his execution.

All Saints' Day

Date 1 Nov.

While Hallowe'en has been slow to catch on in Hungary, the traditional Christian holiday for remembering saints and dead children is marked by people from all religions. Large crowds wander the cemeteries all afternoon and into the evening to leave flowers and burn candles before the Day of the Dead.

Winter

Winter lasts forever, with snow piled on the pavements and sub-zero temperatures. Shops slowly fill for Christmas, without the hard sell of the West. Villages hold a *disznóvágás*, or pig-killing – a bloody, drunken ritual. February is carnival (*farsang*) season, the biggest of which is in Mohács (www.mohacs.hu), a pagan Mardi Gras and Balkan free-for-all.

Mikulás

St Nicholas' Day. **Date** 6 Dec

On the eve of 6 December, children put out their shoes on the window sill for Santa to fill with chocolates, fruit and small presents. He is assisted by

The traditional Christmas market in downtown Budapest.

Budapest's biggest bash

The **Sziget** (*see p157*) is the biggest music festival in the region, if not continental Europe. It may not attract the star names of the big Spanish events – although in recent years Budapest has hosted Franz Ferdinand, Radiohead and the Chemical Brothers, as well as DJs Laurent Garnier, Carl Craig and Roger Sanchez – but for sheer numbers, some half a million visitors over the course of a week, the Sziget is massive.

It's also a different concept. Instead of some field in the city suburbs, the Sziget occupies an island, Óbuda-sziget, ideally accessed by a regular gentle boat ride up the Danube from the Pest side of Margaret Bridge. It's a cross between a holiday camp and Glastonbury, with attractions such as street theatre, play areas including a funfair and even wrestling in chocolate, all set around five main music stages, cinema tent, theatre tent, dance areas and stalls. The city centre empties, bars and clubs close up for the week and everyone heads to the island.

For those coming by boat, admission and a wristband are included in the price of the ticket bought on the day. For those arriving overland, by the HÉV suburban train to Filatorigát, there's a definite sense of crossing the Rubicon as you buy your day ticket (Ft8,000) from the booth and traverse the metal footbridge to an oasis of wanton fun. Everyone is totally up for it. Drinking is dangerously cheap (one local beer company wins the rights to provide inexpensive ale), everyone's body clock is set to 24/7 and monogamy is out the window. For those with a weekly ticket (Ft30,000; Ft37,000 with a tent pitch), this is normality for seven days and seven longer nights.

Since its modest beginnings and 40,000 admissions in 1993, Sziget has become increasingly international. The website gives details in eight languages, music fans stream in from all over Europe and you'll see Sziget posters up in the Métro stations of Paris. Accordingly, with the rise in ticket prices (it isn't that long ago that you could have seen Bowie for a fiver) comes a professional infrastructure that includes proper toilets dotted everywhere, signposted as clearly as everything else, play areas for children and decent medical provision. There are HÉV trains round the clock and three night buses, and the taxi stand is well regulated – you shouldn't have to wait more than ten minutes in the queue to get one.

All told, there are some 50 stages and stalls to choose from, including fortune tellers, random entertainers, counsellors, therapists, teachers and spiritual advisers of every stripe. There's even a wedding tent. One year a music fan married his beer.

krampusz, the bogeyman, a threat to naughty children. To remind them, small *krampusz* puppets, hung on a gilded tree branch, *virgács*, are also left.

Karácsony
Christmas.
Public holiday. **Date** 25, 26 Dec.
The traditional meal is carp, devoured on Christmas Eve, when modest present-giving takes place. The city closes for three days from noon on 24 December.

Szilveszter
New Year's Eve. **Date** 31 Dec.
Szilveszter is when everyone takes to the streets in style. After the national anthem has boomed out at midnight it's champers, kisses and fireworks. Public

transport runs all night and most bars and restaurants lay on some kind of special event. Merriment continues into the next day when *kocsonya*, a dish made from parts of pig feet, wobbles its way into people's hangovers.

Hungarian Film Festival
Magyar Filmszemle.
Magyar Film Müvészek Szövetsége, VI.Városligeti fasor 38 (342 4760/www.magyarfilm.hu/ www.mmka.hu). **Date** late Jan/early Feb.
Screenings at several venues across the city of all Hungarian features, documentaries and shorts produced within the previous calendar year, with everything up for various awards. Translations are provided for the main features.

Arts & Entertainment

Baths

Hubble bubble, soak away your toil and trouble.

The grand **Gellért Gyógyfürdő**. *See p161.*

See p161.

Spa hotels and sauna centres may be a recent worldwide fad, but locals have been enjoying the benefits of the 120 thermal springs gushing from Buda's limestone bedrock for 2,000 years. Indeed, Hungary is now an exporter of spa know-how, with the renovation of the Buxton Spa Crescent complex in the UK's Peak District being carried out with the help of Hungarian spa operators the **Danubius Hotels Group**. Back in Budapest, hardly a year passes without a top-class centre opening to add to the global boom in all things bubbly, wet and warm.

While canny private investors try to reinvent Budapest as the upmarket thermal bathing capital of Europe, the capital's clutch of historic state-run baths have also been given a serious upgrade in the last five years. They remain affordable for locals, a source of civic pride and without doubt reason alone to visit the city. New, almost 24-hour availability at weekends at the **Rudas** means that you can soak through the night in civilised company.

The pull of the mineral-rich waters is one of the reasons a settlement developed here in the first place. Evidence suggests that neolithic peoples were drawn to Buda's warm springs, and later the Romans brought in bathing customs. From the ninth century, the Magyars continued the tradition, but it was under the Ottomans in the 16th and 17th centuries that bathing in Buda reached its zenith.

The natural and abundant supply of water, combined with the demands of Islam that its followers adhere to a strict set of rules for ablutions before praying five times a day, inspired an aquatic culture that still thrives. The Ottoman mosques, monasteries and schools that once filled the streets of Buda are all long gone, but centuries later it is still possible to bathe under an original Ottoman dome in the **Király** or **Rudas** – which, alongside the Tomb of Gül Baba, are the only significant architectural remains of the period.

With so much history involved, it's no wonder that Budapest's bathers held their collective breaths when extensive renovations started on both the Rudas and the **Rác**, the most ambitious of the projects. Not only is the historic building being completely refurbished, but a new 60-room luxury spa hotel operated by the Italian-owned Baglioni Hotel group is being built alongside, with the city co-financing the renovation of the baths. A funicular will connect the site to the top of Gellért Hill. The project is moving slowly, not least owing to historic protection laws that required an archaeological survey when the hotel site was excavated. February 2008 is now the expected completion date.

In 2005, the Rudas was given a complete cosmetic makeover under the watchful eye of the Budapest Historical Society. While the red marble and occasional mixed bathing have angered traditionalists, the consensus is that renovation has been a success. Newer facilities, yet still historic, can be found at the **Gellért**, connected to the art-nouveau Danubius Gellért Hotel, and the 19th-century **Széchenyi** baths complex in the Városliget. The latter has already undergone renovation, with renewal of its neo-baroque façade, and renovation of the Gellért's interior thermal baths is meant to be completed by the end of 2007 – as is work at the **Lukács**, including a new mud-bathing facility.

BACK TO BASICS

For anyone with little or no command of Hungarian, entering the baths for the first time can be a baffling experience. Lengthy menus offer such treats as ultra-sound or a pedicure, as well as massage. In addition, the country of great inventors appears to find it impossible to arrive at a foolproof system to get bathers in through the entrance, into the pool and back out again with ease. Most pools have adopted an electronic-card entry system, activating turnstiles in and out. It also has an electronic time stamp, and will give you a refund if you spend under a certain number of hours in the water. Yet the system is flawed. The number of faulty cards and ratio of bewildered tourists jamming them in upside down means that the electronic turnstile is also manned by a white-coated attendant, who will take the card from your hand and feed it in to the maw of the fickle beast. And few jobsworths shout at customers these days, even the non-Magyar speakers.

The changing and bathing routine is similar in all the Turkish baths, though it varies at the mixed facilities. After negotiating the turnstile, hand over your ticket for a white flap of cloth to be tied round your waist for modesty's sake (though swimming costumes are now tolerated in the single-sex baths). For the mixed facilities you'll need a costume. Flip-flops will make your experience more enjoyable, and a cap is required for those using the swimming pool.

Once in the changing rooms, find an empty cubicle. You will be given a metal tag to tie to your flap or costume. The cubicle is then locked by the attendant and reliably secure – valuables should be left at the entrance, where they are kept in a locked drawer along with your ID.

Baths usually have one or two main pools and a series of smaller ones around the perimeter, of temperatures ranging from dauntingly hot to icy cold. The precise drill depends on preference, but involves moving between different pools, taking in the dry heat of the sauna and the extreme humidity of the steam rooms, alternating temperatures and finally relaxing in gentle warm water.

An hour or two bathing is usually sufficient; it's extremely relaxing and good for relieving aches and pains. Then you shower (bring your own soap); in the Király and Rudas, you will be provided with a towel. Take your own to the others. Most baths also have a resting room where you can take a short nap before changing back into your street clothes. Most have bars – you can enjoy a beer between soaks and swims. On the way out it's customary to tip the attendant Ft100-Ft200. Note that some pools give you a Ft400 refund if you stay less than two hours – show your ticket at the counter.

Apart from pools, saunas and steam rooms, most sites also offer massages. These come in two types: *vízi* (water) massage and *orvosi* (medical) massage – the latter is the gentler experience. Pay for the massage when you get your entrance ticket. The attendant will give you a small metal token with a number on it. Upon entering the baths area, go to the massage room and give your token to a masseur with a tip of Ft100 or so. Also let him know you don't speak Hungarian (otherwise he'll just call out your number when it's your turn and get angry when you don't run over); keep an eye out and he'll wave for you when your time has come.

Don't expect to have the energy to do very much after a visit, except settle down for a long lunch or stretch out for a nap, but do remember to drink lots of water to rehydrate.

Apart from the baths listed here, there are also limited thermal facilities at certain pools and lidos open from May to September, such as the **Palatinus** (*see p200*).

The baths

Gellért Gyógyfürdő

XI.Kelenhegyi út 4 (466 6166). Tram 18, 19, 47, 49/bus 7. **Open** *Mixed* 6am-7pm daily. **Admission** *With changing room* Ft3,100. *With locker* Ft2,800. **Credit** DC, MC, V. **Map** p249 E7.

The most expensive of all the baths, but you do get an art nouveau swimming pool. In the summer your Ft3,000 also allows access to the several outdoor pools and sunbathing areas, with a terrace restaurant. The separate thermal baths – one for men, one for women – lead off from the main swimming pool, which also has its own small warm-water pool. During 2007, these areas are being renovated, so for this limited period the thermal baths a are mixed, and a swimming costume is required. The Secessionist embellishment continues in the maze of steam rooms and saunas that gives the Gellért a different atmosphere to the Turkish Rudas or Király. The clientele is also quite entertaining, composed of startled tourists and, in the male half, gay men on the prowl. The thermal water contains carbonic gases and is recommended for those with blood-pressure problems and coronary disease. **Photo** *p160*.

Király Gyógyfürdő

II.Fő utca 84 (202 3688). M2 Batthyány tér. **Open** *Men* 9am-8pm Tue, Thur, Sat. *Women* 7am-6pm Mon, Wed, Fri. **Admission** Ft1,300. **No credit cards. Map** p245 C3.

The Király is one of the city's most significant Ottoman monuments, particularly the 16th-century pool. Originally called the Bath of the Cock Tower, it takes its name from the 19th-century owners, the König (King) family, who changed their name to its Hungarian equivalent: Király. Construction of the Turkish part was begun in 1566 and completed by Pasha Sokoli Mustafa in 1570. Located within the

Arts & Entertainment

Viziváros town walls, it meant the Ottoman garrison could enjoy a good soak even during the siege. The Classical bits were added in the 18th century. The Király follows the traditional pattern of a main pool surrounded by smaller ones at different temperatures, plus saunas and steam rooms. The bath's environs are light and airy, and three Turkish-style reliefs mark the entrance corridor. There is something of a gay scene in the afternoons on men's days, although not as active as it once was.

Lukács Gyógyfürdő és Strandfürdő

II.Frankel Leó utca 25-29 (326 1695). Tram 4, 6. **Open** *Mixed Oct-Apr* 6am-6pm daily. *May-Sept* 6am-7pm daily. **Admission** *With changing room* Ft1,900. *With locker* Ft1,700. **No credit cards**. **Map** p245 C1.
A complex of two outdoor swimming pools set in attractive grounds, and thermal baths. The Turkish-period Császár baths haven't retained many original features, and the layout is different from the other Turkish places. There's something of an institutional feel to the warren-like facility, not least because the country's main hospital for rheumatism and arthritis is next door, but the setting is verdant and restful. A recent renovation has spruced up the facility, with an expansive roof terrace for sunbathing reached by the wooden staircase next to a smaller swimming pool. On the wall by the entrance to the changing rooms, you'll find old stone plaques, testimonials from satisfied customers – the waters are said to be efficacious for orthopaedic diseases. A mud-bathing area is slated for the end of 2007.

Rudas Gyógyfürdő

I.Döbrentei tér 9 (356 1322). Tram 18, 19/bus 7. **Open** *Men* 6am-8pm Mon, Wed-Fri. *Women* 6am-8pm Tue. *Mixed* 10pm-4am Fri; 6am-5pm, 10pm-4am Sat; 6am-5pm Sun. **Admission** *Baths* Ft2,200. **Credit** MC, V. **Map** p249 D7.

The renovation of the Rudas has seen a revolution. After 450 years, women are allowed in, on Tuesdays and mixed days. The larger swimming pool, too, is mixed. This is the finest and most atmospheric of Budapest's original Turkish baths, especially when rays of sunlight stab through windows in the dome's roof and fan out through the steam above the central pool. The intensity of the experience is enhanced by extraordinary acoustics, as the sound of running water and the chatter of bathers echo from dark corners and up into the dome. The first baths here date from the 14th century. A new site was built by the Pasha of Buda in the 16th century; his plaque stands in the main chamber. The original cupola, vaulted corridor and main octagonal pool remain, and have been restored. There are three saunas, two steam rooms and six pools at various temperatures.

Széchenyi Gyógyfürdő és Strandfürdő

XIV.Állatkérti körút 11 (363 3210). M1 Széchenyi fürdő. **Open** *Mixed* 6am-10pm daily. **Admission** *With changing room* Ft2,800. *With locker* Ft2,400. **No credit cards**. **Map** p247 J1.
In the City Park, this is a large, attractive complex of swimming pools and thermal baths. Its waters are used for treating arthritis, gout and respiratory diseases and, if you drink them, gall bladder disease. Outside is a statue of Zsigmond Vilmos, who discovered the thermal spring that fills the outdoor pool. The Széchenyi is the best choice for a day of relaxation, as it offers outdoor thermal and swimming pools, plus the usual assortment of baths and steam rooms indoors. Guests can exercise, laze and sunbathe all on one site, which fosters an endearing holiday atmosphere. The outer pools are nicely laid out and open all year round; bathers play chess with steam rising around them. Renovations have installed a whirlpool and ice machine.

Rudas Gyógyfürdő.

Children

Bundles of entertaining attractions old and new.

Budapest is a child's playground, and one that is transforming from old-fashioned attractions – puppet theatres, eccentric conveyances and fairground rides – to malls and multiplexes.

Locals spend Saturday or Sunday at the mall, sending the kids to supervised play areas or video arcades; others still prefer folk clubs, craft workshops and puppet shows in local theatres.

Budapest can be difficult with kids too. You may enjoy finding an old tram or toy exhibition, but discover the pushchair doesn't fit through the door or that the show closed an hour early.

The Hungarian family is still traditional in its approach to child-rearing. You don't see many toddlers in restaurants, as they're supposed to stay at home with mum until they learn how to behave like little adults. But don't be surprised if old ladies stop to stroke and praise your children – or criticise their behaviour.

Under-12s are not allowed to travel in the front seats of cars, and seat belts and baby-seats are compulsory in the back. Children under six travel free of charge on all public transport. If you're eating out, don't take highchairs and child-size meals for granted.

Pushchairs now fit on the new main 4/6 tram. Access can be a problem when shopping – except, of course, in the new, spacious malls.

For entertainment information, see the English-language weekly *Budapest Sun*, *Pesti Műsor* under *Gyerekek* ('children'), or phone **Tourinform** (438 8080, www.budapestinfo.hu).

Babysitters

Babaország
XI.Tetényi út 75B (371 0136/www.babaorszag.com). Bus 7, 73. **Open** *Office* 8am-6pm Mon,Wed, Thur. **No credit cards.**
English-speaking babysitters and full- or part-time nannies. Sitting costs Ft900 and up per hour.

Children's activity centres

Centres offer programmes for kids in the school year, and day camps and events in the holidays.

Almássy tér Recreation Centre
Almássy téri Szabadidő Központ
VII.Almássy tér 6 (352 1572/06 70 33 9947 mobile/www.almassy.hu). M2 Blaha Lujza tér/tram 4, 6. **Open** Sept-June. **Admission** varies. **No credit cards.** **Map** p247 G4.

Activities include craft workshops, swimming courses, singing, dancing and puppet shows. Special events can range from giant hands-on toy exhibits to performances by children's entertainers.

Capital City Cultural Centre
Fővárosi Művelődési Ház
XI.Fehérvári út 47 (203 3868/www.fmhnet.hu). Tram 47, 49. **Admission** varies. **No credit cards.**
Children's theatre shows, folk-dance club for kids with the famous Muzsikás ensemble, playgroups for three- to six-year-olds, and dance, gymnastics and aerobics courses for little ones.

Kids' Park
Kölyökpark
Mammut II, II.Lövőház utca 1-5 (345 8512). M2 Moszkva tér/tram 4, 6. **Open** 10am-9pm Mon-Fri; 9am-9pm Sat; 9am-8pm Sun. **Admission** Ft700 for 30mins. **No credit cards.**
Indoor playground with monkey bars, slides, towers and tunnels, for children up to 12. Drop off the kids while you go shopping in the Mammut mall.

Marczibányi tér Culture House
Marczibányi téri Művelődési Ház
II.Marczibányi tér 5A (212 2820/www.maczi.hu). M2 Moszkva tér/tram 4, 6. **Admission** varies. **No credit cards.**
Craft workshops, a folk-dance club, drawing for four- to seven-year-olds, a playgroup with music for six months to six years, a magicians' school for nine- to 15-year-olds and an excellent playground for younger kids. Special events include puppet shows, pet fairs and concerts by popular performers.

Millenáris Park
II.Fény utca 20-22 (336 4000/www.millenaris.hu). M2 Moszkva tér/tram 4, 6. **Admission** varies. **No credit cards.**
Craft workshops, puppet shows, children's theatre and playgroups in a custom-built venue. Attractions include the Palace of Wonders (*see p165*).

Children's shows

Budapest Puppet Theatre
Budapest Bábszínház
VI.Andrássy út 69 (321 5200). M1 Vörösmarty utca. **Shows** Sept-June 10am, 10.30am, 3pm daily. Closed July, Aug. **Open** *Box office* 9am-6pm daily. **Admission** Ft500-Ft1,200. **No credit cards.** **Map** p246 G3.
International fairy tales and Hungarian folk stories form the repertoire. Language is usually not a problem and the shows are highly original.

Old-fashioned fun all day long at the **Vidám Park**. *See p165.*

Circus

XIV.Állatkerti körút 7 (343 9630/www.maciva.hu).
M1 Széchenyi fürdő. **Shows** 5pm Wed-Fri; 3pm,
7pm Sat; 10.30am, 3pm Sun. **Open** *Box office*
10am-6pm daily. **Admission** Ft1,100-Ft2,200.
Credit AmEx, MC, V. **Map** p247 J1.
A permanent building with shows year-round, but
inside it looks just like an old-fashioned travelling
circus. Global and Hungarian performers with
acrobats, magicians, jugglers, clowns and animals.

Holdvilág Kamaraszínház

XVI.Ságvári utca 3 (405 8759). M2 Örs Vezér tere,
then bus 144 to József utca. **Admission** Ft650-
Ft1,000. **No credit cards.**
Children's plays staged by young actors and directors. Tickets can be reserved by phone from 4pm to
8pm on Wednesdays or bought on the door.

Kolibri Theatre

VI.Jókai tér 10 (353 4633). M1 Oktogon/tram 4, 6.
Shows 10am, 3pm daily. **Open** *Box office Sept-June*
9am-5pm Mon-Fri. Closed July, Aug. **Admission**
Ft850-Ft1,400. **No credit cards. Map** p246 F4.
Small theatre presenting fairy tales.

Planetarium

Népliget, SW corner (265 0725). M3 Népliget.
Open *5 shows* 9.30am-5.30pm Tue-Sun. *Laser*
shows 7.30pm daily. **Admission** Ft940; Ft840
concessions. *Laser shows* Ft2,190; Ft600
concessions. **No credit cards.**

Temporary exhibits as well as educational children's
shows. Popular with older kids. English-language
shows on request for groups of 30 or more.

Health

In an emergency call 104 or 311 9133 and ask
for someone who speaks English. You can also
go to **Heim Pál Children's Hospital:**

Heim Pál Children's Hospital

Heim Pál Gyermekkórház
VIII.Üllői út 86 (210 0720). M3 Nagyvárad tér.
Map p250 K8.

Museums

Budapest has a few good museums for children.
The **Transport Museum** (*see p70* **Offbeat**
treasures) can be fun with its life-size and
model trains, cars and ships. You can climb
the steps of an old engine and peek into the
wagons, and turn a ship's wheel. The aviation
section next door has a collection of old planes.
The **Natural History Museum** (*see p99*)
and the **Palace of Wonders** are the most
interactive. Others of interest include those
for **Telephones**, the **Underground Railway**
(for both *see p70* **Offbeat treasures**) and
the one for **Military History** (*see p68*).

Arts & Entertainment

Palace of Wonders

Csodák palotája

II.Fény utca 20-22 (350 6131/www.csodapalota.hu).
M2 Moszkva tér/tram 4, 6. **Open** 9am-6pm Tue-Fri;
10am-7pm Sat, Sun. **Admission** Ft990; Ft790
concessions. **No credit cards.**

The most modern and interactive of Budapest's
kid-friendly museums, with features such as a climb-
in MIG aeroplane, strange mirrors and light effects.

Music

In the country of Bartók and Kodály, you're
bound to find classical music performances
adapted for children. Their nickname is *Kakaó
koncert,* because the children get hot chocolate
at the end. The most popular are the ones given
by the **Budapest Fesztivál Zenekar**.

Budapest Fesztivál Zenekar

Office *XII.Alkotás út 39C (355 4330).* **Open**
Sept-May 9.30am-5.30pm Mon-Fri. **Map** p248 A6.
Venue *III.Selmeci utca 14-16 Tram 17.*
Concerts 2.30pm, 4.30pm Sun.
Admission Ft1,800. **Credit** AmEx, MC, V.
Information and tickets for the Kakaó koncert series,
as well as the rest of the orchestra's activities.

International Buda Stage

II.Tárogató út 2-4 (391 2525). Tram 56/bus 56.
Admission Ft1,000. **Open** 15 Sept-15 June,
times vary. **No credit cards.**
Classical music concerts for kids.

Folk music

The folk music movement doesn't leave kids
out of the fun. Venues (*see pp189-190*) may be
closed in July and August, but if you're ready
for a week of intensive boot-slapping and craft
workshops, you should call any of the dance
houses (*táncházak*) and enquire about summer
camps. **Muzsikás,** the best-known Hungarian
folk band, offers a weekly *táncház* for kids at
the **Fővárosi Művelődési Ház** (XI.Fehérvári
út 47, 203 3868), with live folk music and the
teaching of traditional dances, including folk
tales and games. The **Kalamajka Dance
House** turns into a wild *táncház* at night,
after children's songs, dances and folk tales.

Outdoor activities

Amusement park

Vidám Park

*XIV.Állatkerti körút 14-16 (363 8310/www.vidam
park.hu).* M1 Széchenyi fürdő. **Open** mid Mar-Oct
11am-7pm Mon-Fri; 10am-8pm Sat, Sun. Closed
Nov-mid Mar. **Admission** *Day pass* Ft3,100-Ft3,500;
Ft2,100-Ft2,500 concessions; free children under
100cm. **Credit** AmEx, MC, V. **Map** p247 J1.

Pride of place goes to the laser dodgems and other
recently installed hi-tech games. The old wooden
rollercoaster and ancient merry-go-round have been
lovingly restored. Next door is the renovated funfair
(Kis Vidám Park) for toddlers. **Photos** *p164.*

Parks & playgrounds

City Park

Városliget

M1 Hősök tere/Széchenyi fürdő. **Map** p247 H1-K3.
There's a lot here apart from the zoo, amusement
park and circus listed elsewhere. The first feature is
the boating pond and skating rink immediately
behind Heroes' Square. Ice skating in winter is a
must (*see p198*), and skates can be hired cheaply on-
site. Nearby is Vajdahunyad Castle, housing the
Agriculture Museum (*see p70* **Offbeat treasures**),
filled with stuffed animals and tools. There are slides
and wooden castles in the south corner, and a fenced
playground with a treehouse, safe slides and monkey bars. The playground between the zoo and the
pond is also in good shape and has a trampoline
area. For ball games, check out the five-a-side football pitches, basketball and tennis courts behind
Petőfi Csarnok on the east side of the park.

Honvéd tér

M3 Nyugati pu./tram 4, 6. **Open** 8am-sunset daily.
Admission free. **Map** p246 E3.
A centrally located, fenced playground, with lots of
fun rides for all ages.

József Nádor tér

M1, M2, M3 Deák tér/tram 47, 49. **Open** 7am-
sunset daily. **Admission** free. **Map** p246 D5.
A great playground with wooden castles, a ship
with slides, swings, ride-on toys, a sandpit and a
stream with tiny dams for watery experiments.

Károlyi Garden

Károlyi kert

*V.Magyar utca/Henszlmann Imre utca/Ferenczy
István utca. M2 Astoria/M3 Kálvin tér/tram 47,
49.* **Open** 8am-sunset daily. **Admission** free.
Map p249 F6.
One of the cleanest fenced-in playgrounds in the
downtown area. Includes a sandpit, a slide, ride-on
toys and two ball areas.

Klauzál tér

M2 Blaha Lujza tér/tram 4, 6. **Open** 8am-sunset
daily. **Admission** free. **Map** p246 F5.
A nice playground in the heart of busy and sometimes smelly District VII. Dogs have their own park
(that is, toilet) next door.

Margaret Island

Margit-sziget

Tram 4, 6/M3 Nyugati pu., then bus 26, 26A.
Map p245 C1-D1.
A massive recreational area in the middle of the
Danube, with grassy spaces, old trees, swimming
pools, playgrounds and a small petting zoo with

Arts & Entertainment

domestic animals. You can rent bicycles, four-wheeled pedalos and tiny electric cars for children. Horse-drawn carts and open-topped minibuses leave on round trips every half hour. The best playground is near the Alfréd Hajós swimming pool on the south-west side, and the best swimming is to be had at the summer-only Palatinus Strand, which also features an open-air thermal pool (see p200). Everything is an easy journey from town; avoid hot weekends, when crowds snake from the ticket desk window.

Óbuda Island
Óbudai Sziget
HÉV to Filatorigát/bus 142/boat from Vigadó tér.
An island full of green areas and long slides just north of Árpád Bridge. It's ideal for picnickers, kite-flyers, skaters and cyclists.

Szabadság tér
M2 Kossuth Lajos tér/M3 Arany János utca. **Open** 8am-sunset daily. **Admission** free. **Map** p246 E4.
Newly built playgrounds on the two sides of a park in the heart of the city.

Skating & skateboarding

Although Heroes' Square (Hősök tere) is teen Budapest's favourite rollerskating and skateboarding area, more fanatical skaters can go to **Görzenál Skatepark** (see p198) for hours of well-paved fun. In-line skates and skateboards can be rented on the spot. Near the Mammut mall in Buda, **ProCross** (see p198) sells all kinds of skate gear.

Once the rink in the **City Park** closes in March (see p198), you can go skating in the **Pólus Center** (www.polus.com).

Zoo

Állatkert
XIV.Városligeti körút 6-12 (273 4900/www.zoo budapest.com). M1 Széchenyi fürdő. **Open** *Winter* 9am-4pm daily. *Summer* 9am-5.30pm Mon-Thur; 9am-7pm Fri-Sun. **Admission** Ft1,700 adults; Ft1,200 children; free under-2s; Ft5,500 family of 4. **No credit cards. Map** p247 H1-J1.
The zoo has developed tremendously in the last few years. There are new green areas, more animal-friendly cages and a great new playground. Animal names are written in English and Hungarian, and an English-language booklet with map is available for Ft500. You'll need a whole afternoon to see everything, including animal shows, a petting corner and a maze with questions on fauna and flora to help you find your way out. Animals are housed in stunning art nouveau buildings. There's an indoor play area (Ft500-Ft600 per hour, free for adults) and one of the few public nappy-changing rooms in town. Don't miss the newly renovated palm house and aquarium, the elephant house and the monkey islands.

Train & boat rides

For the Buda Hills, a cogwheel train sets off from opposite the Budapest Hotel (M2 Moszkva tér, then two stops on trams 18 or 56). If you ride all the way up to Széchenyi Hill, about 25 minutes, you can walk across the park to the **Children's Railway** – operated by children, except for the engine drivers. This doesn't run often in low season, so check the schedule by phone (397 5394) or spend the waiting time in the neighbouring playground.

Chairlift
Libegő
(394 3764). M2 Moszkva tér, then bus 158 to terminus. **Open** 10am-5pm daily. **Tickets** Ft500; Ft200 concessions. **No credit cards**.
This slow and gentle ski lift-style ride sweeps right up to the top of János-hegy, the highest hill within the city limits and equipped with a lookout tower.

Funicular
Sikló
I.Clark Ádám tér (201 9128). Tram 19. **Open** 7.30am-10pm Tue-Sun. **Tickets** *Single* Ft700; Ft400 concessions. *Return* Ft1,300; Ft750 concessions. **No credit cards. Map** p248 C5.
The funicular goes from Clark Ádám tér up to the Castle District. It's a short ride, but the view is great.

Nostalgia Train
Nosztalgia vonat
Information & tickets Nyugati station, VI.Nyugati tér (269 5242). M3 Nyugati pu./tram 4, 6. **Tickets** *Single* Ft1,800-Ft2,200; Ft900 concessions. *Return* Ft2,500-Ft2,800; Ft1,200 concessions. **No credit cards. Map** p246 F3.
Hungarian Railways operate a steam engine with old-fashioned carriages, which leaves Nyugati station at 9.40am and takes 90 minutes to puff its way up to Szob on Saturdays from May to September. After time for lunch and a walk along the river, the train returns at 4.35pm, reaching Nyugati at 6pm. At the same time, another child-friendly train leaves for Esztergom up the Danube Bend. Tickets are priced around the same as regular trains, but for an extra Ft500 you can visit the driver and get a steam-engine driver's licence.

Boat trips

The cheapest boat ride down the Danube runs between the Pest end of Petőfi Bridge and Pünkösdfürdő in the north of Budapest, stopping at each of the bridges and Vigadó tér on the way. This is free for under-fours, Ft350 for over-fours and Ft700 for adults.
Any number of sightseeing tours leave from the Vigadó tér terminus on the Pest embankment. They usually cost Ft3,000, half price for under-14s. Call Tourinform (438 8080) or IBUSZ (485 2767) for details. *See p60* **Budapest by boat.**

Film

Viewer-friendly Hungarian films now play alongside Hollywood blockbusters.

Although American blockbusters still rule the domestic market, Hungary is making a good fist of attracting local audiences to Magyar films as well: the country has started to produce films ranging from light comedies to more digestible art films. Until recently, commercial films were frowned upon and the tradition of making art films was very strong. But now filmmakers have realised that they have to bring the audience back to the cinemas. The number of Hungarian films being screened has significantly increased, partly thanks to multiplexes like the **Corvin** or the **Mammut**. This trend has also affected arthouse cinemas, although they still keep their original profiles. Helping this transition is a new generation of filmmakers, with **György Pálfi** (*see p171* **Arsenic and old lace**) at the forefront. Some stick to well-known recipes for commercial films, others experiment more and attempt to break into the international market. An increasing number of co-productions and the import-export of actors brings the hope of putting the country back on the map. It looks like Hungarian cinema is slowly awakening from its long sleep.

The old tradition of arthouse films hasn't died out, with the same cinemas equally popular. Many have received grants for renovation, so their niche audience need no longer put up with uncomfortable seats, dirty screens and bad sound quality. The **Művész** is the biggest to show independent European and American releases, while smaller places like the **Toldi** or **Cirko-gejzír** screen more bizarre stuff. The latter even has its own distribution company, buying rare delicacies that would never reach the country otherwise. These are also meeting places with cafés that open late; the **Puskin** and the **Bem** are busy destination bars in their own right.

Some cinemas are architectural treasures, the restored, century-old **Uránia Nemzeti Filmszínház** being a classic case in point. Take one of the themed boxes here and it won't matter what's playing that night.

TIPS AND LISTINGS

Most movies released in Hungary are screened in the original language with subtitles, but always check beforehand: subtitled is *feliratos* ('*fel.*'), dubbed *szinkronizált* (or '*mb.*'). Dubbing is generally reserved for cartoons, family-oriented movies and the mainstream action films and comedies usually shown at the big multiplexes. English-language films shown at art cinemas are invariably screened with their original soundtrack.

Tickets are cheap. Admission prices run from about Ft300 to Ft1,250, and many theatres have matinee prices or reductions from Monday to Wednesday. Seating is assigned by seat and row number: *szék* is seat, *sor* is row, *bal oldal* designates the left side, *jobb oldal* the right side, *közép* the middle and *erkély* the balcony.

The major English-language movie guide is featured in the weekly *Budapest Sun*, although it often misses out the more esoteric cinemas. Also useful are the Hungarian magazines *Pesti Műsor* and *Pesti Est*. The latter can be picked up free around town. *Pesti Est* includes a film guide in English. In Hungarian schedules, '*É*' refers to the show times: *n9* is 8.15pm, *f9* is 8.30pm, *h9* is 8.45pm. '*De*' means morning, '*du*' is afternoon, '*este*' is evening and '*éjjel*' refers to late screenings.

Certain cinemas have ticket reservation through a central number. For the Corvin, the Művész, Puskin, **Szinbád** and **Tabán**, call 459 5050 and name the cinema you want to go to. All multiplexes belonging to the Palace chain (**Palace Kossuth**, **Palace Mammut** and **Palace Westend**) have the same system with the central number being 999 6161. For other cinemas check in *Pesti Est* and look for '*jegyrendelés*' or '*jegy*', or ticket reservation.

Cinemas

Uránia Nemzeti Filmszínház
VII.Rákóczi út 21 (486 3413/486 3414/www.urania-nf.hu). Bus 7, 78. **Box office** from 1hr before 1st show. **Last show** 9pm. **Tickets** Ft620-Ft890; Ft440-Ft730 Mon. **No credit cards.** 3 screens. **Map** p247 H5.
If you're looking for a unique cinematic experience at an affordable price, treat yourself to one of the seven exclusive boxes: try *Kék Angyal* (Blue Angel), *Nagy Ábránd* (Grand Illusion) or *Díszterem* (Main Hall), where you are served from the café during the show if you order beforehand. The impressive Venetian/Moorish-style building has been restored to its original glory after more than a century – the first independent Hungarian feature was shot here in 1901. As Hungary's National Film Theatre, it features new local releases as well as international ones.

Art cinemas & second-run houses

Bem

II.Margit körút 5B (316 8708). Tram 4, 6. **Box office** from 30min before 1st show. **Last show** 9.30pm. **Tickets** Ft720. **No credit cards**. 1 screen. **Map** p245 C2.

This newly restored cinema combines comfortable seats and good sound quality with a selection of art films and the latest Hungarian releases; it also screens second runs. Late, lively bar too.

Cirko-gejzir

V.Balassi Bálint utca 15-17 (269 1915). Tram 2. **Box office** from 30min before 1st show. **Last show** 9pm. **Tickets** Ft500-Ft850. **No credit cards**. 2 screens. **Map** p246 D2.

This small cinema showcases obscure independent movies from all over the world. All films are screened with original sound and Hungarian subtitles. Free mineral water is offered on hot days and tea in winter. Leave your bike in the lobby.

Hunnia

VII.Erzsébet körút 26 (06 30 941 4572 mobile). M2 Blaha Lujza tér/tram 4, 6. **Box office** from 30mins before 1st show. **Last show** 9-10pm. **Tickets** Ft390-Ft500. **No credit cards**. 1 screen. **Map** p247 G5.

The Hunnia specialises in showing cult classics such as *Clerks* and *Pulp Fiction,* peppering the schedule with the occasional money-maker. The café, open till midnight, is busy whatever happens to be playing.

Művész

VI.Teréz körút 30 (332 6726/central ticket reservation 459 5050). M1 Oktogon/tram 4, 6. **Box office** from 1hr before 1st show. **Last show** 10.30pm. **Tickets** Ft700-Ft1,050. **Credit** MC, V. 5 screens. **Map** p246 F3.

The most successful art cinema in the region. The Művész usually offers a new independent release or two, with the remainder of its five halls featuring nightly changing programmes of the world's art films from the last decade. Soundtrack CDs and art books are sold in the lobby. Guarded bike parking available during shows.

Odeon-Lloyd

XIII.Hollán Ernő utca 7 (329 2064). Tram 2, 4, 6. **Box office** from 1hr before 1st show. **Last show** 9pm. **Tickets** Ft400; Ft750 for 1st show Sat, Sun. **No credit cards**. 1 screen. **Map** p246 D2.

The Odeon video-rental service (*see p170*) took over the Duna and created the Odeon-Lloyd, which shows classics from *Psycho* to *Betty Blue*. The screening hall has the latest technology and comfortable seats, the decoration is stylishly simple, and there's a café.

Örökmozgó Filmmúzeum

VII.Erzsébet körút 39 (342 2167). Tram 4, 6. **Box office** from 4pm. **Last show** 8.30pm. **Tickets** Ft500-Ft800. **No credit cards**. 1 screen. **Map** p246 G4.

Known for its eclectic schedule of everything from silents to documentaries. Foreign-language films in this small house, subsidised by the Hungarian Film Archive, are played with their original sound and simultaneous Hungarian translation via headsets. Newer films often have English subtitles.

Puskin

V.Kossuth Lajos utca 18 (central ticket reservation 459 5050). M2 Astoria/tram 47, 49/bus 7. **Box office** from 9.30am. **Last show** 9.30pm. **Tickets** Ft700-Ft1,050. **Credit** MC, V. 3 screens. **Map** p249 F6.

This 420-seat house features major Hollywood releases, while its second and third screens play previously released movies, art films and Hungarian releases. The Puskin has a branch of the Odeon video rental shop (*see p170*) upstairs and is also connected to the popular Puskin café around the corner, which has free Wi-Fi.

Szindbád

XIII.Szent István körút 16 (349 2773/central ticket reservation 459 5050). M3 Nyugati pu./tram 4, 6. **Box office** from 30mins before 1st show. **Last show** 8.30-9pm. **Tickets** Ft500-Ft720. **No credit cards**. 2 screens. **Map** p246 E2.

This decent two-screen art cinema is often the only place to see contemporary Hungarian releases with English subtitles. The Szindbád also screens second-runs. The smaller screening hall is accessible for wheelchair users.

Tabán

I.Krisztina körút 87-89 (356 8162/central ticket reservation 459 5050). Tram 18/bus 5, 78, 105. **Box office** from 1hr before 1st show. **Last show** 8.45pm. **Tickets** Ft660. **No credit cards**. **Map** p245 A3.

Nestled in the old Serbian quarter of the city, this tiny theatre usually plays several English-language gems a week. German and French films also feature. Sound and picture quality are sometimes below par. There's also a video-rental library and friendly café.

Toldi

V.Bajcsy-Zsilinszky út 36-38 (472 0397). M3 Arany János utca. **Box office** from 30mins before 1st show. **Last show** 9.30pm. **Tickets** Ft540-Ft850. **No credit cards**. 2 screens. **Map** p246 C3.

Large venue featuring modern independent releases and Hungarian features old and new. Hungarian, Czech and Polish animation films from the 1970s and 1980s are shown on Sunday afternoons. The bar is ideal for an afternoon coffee or an evening beer.

Vörösmarty

VIII.Üllői út 4 (317 4542). M3 Kálvin tér/tram 47, 49. **Box office** from 30mins before 1st show. **Last show** 9pm. **Tickets** Ft300-Ft700. **No credit cards**. 2 screens. **Map** p249 F7.

Small, quiet and centrally located, this cinema offers weekend matinées for Ft300 and 50 per cent concession on Mondays. There's also a popular bar, and a separated space for exhibitions.

Arts & Entertainment

Hungarian classics and Hollywood blockbusters, all available at the **Odeon**. *See p170.*

Multiplexes

Some multiplexes are set in suburban malls; the Palace Westend (VI.Váci út 1-3, central ticket reservation 999 6161, www.palacecinemas.hu) behind Nyugati station is the most central.

Corvin Budapest Filmpalota

VIII.Corvin köz 1 (459 5059/central ticket reservation 459 5050/www.corvin.hu). M3 Ferenc körút/tram 4, 6. **Box office** from 9am. **Last show** 10.30pm. **Tickets** Ft950-Ft1,150. **Credit** AmEx, DC, MC, V. Free parking with cinema ticket. 6 screens. **Map** p250 G7.

The city's best multiplex. The attractive building, a resistance stronghold in the 1956 Uprising, has the latest projection and sound equipment, a branch of the Odeon video-rental service (*see right*) and a café.

Palace Kossuth

XIII.Váci út 14 (320 4250/central ticket reservation 999 6161/www.palacecinemas.hu). M3 Nyugati pu./tram 4, 6. **Box office** from 9.30am. **Last show** 10pm. **Tickets** Ft690-Ft990. **No credit cards.** 4 screens. **Map** p245 E2.

Decent seats and a first-rate sound system are the important elements here, as is the Kossuth's policy of featuring English-language first-runs that other cinemas will only show in dubbed versions.

Palace Mammut

II.Lövőház utca 2-6 (345 8131/central ticket reservation 999 6161/www.palacecinemas.hu). M2 Moszkva tér/tram 4, 6. **Box office** from 9.30am. **Last show** 10.45pm. **Tickets** Ft800-Ft1,250. **Credit** AmEx, DC, MC, V. Free parking with cinema ticket. 13 screens. **Map** p245 A3.

Mostly features Hollywood blockbusters and new Hungarian releases. Mammut I is the main venue for the Magyar Filmszemle (*see below*).

Film festivals

Magyar Filmszemle

Magyar Film Művészek Szövetsége, VI.Városligeti fasor 38 (342 4760/351 7760/www.magyarfilm.hu/ www.mmka.hu). **Date** late Jan/early Feb.

The main event in the Hungarian cinema calendar. Each January or February, at several venues around town, the Magyar Filmszemle (Hungarian Film Festival) shows all domestic features, documentaries and shorts produced within the previous calendar year. Awards are presented for numerous categories.

Mediawave

Festival Office H-9021 Győr, Kazinczy út 3-5 (06 96 517 666/fax 06 96 517 669/http://mwave. irq.hu/www.mediawave.hu). **Date** Apr.

Held in Győr, 125km west of Budapest, Mediawave has become Hungary's major international competitive festival for short, experimental and documentary films. Music, theatre and dance performances are equally important at this week-long event, usually held towards the end of April.

Titanic International Film Festival

Titanic Nemzetközi Filmfesztivál www.titanicfilmfest.hu. **Date** Apr.

A showing of new arthouse and cult movies from Asia, Europe and North America, plus an excellent dual-language catalogue. Award for best movie.

Anilogue Budapest International Animation Festival

Anilogue Budapesti Nemzetközi Animációs Fesztivál Festival office Szimplafilm,VII.Kertész utca 48 (321 5880). **Date** Nov-Dec.

The largest Hungarian animation film festival. Four days are packed with shows, a competition for European short animations and animation features, and a daily after-party that includes drinks and a seven-hour non-stop screening. Also has an international workshop.

Video & DVD rental

Most English-language videos are dubbed into Hungarian, but older releases are subtitled. All video shops will have titles in English.

Municipal Ervin Szabó Library

Fővárosi Szabó Ervin Könyvtár VIII.Szabó Ervin tér 1 (411 5052). M3 Kálvin tér. **Open** 10am-8pm Mon-Fri; 10am-4pm Sat. **Membership** 6mths Ft2,400; 1yr Ft3,600. **Map** p249 F7.

From autumn 2007 the collection of the British Council Library will be relocated to the Municipal Szabó Ervin Library. Superb selection of UK TV shows, documentaries and sitcoms.

Odeon

XIII.Hollán Ernő utca 7 (349 2776). Tram 4, 6. **Open** 10am-11pm daily. **Rental** *Video* Ft400-Ft500/ night (plus refundable Ft3,000 deposit). *DVD* Ft510-Ft680/night (plus refundable Ft5,000 deposit). **Map** p246 D2.

Original soundtrack videos of US and UK features and a large collection of DVDs from blockbusters to arthouse films. Renowned for its collection of Magyar classics subtitled in English (most of them in the Puskin branch). **Photos** *p169*.

Other locations: Corvin Multiplex, VIII.Corvin köz 1 (313 9896; open 10am-11pm daily); Puskin, V.Kossuth Lajos utca 18 (318 6464; open 10am-10pm daily); Tabán, I.Krisztina körút 87-89 (213 7730; open 4-10pm Mon-Fri; 3-9pm Sat, Sun).

Video Mania

VI.Nagymező utca 27 (331 7175). M1 Opera. **Open** 10am-10pm Mon-Thur, Sun; 10am-midnight Fri, Sat. **Rental** *Video* Ft430-Ft720/night (plus one-off Ft2,500 deposit). **Map** p246 D3.

This popular video outlet offers a comprehensive selection of movies in several European languages, as well as English.

Other locations: Rózsadomb Center, II.Törökvészi út 87-91 (345 8449; open 10am-10pm daily).

Arts & Entertainment

Arsenic and old lace

Hungarian films have the reputation of being depressing, with a grim outlook that only locals can appreciate. But a new generation of directors is trying to prove that Magyar film can be entertaining too. One of the pioneers of this movement is **György Pálfi**, born in 1974, who stresses the importance of using humour and innovation. For him the new cinema has to be more viewer-friendly and attract interest on various levels.

Pálfi has no role model, only a long list of favourite films from all genres. 'I grew up on *Star Wars* and *Jaws*,' he confesses, 'and only discovered arthouse films at a later stage in my life.' 'A later stage' might be exaggerating, as Pálfi is still starting out on a promising career. At 33, not only has he won awards for his two features *Hukkle* and *Taxidermia*, he has also received the Knight's Cross of the Order of Merit of the Hungarian Republic.

Hukkle, his first feature, produced while at the Academy of Drama and Film, catches moments from life in a remote Hungarian village where women poison the husbands they no longer desire. This gloomy premise may sound like the depressing type of film Pálfi set out to fight. What's more, there's not a word of dialogue in the whole 78 minutes. Yet *Hukkle* nails viewers to their seats with breathtaking images and funny storytelling. It's impossible not to like the old man sitting peacefully on a bench, hiccupping throughout, who takes no active part in the events.

Most of the actors are amateurs and Pálfi spent a lot of time in the village before shooting the film. The great cinematography is the work of Gergely Pohárnok, Pálfi's former fellow student from the Film Academy, who also shows his talent in *Taxidermia*. 'I've been with Gergely since college,' says Pálfi. 'Our generation should work together to revive Hungarian cinema and start a new chapter.'

Pálfi's second feature, *Taxidermia* (*see photo*), is equally strong in originality and visuals, although more challenging for the viewer. Some people find it scandalous and leave before the end – some say it's a work of genius. *Taxidermia* was screened to a full house at Cannes and was highly praised by critics. Telling the tale of three generations based on short stories by contemporary Hungarian writer Lajos Parti Nagy, the film is an audacious undertaking, grotesque, morbid and often nauseating. Pálfi joked that the tagline should be: 'Don't take your girlfriend'. Or anyone under 18 in fact, because of the rating the movie got in many countries. Also, resist the temptation to buy any snacks or you might feel the need to throw up along with the speed-eating champion father or the taxidermist son stuffing himself to crown his oeuvre. It might help to know that no human was harmed while making the film – the flesh was all pork from the local market.

Hukkle and *Taxidermia* are available on DVD in 20 countries, including the UK and USA.

Galleries

Dynamic artist-run spaces vie for attention with major institutions.

Figurehead of the alternative movement – the **Liget Galéria**. See p176.

See p176.

There are two ways of approaching the local art scene: through what major institutions offer as the best Hungarian art; and via the grassroots, from which a quite different picture emerges. The usual starting point for the art lover to discover in Budapest is the **Ludwig Museum**, located in a new wing of the Palace of Arts on the Pest bank. Its permanent collection serves as an introduction to the key players of post-war art, but the story of local art it presents is far from complete. The **Műcsarnok** has vast rooms in a grand 19th-century pavilion on Heroes' Square but takes imagination to transform into a space for contemporary art.

Yet scratch the surface and you'll find many small and medium-sized galleries and artist-run spaces which offer dynamic and diverse programmes and events. The **Trafó** has regular high-quality shows and international collaborations. The Studio Association of Young Artists (**FKSE**) has a pedigree of presenting the latest talent, and is sure to gain a fresh lease of life in its new home on Rottenbiller utca. **IMPEX** is a prominent artist-run space, whose volunteer staff run shows, talks and projects of a standard that competes with the Ludwig. See p175 **Watch this space**.

The commercial galleries should also not be overlooked – many try to present challenging contemporary art. While some specialise in photography, such as the **Vintage Gallery**, or drawings and animation, such as **Karton Gallery**, others have a revolving programme of painting, video, installations and conceptual interventions. **Knoll Gallery**, **ACB** and the recently opened **Kisterem** are among the most prominent, representing local bluechips such as **Attila Szűcs**, **Csaba Nemes** and **Imre Bak**.

New art quarters are crystalising. One area of activity is on and around **Ráday utca**, where the local council has brought new galleries such as **2B** and **Videospace Budapest**. The other zone is the quirky outer 7th District from Keleti station to Városliget, currently thriving on the

See p175 **Watch this space**.

energy of pre-gentrification. Meanwhile, the traditional inner-city art sites are in decline – sites such as Andrássy út, where contemporary art appears only in the commissioned window displays of **Louis Vuitton** (*see p146*).

The cosy camaraderie of the post-Communist decade has given way to an intense competitive spirit in today's art scene. The frenetic pace of projects and collaborations is driven by the euro slush fund for cultural regeneration, while an glut of art funding is causing overproduction and overload for local audiences. The ever-present generational quarrel is manifested in major institutions where either the old guard cling to power or younger appointees are unwilling to follow their predecessors. Debates flare up between young art professionals and their former teachers, reluctant to relinquish their authority and privileged position.

Details of exhibitions (*kiállítások*) and performances are on **Index** (www.exindex.hu), a listing of all that's worthy in public and private spaces. It also has a map of the city's exhibition spaces and a printed copy can be picked up at the larger venues listed below. The online version has listings in English and announces openings (*megnyitók*) for the forthcoming seven days. While most contemporary art still resides in the capital, the regional scene is increasingly active, especially in **Pécs**, where Fine Art is also taught at the local university, in **Dunaújváros**, the home of Hungary's Institute of Contemporary Art (www.ica-d.hu), and at the recently opened **MODEM** art centre (Baltazár Dezső tér 1, 052 518 476) in **Debrecen**.

Public galleries

Barcsay Terem

VI.Andrássy út 69-71 (342 1738). M1 Vörösmarty utca. **Open** 10am-6pm Mon-Fri; 10am-1pm Sat. **Admission** free. **No credit cards**. **Map** p246 G3.
Tell the stern security guard that you've come for the exhibition, and he'll let you through the turnstile and into the heart of the Hungarian Art Academy. The Barcsay is up the grand staircase and has regular noteworthy shows.

Budapest Gallery Exhibition House

III.Lajos utca 158 (388 6771). Tram 1. **Open** 10am-6pm Tue-Sun. **Admission** Ft400; Ft200 concessions. **No credit cards**.
Located on the outskirts of Óbuda, the Exhibition House feels like a relic from the Communist past, an old-fashioned space with elderly attendants – there is even a permanent exhibition to Pál Pátzay, the sculptor of Budapest's Lenin monument. The gallery is a non-profit institution funded by the Budapest City Council, at which to catch eclectic and offbeat exhibitions of emerging Hungarian artists.

Ernst Museum

VI.Nagymező utca 8 (341 4355/www.ernst museum.hu). M1 Opera/M1 Oktogon. **Open** 11am-7pm Tue-Sun. **Admission** Ft500; Ft300 concessions. **No credit cards**. **Map** p246 F4.
Recognisable at street level by its beautiful brass art nouveau doors, the Ernst was designed as an exhibition space in a block of artists' studios commissioned by the private collector of the same name in 1912. Despite the excellent location and exhibition facilities, since the troubled separation from the Műcsarnok in 2000, the Ernst has struggled to redefine its identity. It is best known for hosting the annual show for Derkovits scholarship artists.

Kicselli Museum

III.Kiscelli utca 108 (388 7817/www.btmfk.iif.hu). Tram 17. **Open** 10am-6pm Tue-Sun. **Admission** Ft700; Ft350 concessions. **No credit cards**.
Officially a branch of the Hungarian History Museum, out in leafy Óbuda, mainly known for its collection of 19th-century plaster busts, the Kicselli is not a place people would automatically connect with contemporary art. The in-house Municipal Picture Gallery has reversed this trend in recent years by raising its profile on the local art scene with a regular series of shows.

Ludwig Museum

IX.Komor Marcell utca 1 (555 3444/www.ludwig museum.hu). Tram 1, 2, 24. **Open** 10am-8pm Tue-Sun. **Admission** *Temporary exhibitions* Ft1,200; Ft600 concessions. **No credit cards**. **Map** p250 inset.
The Ludwig Museum was founded in 1989 and hosts one part of the collection of chocolate manufacturers Peter and Irene Ludwig – other parts are in Ludwig Museums in Germany, Moscow and Beijing. This is Budapest's main museum of contemporary art, and a good place for a post-1960s overview of Hungarian and Central European art – although it is criticised locally for failing to promote genuinely challenging art and for an over-reliance on blockbusters and travelling exhibitions.

Mai Manó

VI.Nagymező utca 20 (302 4398/www.maimano.hu). M1 Opera/M1 Oktogon. **Open** 2-7pm Tue-Sun. **Admission** Ft700; Ft300 concessions. **No credit cards**. **Map** p246 F4.
Set in an appropriately photogenic fin-de-siècle gem, known as the Mai Manó after the photographer who built it, the House of Hungarian Photographers is a consistent part of Budapest gallery life and the place at which to find out more about the rich local photographic tradition dating back over a century.

Műcsarnok

XIV.Dózsa György út 37 (460 7000/www. mucsarnok.hu). M1 Hősök tere. **Open** *Museum* 10am-6pm Tue, Wed, Fri-Sun; noon-8pm Thur. *Library & archive* 2-5pm Mon, Wed; 10am-2pm Thur. **Admission** Ft1,500; Ft800 concessions. **Credit** MC, V. **Map** p247 J2.

Standly grandly on Heroes' Square, the Műcsarnok was established in 1896 as the exhibition hall of the Society of Artists. This is Hungary's largest space devoted to temporary exhibitions of domestic and international artists; huge eclectic shows focused on a single medium, painting or sculpture, give a real idea of the range of Hungarian artistic production. Recent ones have included 'Az Út', related to the 1956 Uprising, and 'Dreamlands Burn', a survey of new Nordic art. The Műcsarnok co-organises late autumn's Plug Contemporary Art Fair.

Polish Institute – Platán Gallery

VI.Andrássy út 32 (331 1168/www.polinst.co.hu). M1 Opera. **Open** 11am-7pm Tue-Fri. **Admission** free. **No credit cards. Map** p246 F4.
Foreign cultural centres in Budapest used to have worthy art agendas and significant shows. Today only the recommended Platán continues in this vein, showing the best of Polish contemporary art.

Commercial galleries

ACB

VI.Király utca 76 (413 7608/www.acbgaleria.hu). Tram 4, 6. **Open** 2-6pm Tue-Fri; 11am-2pm Sat. **Admission** free. **No credit cards. Map** p246 F4.
Since opening in 2003, the ACB has secured an enviable reputation for its business-like approach to contemporary art. By cultivating the careers of leading Hungarians like video artist Tamás Komoróczky, sculptor Attila Csörgő and painter Attila Szűcs, the ACB is well positioned to capitalise on an emerging circle of local collectors.

Deák Erika Gallery

VI.Jókai tér 1 (302 4927/www.deakgaleria. t-online.hu). M1 Oktogon/tram 4, 6. **Open** noon-6pm Wed-Fri; noon-3pm Sat. **Admission** free. **No credit cards. Map** p246 F4.
This established gallery has friendly openings and collectable shows by the likes of László Lakner, KisPál Szabolcs and Tibor Iski Kocsis.

Dovin Gallery

V.Galamb utca 6 (318 3673/www.dovingaleria.hu). M3 Ferenciek tere/tram 2/bus 15. **Open** noon-6pm Tue-Fri; 11am-2pm Sat. **Admission** free. **No credit cards. Map** p249 E6.
This private gallery in a prime location has built a stable of prominent Hungarian artists such as sculptor Andrea Huszár and painter Levente Baranyai. It has a programme of discussions primarily devoted to the issue of landscape in contemporary art.

Karton Galéria

V.Alkotmány utca 18 (472 0000/www.karton.hu). M3 Nyugati pu./M2 Kossuth tér. **Open** 1-6pm Mon-Fri; 10am-2pm Sat. **Admission** free. **No credit cards. Map** p246 E3.
This well-designed gallery specialising in animation, caricature and comics in the heart of Budapest's business district has private views that are a cut above the local norm.

Kisterem

V.Képíró utca 5 (267 0522/www.kisterem.hu). M3 Kálvin tér. **Open** 2-6pm Tue-Fri. **Admission** free. **No credit cards. Map** p249 F6.
A recent addition to the commercial scene, within the Ráday utca radius, the Kisterem specialises in challenging contemporary art. The gallery is run by Margit Valkó, with a discerning eye for new trends.

Knoll Gallery

VI.Liszt Ferenc tér 10 (267 3842/www.knoll galerie.at). M1 Oktogon/tram 4, 6. **Open** 2-6.30pm Tue-Fri; 11am-2pm Sat. **Admission** free. **No credit cards. Map** p246 F4.
Established in 1989 by Austrian Hans Knoll, this is one of Budapest's most respected private galleries. He exhibits well known Hungarian artists, such as Ákos Birkas and Csaba Nemes, and artists from neighbouring countries in line with the gallery's cultivated Central European profile.

Várfok 14 Gallery

I.Várfok utca 14 (213 5155/www.varfok-galeria.hu). M2 Moszkva tér/tram 4, 6, 18. **Open** 11am-6pm Tue-Sat. **Admission** free. **No credit cards. Map** p245 A4.
In 1990 enterprising collector Károly Szalóky chose the strategic road leading from Moszkva tér to the Castle District for his first gallery, which he used to promote the work of a dozen bankable artists, including Imre Bukta, István Nadler and El Kazovszkij. He also runs several other galleries on the same street including the XO Galéria at no.11.

Vintage Gallery

V.Magyar utca 26 (337 0584/www.vintage.hu). M2 Astoria/tram 47, 49/bus 7. **Open** 2-6pm Tue-Fri. **Admission** free. **No credit cards. Map** p249 F6.
This small gallery with an ambitious profile features contemporary photographic work by leading local artists including Balázs Beöthy and Hajnal Németh.

Independent spaces

FKSE

VII.Rottenbiller utca 35 (342 5380/www.c3.hu). Trolleybus 74. **Open** 4-8pm Tue-Fri; noon-4pm Sat. **Admission** free. **No credit cards. Map** p247 H4.
The Studio of Young Artists is the flagship of a national organisation whose full membership is limited to those under 35. The Studio is committed to the promotion of the work of its 300 or so members through exhibitions, the provision of cheap studio space, international exchange programmes and publications. Its agenda includes the annual springtime Gallery by Night event, a week-long series of late-night shows focusing on a different artist each night.

IMPEX

VIII.Futó utca 48 (06 20 966 9674 mobile/www. impex-info.org). M3 Ferenc körút/M3 Klinikák/ tram 4, 6. **Open** 4-7pm Wed; 8-11pm Thur-Sat. **Admission** free. **No credit cards. Map** p250 H6.

Watch this space

The most innovative venues for contemporary art have arisen from the rapid process of urban change transforming Budapest. A number of projects reflect the side effects of this trend, such as Csaba Nemes' comments on the erosion and exploitation of cultural identities in his photographic series *CBA*, documenting the disappearance of Socialist-era ABC supermarkets and their cynical reincarnation as national supermarket chain CBA. Miklós Erhardt's *Havana* is a project set in the housing estate bearing the same name that involved renovating a disused shop to create an office in which the unemployed could offer advice to artists on how to get by. In the case of Tamás Kaszás, it was the artist who gave advice to potential activists on the ins and outs of squatting to introduce the movement to Hungary.

Launched in 2006, artist-run 'contemporary art provider' **IMPEX** (*see p174; pictured*) is already an unmissable venue on the local art scene. It occupies the upper floors of the West Balkan nightspot, in a building to be demolished in one of the biggest urban regeneration projects in Central Europe. The gallery thrives on the critique of the process of local gentrification and its effects on what was a traditionally working-class and Roma district of the city. The leading figures of this alternative art centre are László Gergely and Katarina Šević, successful artists in their own right individually and collaboratively. The gallery hosts regular shows of alternative artists, public discussions, workshops and other events, some in English.

KÉK (*see p176*) is both an acronym for 'contemporary architecture centre' and the word for 'blue' – although its setting is on a shabby grey street near Keleti station. It occupies an empty building in an inner courtyard, where the centre stages cutting-edge retro exhibitions, popular public events and occasional DJ nights. Operating at the crossover between art and architecture, KÉK investigates the processes of social and urban change and the heritage of threatened architectural sites. It also runs guided tours of architectural relics of Socialism, giant factory complexes and so on, before this living history is wiped out in a wholesale conversion into homogenous offices and flats.

The survival of what seem outdated local institutions has turned out to be a successful strategy to preserve a space for freedom of action out of reach of the market mechanism. The **Liget Galéria** (*see p176*) is one of the most significant of these rare non-institutional spaces with a direct relationship to the confrontational culture of late Socialism – curtains, signage and personnel have not changed since the mid 1980s. It rejects the new free market free-for-all, is instinctively ecological in outlook, declines big-budget collaborations and stubbornly resists the temptation to rebrand and renovate. The gallery is run by the artist Tibor Varnagy, a cult figure on the alternative scene. Despite its small size and out-of-centre location by the Városliget, it has renowned artists queuing up to exhibit.

Arts & Entertainment

Artist-run, underground venue at a prominent bohemian nightspot launched in the summer of 2006. The building may be demolished by 2008, so get here quick. *See p175* **Watch this space.**

KÉK
VII.Nefelejcs utca 26 (225 3530/www.kek.org.hu). M2 Keleti pu./bus 7. **Open** times vary. **No credit cards. Admission** free. **Map** p247 J4.
Quality retro exhibitions, public events as well as DJ nights. *See p175* **Watch this space.**

Kogart
VI.Andrássy út 112 (354 3820/www.kogart.hu). M1 Bajza utca. **Open** 10am-6pm daily. **Admission** Ft1,200; Ft600 concessions. **Credit** MC, V. **Map** p247 H2.
Housed in the former FMK, the cult premises of the Young Artists' Association, the Kogart's opening in 2004 marked a surprise return of contemporary art here. Its prestigious location and rich history gave it a name among Hungary's new private galleries, though the art world remains sceptical about its founder, industrialist collector Gábor Kovács.

Liget Galéria
XIV.Ajtósi Dürer sor 5 (351 4924). Bus 7/trolleybus 74, 75. **Open** 2-6pm Mon, Wed-Sun. **Admission** free. **No credit cards. Map** p247 K3.
Renowned figurehead of the alternative scene. *See p175* **Watch this space.** **Photo** *p172.*

Lumen Galéria
VI.Király utca 46 (06 30 395 1513 mobile). M1 Opera. **Open** 2-8pm Mon-Sat. **Admission** free. **No credit cards. Map** p246 F4.
Located in temporary, run-down premises that are a favourite with the alternative crowd, the Lumen is representative of the new type of crossover artist-run space. It is accessible only through a large and noisy bar, but the art on show is usually worth it.

Trafó Galéria
IX.Liliom utca 41 (215 1600/www.trafo.hu). M3 Ferenc körút/tram 4, 6. **Open** 4-7pm Mon-Sat; 2-8pm Sun; & 1hr before & after theatre shows. **Admission** free. **No credit cards. Map** p250 H8.
The gallery in this notable cultural centre shows the latest works, collaborations and experiments by Hungarian and international artists, and is recognised as one of the leading spaces for contemporary art in the city. The exhibition programme is as good as the modern dance and theatre on the stage above the gallery, and the Trafó is also known for its innovative style of curating.

2B Gallery
IX.Ráday utca 47 (215 4899/www.pipacs.hu/2b). M3 Ferenc körút/tram 4, 6. **Open** 2-6pm Mon-Fri; 11am-4pm Sat. **Admission** free. **No credit cards. Map** p249 G8.
The 2B contemporary art gallery was founded by the internationally connected Böröcz brothers, András and László. Until 2006 it operated in a suburban flat and recently moved to this location on trendy Ráday utca. Their free-ranging exhibition programme has included contemporary painters such as Ádám Zoltán, quirky conceptual shows and thematic surveys of drawing and sculpture.

Videospace Budapest
IX.Ráday utca 56 (06 20 984 3669 mobile/www. videospace.c3.hu). M3 Ferenc körút/tram 4, 6. **Open** hours vary. **Admission** free. **No credit cards. Map** p249 G8.
Strategically set by the Goethe Institut, VB is the artist-run project of Eike, a long-standing resident and active member of the art scene. The gallery aims to show the best in local and global new media art.

WAX Culture Factory
IV.József Attila utca 4-6 (272 0528/www.wax budapest.com). M3 Újpest-Városkapu. **Open** noon-6pm daily. **Admission** free. **No credit cards.**
The WAX had an impressive start in its first incarnation as MEO from 2001 to 2004, when it was a prestigious tannery conversion with aspirations to become the Hungarian Tate Modern. There then followed a sobering period when the hordes of visitors failed to materialise and its reputation declined. Recently it reopened under the new management of ACAX, the Agency for Contemporary Art Exchange, with a solo show by maverick artist Kriszta Nagy, and there remains great potential in its vast and original exhibition space.

Gay & Lesbian

A trio of movers and shakers is revitalising a once-staid scene.

While Budapest enjoys a reputation as a porn and party capital, its pink scene has found momentum. *Queer as Folk* was a local TV hit and there's now a Mr Gay Hungary contest. Most gay activities have found a permanent address: you no longer have to cruise on the Danube by the Marriott or seek alternative pleasure in the baths – some of which are being renovated anyway. Enthusiastic entrepreneurs have opened cafés, bars, dance clubs, dark rooms and saunas, complete with activities. In the absence of decent above-ground party spaces downtown, most gay venues, old and new, are burrows: a bottleneck entrance leads down into the dark. The fare on offer is staple stuff: cosy bars and large clubs, some with extra-curricular action.

There's been a move away from transgender and transsexual performances: new clubs are trying to get off the tranny train and diversify their offerings. Besides, Budapest's small drag community has boosted its visibility by appearing en bloc on a TV quiz show and a glamorous TV spot. Expect a fair share of heteros at the drag dos – centrally located **Capella** can almost be categorised as a straight club for that reason. **Alibi** continues to boast the best make-up and get-up, otherwise some of the wigs are risible and frocks tend to come in polyester. New venues like **Bamboo** (Pure Parties; www.pure.i-shop.hu) and **Alterego** (Candy Parties; www.candyparty.hu) have brought fresh energy, but it remains to be seen if their permanent locations hold.

For more sex-oriented entertainment, there are theme parties, and a couple of specialised venues. Most clubs hand out a card to tally your drinks: it is a form of cover charge. Such venues have a minimum consumption requirement and levy a hefty penalty if you lose the card. Save yourself a headache and stick to beer: wine and cocktails are cheap for a reason.

Local gays and lesbians have little experience of the liberation movement as the West knows it, and it is easier to stay in the closet. The Lesbian and Gay Pride event attracts a small crowd, although numbers increase every year. NGOs have also run billboard campaigns on homosexuality, and the liberal SZDSZ party introduced gay cohabitation legislation, sparking a tasteless political debate in the process. The age of consent for gay men is

Cocky **coXx Men's Club**. *See p179.*

14, in line with heterosexuals. Gay marriage isn't possible, but gay couples can register themselves as 'partners living together' just like their straight counterparts.

There are two gay magazines: the monthly *Mások* (www.masok.hu) and the free monthly *Na Végre!* (www.navegre.hu), with listings information in English on the website. Useful sites include www.pride.hu and www.gay.hu. Gay stations Gay Rádió (www.gayradio.hu), Paradiátor (www.pararadio.hu) and Radio G (www.radiog.hu) all broadcast on the internet, while Tilos Rádió (www.tilos.hu), Fikszrádió (www.fikszradio.hu) and Magyar Rádió (www.magyarradio.hu) air occasional gay shows. For local organisations, information and helplines, *see p226.*

Movers and shakers

By day a modest, serious man, with a background in the catering business, Oszkar becomes a warm, slightly camp host behind the bar. 'Ownership rather than lease of the club is vital,' he says. 'It allows for long-term planning and security in a market that does not require constant change and relies heavily on tourists.' While the early days saw indecision over where to take coXx, according to Oszker 'the aesthetics, the back rooms and the frequent theme parties cater to the gay male's fantasies and sense of frivolity'. The upstairs space is graced with contemporary artwork by the students of the University of Fine Arts, something else to stir the imagination.

Budapest's gay scene after dark is run by a trio of offbeat personalities.

Desire Dubonet is the most colourful figure of Pest's pink nightlife. A gracefully larger-than-life personality, Desire roams in and out of projects, identities and countries with that unmistakable American drive and sense of destiny. Owner of the **Club Bohemian Alibi** (see p179), she reigns supreme in her stable of drag performers. She also writes music and produces her own films tackling subjects like the 1956 Hungarian Uprising, US pharmaceuticals and Dracula. Her current celluloid offering accuses Harry S Truman of war crimes over the atomic strike on Japan. Desire buys commercial time on local cable channel Budapest TV to air her films, some of them featuring the stars from the club.

CoXx Men's Club (see p179), like Alibi, operates in a residential building. Tenants have no idea that in their basement, a nightly labyrinth of pleasure attracts crowds of gay men. And that façade of discretion is just fine, according to owner **Oszkar Osvald**. 'Even the carpenter was comfortable about making glory holes,' he says. 'Although I had to explain to him how high the holes should be,' he continues, perhaps giving new meaning to the term 'odd job'.

'At first, young gay men were appalled,' says Oszkar, who broke new ground in this conservative market. Even the serenely minimalist bar, cleverly separated from the activity rooms, provoked initial criticism.

For **Ágota Weiszgerber**, the lesbian tag may have come as a blessing and a curse. With no particular intention to run a lesbian café, she and her then partner were waitressing at the original **Café Eklektika** (see p180; see photo) on Semmelweis utca, then a different venue. 'The owner was running it into the ground,' she explains, 'so we decided to take it over. We turned it around.' The atmosphere encouraged a growing lesbian crowd. 'We went in for the retro look because we had no money. That sort of furniture was dirt cheap,' she says. 'Then we had exhibitions and live DJs, and the culinary and wine offerings were slowly upgraded. Our regulars began to appreciate good wine. With the menu and entertainment, it also became a young gay men's hangout too.'

Ágota took a new location on Nagymező utca, the Broadway of Budapest. Eklektika has transformed into a restaurant-lounge, with an fine kitchen that presents Hungarian and global dishes. Some ingredients are grown by Ágota's mother, with cakes baked at home. The crowd remains the same mix of unintimidated lesbians and gay men, their friends, and a new influx of theatre-goers.

Where to stay

BudapestGayCity.net
Various locations (06 20 556 7018 mobile/
www.budapestgaycity.net). **Rates** *from €70.*
No credit cards.
Accommodation services offering apartments in fine
locations such as Váci utca and Liszt Ferenc tér.

Gayguide.net/gaystay.net
Various locations (06 30 932 3334 mobile/www.
budapest.gayguide.net). **Rates** *from €60.*
No credit cards.
This gay-owned and operated venture has flats in
town. Along with central Kigyó utca, Március 15 tér
and Kristóf tér locations, KM Saga is set between
the central gay strip and the bar zone of Ráday utca.

Guesthouse Connection
VII.Király utca 41 (267 7104/fax 352 1703/www.
connectionguesthouse.com). M1, M2, M3 Deák tér.
Rates *from €45.* **Credit** *via web only* MC, V.
This gay hotel offers modest rooms, some with
showers. A late breakfast is served.

Events

Gay Pride Day and **Gay & Lesbian**
Cultural Festival (www.gaypride.hu) in
summer feature a march, parties and cultural
events. The **Sziget Festival** (www.sziget.hu)
hosts a range of gay-oriented events.

Gay

Restaurants, bars & clubs

Action Bar
V.Magyar utca 42 (266 9148/www.action.gay.hu).
M3 Kálvin tér/night bus 914, 950. **Open** 9pm-4am
daily. **Admission** *min consumption* Ft1,600. **No**
credit cards. Map p249 F6.
Popular cellar bar, recently refurbished, with the
busiest darkroom in town. Look out for a letter 'A'
on the decrepit door. Live shows and striptease.

Capella
V.Belgrád rakpart 23 (318 6231/www.capella
cafe.hu). M3 Ferenciek tere/tram 2/night bus 908.
Open 9.30pm-4am Wed, Thur; 9.30pm-6am Fri, Sat.
Admission *Wed, Thur* Ft500. *Fri, Sat* Ft1,500.
No credit cards. Map p249 E7.
Capella is a gutted mini-opera house with balconies
lining the central space, looking into the deep end.
The drag shows, three times nightly, attract many
heteros – too many, according to some.

Club Bohemian Alibi
IX.Üllői út 45-47 (219 5260/www.clubbohemian.hu).
M3 Ferenc körút/tram 4, 6. **Open** midnight-2am
Mon-Thur; midnight-5am Fri; midnight-6am Sat.
Admission *Fri, Sat min consumption* Ft1,200.
No credit cards. Map p250 H7.

And the prize for best make-up goes to... Alibi and
its wild drag performers, run by Desire, an extravagant, multi-talented American. They perform twice
a night, with guest stars, an air-conditioned dance
floor and three bars. Check out the improv theatre
on Tuesdays. Probably the best club in its category,
Alibi operates as a restaurant by day. *See p178*
Movers and shakers. Photo *p180.*

Club 93 Pizzeria
VIII.Vas utca 2 (06 30 630 7093 mobile). Bus 7.
Open 11.30am-midnight daily. **No credit cards.**
Map p249 G5.
This small pizzeria has been serving Italian faves,
cocktails and desserts since 1993.

coXx Men's Club
VII.Dohány utca 38 (344 4884/www.coxx.hu).
M2 Astoria/tram 47, 49/bus 7/night bus 908, 914,
950. **Open** 9pm-4am Mon-Thur, Sun; 9pm-5am Fri,
Sat. **Admission** Ft1,000. **No credit cards.**
Map p249 D4.
CoXx is one of the smarter gay bars, with a clever
and discreet separate themed cruising labyrinth:
cages, slings, glory holes and wet rooms. Theme par-
ties include military and nude events. *See p178*
Movers and shakers. Photo *p177.*

Habroló Bisztró
V.Szép utca 1B (06 20 211 6701 mobile/www.
habrolo.hu). M3 Ferenciek tere/bus 7/night bus
908. **Open** 5pm-3am daily. **No credit cards.**
Map p249 E6.
Habroló is a local delicacy, a dough-like shaft filled
with loads of cheese, about 6 inches long. The allusion is deliberate. This comfortable bar features a
tiny lounge-like space upstairs, a performance podi-
um and dating parties for the over-30s on Sundays.

Mylord Café & Bar
V.Belgrád rakpart 3-4 (06 20 498 2944 mobile).
Tram 2. **Open** 10am-2am daily. **No credit cards.**
Map p249 E6.
An intimate bar on the embankment near Capella.

Smile
VII.Nagy Diófa utca 17 (06 30 403 1372 mobile).
M2 Blaha Lujza tér/bus 7/night bus 907. **Open**
9pm-4am daily. **No credit cards. Map** p249 G5.
This new attitude-free venue, exclusively for men,
gained quick fame for its discos downstairs. The
upstairs café has great atmosphere.

Baths & beaches

Gay activity at Budapest's baths has been
curtailed of late. The **Király** requires trunks,
and staff keep their eyes peeled for anything
untoward. Men-only is on Tuesdays, Thursdays
and Saturdays. The **Gellért** demands you wear
an apron, and is undergoing renovation anyway
– sections will be closed and others co-ed.
The **Rác** is being converted into a spa hotel.
See p50 **Spa city** and *pp160-162* **Baths.**

Outlandish **Club Bohemian Alibi**. *See p179*.

Cruising areas

The **Danube Cruise**, between the Marriott Hotel and Petőfi's statue near Erzsébet Bridge, once the busiest cruising strip, has been cleared of most action except for a few hustlers at dusk. **Népliget**, a park by the metro station of the same name, has some action in the daytime, and more at night near the Planetarium. Carry ID.

Saunas

Magnum Szauna

VIII.Csepreghy utca 2 (267 2532/www.magnum szauna.hu). M3 Ferenc körút or Kálvin körút/night bus 906. **Open** noon-1am Mon-Thur; noon-4am Fri; 1pm Sat-1am Mon. **Admission** Ft1,350. **Map** p250 G6.

Magnum is a huge labyrinth with diversions like a sauna, steam room, showers for two, lounge area with TV, a big gym, dark room and cabins. There are tranny and other shows on Fridays, theme days, and from Saturday to Monday morning the operation is non-stop. You can get a hair trim in various areas while (or before) you're at it, a pedicure or manicure, and there's massage too.

Sex shops

Condoms and lubricants are available in sex shops, pharmacies and chains such as **Drogerie Markt** (*see p151*), which stocks K-Y – otherwise ask for *síkosító zselé*.

Connection Szex Shop

VIII.Berzsenyi utca 3 (323 1203/www.connection bt.hu). M2 Keleti pu./bus 7. **Open** 10am-10pm Mon-Fri; 10am-2am Sat. **Credit** MC, V. **Map** p250 E4.

Well-stocked sex shop, with cabins.

Sport & activities

Atlasz Sport (www.atlaszsport.hu) is the local gay sports association, offering activities from badminton to belly dancing, with football and handball in between. Hiking group **Vándor Mások** operates under the Atlasz umbrella.

Gemini ballroom dancing

V.Veres Pálné utca 19 (06 70 202 0833 mobile/www. geminitanclub.hu). M3 Ferenciek tere. **Open** varies. **Admission** *Class* Ft1,200. *Monthly ticket* Ft4,000. **No credit cards. Map** p249 E6.

Ballroom, Latin and dancing classes and courses for lads and lasses, from cha cha cha to *csardás*. While the couples here are mostly same sex, everybody is welcome to practise or learn their waltzes. On Sundays, the Bamboo (VI.Desewffy utca 44) hosts a ballroom dance party, for which admission is free. At this main Veres Pálné location, ring *táncterem* to enter the building.

Yogasanas

VIII.Horanszky utca 5 (06 20 802 0262 mobile/ www.yogasanasbudapest.com). M3 Kálvin tér/tram 4, 6. **Open** 6.30pm Mon; 11.30am Sat. **No credit cards.** **Map** p249 G6.

This yoga studio provides weekly beginners' yoga classes for gays, lesbians and friends.

Lesbian

Cafés, bars & clubs

Café Eklektika

VI.Nagymező utca 30 (266 1226/www.eklektika.hu). M1 Opera/M1 Oktogon. **Open** 10am-midnight Mon-Fri; noon-midnight Sun. **No credit cards.** **Map** p246 F4.

Not lesbian only, the Café Eklektika is lesbian-run and attracts a faithful following, thanks to Superhen Ágota. Now in a beautifully unpretentious location, it has occasional DJs and live performances, plus exhibitions. The restaurant offers fabulous fare on a budget and fine wine too. A summer terrace adds to the attraction. *See p178* **Movers and shakers**.

Events

Femme football and babe bowling evenings are organised by **Atlasz Sport** (*see left*).

Ösztrosokk Parties

Living Room, V.Kossuth Lajos utca 17 (osztrosokk @femfatal.hu/www.osztrosokk.hu). M2 Astoria/tram 47, 49/bus 7/night bus 908, 914, 950. **Open** 10pm-4am last Sat of mth. **Admission** Ft600. **No credit cards. Map** p249 D4.

Women-only groups take over this prominent, centrally located venue involving the lesbian community with resident DJs and theme parties.

milkS/HakE Parties

At Bamboo, VI.Dessewffy utca 44 (milkshake@ femfatal.hu/428 2225/www.bamboomusicclub.hu/ www.osztrosokk.hu). M1 Oktogon/tram 4, 6/night bus 906. **Open** 9pm-4am days vary. **No credit cards. Map** p246 F3.

MilkS/HakE welcomes lesbians and their friends in various locations. Check the website for regularly updated schedules and themes.

Arts & Entertainment

Music

A new lease of life for the city's top-notch orchestras, an international breakthrough for local Britpop bands – and Romano Drom fiddle anew.

Classical & Opera

Classical music has always been vital to the cultural life of the capital, yet over the last two decades the financial realities of supporting such a vast music scene have been fiercely at odds with the unusually high number of professional musicians and the unquenchable thirst of music lovers. Even though groups are underfunded, and musicians' salaries seriously low compared with those of their Western counterparts, no major outfit has folded. In fact, 2007 was a watershed year for classical music in the capital, as three of the city's major orchestras received new leases of life, and the State Opera hired a dynamic new team to guide it out of its struggles. There's never been a better time to enjoy classical music in Budapest.

Hungarians are raised with an profound sense of their musical history. After the two greatest Hungarian composers of the first half of the 20th century, Béla Bartók and Zoltán Kodály, had incorporated elements of traditional folk music into their work and teachings, Hungarian music freed itself from the influence of Germany and Vienna. The gradual introduction of these melodic structures would be as important to Hungary's new-found national identity as the works of any local writer, architect or politician.

Bartók and Kodály had ventured out to the remote regions of Greater Hungary to document the vanishing folk heritage. By combining the melodic characteristics and rugged dance rhythms of Eastern European folk with the compositional techniques of the Western avant-garde, Bartók created a distinctly Magyar music style that has proved an inspiration for future composers. Kodály created a method of music education based on the folk songs he and Bartók collected. It would shape musical appreciation for every generation to follow. The distinctive Hungarian musical identity has continued into the 21st century with three of the biggest composers of the last 50 years: György Ligeti, György Kurtág and Péter Eötvös.

Budapest currently boasts eight professional symphony orchestras, enjoyed by a large and knowledgeable, if conservative, concert-going public. The season runs from September to June, with anything from two to ten or more concerts every night. Programming invariably includes plenty of Bartók and Kodály, and the standards of the classical canon. The local market for early and contemporary music is small but of enthusiastic.

In summer there are regular outdoor concerts at the **Vajdahunyad Castle** in the Városliget (*see p93*), the **Kiscelli Museum** (*see p77*) in Óbuda and **Matthias Church** (*see p68*) up in the Castle District.

INFORMATION AND FESTIVALS

Koncert Kalendárium, an extensive listing in English of classical and opera events, is online at www.koncertkalendarium.hu/en. A printed version (in Hungarian only) can be found at ticket agencies and record shops. Listings in English are also in the *Budapest Sun*.

Few classical concerts in Budapest sell out. With the exception of the Festival Orchestra's subscription series, tickets are usually available and affordable unless a major international artist is involved. For details of ticket agencies, *see p154*. What is not available there can be bought at venues themselves an hour before the performance – tickets for the **Opera House** at their box offices and at the **State Opera Ticket Office** a few doors down Andrássy út.

The most important classical music event is the **Budapest Spring Festival** (*see p156*), a cultural extravaganza lasting a fortnight in March. It attracts leading international soloists and orchestras, as well as the best local musicians. Its sister is the **Budapest Autumn Festival** (*see p158*) in October, which focuses on contemporary Hungarian music and arts. The **Music of Our Time** (*see p158*) festival in October is a week of new Hungarian music.

Orchestras & choirs

Although the city's seven orchestras maintain a high performing standard – only a notch down from the world's most famous bands, in fact – musicians' salaries are still well below those in the West. In the past, some of the best players were forced to head West to look for better paid work, but with money flowing steadily into Budapest, the best orchestras are now able to earn a decent living here at home.

Arts & Entertainment

One of the world's acoustic masterpieces – the **Zeneakadémia**. *See p184*.

The **Budapesti Fesztivál Zenekar**, winners of a Gramophone Award for best orchestral recording, were the first out of the gate in the sponsorship race. Founded by its principal conductor Iván Fischer and pianist Zoltán Kocsis in 1983, the Budapest Festival Orchestra was originally an ad-hoc group of the country's best musicians. When they became a full-time group in 1992, they quickly learned how to get the financial support they needed. Consequently, they also got most of the best young musicians. Since then, they have consistently been able to keep the standard and the budget high, and are consequently able to invite big-name soloists and conductors from abroad. As well as its orchestral concerts – most of which sell out – the players also give chamber music concerts.

The **Nemzeti Filharmonikus Zenekar**, once the state dinosaurs, have fast become a formidable force in the capital since Zoltán Kocsis took the reins in 1997. The National Philharmonic Orchestra received enthusiastic reviews on their US concert tour in 2003 and have a new home at the **National Concert Hall** in the riverside arts complex in south Pest. With their own stable of top-class local musicians and conductor Kocsis' superior musicianship and imaginative programming, the orchestra are fast becoming the ones to beat.

Their Bartók under Kocsis' baton is second to none and absolutely not to be missed. The ensemble also lures renowned soloists like Joshua Bell and Kim Kashkashian.

The **Magyar Rádió Szimfonikus Zenekar** are getting their act together as well. Although continued funding from Hungarian Radio is uncertain, the orchestra have managed to re-energise themselves under their new music director Ádám Fischer (the brother of Iván, of the Budapesti Fesztivál Zenekar). The orchestra present a Wagner Festival every summer (www.radio.hu).

Two other orchestras are worth catching. After losing most of their state funding two years ago, the **Budapesti Filharmóniai Társaság Zenekara** (Budapest Philharmonic Orchestra), second oldest orchestra on the continent and pit band for the State Opera, have admirably re-organised themselves and are on the way to re-capturing their former glory days. The **Danubia Szimfonikus Zenekar**, officially a youth orchestra though you'd never know it from their enthusiastic and highly-polished performances, shine under their young conductor Domonkos Héja.

Other young conductors to watch out for are the dynamic Zsolt Hamar and his **Pannon Philharmonic Orchestra** from Pécs, who visit the capital often; and György Vashegyi

The comfortable **Bartók Memorial House**.

with his early music groups, the **Purcell Kórus** and the **Orfeo Zenekar**, who perform baroque music on period instruments.

Choirs are part of Kodály's legacy. The **Nemzeti Énekkar** (National Choir) and the **Magyar Rádió Énekkara** (Hungarian Radio Choir) perform both sacred and secular works. The **Magyar Rádió Gyermekkórusa** (Hungarian Radio Children's Choir) have no equal and sings works from a broad repertoire, especially contemporary Hungarian. First-class chamber choirs include the **Tomkins Vocal Ensemble** and the **Victoria Choir**.

Soloists & smaller ensembles

There are plenty of chamber music or solo recitals in Budapest. For piano music, try and catch recitals by **Dezső Ránki** and **Gergely Bogányi**. **Zoltán Kocsis**, usually busy with conducting, doesn't give many solo recitals any more but frequently joins others for chamber music. **András Schiff** comes to the capital regularly. Young violinist **Barnabás Kelemen** appears in recital or as soloist with an orchestra, and you won't find a more sublime cellist than **Miklós Perényi**. Mezzo-soprano **Andrea Meláth** is the best singer of the younger generation. Any concerts by the **Keller Quartet** are a sure hit.

Contemporary music fans shouldn't miss the percussion quartet **Amadinda**, one of the best percussion ensembles in the world, and the **UMZE Kamaraegyüttes**, often conducted by Kocsis or Péter Eötvös.

Concert venues

Most concerts take place in the same four or five halls, the most important being the new National Concert Hall and the **Zeneakadémia** (Music Academy). Churches and smaller halls also host a large number of performances.

Bartók Memorial House

Bartók Emlékház
II.Csalán út 29 (394 2100/www.bartokmuseum.hu).
Bus 5, 29. **Open** *Museum* 10am-5pm Tue-Sun.
Tickets on sale 1hr before performances & during museum hours. **No credit cards**.
Bartók's last Budapest residence, now a museum, hosts a series of Friday evening chamber concerts by Hungary's recitalists. The low ceiling can be somewhat claustrophobic, but the chairs here are the most comfortable of any venue in Budapest. It's open for visits during the day (*see p74*). No box office.

Budapest Congress Centre

Budapest Kongresszusi Központ
XII.Jagelló út 1-3 (372 5400). M2 Déli pu., then tram 61. **Open** *Box office* 4-6.30pm Wed, Fri; 10am-1pm Sat.
No credit cards. Map p248 A7.
An ugly convention centre with poor acoustics, this is where many world-famous stars perform, mainly during festivals, because of its large seating capacity of 1,750. Don't bother with famous smaller ensembles unless you can get seats up front.

Ceremonial Hall of the Hungarian Academy of Sciences

MTA Díszterme
V.Roosevelt tér 9 (411 6100). M1 Vörösmarty tér/ tram 2. **Tickets** on sale 1hr before performances.
Closed July, Aug. **No credit cards. Map** p246 D5.
This ornate hall near the Chain Bridge has fine acoustics for chamber music and smaller orchestras. Seating is on a first come, first served basis.

Matthias Church

Mátyás templom
I.Szentháromság tér 2 (355 5657/www.matyas- templom.hu). M2 Moszkva tér, then Várbusz/bus 16.
Tickets on sale 1hr before performances. **No credit cards. Map** p245 B4.
A top venue for organ recitals and concerts of sacred music for a cappella choir or choir and orchestra all year round. Arrive early and get a seat close to the front to beat the cavernous acoustics.

Nádor Hall

Nádor terem
XIV.Ajtósi Dürer sor 39 (344 7072). Trolleybus 72, 74, 75. **Tickets** on sale 1hr before performances.
Closed July, Aug. **No credit cards**.

Opera House. *See p186.*

A gorgeous little art nouveau concert hall in the Institute for the Blind, with excellent acoustics and a rich programme of song recitals, chamber music and baroque ensembles.

National Concert Hall
Nemzeti Hangversenyterem
Palace of Arts, IX.Komor Marcell utca 1 (555 3300/ www.mupa.hu). HÉV to Lágymányosi-híd/tram 2.
Tickets 1-6pm daily. Also on sale until show time. Closed July, Aug. **Credit** MC, V. **Map** p250 inset.
This acoustically correct concert hall is the main venue in the overblown Palace of Arts, a recently built, state-funded centre beside the National Theatre in the burgeoning riverside arts complex of south Pest (*see p100*). This is the new home for the top-class National Philharmonic Orchestra, directed by renowned virtuoso Zoltán Kocsis – and it's a real treat when he occasionally sits down at the keyboard. The National Concert Hall has sufficient wherewithal and capacity (1,700 seats) to accommodate the most prestigious orchestras visiting Hungary from abroad.

Óbuda Social Circle
Óbudai Társaskör
III.Kis Korona utca 7 (250 0288). HÉV to Árpád-híd/ bus 6, 86. **Open** *Box office* 10am-6pm daily.
No credit cards.
This charming little building is one of the few left from early 19th-century Óbuda. Intimate and atmospheric, set near the Danube, it hosts excellent recitals and chamber music concerts.

Pesti Vigadó
V.Vigadó tér 2 (318 9903). M1 Vörösmarty tér/ tram 2. **Tickets** on sale 1hr before performances.
No credit cards. Map p249 D5.
Because of its riverside location, the Vigadó tailors its programme to tourists. But the Socialist-modern restoration of the faux-romantic interior (itself a scandal in 1864) makes it not only ugly, but an acoustic washout. A shame, because the Vigadó staged the première of Mahler's First Symphony. The Vigadó is currently undergoing renovation and will reopen towards the end of 2007.

Zeneakadémia
VI.Liszt Ferenc tér 8 (342 0179). M1 Oktogon/tram 4, 6. **Open** *Box office* 10am-8pm Mon-Fri; 2-8pm Sat, Sun. **No credit cards. Map** p246 G4.
A gem of Hungarian Secession architecture, the Zeneakadémia has been home to the Franz Liszt Academy of Music since 1907. Almost all of Hungary's top musicians learned their craft here, as did those who taught them. Recognised as one of the great acoustic masterpieces of the world, the 1,200-seat Nagyterem (Large Concert Hall) hosts concerts most nights. The lack of any air-circulation system can make it quite stifling in the warmer months, but it's generally closed in July and August. The somewhat smaller Kisterem upstairs provides a space for chamber and contemporary music. **Photo** *p182.*

Opera

The **Hungarian State Opera** stages 60 opera and ballet productions each year at two venues. The pride of all theatres is the opulent **Opera House** on Andrássy út, where the bulk of the German repertoire and most prestigious Italian productions are given. Once the site of mainstream operas, the starkly Socialist Erkel Színház is closed for extensive renovations until 2010 (they hope). Until then, the smaller **Thália Színház** is serving as substitute, taking on a handful of productions each season.

The Opera House has a rich history – Gustav Mahler and Otto Klemperer were intendants. Opened in 1884, of late it had everything but top-notch performers and directors. Weak finances and mismanagement sent the best talent abroad, leaving home audiences to suffer through mostly average to mediocre and unimaginative productions. But that looks set to change; in May 2007 a new leadership team was appointed, including world-renowned conductor Ádám Fischer. With his connections and political influence, Fischer has vowed to raise the standard to a truly international level.

There are a handful of opera and ballet premières a year. From mid July to mid August, the **Budafest** opera and ballet festival (*see p157*) is held here. The Opera House also hosts symphonic concerts featuring its own orchestra.

We speak English

Saddled with a language they can't export, failing to break into a world of falling CD sales, a few new local bands have changed tack. Magyar is out and English, the language of their self-penned songs, is in.

The **Puzzle** are a fine example. In 2000, while still based in Hungary, they won a talent contest and gained a record contract with Universal. Yet it was three years before they held their debut album in their hands. The band decided to relocate to London. Ex-Oasis manager Alan McGee, a DJ at Death Disco at the **Trafó Bar Tango** (*see p188*), described their gigs as 'a Zeppelinesque journey with a singer like Lennon circa '65'. Since their move to England, the four-piece who, according to their MySpace page, play 'psychedelic old-skool indie rock', have had many gigs, played a live acoustic session on BBC Merseyside radio, opened for Zoot Woman, and are regular guests of McGee's various club nights in London. They signed to Weekender Records, home of the Bishops, in March 2007.

Borrowing their name from a nightspot in Barcelona, the **Moog** (*see photo*) became the first Magyar band to sign to an American label: garage- and surf rock-oriented MuSick Recordings. The lads were playing Nirvana covers when they started writing their own material, influenced by 1960s garage, punk and a touch of Britpop. Their debut album,

Sold For Tomorrow, was recorded at Budapest's Tom Tom studio, mixed by Jack Endino (Nirvana, Soundgarden) in Seattle and mastered by Dave Schultz (Pretenders, Otis Redding) in Los Angeles. To promote the album, the Moog toured the US for two months. Another guitar band, **Amber Smith**, are defined by a British sound. On *Reprint*, released in 2006 in Europe by Kalinkaland Records, they worked with Robin Guthrie from the Cocteau Twins; and, on their next effort, with Chris Brown, known for his work with Radiohead. **Kistehén tánczenekar** started out as a spoof band providing the music for a cartoon about a little yellow cow, before taking it seriously and becoming the Eastern European version of Mano Negra, translating their name to **Little Cow** to be more exportable on the global market. Their third album, *I'm In Love With Every Lady*, was released by Berlin-based Eastblok Music, with some songs delivered with a deliberately clumsy Hunglish translation to lend a curious charm to tunes that blend Gypsy, Balkan, rock, ska, pop and dance rhythms.

Other new bands include **Middlewave** from Békéscsaba; **Annabarbi**, melodic indie rock-cum-emo punk and a side project by Amber Smith; **E.Z. Basic**, indie pop, post-punk and electronica; the **Trousers**, influenced by classic guitar rock; **Supersonic**; **Galapagos**; **30Y** and the **Samy Sosa Band**.

The State Opera publishes a schedule every month, available here and at ticket agencies, along with an online listing. Performances are listed in the **Koncert Kalendárium** (*see p181*) as well as in the *Budapest Sun*.

Opera House

Magyar Állami Operaház
VI.Andrássy út 22 (353 0170/www.opera.hu).
M1 Opera. **Open** *Box office Concert days* 11am-show time Tue-Sat; 4pm-show time Sun. *Non-concert days* 11am-5pm daily. Closed July. **Credit** MC, V.
Map p246 F4. **Photo** *p184.*

Thália Színház

VI.Nagymező utca 22 (331 0500/www.thalia.hu).
M1 Oktogon/M1 Opera. **Open** *Box office* 10am-6pm Mon-Fri; 2pm-show time Sat, Sun. **Credit** MC, V.
Map p246 F4.

Rock, Roots & Jazz

Budapest is home to a handful of decent venues occasionally hosting quality indie acts and world music bands. The only time the city takes centre stage music-wise is for the week-long **Sziget festival** (*see p159* **Budapest's biggest bash**) in August, by far the biggest music event in the region, with fmusic of every style imaginable on several stages at once.

For the rest of the year, most international acts play at the **Budapest Arena** (*see p196*), in the same complex as the bigger national **Puskás Ferenc Stadion** (*see p196*), where George Michael played in May 2007.

The Petőfi Csarnok, a large hall in the Városliget, hosts well-known artists who are either past their best or warming up for world tours. The 'Pecsa' also has an adjoining open-air summer stage, a pleasant place to catch acts which have recently included Nick Cave and Morrissey. The festival atmosphere makes up for the relative sound quality.

Smaller venues that might surprise you with an exciting and diverse line-up of artists include the **A38**, the **Gödör klub**, **Trafó Bár Tangó** and the **Süss fel nap**.

One of the key recent musical developments here has been the emergence of a new wave of bands more accessible to foreigners, penning lyrics in English rather than impenetrable Hungarian. Striving to remove the 20-year-long hegemony of indie bands such as Kispál és a Borz and Sziámi, the first to materialise was the Britpoppy **Heaven Street Seven**. Winning the the European Breakthrough Award at MIDEM in Cannes in 2006, Heaven Street Seven joined Australia's Church on a 2007 European tour while promoting their English-language release, *Sordid Little Symphonies*. On their

coat-tails, raunchy guitar bands such as the **Puzzle**, the **Moog** and **Amber Smith** have burst onto the scene, with a fresh sound, foreign names, trendy haircuts – and English lyrics. A similar shift has occurred on the electronic side with **Yonderboi**, **Zagar** and **Neo** replacing established Anima Sound System, Másfél and Korai Öröm. In heavy rock, **Depresszió** are competing with their mentors, Tankcsapda. Hungary's gangsta rappers, such as Dopeman and Sub Bass Monster, have been left in the shade by the real goulash hip hop provided by **Belgä** and **Ludditák**'s MC-ing girl chorus. See *p185* **We speak English**.

TIMES AND TICKETS

Most clubs open until 3am, but some push on until 6am. Admission varies from Ft500 to Ft2,000, while bigger concerts are nearer the Ft5,000 to Ft15,000 mark. Beware that bouncers can be aggressive, so just smile and politely hand over the modest entrance fee. Concert details can be found in the *Budapest Sun*, *Pesti Műsor* and free listings magazines *Exit* and *Pesti Est*. For ticket agencies, *see p154.*

Concert venues

Budapest Arena

Papp László Budapest Sportaréna
XIV.Stefánia út 2 (422 2682/www.budapestarena. hu). *M2 Stadionok.* **Open** *Box office* 9am-6pm Mon-Fri; 10am-2pm Sat, Sun or until show. **Admission** varies. **No credit cards.**
The latest addition to the venue roster is a multi-purpose stadium with 12,500 seats and six bars. Its very functionality (ice rink transformed into rock venue in 30 minutes) takes away any ambience it might offer, but it's very welcome all the same.

Millenáris Centre

II.Fény utca 20-22 (438 5312/www.millenaris.hu). *Tram 4, 6.* **Open** *Box office* 10am-6pm daily. *Concerts* 8pm. **Admission** from Ft500.
No credit cards.
This culture complex of exhibition hall, theatre and concert hall is set amid greenery near the Mammut mall. Most concerts are staged in the *fogadó* or pub area, a modest but reasonably satisfactory atmosphere for live music.

Petőfi Csarnok

XIV.Városliget, Zichy Mihály út 14 (363 3730/ www.petoficsarnok.hu). *M1 Széchenyi fürdő.*
Open *Concerts* 8pm. **Admission** varies.
No credit cards. Map p247 K2.
For a long time, this large events hall in the City Park was the only concert venue in town capable of accommodating non-megastar bands. The indoor arena is still too large for most Hungarian acts, but has-been Western acts stop off here. The outdoor stage is ideal for summer. Both hold 2,500 people.

Take it to the bridge – the great **A38** is set on a former Ukrainian barge.

Live music clubs

A38

XI.Pázmány Péter sétány (464 3940/www.a38.hu).
Tram 4, 6. **Open** 11am-4am Mon-Sat. *Concerts*
vary. **Admission** varies. **Credit** AmEx, MC, V.
Map p249 F9.
This former Ukrainian barge has been converted
into one of Budapest's busiest venues, with big local
alternative acts and good mid-range ones from
abroad. This is certainly the spot at which to catch
some of the best live shows in town – it has good
acoustics too. Concerts take place on the lower deck,
with a restaurant in the middle (reservations on 464
3946) and dancing up on the top deck in summer.

Filter Klub

VII.Almássy utca 1 (06 30 921 4212 mobile). M2
Blaha Lujza tér/tram 4, 6. **Open** 7pm-4am Mon-Sat.
Admission free. **No credit cards**. **Map** p247 H4.
This punk rock bar (*see p135*) has gigs by local
bands through the week, attracting new generation
of enthusiasts. Moody young Magyars come here
to share camaraderie and a love of speed guitar.

Gödör klub

V.Erzsébet tér (06 20 943 5464 mobile/www.godor klub.hu). M1, M2, M3 Deák tér. **Open** 4pm-2am daily. **Admission** varies. **No credit cards.** **Map** p246 E5.

A club venue under the urban park of central Erzsébet tér. Originally the building site of the National Theatre, this place is set in a bunker over which an artificial park was built. Surprisingly, this neon-lit hall with minimalist design has perhaps the best acoustics in town. Concerts start at 9pm, and in summer are often staged outside. Folk, jazz, indie and electronica – the place is open to everything.

Old Man's Music Pub

VII.Akácfa utca 13 (322 7645/www.oldmans.hu). M2 Blaha Lujza tér/tram 4, 6. **Open** 3pm-4am daily. *Concerts start 9pm.* **Admission** varies. **No credit cards.** **Map** p246 G5.

Large and comfortably furnished, this is the place at which to catch local blues acts such as Tamás Takács Dirty Blues Band, Ádám Török and Hobo. Jazz also gets a look-in. Good acoustics, but book a table if you want a view of the small stage.

Süss Fel Nap

V.Szent István körút 11 (374 3329/www.sussfel nap.hu). M3 Nyuguti pu./tram 4, 6. **Open** 6pm-dawn daily. **Admission** varies. **No credit cards.** **Map** p246 E3.

Labyrinthine cellar club with a musically astute management books good DJs and small bands from the UK and US, plus some of the best local alternative acts. Their Tesco Disco nights were named after a song by upcoming band E.Z. Basic.

Trafó Bár Tangó

IX.Liliom u. 41 (456 2049/www.trafo.hu). M3 Ferenc körút/tram 4, 6. **Open** 6pm-4am daily. **Admission** varies. **No credit cards.** **Map** p250 H8.

Beside housing modern theatre and dance performances in town, this cultural complex also boasts a cellar club. TBT is where you can catch some truly great gigs and most of Budapest's underground DJs. Alan McGee is a regular for his Death Disco nights.

Vörös Yuk/Kék Yuk

III.Fényes Adolf utca 28 (06 20 495 8016 mobile/ www.yuk.hu). HÉV to Timár utca. **Open** show nights. **Admission** varies. **No credit cards.**

These adjacent venues offer metal and punk acts, in an industrial setting. The hard-to-spot entrance is inside a factory complex. Check the web for concerts.

Wigwam Rock

XI.Fehérvári út 202 (208 5569/www.wigwamrock klub.hu). Tram 47/night bus 973. **Open** 8pm-5am Thur-Sun. **Admission** varies. **No credit cards.**

A barn-sized venue with an overdone Wild West theme, this is one of Budapest's large stages for rock bands, offering weekly rock 'n' roll parties and heavy metal acts plus three bars, a dancefloor and a games room. It's quite far out from the centre but right by the no.47 tram stop.

Unlike pop acts, Hungary's jazz musicians have always been more appreciated abroad. From fusion to mainstream and ethno-jazz, from Dixieland to big band, there have been a number of outstanding musicians. Key figures include violin virtuoso **Félix Lajkó**; saxophonist **Tony Lakatos**; drummer **Elemér Balázs**; guitarists **Ferenc Snétberger** and **Gyula Babos**; sax player **László Dés**; percussionist **Kornél Horváth**; and pianists **Béla Szakcsi Lakatos** and **Zsolt Kaltenecker**. Mihály Dresch is a world-class saxophonist who creates his own folk-jazz, spinning ancient Hungarian tunes into avant-garde experiments. Other ethno-jazzers worth seeking out include **Tin Tin Quintet**, **Makám** and upcoming band **Borago**, who incorporate Bartók's heritage into jazz. **Veronika Harcsa** is a remarkable singer who is at home in many different styles; **Gergő Borlai** is the most sought-after young jazz drummer at the moment – he is also a talented composer and has recently started his own band, **European Mantra**. Trumpet-player **Kornél Fekete-Kovács** was the founderof the first professional big band, the Budapest Jazz Orchestra (and its director until 2005), before starting the **Modern Art Orchestra**. Trumpet player **Lőrinc Barabás** and his band **Eklektric** merge jazz, reggae and electronic music. Acid-jazz oriented **Eszter Váczi & the Szörp** are also worth a try.

Brooklyn Music Pub

VI.Jókai utca 4 (06 30 210 3436 mobile/www.new brooklyn.hu). M1 Oktogon/tram 4, 6. **Open** 6pm-midnight Mon-Thur; 6pm-2am Fri, Sat. **Admission** free. **No credit cards.** **Map** p246 F4.

Owned by Roma musicians who are also the house band, the Patai Gypsy Band – yet they're not really folk music. They're a jazz string quartet, incredibly tight and fast-paced, channelling Django Reinhardt and similar influences. A cosy lounge atmosphere adds to an unusual, entertaining vibe.

Columbus Jazzklub

Jetty 4, V.Vigadó tér (266 9013). Tram 2. **Open** noon-midnight daily. **Admission** Ft1,500. **Credit** AmEx, DC, MC, V. **Map** p249 D5.

This modestly designed jazz club might be deep in tourist central, aboard a boat on the Pest embankment, but if you want to catch Hungary's jazz icons with their various offshoot projects and ensembles, this floating pub-restaurant is the place for it.

Jazz Garden

V.Veres Pálné utca 44A (266 7364). M3 Kálvin tér/tram 2, 47, 49. **Open** 6pm-1am daily. *Concerts* 8.30pm daily. **Admission** varies. **Credit** AmEx, MC, V. **Map** p249 F7.

Cellar club decorated with plants for a virtual outdoor effect. Beyond the indoor garden space is a rose-hued restaurant area where the live jazz is audible but unobtrusive. It's a welcome spot in winter.

New Orleans

VI.Lovag utca 5 (06 30 451 7525 mobile/www.new orleans.hu). M1 Oktogon/tram 4, 6. **Open** 10pm-4am Fri, Sat. Closed June-Aug. **Admission** varies. **No credit cards. Map** p246 F3.

Hidden in a little side street in the Theatre District, New Orleans is a spacious, lavishly ornamented club with a half-circular arrangement of comfy sofas and small coffee tables grouped around the stage. Dinner tables line the balcony. International acts to have appeared here include the likes of Al Di Meola, Robben Ford, John McLaughlin and Dewey Redman.

Folk & world music

Hungary's prominence in the music world owes much to the rich traditions of Magyar folk music. The often serious and morose Magyar turns into a completely different animal as soon as the sounds of a fiddle-led band swing into a lively *csárdás*, and village-style folk dancing enjoys a lively and youthful following at any of the dance houses (*táncház*) in Budapest on most nights of the week.

The old style of authentic folk music was revived in the early 1970s from oblivion by fiddler Béla Halmos and singer Ferenc Sebő. This new 'dance house' movement involved scores of young local musicians creating a counterculture away from the meddling authorities. Among the best known exponents were Muzsikás, whose singer, Márta Sebestyen, went on to global fame on albums such as *Deep Forest* and soundtracks to movies like *The English Patient.*

BANDS AND VENUES

Hungarian musicians tend to put great stock in accurately reflecting village styles, and you will see bands using instruments such as the hairy Hungarian bagpipe (*duda*), the three-stringed violas and basses of Transylvania, and the *utogardon*, a percussion instrument carved from a log in the shape of a cello. Music of the Csángós – a Magyar minority living in Moldavia – is all the rage these days, with its thumping, wild rhythms played on long wooden flutes, *koboz* lutes, fiddles and drums.

In a recent development, the largest dance takes place on Thursday evenings at the centrally located **Almássy téri Szabadidő Központ**. As opposed to most of Budapest's other venues where folk music is played, the *táncház* sessions at the Almássy tér Recreation Centre currently run throughout the summer. If you thought folk dancing was a staid and

Fonó Budai Zeneház. *See p190.*

frumpy affair, this should change your mind. On a good night hundreds of young dancers come to twirl in two halls to either Moldavian Csángó or Transylvanian village music by simultaneous live bands until the wee hours of the morning. Earlier in the evening there is usually tuition in a circle in the thick of the dancing, so just jump in.

The most reliable club venue for folk music is the **Fonó Budai Zeneház** for village bands (usually Wednesday or Thursday nights), revivalists and the ethno-rave of Balkan fusionists such as **BeshoDrom**. The archaic sounds of the Transylvanian Gypsy village band of **Palatka** can be heard here on the last Thursday of each month. The club also boasts the best folk, world music and jazz CD shop in Hungary, featuring the catalogue of the in-house Fonó record label (*see p154*).

Most regular dance houses close down from June to mid September, but festivals take place all summer in Budapest and beyond. For details, the Dance House Workshop runs the English-language www.tanchaz.hu/thmain.htm. A more comprehensive listing of folk events (in Hungarian) can be found, along with Magyar folk music, at www.folkradio.hu – click on *Folknaptar* for events.

Almássy tér Dance House

Almássy téri Szabadidőközpont
VII.Almássy tér 6 (342 0387/www.almassy.hu).
M2 Blaha Lujza tér/tram 4, 6. **Open** *Concerts* from
8pm Thur. **Admission** free. **No credit cards.**
Map p247 G4.

Csángó Dance House/ Marczibányi tér Culture House

Marczibányi téri Művelődési Ház
*II.Marczibányi tér 5A (212 2820). M2 Moszkva
tér/tram 4, 6.* **Open** *Concerts* 8pm-midnight Wed.
Admission varies. **No credit cards.**

Fonó Budai Zeneház

XI.Sztregova utca 3 (206 5300/www.fono.hu).
Tram 41, 47. **Open** *Concerts* from 8pm.
Admission varies. **No credit cards.**
Photos *p189.*

Kalamajka Dance House/ Aranytíz Culture Centre

Aranytiz Művelődési Központ
VI.Arany János utca 10 (354 3400/www.aranytiz.hu).
M3 Arany János utca/night bus 914, 931, 950.
Open *Concerts* 9pm-late Sat. **Admission** Ft800;
Ft500 concessions. **No credit cards. Map** p246 E4.

Romano's road

The Roma are experiencing a strong cultural
revival, nowhere better reflected than in the
musical legacy of the Kovács family, the
backbone of **Romano Drom** ('Gypsy Road').
Using driving rhythms punctuated by vocal
scat singing, milk-can percussion, and wild
guitar and accordion riffs drawn from Gypsy
traditions, Romano Drom have emerged
as Hungary's premier Gypsy group.

The music is grounded in their Lovari roots.
Among Vlach Roma, vocal music prevails,
and instrumental parts for dancing are sung
using a technique called oral bassing.

Romano Drom were founded by Gojma
Kovács and his son Anti to represent the
more traditional side of Romani song lore,
but quickly grew in popularity as one of the
most experimental Gypsy bands, absorbing

styles from Catalan Gypsy to Romanian taraf.
Throughout, the band brings a strong public
sense of Roma pride to their work, composing
new songs in the Lovara dialect of Romani
spoken by the Kovács family.

The death of Gojma in 2005 left the group
devastated, but they decided to carry on,
bringing in Anti's 15-year-old son Mate
on percussion and touring the world music
circuits of Europe and the Americas. In
Budapest they are the hardest working band
in the Roma community, playing for Gypsy
events and gatherings, festivals and a
residency at the downtown **Gödör Klub** (*see
p188*). Look for Romano Drom's releases on
the French world music label Daqui: the
recent *Po Cheri* (2007) or *Ando Foro* and *Déta
Dévla,* featuring the irrepressible Gojma.

Arts & Entertainment

Nightlife

Few frills but a lot of thrills make Budapest a great party town.

Budapest by night is unpretentious and gloriously easy. There's no great white way or exclusive see-and-be-seen scenes. Instead there is an energetic young crowd that eagerly fills a wide range of venues, where, for little money and even less aggravation, you can dance and drink until dawn. Innocent plans to have a quiet one before retiring can go wonderfully awry, as you discover how many great places are packed into downtown Budapest, especially District VII. Budapest is also a relatively safe town at night. Most of the people you meet will be out for serious fun, not trouble, and happy to meet visiting foreigners. Taxis are cheap and relatively easy to find, and there is a handy network of night buses working major routes.

Summer is the time to be here. Although the full-time bars and clubs get quieter, these are supplemented by an almost equal number of temporary outdoor venues whose locations change from year to year. The best of these are set up in ruined courtyards of downtown buildings, mainly in Districts VII and VIII. Locals know them as garden (*kert*) bars. *See p194* **Party under the stars**.

Local jocks, like Palotai, Cadik and Suhaid, and collectives, like Manna Manna, El Bombo Atomico, the Gimmeshot Crew and the Tilos Rádió DJs, all know how to move the dance floor. Meanwhile, more and more international talent is coming this way. Still, admission to most shows remains relatively cheap and affordable for the local market, with tickets ranging from free to about Ft3,000.

Like any other vibrant city, Budapest's night scene is fluid: places open and close quickly, and the party crowd shifts with the current, especially the outdoor bars. Keep your eyes peeled, pick up a copy of the free listings publications *Exit* or *Pesti Est*, and check flyers at the key bars listed below.

Late-night bars & clubs

Café Droszt Tulipán Espresszó
V.Nádor utca 32 (269 5043). M2 Kossuth tér/ tram 2. **Open** 24hrs daily. **No credit cards.** **Map** p246 D4.
The retro, taxi-themed decor, card-playing cab drivers in the back and charming young staff make this bar a pleasantly lively oasis in the business quarter of District V that mostly shuts down after working hours. The Tulipán's success has spawned

other bars in the neighbouring doorways, but this place is clearly the original. The mini-terrace out front offers the perfect setting for those serious late-night conversations.

Fészek Club
VII.Kertész utca 36 (342 6549). Tram 4, 6/night bus 923. **Open** 8pm-5am daily. **Admission** free-Ft300. **No credit cards.** **Map** p246 G4.
Downstairs in the old actors' and artists' club, where there's also a courtyard bar in summer (*see p194* **Party under the stars**), you'll find a decadent cellar club with a surreal look and atmosphere straight out of a David Lynch movie. The decor is brothel style, with crushed velvet chaises longues and a natty piano keyboard bar top. Be deferential to the codger on reception to get inside. Depending on the mood, you'll either encounter a glamorous crowd dancing till dawn to a superb live jazz-funk combo – or a handful of people sharing a last drink. Most weekends, at around 4am, there'll be an impromptu snogathon, in which strangers inexplicably fall into each others arms and canoodle. A fun place.

The meticulously sexy **B7** – *see p193*.

Three clubs, one big party – **Buddha Beach/Inside/Szociális Klub**. *See p193.*

Katapult Kávézo

VII.Dohány utca 1 (266 7226). M2 Astoria/night bus 909, 931, 966, 979A. **Open** 9am-2am daily. **No credit cards. Map** p249 F6.

Energizing late night bar with decadent, sociable regulars and a staff that has seen everything, and liked most of it. DJs spin weekend nights, encouraging the twenty- and thirtysomething crowd to shove the wicker furniture in a corner and dance in front of the bar. The dark red walls and abundance of tattoos encourage casual intimacy. The Katapult is set at the tip of the District VII bar zone, right opposite the Synagogue, so it gets a good buzz in the early evening as party-goers meet to compare notes. It can be sublime later, when tongues and morals hang loose.

Múzeum Cukrászda

VIII.Múzeum körút 10 (338 4415). M2 Astoria/tram 47, 49/bus 7/night bus 909, 914, 950, 966, 979, 979A. **Open** 24hrs daily. **No credit cards. Map** p249 F6.

Right in the heart of town, this Budapest nightlife staple is basically a cake shop where you can get a pint or a shot with your coffee and sweets. The small terrace is a great place at which to have a breakfast beer and pity solid citizens as they scurry to work.

Noiret

VI.Dessewffy utca 8-10 (331 6103). M3 Arany János utca/night bus 914, 931, 950, 979. **Open** 2pm-4am daily. **No credit cards. Map** p246 E4.

A youngish crowd comes here throughout the day to play darts and pool on one of the many big, if worn, Brunswick tables. As evening sets in, the upstairs cocktail bar provides fuel for party-goers setting off around District VI. By late at night this is a destination, with a friendly bar staff and pop jukebox sprinkled with classics encouraging drinkers on their way home to have one more beer. Bar snacks include hefty pizzas.

Piaf

VI.Nagymező utca 25 (312 3823). M1 Opera/M1 Oktogon/tram 4, 6/night bus 914, 923, 931, 950, 979. **Open** 11pm-6am Mon-Thur, Sun; 11pm-7am Fri, Sat. **Admission** up to Ft800 incl 1 drink. **No credit cards. Map** p246 F4.

A marvellously depraved old Pest stalwart that gets going in the wee hours. A century ago, the city was dotted with dimly lit orpheums, a cross between a nightclub and a *café chantant*, louche and alluring. In similar vein, the Piaf has an upstairs bar done up in bordello red and comes with a piano player. The punters are showbiz/lounge lizard types, with the odd lady scooping up drunks. A tricky staircase leads to a cellar with tiny dancefloor, where live bands or jazzy pop provide the soundtrack.

Vittula

VII.Kertész utca 4 (no phone). M2 Blaha Lujza tér/night bus 907, 908, 923. **Open** 6pm-2am Mon-Wed, Sun; 6pm-4am Thur-Sat. Closed July, Aug. **No credit cards. Map** p247 G5.

First, the name. The reason why there's a bunch of Finns outside solemnly taking pictures of each other pointing at the bar sign is because Vittula is Finnish for the c word, collectively ('c*** club?') – and the name of a short story and film. Tim, the friendly slacker who started up this charming cellar bar, liked it in any case. Vittula fills up with an alternative crowd, and a smattering of foreigners later at night. A fun, sociable, no-frills atmosphere encourages long, late drinking sessions. Music, often good, is augmented by DJs.

Nightclubs

B7

VI.Nagymező utca 46-48 (269 0573/www.b7.hu). *M1 Opera/M1 Oktogon/tram 4, 6/night bus 914, 923, 931, 950, 979.* **Open** 5pm-5am Wed-Sat. **Admission** varies. **No credit cards. Map** p246 F4. The house music and dance classics in this high-ceilinged downtown box of a club are energizing, but the MC and go-go shows in the middle of the main floor can be a distraction. Most women here are meticulously sexy and seriously outnumbered by eager, sharply dressed men. Lucky guys who do get to chat someone up have to speak loudly, as there's nowhere to escape the throbbing dance music. **Photo** *p191*.

Buddha Beach/ Inside/Szociális Klub

IX.Közraktár utca 9-11 (210 4872/06 20 361 3445 mobile/www.beachside.hu). Tram 2/night bus 979, 979A. **Open** 5pm-5am daily. **Admission** varies. **No credit cards. Map** p249 F8. The riverside warehouses by the Pest foot of Petőfi Bridge have been converted into this slick, sprawling, classy but fun party complex. Admission is usually free to the outdoor Buddha Beach, done up in gold Buddhas and '70s decor, with intimate riverside seating and a capacity of 4,000. In winter, the party moves to the adjacent Inside, a long, skinny warehouse club, with DJs playing disco and techno in separate dance rooms and a chill-out space in between with lounge music. Funky retro decor and a fun crowd electrify the dance floors, though go-go girls on stage in the techno room encourage gawking instead of dancing. The many bar counters give snappy service, and the busboys will offer to light your cigarette. The Szociális Klub, a separate bar in one corner of the complex, has concerts and parties, but also a high testosterone count on quiet nights, when entry is free for all, because women get into the superior Inside for free anyway. **Photos** *p191*.

Capella

V.Belgrád rakpart 23 (318 6231). M3 Ferenciek tere/ tram 2/night bus 907, 908, 921, 973. **Open** 10pm-4am Wed, Thur; 10pm-5am Fri, Sat. **Admission** Ft1,500. **No credit cards. Map** p249 E7. Although invariably billed as a gay club (*see p179*), Capella is happy to welcome in straights for the midnight drag show and for house and disco tunes till dawn. A cover charge will be included on your drinks bill. Can be one of the best nights in Budapest.

A warm welcome at **Living Room**. *See p195.*

Citadella Club

XI.Citadella sétány 2 (209 3271). Bus 27. **Open** 10pm-5am on party nights. **Admission** varies. **No credit cards. Map** p248 D7. While the quality of the party varies, the indoor club and garden complex in the Citadella affords an unbeatable view of the city. One-off parties can be great, but it's a long way uphill, so check flyers. There's a restaurant and hostel (*see p49*) here too.

Dokk Bistro & Club

III.Hajógyáriszige 122 (06 30 535 2747 mobile). HÉV to Filatorigát/bus 86/night bus 923. **Open** 8pm-4am Mon-Sat. **Credit** AmEx, MC, V. In a nicely renovated brick warehouse by the river, this pricey club far from the rest of town draws a flash crowd of yuppies and beautiful people, including performers and producers from the nearby porn movie studios. As the upwardly mobile regulars tend to have jobs, weekdays here can be quieter.

E-Klub

X.Népliget, next to Planetarium (263 1619/www.e-klub.hu). M3 Népliget/night bus 901, 914, 937, 950. **Open** 9pm-5am Fri; 10pm-5am Sat. **Admission** Ft700-Ft900. **No credit cards.** Drunk and suitably lively suburban kids enjoy foam parties, go-go dancers and teeny discos in this Communist-era rock disco – reinvented as a mainstream house/techno nightclub with three dance floors and a decent sound system.

Arts & Entertainment

Party under the stars

Budapest nightlife is best enjoyed alfresco on a blazing hot summer night. From May to September, the number of venues nearly doubles with the opening of outdoor garden (*kert*) clubs and bars. Partying under the stars encourages a kind of abandon that you just don't get indoors. Nailing down exactly where to party is not so easy. The scene is in flux. Fine outdoor spots spring up in temporary locations, which means one summer's hotspot may be a building site by spring. Keep an ear to the ground to find some of the best Budapest has to offer.

A few year-round spots, like the **A38 boat** (*see p187*), **Buddha Beach/Inside** (*see p193*), **Szimplakert** (*see p195; see photo*) and **West Balkan** (*see p195*) have outdoor spaces incorporated into their regular clubs, so they just become more spacious in summer. Other locations close in winter but are guaranteed to bloom once school's out.

These include two clubs on the Buda side of the Petőfi Bridge: the somewhat yuppie-ish, ersatz **Latin Café Del Rio** (XI.Goldmann György tér/Vitézek tere, 06 30 297 2158 mobile, www.rio.hu); and the well established **Zöld Párdon** (XI.Goldmann György tér/Vitézek tere, www.zp.hu), with a rowdier crowd.

A more temporal site is the new **Corvintető** (VII.Blaha Lujza tér 1-2, 461 0076) on the roof of the 1970s-style Corvin department store, where stairs and a lift on the side lead straight up to the party. With an enclosed disco area, great views and a location in the heart of District VII, this place is likely to be packed until the building comes down, in 2009 or 2010. Another District VII hangout is the garden of the **Fészek** (*see p191*), inside the beautifully cloistered courtyard of a complex that also houses the cellar club.

Margaret Island offers several places, including the **ChaChaCha Teaház** (Atlétikai Centrum, XIII.Margit-sziget), a busy location in a small sports stadium just to the left as you enter the island from the Nagykörút. The **Holdudvar** (Casino kert, XIII.Margaret-sziget, 236 0155, www.holdudvar.net) is another popular spot. Its neighbour is the quieter, but more alternative, **Sark kert**, on the Pest side of the island by the jogging path.

Facing Margaret Island on the Buda side is another rooftop garden. The **Fecske** (II.Árpád fejedelem útja 8, 06 70 341 7085 mobile, www.fecske.net; open 11am-2am Mon-Thur, Sun, 11am-4am Fri, Sat) sits atop the Komjádi swimming pool (*see p197*).

Deep in District IX, in a gritty neighbourhood full of abandoned buildings, the biggest empty structure, a former fire department warehouse, has been taken over by the **Tűz Tate** (IX.Tűzoltó utca 54-56, 06 30 954 5993 mobile, www.tuztate.hu), with a huge courtyard, cellar concert space and upstairs art gallery. A busy music programme favours a mixture of dancehall reggae, break beats and live rock.

Kultiplex

IX.Kinizsi utca 28 (219 0706). M3 Ferenc körút/ tram 4, 6/night bus 906, 966, 979, 979A. **Open** 10am-4am daily. **Admission** free-Ft1,000. **No credit cards.** **Map** p249 G7.

This club with two dance floors and a big terrace serving grilled food is slated for the wrecking ball by 2009. In the meantime, regular DJs entertain, with an accent on drum 'n' bass and dancehall reggae.

Kuplung

VI.Király utca 46 (06 30 986 8856 mobile). M1 Opera/night bus 923. **Open** 2pm-4am Mon-Sat; 5pm-4am Sun. **Admission** varies. **No credit cards.** **Map** p246 F4.

This former bus garage on the edge of District VII's party zone provides a big space that can develop a great buzz. Kuplung hosts performances by DJs and concerts in a small, soundproof inner chamber, but half

Arts & Entertainment

the fun is in being swallowed up by the cavernous, chaotic main room, where you can drink and cavort until dawn without realising it. Funky decor includes a wall full of graffiti. A gallery area hosts exhibitions.

Living Room
V.Kossuth Lajos utca 17 (06 70 337 3434 mobile/ www.livingroom.hu). M2 Astoria/bus 7/night bus 909, 914, 950, 966, 979, 979A. **Open** Fri, Sat & parties. Closed May-Sept. **Admission** varies. **No credit cards**. **Map** p249 F6.
This downtown cellar has three floors for different beats. Though sometimes hokey, the tunes still fill the floors with charming twentysomethings who are looking for fun and not taking themselves too seriously. Great chill-out rooms, with pillows on the floor and curtains for privacy, give the place its name. Two bars offer friendly service and cheap booze. **Photo** *p193*.

Macskafogó Music Pub
VI.Nádor utca 29 (473 0123/www.macskafogo.hu). M2 Kossuth Lajos tér/tram 2. **Open** 6pm-3am Thur; 6pm-4am Fri, Sat. **No credit cards**. **Map** p246 D4.
Discreetly sequestered in a dark cellar, on a street near Parliament, the Cat Catcher attracts a happy mob of locals who boogie like maniacs. Joan Jett, the Clash and George Michael are passé, but tell that to the giddy crowd, dancing as if it didn't know better. A great place to meet Magyars in a good mood.

Roktogon Music Club
VI.Mozsár utca 9 (06 70 537 6230 mobile). M1 Oktogon/tram 4, 6/night bus 923, 979. **Open** 5pm-4am Wed-Sat. **Admission** free. **Concerts** Ft500. **No credit cards**. **Map** p246 F4.
Fun, medium-sized cellar bar-disco specialising in local live bands, from Doors impersonators to hardcore acts. DJs play MTV hits between acts. Clientele is generally young, excitable and friendly.

School Club
IX.Fővám tér 8 (215 4359/www.schoolclub.hu). M3 Kálvin tér/tram 2, 47, 49/night bus 979, 979A. **Open** 10pm-5am Tue-Sat. **Admission** Ft600-Ft1,000. **No credit cards**. **Map** p249 E7.
Formerly the Közgáz Klub, this huge cellar in the Economics University is packed in term-time with students sinking cheap booze, listening to loud Magyar pop, falling over and snogging drunkenly.

Szimplakert
VII.Kazinczy utca 14 (no phone/www.szimpla.hu). M2 Astoria/bus 7/night bus 909, 914, 950, 966, 979, 979A. **Open** noon-3am daily. **Admission** free. **No credit cards**. **Map** p248 F5.
This nightlife institution, occupying the courtyard and first two floors of an abandoned building in District VII, is packed by midnight most nights. The big indoor space includes a cluster of rooms, done up in a squat-like decor. Throughout summer, they show films outdoors. The one thing missing is the beat. There are too many people to make space for a dance floor, and, outside of the upstairs maze of chill-out rooms, where there's usually a DJ spinning

lounge tunes, it's hard to hear the music anyway. At least you can chat in the spacious bar areas. Enjoy the chaos and conversation and dance elsewhere.

Szóda
VII.Wesselényi utca 18 (461 0007/www.szoda.com). M2 Astoria/bus 7/night bus 909, 914, 950, 966, 979, 979A. **Open** 9am-midnight Mon-Fri; 2pm-midnight Sat. **Admission** free. **No credit cards**. **Map** p249 D4.
A lively, two-floor operation deep in District VII's party vortex, where a relaxed, alternative crowd takes its nightlife seriously. The upstairs bar, half-exposed to passers-by through its picture windows, opens with a busy bar counter at which with-it staff serve superior sandwiches and cheapish spirits. At the back are secluded, intimate tables. Rows of soda bottles, manga art and retro touches comprise the decor. Dancing takes place in a cellar full of folks giving it full welly.

Trafó Pince Bar Tangó
IX.Liliom utca 41 (456 2049). M3 Ferenc körút/ tram 4, 6/night bus 923. **Open** 6pm-4am daily. **Admission** free-Ft750. **No credit cards**. **Map** p250 H8.
The basement of Budapest's main culture centre hosts some of the best DJs to hit town. On sporadic Death Disco nights, Alan McGee of Oasis fame flies in from London to spin high quality retro and indie. Techno wizards from Austria and Serbia also grace the decks. A friendly young crowd, with good ears for music and good feet for dancing, make this one of the best spots to be at on any weekend night in Budapest. A cheap bar (mind the wine), roomy booths and big dance floor complete the picture.

Trocadero
V.Szent István körút 15 (06 30 987 7450 mobile). M3 Nyugati pu./tram 4, 6/night bus 906, 923, 931. **Open** 9pm-3am Mon-Thur; 9pm-5am Fri, Sat. **Admission** varies. **No credit cards**. **Map** p246 D2.
The main Latin disco in town is a fun place where enthusiastic and unpretentious Hungarians eagerly work on their moves. On weekends, the night starts with salsa lessons. Sporadic live salsa and merengue acts then pack the house. One of the few places in Budapest with a truly multinational crowd.

West Balkan
VIII.Futó utca 46 (06 20 473 3651 mobile/www. west-balkan.com). M3 Ferenc körút/tram 4, 6/ night bus 906. **Open** 2pm-dawn daily. **Admission** free. **No credit cards**. **Map** p250 H7.
The WB is now in its third location, and likely to move again by 2009 – but wherever it ends up, there's sure to be a party. The smart management, darling staff and hip regulars of this huge boho club have followed it from one abandoned building to the next, making sure that it stays one of the top spots in town. The current site is a stunning old structure with a half-outdoor dance area and a labyrinth of upstairs rooms, done up with junk/antique furniture. Plans call for taking over a similarly dilapidated site in District VIII, perhaps on Fecske utca.

Arts & Entertainment

Sport & Fitness

Gym, swim and cycle around Budapest to your heart's content.

Hungary has a proud sporting tradition and offers the visitor a variety of indoor and outdoor activities. As in all former Socialist societies, sports facilities were cheaply accessible for all. Much of that infrastructure is still in place, by now most of it modernised.

The biggest spectator sport is football, although water polo is popular in summer, ice hockey in winter. The biggest event of the year is the **Hungarian Grand Prix** in August.

Details of all sports events are in *Nemzeti Sport*. This well established sports daily (Ft104) is also finest source for international football results in you'll find in newsprint.

Major stadia

Budapest Arena

XIV.Stefánia út 2 (422 2600/www.budapest arena.hu). M2 Stadionok. **Open** *box office* 9am-6pm Mon-Fri; 9am-2pm Sat.
A 12,500-capacity indoor sports venue in the same large complex as the national stadium. The Arena hosts basketball, boxing and rock concerts.

Puskás Ferenc Stadion (Népstadion)

XIV.Istvánmezei út 3-5 (471 4100/471 4321). M2 Stadionok. **Open** *box office* 10am-6pm Mon-Fri.
The national stadium, built by and for the people (*nép*) in 1953, was renovated for the 1998 European Athletics Championships. In 2002 it was renamed to honour footballer Ferenc Puskás. Stalinist statues still line the approach to this open bowl, still in urgent need of serious renovation.

Spectator sports

Basketball

A few American NBA rejects are attracting bigger crowds to the domestic game, which runs from September to May. For fixtures see *Nemzeti Sport* or call the Hungarian Basketball Federation (460 6825).

Football

After the glory of the post-war era, the domestic game has deteriorated to a shameful degree. Once it was discovered that matches were being rigged – the word *bundameccs*, or fixed match, is whispered whenever anything iffy happens

on the pitch – local football lost all credibility and funding. Players left for foreign leagues in droves, fans likewise. Average attendances would put an English lower-league club to shame. Hungary's failure in 2007 to be awarded the co-hosting of Euro 2012 means that the much-needed improvements to football's infrastructure have been put on ice indefinitely.

The three main Budapest clubs, Ferencváros, Újpest and MTK, head a lacklustre league, with competition from recent consecutive champions Debrecen. The big game is Ferencváros against fierce rivals Újpest, usually played in the morning with a heavy police presence.

The season runs from August to November, and from March to June, with most games taking place on Saturdays. *Nemzeti Sport* has details. A ticket (*belépő*) is about Ft1,200; a *lelátó* offers a better view.

Ferencváros

IX.Üllői út 129 (215 6023/www.ftc.hu). M3 Népliget.
Hungary's biggest club, Ferencváros (FTC or 'Fradi') have the largest following. Many of these people are bone-headed imbeciles, and FTC can be an intimidating place. A financial scandal in 2006 saw the club forcibly relegated to the lower league, and demonstrations on the streets.

MTK

VIII.Salgótarjáni út 12-14 (333 8368/fax 303 0592/ www.mtkhungaria.hu). Tram 1/trolleybus 75/bus 9.
MTK barely attract 3,000 spectators despite recent success. Fans of the cult war movie *Escape to Victory* may recognise their ground, as the football scenes were filmed here.

Újpest

IV.Megyeri út 13 (231 0088/fax 231 0089/www. ujpestfc.hu). M3 Újpest-Központ, then bus 96, 104.
Of all Budapest's half-dozen clubs in the top flight, Újpest (UTE) have the most promising set-up. A revamped 13,000 all-seater stadium, a partnership agreement with a Belgian club and a young, motivated side point towards a reasonably bright future.

Ice hockey

Ice hockey is a popular spectator sport during the football break. Two of the four professional clubs in the capital, Ferencváros and Újpest, are in the Extra Liga, playing at the Budapest Arena (*see above*) and the rink by Újpest football stadium (IV.Megyeri út 13, 369 7333).

Built by the people for the people – the national **Puskás Ferenc Stadion**. *See p196.*

Motor racing

Hungary's biggest sporting event of the year, held at the renovated Hungaroring some 20km from town, packs out Budapest's hotels and restaurants for one weekend in August, and gives locals a chance to star-spot.

Hungaroring
20km east of Budapest off M3 motorway at Mogyoród, H-2146 (tel/fax 06 28 444 444/ www.hungaroring.hu). **Information** *Osztermann Forma 1 Kft, V.Apáczai Csere János utca 11, 3rd floor (ticket hotline 266 2040/fax 317 2963). M1, M2, M3 Deák tér/tram 47, 49.* **Open** *8am-4pm Mon-Thur; 8am-2pm Fri 2mths before event.* **Date** Aug. **Advance ticket booking** *Official agencies www.gpticketshop.com.*

Swimming & water polo

Hungary still produces Olympic champions in swimming, and enjoys a solid tradition in water polo, the nation's main summer sport.

Császár-Komjádi Sportuszoda
III.Árpád fejedelem útja 8 (212 2750). Bus 6, 60, 86. **Open** 6am-6pm daily. **Tickets** Ft1,200; Ft720 concessions. **No credit cards. Map** p245 C1.
Hungary's national swimming stadium is packed for top water polo matches and major swimming galas.

Activities

Cricket

The summer of 2007 ushers in the inaugural **Hungarian Cricket League**. Curious locals, expat Brits and Aussies, and the Indian community have signed up for seven teams. Players practise every summer weekend in the Városliget. Matches take place at several venues in and near the capital. For more information, see www.hungary4cricket.com.

Cycling

Budapest is improving as a cycle city. *See p199* **Life in the narrow lane**.

Friends of the City Cycling Group
V.Nádor utca 34 (311 7855). M2 Kossuth tér. **Map** p246 D4.
Produces a *Map for Budapest Cyclists*, detailing bike lanes, riding conditions and service shops.

Extreme sports

Today's Magyar teenager is nobody without a skateboard and/or in-line skates. All major malls have a skate shop, complementing the specialist venue and store listed below.

Görzenál Skatepark

*III.Árpád fejedelem útja 125 (250 4800). HÉV to
Tímár utca.* **Open** 1-7pm Mon-Fri; 9am-7pm Sat,
Sun. **Admission** Ft400-Ft600; Ft150 non-skating
parents. **Rental** Ft600 for 3hrs. **No credit cards.**
Teenage paradise. Rollerskating track, skateboard
park, BMX/cycle track and jumps, two basketball
courts and several 'freestyle' areas with ramps and
jumps for bike, skate or board.

ProCross

*II.Margit körút 67 (315 1995). M2 Moszkva tér/
tram 4, 6.* **Open** 10am-7pm Mon-Sat. **No credit
cards. Map** p245 A3.
Just before the Mammut mall – boards, skates, BMX,
accessories, clothing and protection gear.

Gliding & paragliding

The Buda hills offer plenty of opportunities to
hang-glide. Traditional gliding, with or without
an instructor, is also available. At weekends,
spectators can take no.11 bus from Batthyány
tér to its terminus, then walk on through the
forest to the clearing at Hármashatárhegy,
following the noise of gliders humming and
microlites buzzing overhead. The Airborne
Club of Hungary (www.airborneclub.hu) offers
courses in paragliding and trips out of town.

Hármashatárhegy Airfield

*II.Arad utca 2 (376 5110/www.bme.hu/hhh).
M2 Batthyány tér, then bus 11 to terminus.*
Open 10am-8pm Sat, Sun. **Rates** vary.
Gliding, hang-gliding, microlites and paragliding,
with instruction available for beginners.

Golf

Until the recent addition of the **Pólus**, courses
near Budapest were poor and serious hackers
headed down to the **Hencse** by Lake Balaton.
Also quite close to town is the **Old Lake Golf
& Country Club** (www.oldlakegolf.com), in a
wooded park in the Gerecse foothills near Tata.
For further details, check www.golfhungary.hu.

Birdland Golf Country Club

*240km from Budapest. M1 towards Győr, route 85 to
Csorna, route 86 to Hegyfalug, through Tompaládony
to Bükfürdő. Thermal körút 10 (06 94 358 060/www.
birdland.hu).* **Open** 8am-6pm daily. **Fee** Ft9,000-
Ft14,000. **Credit** AmEx, DC, MC, V.
Hungary's best course, championship-rated and
sited in beautiful hills close to the Austrian border.

Hencse National Golf
& Country Club

*175km south-west of Budapest at Hencse. Kossuth
Lajos utca 3 (06 82 481 245/fax 06 82 481 248).*
Open Feb-1 Dec dawn-dusk. **Fee** Ft13,750-Ft17,500.
Credit MC, V.
Marvellously sited in a verdant National Park.

Pólus Palace Thermál Golf Club

*H-2132 Göd, Kádár utca 49 (06 27 530 500/06 27
530 570/www.poluspalace.hu).* **Fee** Ft13,240-
Ft16,740. **Credit** AmEx, DC, MC, V.
The closest 18-hole championship course to
Budapest, 20km north of town. Part of a five-star
thermal leisure hotel resort, opened in 2005.

Health & fitness

Modern gyms and solariums are all over town.
Better clubs, such as the ones listed here, meet
standard regulations. Most of Budapest's major
hotels also have fitness facilities.

Andi Studio

*V.Hold utca 29 (311 0740). M2 Kossuth tér/M3
Arany János utca.* **Open** 6am-9pm Mon-Fri; 9am-
2pm Sat. **Rates** *Aerobics & sauna* Ft900. *Gym &
sauna* Ft900. *Aerobics, gym & sauna* Ft1,200.
No credit cards. Map p246 E4.
Budapest's first Western-style gym and fitness club,
with an on-site beautician, a bar and café.

Astoria Fitness Centre

V.Károly körút 4 (317 0452). M2 Astoria. **Open**
6.30am-midnight Mon-Fri; 9am-9pm Sat; 1.30-9pm Sun.
Admission Ft1,400. **No credit cards. Map** p249 F6.
Popular, well-appointed city-centre gym.

Yogasanas

*VIII.Horanszky utca 5 (06 20 802 0262 mobile/www.
yogasanasbudapest.com). M3 Kálvin tér/tram 4, 6.*
Open 6.30-8pm Mon-Wed, Fri; 7-8.30pm Thur;
11.30am-4.30pm Sat. **Rates** from Ft2,000.
No credit cards. Map p249 G6.
A drop-in yoga studio that offers classes in English
from beginner to advanced.

Ice skating

Every winter locals dust off their skates and
head to the open-air rink behind Hősök tere in
the City Park. A rinkside bar is open for those
happy just to watch. Skates can be rented out.

Városligeti Műjégpálya

XIV.Olof Palme sétány 5 (364 0013). M1 Hősök tere.
Open Nov-Mar 9am-1pm, 4-8pm Mon-Fri; 10am-2pm
Sat, Sun. **Rates** Ft900; Ft400 children. **No credit
cards. Map** p247 J2.

Kayak & canoe

Although kayak- and canoe-hire places are few
and far between around Budapest, Hungary
remains one of the top nations in the sport.

Béke Üdülőtelep

III.Nánási út 97 (388 9303). Bus 34. **Open** Apr-
mid Oct 8am-7pm daily. **Rates** Ft1,000-Ft3,000.
No credit cards.
Beautifully situated on the banks of the Danube,
in the vicinity of the Hotel Lido.

Life in the narrow lane

Budapest's cyclists knew their time had come in March 2007, when 50,000 of them took a day-long, traffic-stopping tour around the capital to stage the world's largest Critical Mass rally for bikers' rights. A city where bicycles were once treated more like targets than vehicles had begun to make room for two-wheeled traffic. With its growing network of bike lanes, quiet side streets and riverside trips, Budapest can be great to cycle round.

Several places will rent you a bicycle, and give you a tour if you want; or you can just ask for a map of the bike routes and find your own way. The quality of these routes varies, with some of the smaller ones poorly marked.

The car-free path that runs through Buda, right along the Danube, is the autobahn of Budapest bike lanes. Easy to find, flat and relatively well signposted, this shaded route offers great river views and convenient connections. From its southern origin on **Csepel** island (*see p101*), it goes through the heart of town, intersecting with all the bridge crossings and continuing on to a network that reaches the **Danube Bend** (*see pp208-209*).

By heading north on this main Buda path, and following the green signs, you can take a flat 20-kilometre pedal to quaint **Szentendre** (*see p208*), with riverside restaurants. About halfway through the trip, you'll hit the Római Part, a shaded park on the Danube with a rocky shore, summer hotels and terraces selling sausages, beer and fried fish. If you turn off the Buda bike lane where indicated at Kacsa utca, near Bem tér, you can take a pulse-pushing eight-kilometre (five-mile) uphill route to scenic green Hüvösvölgy, where the last couple of kilometres are along a dirt path through a forest.

Inside Pest, the big bike path along Andrássy út runs from the Chain Bridge to the Városliget, with side paths heading down Bajcsy Zsilinksy and toward Deák tér. In heavily pedestrianised District V, and most of downtown, the side streets have easy traffic and lead to where you need to go.

Biking these small streets is a good way to catch most of the major sights in town. A guide who knows the easy routes can be helpful, and there are several English-language bicycle tours, led by laid-back young cyclists.

Cycling has a hip, alternative cachet in Budapest, so most of the courtyard garden bars offer a safe place to lock up. If you can remember to drink carefully, it's fun to join the crowd biking between outdoor venues in the summer – **Budapestbike.hu** offers tours. The streets get quieter as the evening wears on, and by midnight the road is yours.

Bikebase

VI.Podmaniczky utca 19 (269 5983/06 70 625 8501 mobile/www.bikebase.hu) M3 Nyugati pu.. **Open** 9am-7pm. **Rates** *Rentals* Ft2,500/day. **No credit cards. Map** p246 F3. This friendly shop near Nyugati station rents bikes and accessories cheaply and can organise tours with 24-hour notice.

Budapestbike.hu

VII.Wesselényi utca 18 (06 30 944 5533 mobile/www.budapestbike.hu). M1, M2, M3 Deák tér. **Open** 10am-8pm daily. **Rates** *Rentals* Ft3,000/day. *Tours* from Ft5,000. **No credit cards. Map** p249 F5. Based at the hip Szóda bar, this was started by couriers. They rent bikes and give tours, including one of Saturday nightlife.

Yellow Zebra

V.Sütő utca 2 (266 8777/269 3843/ www.yellowzebrabikes.com). M1, M2, M3 Deák tér. **Open** *Nov-Mar* 10am-6pm daily. *Apr-Oct* 8.30am-8pm daily. **Rates** *Rentals* Ft1,500/5hrs; Ft3,500/24hrs. *Tours* Ft4,500; Ft4,000 concessions. **No credit cards. Map** p249 E5. This professional operation lets you tour in a pack of bright yellow bikes or take off on your own. Also has a branch at VI.Lázár utca 16.

Poker

Since the inaugural Budapest Poker Open in late 2005, card clubs big and small have sprung up across town, luring hopeful gamblers with dreams of getting rich quick. If you're looking for a game, a good place to start out is the downtown **Tropicana Casino** (V.Vigadó utca 2, 266 3062, www.tropicanacasino.hu), where tournaments are held every day from 6pm – exclusively Texas Hold'em, but with varying sizes of buy-in. If it's a cash game you're after, sign up and stick around until a table or two gets freed up around 8pm-9pm. Most players speak English – and they'll no doubt point you to some of the private card clubs. One of the friendliest and most professionally run, opened in May 2007, is the **Royale Poker Club** (XIII. Fiastyúk utca 4, www.royaleclub.hu).

Riding

Hungarians are famed for their horsemanship and have a well-developed industry for riding holidays around the Puszta and Lake Balaton.

Hungarian Equestrian Tourism

V.Ferenciek tere 4 (266 8697/www.equi.hu). M3 Ferenciek tere/tram 2/bus 7. **Open** 9.30am-4pm Mon-Thur; 8.30am-2pm Fri. **Map** p249 E6.
Provides comprehensive information on riding holidays around Hungary. Next door is Pegazus (317 1644), which offers a similar service.

Petneházy Riding School

II.Feketefej utca 2-4 (397 5048/06 20 567 1616 mobile). M2 Moszkva tér, then tram 56, then bus 63. **Open** *Pony riding* 10am-noon, 1-3pm Sun. **Rates** Ft1,500 for 15mins on ponies to Ft15,000 for 2hr coaching session. **No credit cards**.
Next door to the Petneházy Club Hotel (*see p44*), 10km from the city centre. Riding lessons for children and beginners, plus English-language tuition.

Snooker

Quite easily the best of Budapest's half-dozen or so snooker venues is the **Rex Williams Snooker Club** (XI.Ménesi út 1, 466 5703, www.rwsnooker.uw.hu). This is a haven for true aficionados, with its non-smoking, air-conditioned playing room of four immaculately groomed tables. If you prefer a somewhat rowdier atmosphere, with smoking and pool tables as well, try the hangar-like **Gold Crown Biliárd Center** (XI.Budafoki út 111-113, 206 5234), or the **Billiard Art Club** (IV.Elem utca 5-7, 370 5487, www.billiard-art.hu/biliard-klub). The latter is a bit of a trek, best reached by local train from Nyugati station, but it's where many of Hungary's top players hang out.

Squash

City Squash Club

II.Marczibányi tér 1-3 (336 0408). Tram 4, 6/bus 11, 49. **Open** 7am-midnight Mon-Fri; 8am-10pm Sat, Sun. **Rates** *Off-peak* Ft2,200/hr. *Peak* Ft4,200/hr. **No credit cards**.
Four courts and a sauna. Booking advised.

Swimming

In summer, open-air pools double up as a lido, or *strand*. All require swimming hats to be worn by both sexes – the ones available for hire look ridiculous, so bring your own.

Gellért Gyógyfürdő

XI.Kelenhegyi út (466 6166). Tram 18, 19, 47, 49/bus 7. **Open** 6am-7pm daily. **Admission** Ft2,800-Ft3,100. **Credit** DC, MC, V. **Map** p248 E7.
A grand spot to knock out a few lengths. Warm indoor pool, relaxing outdoor one, wave pool, kids' pool, thermal pool and sauna (*see p50* **Spa city**).

Hajós Alfréd Nemzeti Sportuszoda

XIII.Margitsziget (450 4200). Bus 26. **Open** 6am-5pm Mon-Fri; 6am-6pm Sat, Sun. **Admission** Ft1,200; Ft720 concessions. **Credit** MC, V. **Map** p245 C1.
Two outdoor pools, an indoor one, and sunbathing.

Palatinus Strand

XIII.Margitsziget (340 4482). Bus 26, 26A. **Open** *May-mid Sept* 9am-7pm daily. **Admission** Ft1,800; Ft1,600 concessions. **No credit cards**.
This popular outdoor complex on Margaret Island comprises seven pools, including a thermal pool, two children's pools, slides and wave machines. Although it has a capacity of 10,000, on a hot afternoon in July it's standing room only. Renovated in 2002, the Palatinus doubles up as a lido.

Tennis

There are some 40 clubs in Budapest, most with clay courts. Major hotels can also hire courts.

Római Teniszakadémia

III.Királyok útja 105 (240 8616). Bus 34. **Open** 7am-9pm daily. **Rates** Ft1,600-Ft2,600/hr. **No credit cards**.
Ten outdoor courts, ten indoor.

Városmajor Teniszakadémia

XII.Városmajor utca 63-69 (202 5337). Bus 21, 121. **Open** 7am-10pm Mon-Fri; 7am-7pm Sat; 8am-7pm Sun. **Rates** Ft1,400-Ft2,600/hr. **No credit cards**.
Five outdoor courts, three indoor.

Vasas SC

II.Pasaréti út 11-13 (212 5246). Bus 5. **Open** 7am-9pm daily. **Rates** Ft1,700-Ft3,300/hr (booking advised). **No credit cards**.
Nine outdoor courts, two indoor.

Theatre & Dance

What's on in English – and what's accessible in Hungarian.

Hungarians love their theatre and, despite subsidy cuts, there remain plenty of quality productions to choose from in Budapest – even in English. Two troupes with contrasting styles – **Madhouse** and **Scallabouche** – are well established in residence at the **National** and **Merlin** theatres respectively. Madhouse (www.madhouse.hu) is a three-man repertory outfit while Scallabouche focuses on improv, cabaret and one-man pieces penned by its founder and leading actor Alexis Latham (*see p203* **One's a company**). Visiting UK theatre groups are also a regular feature at the Merlin.

Leading Hungarian theatres realise the limited appeal of their offerings to foreigners and tend to choose from the standard repertoire – with a strong accent on visuals. Some even provide subtitles projected over the stage for certain plays. The **Budapest Spring** and **Autumn Festivals** (*see p156 & p158*) include international productions in their schedules.

The three-day **Budapest Fringe Festival** in late March, part of the main Spring Festival, offers the chance to catch offbeat performances, as does April's renowned **Contemporary Drama Festival** (www.dramafestival.hu).

TIMES AND TICKETS

Curtains usually rise at 7pm or 7.30pm. If they're not open all day, box offices begin selling tickets an hour prior to curtain. Ticket prices are generally in the Ft1,000-Ft3,000 price range. Wheelchair access and hearing systems aren't available. Productions run in repertory and can continue for ages. *Pesti Est* and *Pesti Műsor* cover most events. *Pesti Súgó* is a free monthly dedicated to theatre. The *Budapest Sun* also prints listings.

Tickets are available at the two main ticket outlets near the Opera House listed below. For online tickets, see http://jegyiroda.kulturinfo.hu; www.jegymester.hu; http://jegy.szinhaz.hu and www.jegyvilag.hu.

Nagymező Ticket Office

VI.Nagymező utca 19 (302 3841). M1 Opera/M1 Oktogon. **Open** 10am-7pm Mon-Fri. **Credit** V. **Map** p246 D3.

Ticket Express Booking Office

VI.Andrássy út 18 (312 0000/06 30 30 30 999 mobile/www.tex.hu). M1 Opera/M1 Bajcsy-Zsilinszky *út.* **Open** 9.30am-6pm daily. **No credit cards**. **Map** p246 D3.

On Broadway – **Nagymező utca**. *See p202.*

Theatre

English-language venues

International Buda Stage (IBS)

II.Tárogató út 2-4 (391 2525/www.ibs-szinpad.hu). M2 Moszkva tér, then tram 56. **Open** *Box office* 10am-6pm Mon-Fri; from 1hr before curtain. **No credit cards**.

Mostly Hungarian theatre these days, but keep an eye out for simultaneous English translation for major productions and English-language guest shows. The IBS also offers movies, dance, concerts and cultural symposiums.

Merlin International Theatre

V.Gerlóczy utca 4 (317 9338/www.szinhaz.hu/merlin). M1, M2, M3 Deák tér. **Open** *Box office* 2-7pm daily. **No credit cards**. **Map** p249 D5.

Now the home of the English-language Scallabouche Theatre Company (*see p203* **One's a company**) since it moved out of the cellar space at the Kolibri.

The Merlin has a strong tradition of bringing in companies from abroad, often from the UK, for guest performances and co-productions. Dance is also featured; in spring 2007 the Merlin welcomed two *cirque nouveau* troupes from France.

National Theatre
Nemzeti Szinház
IX.Bajor Gizi park 1 (476 6868/www.nemzeti szinhaz.hu). HÉV Lagymányosi-hid/tram 2. **Open** *Box office* 10am-6pm Mon-Fri; 2-6pm Sat, Sun. **No credit cards. Map** p250 inset.
The latest incarnation of the National Theatre opened in 2002 to much controversy, first over its location, then over disputes between its architect and artistic director Tamás Jordán. Its design evokes ancient Greece amid a modern façade, and although the jury is still out regarding its aesthetic appeal, though there's no denying that the riverside setting is superb. The acoustics have also come in for much criticism, but the technical capabilities of the stage are unparalleled. The stage can be raised or lowered at 72 different points, the lifts offer a panoramic view of the city, and the façade of the old building lies half submerged in a pool by the main entrance. Jordán has always welcomed new writing and has hosted a wealth of dance and movement pieces in repertory. Apart from Hungarian drama, resident English-language repertory troupe Madhouse have their home in the intimate downstairs Stúdiószinpad, seating an odd 619 in a blue-carpeted interior. Set down a grand staircase, with its own little bar, the location turns a nice evening watching expat theatre into a real event.

Nagymező utca

This attractive stretch, otherwise known as 'Budapest's Broadway', has been pedestrianised and allows for a pleasant stroll before pre-show drinks at the **Mai Manó Kávézó** (*see p134*) or at the Operett Kavéház diagonally opposite.

Radnóti
VI.Nagymező utca 11 (321 0600/www.szinhaz.hu/ radnoti). M1 Oktogon/M1 Opera. **Open** *Box office* 1-7pm daily. **No credit cards. Map** p246 F4.
A highly regarded company performing a wide selection of highbrow classics and contemporary plays. Award-winning resident troupe.

Thália
VI.Nagymező utca 22-24 (331 0500/www.thalia.hu). M1 Oktogon/M1 Opera. **Open** *Box office* 10am-6pm Mon-Fri; 2-6pm Sat, Sun. **No credit cards. Map** p246 F4.
This elegant, air-conditioned venue accommodates performances by established local dance and theatre companies, as well as the occasional mainstream musical. Operetta produced in conjunction with the Operetta Theatre opposite rubs shoulders with contemporary successes such as *The Vagina Monologues* (in Hungarian).

Tivoli Színház
VI.Nagymező utca 8 (351 6812). M1 Oktogon/M1 Opera. **Open** *Box office* 2-7pm daily. **No credit cards. Map** p246 F4.
The main stage of the Budapest Chamber Theatre, the Tivoli is attractively art nouveau, and tends to show modern classics and comedies. It also has two studio stages on Asbóth utca, close to Deák tér.

Establishment theatres

Katona József
V.Petőfi Sándor utca 6 (318 6599/www.szinhaz.hu/ katona). M3 Ferenciek tere/bus 7. **Open** *Box office* 10am-6pm daily. **No credit cards. Map** p249 E6.
The company with the highest reputation in Budapest and well received the world over, Katona might be the most accessible local-language theatre for foreigners. Their repertory of mainstream and alternative plays expands every year, with works by Ibsen, Carlo Goldoni and Sophocles added in 2007. The theatre also houses ambitious dance productions, often collaborating with leading choreographer Yvette Bozsik, who uses her own dancers and the theatre's actors. The sister company performs equally exciting and dynamic productions at a smaller space around the corner.
Other locations: Katona József Kamra, V.Ferenciek tere 3 (318 2487).

Vígszínház Comedy Theatre
XIII.Szent István körút 14 (329 2340/www.vig-szinhaz.hu). M3 Nyugati pu./tram 2, 4, 6. **Open** *Box office* 11am-6.30pm daily. **No credit cards. Map** p246 E2.
A historic baroque venue, immaculately renovated for its centenary in 1996, the Comedy Theatre covers the gamut of genres from musicals to grand productions of Shakespeare. It had its heyday in the early 20th century, when it was the launchpad for local playwrights who went on to fame and fortune abroad, like Melchior Lengyel and Ferenc Molnár.
Other locations: Pesti Színház, V.Váci utca 9 (266 5557).

Alternative theatres

Bárka Theatre
VIII.Üllői út 82 (303 6505/483 1325/www.barka.hu). M3 Klinikák. **Open** *Box office* 2-7pm Mon-Fri; 2hrs before curtain. **No credit cards. Map** p250 H8.
The resident company of some 15 local actors has a diverse repertoire, ranging from Pinter to Pirandello.

MU Színház
XI.Kőrösy József utca 17 (466 4627/2090 4014/ www.mu.hu). Tram 4. **Open** *Box office* 6pm until curtain Mon-Thur; 1hr before curtain Fri. **No credit cards.**
A space for small alternative companies, musicians and dancers, with no resident company. It's worth a visit, if only to check out what's happening on the fringe. The bar is a destination in its own right.

One's a company

Scallabouche, the longest-standing English-language troupe now performing in Hungary, lies at the more experimental end of the Budapest theatre spectrum. But beyond responding to a simple demand for English theatre, it also aims to give foreigners a little of the flavour of Hungarian drama by using local actors in some of its productions.

At the heart of Scallabouche is its founder, playwright and leading man **Alexis Latham** (*photos above*). Englishman Latham first travelled to Hungary in the mid 1990s on a British Council-sponsored programme with a London-based theatre troupe. It was then that he met his future Hungarian wife, taking the decision to move to Budapest soon after.

Latham launched Scallabouche as a one-man theatre in 1998. Unlike **Madhouse** (*see p201*), Budapest's other resident English-language troupe, Scallabouche has thus far largely performed material written by Latham and his collaborators. What also sets Scallabouche aside from other theatre in English in Hungary – reflecting a more ambitious aim to fill a niche in Budapest's theatre scene as a whole – is a strong emphasis on improvisation.

Besides a regular pool of actors, native English speakers and sundry Hungarians, Scallabouche works with two local theatre directors. András Kovács has an interest in the theatre of the absurd that has proven a perfect match for Latham's improv-driven

material, while János Novák directs for the Kolibri Theatre, whose cellar studio on Andrássy út was Scallabouche's residence for nearly six years.

The group recently moved into a new home at the **Merlin International Theatre** (*see p201*), where it took over from Madhouse as the resident English-language troupe when the latter moved to the studio of the National.

Latham managed to register the group as a foundation in 2007, which he hopes will put it on a better financial footing. Another motivating force is Scallabouche's desire to get involved in more collaborative work on the local theatre scene, doing workshops for actors and evening improv classes, already up and running.

Latham does concede that some of Scallabouche's efforts – while gaining critical accolades – have been a tough sell on Budapest audiences. The immediate plan is to include more mainstream drama in the repertoire. He's also eyeing collaborative work with theatre companies abroad, bringing them over for co-productions and exploiting the contacts Scallabouche has generated on well-received visits to Edinburgh and various fringe festivals around Europe.

One handy feature on Scallabouche's website (www.scallabouche.com) is an updated list of current performances by Hungarian companies that are recommended as accessible for foreigners.

Arts & Entertainment

Trafó House of Contemporary Arts.

Szkéné

XI.Műegyetem rakpart 3 (463 2451/www.szkene.hu).
Tram 18, 19, 47, 49. **Open** 9am-4pm Mon-Thur;
9am-1pm Fri & 1hr before curtain. **No credit cards.**
Map p249 E8.

A theatre that sponsors the International Meeting of
Moving Theatres every other October, for which
obscure dance groups gather at this small black box,
and the Alternative Theatre Festival in April. Look
out for Béla Pinter's acclaimed theatre group.

Trafó House of Contemporary Arts

IX.Liliom utca 41 (215 1600/www.trafo.hu).
M3 Ferenc körút/tram 4, 6. **Open** Box office
2-8pm Mon-Fri; 5-8pm Sat, Sun. **No credit**
cards. Map p250 H8.

Contemporary dance, theatre and performance are
at the heart of the programme at the Trafó, a venue
which, uniquely in the city, brings together all
branches of art and culture under one roof. It's the
nearest that Budapest gets to London's Barbican.
Expect performances by the best Hungarian theatre
and dance companies, such as Mozgó Ház Társulás,
Pál Frenák and Yvette Bozsik. Trafó also has close
links with international cultural institutes and often
stages foreign-language guest productions.

Új Színház

VI.Paulay Ede utca 35 (269 6021/269 6024/www.
szinhaz.hu/ujszinhaz). M1 Opera. **Open** Box office
2-7pm Mon-Fri & until 1st interval of evening show.
No credit cards. Map p246 F4.

The 'New Theatre', dramatically designed by Béla
Lajta as the Parisian nightclub, stages a range of
new and established plays. The building alone is
worth the visit. *See p82* **Strolling the Secession**.

Dance

The Budapest ballet scene consists mainly
of competently executed traditional pieces
drawing on Russian and Hungarian traditions.
There's much innovative local work too.
Experimental groups abound. One exciting
young talent to have performed her work here
is the acclaimed **Éva Duda**, a dancer and
choreographer whose rise has been meteoric.
The most internationally recognised figure is
Yvette Bozsik, whose style leans towards
grotesque comedy and whose productions –
at venues such as the Katona József, Trafó and
Merlin theatres – have often used actors.

Pál Frenák has been sending shockwaves
through the Budapest dance scene for some
years. This notorious maverick splits his time
between Hungary and France, where he has
created his own company of contemporary
dancers. The shock quotient is always pretty
high in Frenák's productions – but anything
goes at the Trafó.

Iván Markó was a solo dancer with Maurice
Béjart in Paris, so he had a considerable head
start when he returned to pursue his career in
Hungary. Now in his sixties, Markó is past
trying anything too athletic, but compensates
for this with experience, grace and good ideas.
His troupe of modern ballet dancers is based in
Győr, west of Budapest, but his productions
often make their way to the capital. See him at
the National, the Thália and the **Várszínház**.

Budai Vigadó

I.Corvin tér 8 (225 6049/www.hagyomanyok
haza.hu) M2 Batthyány tér/tram 19/bus 86.
Open varies. **Map** p245 C4.

Home theatre for Hungarian State Folk Ensemble,
regular venue for performances of professional and
amateur folk dance groups from all over Hungary
and national centre of Hungary's active folk dance
movement. Performances three or four times a week,
throughout the summer as well.

MU Színház

XI.Kőrösy József utca 17 (466 4627/209 4014).
Tram 4. **Open** varies.

Contemporary dance performances. *See p202.*

Hungarian National Ballet

Magyar Nemzeti Balett

The HNB perform at the **Opera House** (*see p186*)
and the **Erkel Színház** (*see p184*).

Várszínház – The
National Dance Theatre

I.Színház utca 1-3 (375 8649/201 4407/www.nemzeti
tancszinhaz.hu). Várbusz from M2 Moszkva tér/
bus 16. **Open** Box office 1-6pm daily. **Map** p245 B4.

The Culture Ministry set up this venue in the Castle
District. Dance productions of the highest quality.

Trips Out of Town

Esztergom. *See p209.*

Getting Started

Easy and enjoyable day trips and overnighters from Budapest.

Exploring Hungary is easy, cheap and fun; the rail network, centred on Budapest, is reliable. The most popular getaways are the **Danube Bend** and **Lake Balaton**; a boat service in summer leaves town for spots up the Danube and another serves resorts on Lake Balaton.

The most interesting towns to visit are **Eger** and **Pécs**, both boasting historic monuments and thriving cultural scenes, Pécs gearing up for its role as European Capital of Culture in 2010. The countryside is pretty but without the dramatic scenery of Slovakia or the Adriatic coast, both a half-day's drive away. Hungary's attractions are its spa waters and vineyards.

The phone numbers given here are for dialling from Budapest. From abroad, dial +36 and drop the 06. In the town itself, drop the 06 and two-digit code and dial the main number. For more tourist information, contact:

Ibusz

V.Ferenciek tere 10 (485 2767/www.ibusz.hu). *M3 Ferenciek tere/bus 7.* **Open** 9am-6pm Mon-Fri; 9am-1pm Sat. **Credit** AmEx, DC, MC, V. **Map** p249 C4.

Tourinform

V.Sütő utca 6 (438 8080). M1, M2, M3 Deák *tér.* **Open** 8am-8pm daily. **No credit cards**. **Map** p249 C4.

By train

Trains are cheap and reliable. The fastest, Intercity, require a seat reservation (Ft520). Timetables are posted at Budapest's three main stations, Keleti, Nyugati and Déli, each with their own metro station. *See p219* **Trains**.

MÁV Information

Information 06 40 46 46 46/from abroad +36 1 371 9449. Timetable information 461 5400/international 461 5500. **To Balatonfüred**: *Déli.* 2hrs 20mins (Ft2,560). 15 trains daily. Last fast train returns 7.39pm. **To Eger**: *Keleti.* 2hrs (Ft2,810). 33 trains daily. Last fast train returns 7.36pm. **To Esztergom**: *Nyugati.* 90mins (Ft900). 27 trains daily. Last return 10.08pm. **To Keszthely**: *Déli/Keleti.* 3hrs 30mins (Ft3,000). 3 fast trains daily. Last return 7pm. Train often divides. **To Pécs**: *Déli/Keleti.* 3hrs (Ft3,750). 7 fast trains daily. Last return 6.55pm. **To Siófok**: *Déli/Keleti.* 2hrs (Ft2,160). 17 trains daily. Last fast return 7.38pm. Last return 8.59pm.

By car

Many roads in Hungary are still single carriageway despite recent renovation of the main motorways. Major routes are now easier to travel, but you have to buy a *matrica* sticker for your windscreen. These are available at petrol stations. Look for the word *matrica* on blue signs. Rates vary: a *matrica* for one week to one month ranges from Ft2,550 to Ft4,200.

Getting out of Budapest is easy and the routes are well signposted. From Buda, follow M7 for destinations to the Balaton region and M6/E73 for Pécs. From Pest, follow M3/E71 signs for Eger. From Árpád Bridge, take the 10 for Esztergom and the 11 for Szentendre and Visegrád, along the west bank of the Danube.

By boat

In summer, leisurely boats cruise up the Danube to Szentendre, Visegrád and Esztergom. Nippy jetfoils go to Visegrád and Esztergom on weekends and holidays.

All boats to and from Esztergom stop at Visegrád. Most Szentendre boats continue to Visegrád, making a total of five boats to Visegrád every day. It's easy to visit Visegrád plus either Esztergom or Szentendre in a day trip by boat. Taking in all three by boat in one day is theoretically possible, but pushing it.

Boats run daily from 7 April to 30 September, and you can usually get tickets at the dock.

You can get jetfoils to Visegrád/Esztergom, from June to August. Book tickets in advance.

Boats at Vigadó tér terminal

V.Vigadó tér (318 1223). M1 Vörösmarty tér/ tram 2. **Credit** MC, V. **Map** p249 C4. **Boat to Esztergom**: Ft1,690; Ft2,535 return. 3 boats daily in summer. First boat leaves Vigadó tér 8am. Last boat leaves Esztergom 8.30pm. **Boat to Szentendre**: Ft1,390; Ft2,085 return. 3 boats daily in summer. First boat leaves Vigadó tér 9am. Last boat leaves Szentendre 5.55pm. **Boat to Visegrád**: Ft1,490; Ft2,235 return. 4 boats daily in summer. First boat leaves Vigadó tér 8am. Last boat from Visegrád 6pm.

Hydrofoils

Hydrofoil to Visegrád: Ft2,690; Ft3,990 return. 1 trip daily on summer weekends. Leaves Budapest 9.30am. Leaves Visegrád at 5pm. Same times for **Esztergom** (Ft 3,290; Ft4,990 return).

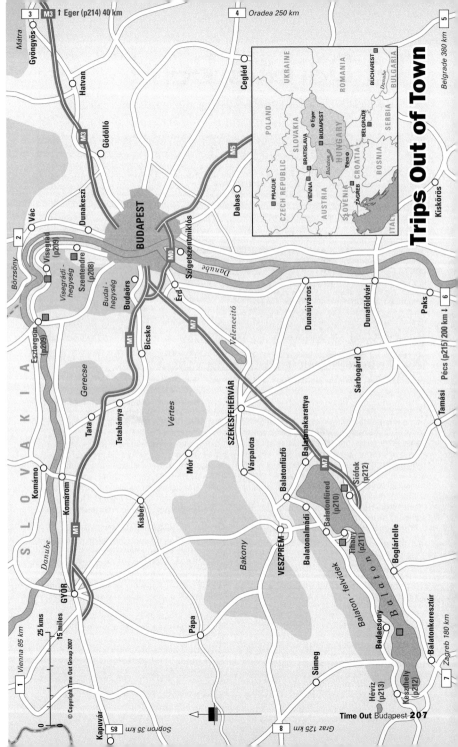

Trips Out of Town

The Danube Bend

Serbian churches, medieval citadels and Hungary's most sacred cathedral.

Hungary's first real capital, overlooking the Danube – **Esztergom**.

The kink in the Danube about 40km north of Budapest is one of the most scenic stretches in the river's 3,000km course. Here the Danube widens and turns sharply south, into a narrow valley between the tree-covered Börzsöny and Pilis Hills, before flowing onwards to Budapest.

The two main towns on the west bank of the Danube Bend, **Visegrád** and **Esztergom**, were respectively a Hungarian medieval capital with a hilltop citadel and a royal seat with the nation's largest cathedral. Both are easily accessible from Budapest by train, bus or boat.

Although both can be fitted into one long day, they lend themselves more to an overnight stay. Day-trippers prefer **Szentendre**, a quaint old Serbian village and artists' colony at the end of the HÉV line from downtown Batthyány tér.

Szentendre

Szentendre is a settlement of 20,000 people 20km north of the capital, offering shaded walks along the Danube, glimpses of Serbian history and a sizeable collection of art galleries.

The HÉV takes a pleasant 45 minutes to pass gentle suburbs and grazing horses. The summer boat service from Vigadó tér takes an hour more but the journey back to town can be delightful.

An old artists' haunt, Szentendre is a tourist destination, with daft museums (marzipan, wine), overpriced crafts and horse-drawn carriages. Ignore the tack – there's plenty to do.

Serb refugees reached Szentendre centuries before the souvenir-sellers. Their legacy is a small immigrant community and a handful of Orthodox churches, some still in operation. The Serbs came here in several waves, escaping war and persecution to enjoy religious freedom under Habsburg rule and to prosper in the wine and leather trades. Although the exteriors are baroque, their churches preserve Orthodox traditions; all sanctuaries face east, irrespective of dimension or streetscape. The resulting layout gives the town a distinctly Balkan atmosphere.

The first church you see is **Požarevačka**, in Vuk Karadzics tér, open to visitors at weekends. Inside is Szentendre's oldest iconostasis, iconic representations of saints that are joined together in a screen. In the main square, Fő tér, **Blagovestenska Church** provides a mix of deep music, incense and a glorious iconostasis. The most stunning place of worship is the **Belgrade Cathedral**, seat of the Serbian Orthodox bishop, with its entrance in Pátriáka utca (open 10am-4pm Tue-Sun). The entryway is decorated with oak wings carved in rococo style. The interior features a pulpit adorned with carvings and paintings, and an ornate bishops' throne. In the same grounds is a museum of Serbian church art, containing bishop's garments, icons and religious trappings made of gold and other precious metals (open Oct-Apr 10am-4pm Tue-Sun; May-Sept 10am-6pm Tue-Sun).

After a series of floods and epidemics, artists moved into Szentendre in the 1920s, delighted to find a living museum of Serbian houses and churches. Later generations set up galleries, with varying degrees of merit. The first was the **Vajda Lajos Stúdió** (Péter Pál utca 6, 06 26/935 7853), named after the famed surrealist painter and key member of the famed Kassák circle. You can also see his works at the **Vajda Lajos Múzeum** (Hunyadi utca 1, no phone; open 10am-4pm Fri-Sun) and the **Erdész Galéria** (Fő tér 20, 06 26/310 139). Pieces by other artists from the studio are displayed at the **Art'eria** (Városház tér 1, 06 26/310 111). The other key figure is popular sculptor/ceramicist **Margit Kovács**, whose **museum** (Vastagh György utca 1, 06 26/310 790) shows the breadth of her oeuvre. The **Dunaparti Művelődési Ház** (DMH) at Dunakorzó 11A (06 26/312 657) is a cultural centre with a gallery and regular live music. The **Művészet Malom** (Bogdányi utca 32, 06 26/301 701) hosts contemporary exhibitions.

There are decent restaurants at Fő tér and by the river. **Görög Kancsó** (Görög utca 1, 06 26/303 178) offers a diverse menu at fair prices; you'll find finer at **Chez Nicolas** (Kigyó utca 10, 06 26/311 288). Locals prefer the fish at **Rab Ráby** (Kucsora Ferenc utca 1A, 06 26/310 819).

Tourinform Szentendre

Dumtsa Jenő utca (06 26/317 965/www.szentendre. hu). **Open** 9.30am-4pm Mon-Fri; 10am-2pm Sat, Sun.

Visegrád

From the **citadel** in Visegrád, views take in a nice stretch of the river, but the sleepy village below is only worth seeing for the palace ruins.

The citadel and Visegrád Palace were built in the 13th and 14th centuries. The latter was the setting for the Visegrád Congress of 1335, when Magyar, Czech and Polish kings quaffed 10,000 litres of wine over trade talks. Representatives of the so-called 'Visegrád Group' of Hungary, Poland, the Czech Republic and Slovakia still meet here to discuss joint concerns.

In the 15th century King Mátyás overhauled the palace in Renaissance style. It fell into ruin after the Turkish invasion, and was buried under mudslides; it was only rediscovered in 1934.

What you see today are ruins or modern re-creations. Several restored rooms house small displays about everyday life here in medieval

times. Original pieces uncovered in 1934 can be found at the **Mátyás Museum**, in the Salamon Tower, halfway up the hill to the citadel.

You can reach the citadel via a strenuous, 25-minute walk up the stony Path of Calvary, by one of the thrice-daily buses, or by taking a taxi (06 26/397 372) up Panoráma út.

Before the boat back, enjoy a beer at the terrace bar above the kitschy **Renaissance** restaurant by the landing. For lunch, try the **Fekete Holló** (Rév utca 12, 06 26/397 289).

Visegrád Tours

Rév utca 15 (06 26/398 160/www.visegradtours.hu). **Open** 8am-5.30pm daily.

Esztergom

Although Esztergom is Hungary's most sacred city, home of the Archbishop and the nation's biggest church, it has a real-life edge that makes it worth a stopover. Not all of its 30,000 inhabitants are pious; there's a Suzuki factory on the outskirts and, in town, a string of bars full of drunken fishermen.

Esztergom was Hungary's first real capital. The nation's first Christian king, Szent István, was crowned here in AD 1000. He built a royal palace, parts of which can be seen in the **Castle Museum** south of the **cathedral**. For nearly three centuries Esztergom was the royal seat, until the Mongol invasion all but destroyed the city. It suffered more damage under the Turks, but most of what's worth seeing was rebuilt in baroque style some 250 years ago: **Víziváros Parish Church** on Mindszenty tere; the **Christian Museum** on Berényi Zsigmond utca and the **Balassi Bálint Museum** on Pázmány Péter utca.

It's the huge cathedral that dominates, though. When the Catholic Church moved its base back to Esztergom in 1820, Archbishop Sándor Rudnay wanted a monument built on the ruins of a 12th-century church destroyed by the Turks. Three architects created this bleak structure. A bright spot is the **Bakócz Chapel**, built in red marble by Florentine craftsmen, dismantled during the occupation of the Ottomans and reassembled in 1823.

For lunch, the **Csülök Csárda** (Batthyány utca 9, 06 33/412 420) is reasonable. The **Ria Panzió** hotel, nearby at no.13 (06 33/401 428), is charming and the **Alabárdos Panzió** (Bajcsy-Zsilinszky utca 49, 06 33/312 640) can also provide cheapish rooms. The dearer **Hotel Esztergom** (Prímás-sziget, Helischer J utca, 06 33/412 555) has a river terrace and sports centre.

GranTours

Széchenyi tér 25 (06 33/502 001/www.grantours.hu). **Open** 8am-4pm Mon-Fri.

Trips Out of Town

The Balaton

The tacky and thermal delights of Hungary's best-known tourist destination.

The Balaton is one of Europe's largest lakes, a huge area of water for such a small, landlocked country. No wonder Hungarians have flocked here for generations: even those on modest salaries have access to a weekend house on the shores of this shallow lake.

As a foreigner, unless you get invited too, your trip here might be different: high-rise hotels, concrete beaches, white plastic chairs, advertising umbrellas and a string of over-priced resorts. Although there are quieter parts, a trip to this lake is first and foremost an excursion into deepest naff – which doesn't mean to say that it can't also be a lot of fun.

Its allure goes way back, attracting Celts, Romans and Huns, and Slavs; whose word for swamp, *blatna*, probably gave the lake its name. The Magyars brought fishing and farming, and built a lot of churches, before the Mongols came in 1242. The Turks occupied the south shore and scuffled with Austrians on the other side in the 16th and 17th centuries. Once they were driven out, the Habsburgs came along and blew up any remaining Hungarian castles.

Most of the best sights, therefore, date from the 18th century, when viticulture flourished and baroque was in vogue. Landmarks include the Abbey Church in **Tihany** and the huge Festetics Palace in **Keszthely**. Nearby is the world's second largest thermal lake, **Hévíz**, a stand-out destination on its own, particularly with the recent introduction of direct UK low-cost flights to FlyBalaton airport at Sármellék. *See p213* **Radioactive recreation**.

Although **Balatonfüred** was declared a spa in 1785, it wasn't until the 19th century that bathing and the therapeutic properties of the area's thermal springs began to draw the wealthy in large numbers. In 1836 Baron Miklós Wesselényi, a leading reformer of the era, was the first to swim from Tihany to Balatonfüred. Lajos Kossuth suggested steamships, and Count István Széchenyi rustled some up. Passenger boat services still link most of the major resorts and are an appealing way to get around, though the ferry from the southern tip of the Tihany peninsula to Szántód – a ten-minute journey spanning the lake's narrowest point – is the only one that takes cars.

The southern shore – now an 80-kilometre stretch of tacky resorts – was developed after the 1861 opening of the railway. The line along the hillier and marginally more tasteful north shore wasn't opened until 1910. Despite the easy transit, the Balaton mainly remained a playground for the well-to-do until the Communists rebuilt the area for mass recreation. Hungary was one of the few places to which East Germans could travel, and the Balaton became the place where West Germans would meet up with their poor relations. Tourism is still geared towards the needs of Germans, and in some shops and restaurants German is the first language and Hungarian the second.

The lake itself is unusual. A 77-kilometre-long rectangle, 14 kilometres at its widest, it covers an area of 600 square kilometres but is shallow throughout – Lake Geneva contains 20 times as much water. At its deepest (the Tihany Well by the peninsula that almost chops the lake in half) Balaton reaches 12 metres down. At Siófok and other south shore resorts, you can paddle out 1,000 metres before the water gets to your waist – it's safe for kids.

But it's not ideal swimming water. It's silty and milkily opaque, and can feel oily on the skin. Motor boats are forbidden, but you can sail or windsurf. Fishing's popular too. Balaton is home to around 40 varieties of fish, many of which are served in local restaurants. The *fogas*, a pike-perch, is unique to the lake and goes well with the very drinkable local wines.

Because Balaton is traditionally the place where Hungarians make money off Western tourists, prices are high. Affordable hotels and restaurants exist, but nothing's very cheap.

Despite its drawbacks, the Balaton can make for an interesting trip. Most destinations can be reached by train in about two or three hours. Siófok and the other resorts at the western end of the lake are manageable in a day.

Balatonfüred

The north shore's major resort is also the Balaton's oldest and has long been famed for the curative properties of its waters.

The State Hospital of Cardiology and the Sanitorium dominate baroque, dilapidated Gyógy tér in the town centre. The neo-classical Kossuth Well in the square dispenses warm, healing, mineral-rich water, which is the closest you'll get to the thermal springs without having to check into the hospital.

Mellow **Keszthely** offers a more relaxing Balaton experience. *See p212.*

Balatonfüred has a busy harbour with a pier, a shipyard, a promenade, half-a-dozen major beaches and an assortment of uninspiring things to see. Romantic writer Mór Jókai cranked out many of his 200 novels here; his villa at the corner of Jókai Mór utca and Honvéd utca is a memorial museum that includes a coffeehouse, the **Jokai Kávézó**. Opposite stands the neo-classical **Kerék templom** (Round Church), built in 1846. The **Lóczy Barlang** (Cave), off Öreghegy utca on the northern outskirts of town, is the largest hole in the ground hereabouts. You can catch ferry boats from Balatonfüred to Tihany and Siófok.

The **Hotel Wellness Flamingo** at Széchenyi út 16 (06 87/581 060) is a modernised four-star spa job. Cheaper but still comfortable is the **Korona Panzió** (Vörösmarty utca 4, 06 87/343 278). After dinner at one of the many restaurants all along **Tagore sétány** and up Jókai Mór utca – the ones by the end of the pier all specialise in fish dishes – you might try the disco in the **Columbus Club,** which offers pop techno, go-go dancers and teenagers on the dancefloor. The **Füredi Fészek Kávézó** on Kisfaludy utca offers pizzas and house music until the wee hours. From the end of the pier, with the lights of Siófok in the distance and the Tihany peninsula looming darkly to the west, the lake looks delightful by moonlight.

Balatontourist Balatonfüred

Petőfi Sándor utca 68 (06 87/580 480/www.balaton tourist.hu). **Open** *Oct-May* 10am-4pm Mon-Fri. *June, Sept* 9am-5pm Mon-Sat. *July, Aug* 9am-7pm Mon-Fri; 9am-6pm Sat; 9am-1pm Sun.

Tihany

Declared a national park in 1952, the Tihany peninsula is one of the quietest and (relatively) most unspoilt places around the lake.

The 12 square kilometres of the peninsula jut five kilometres into the lake, almost cutting it in half. Tihany village lies by the Inner Lake, cut off from the Balaton by a steep hill. Atop it stands the twin-spired **Abbey Church**, opened in 1754. This is one of Hungary's most important baroque monuments. King Andrew I's 1055 deed of foundation for the church originally on this site was the first written document to contain any Hungarian (a few score place names in a mainly Latin text): it's now in Pannonhalma Abbey near Győr. The **Abbey Museum** in the former monastery next door contains exhibits about Lake Balaton and a small collection of Roman statues.

Perhaps the most stunning sight on this hilltop is the view. The church is on a sheer cliff, which affords splendid vistas of the Balaton and the countryside around it. There's

Trips Out of Town

beautiful nature around here, and **Tourinform Tihany** can provide information about walks in the area, which has a bird sanctuary, two small lakes, some geyser cones and Echo Hill.

The **Kakas**, a rambling old restaurant below the **Erika Hotel**, is an agreeable spot and open all year round. There's a bunch of bars and restaurants around the main square and along Kossuth utca. Places to stay at are limited, although the **Park Hotel Kastély** (06 87/448 611) by the lake on Fürdőtelep utca, an old Habsburg summer mansion, offers a modicum of elegance and its own beach. Avoid the ugly new annexe on the same grounds. Private rooms in Tihany village can be arranged through Tourinform.

It may be best to stay in Balatonfüred, ten kilometres away, and do Tihany as a side trip.

Tourinform Tihany

Kossuth utca 20 (06 87/448 804/www.tihany.hu). **Open** 10am-4pm Mon-Fri; 10am-6pm Sat, Sun.

Keszthely

The only town on the Balaton that isn't totally dependent on tourism, Keszthely has a mellow feel quite different from other lakeside resorts. The two busy lidos seem to swallow up all the tourists, while the university means a bit of life off-season as well as some variety at night.

The main tourist attraction is the **Festetics Palace**, a 100-room baroque pile in pleasant grounds north of the town centre. The Festetics family owned this whole area, and Count György (1755-1819) was the epitome of the enlightened aristocrat. He not only built the palace but made ships, hosted a salon of leading literary lights, and founded both the Helikon library – in the southern part of the mansion and containing more than 80,000 volumes – and the original agricultural college, these days the Georgikon Museum at Bercsényi utca 67. There's also the **Balaton Museum**, with artefacts dating back to the first century AD.

The **Gothic Parish Church** on Fő tér has a longer history than most Balaton buildings. Originally built in the 1380s, it was fortified in 1550 in the face of the Ottoman advance. When the rest of the town was sacked, it managed to hold out against the Turks. In 1747 the church was rebuilt in baroque style.

The **Hotel Bacchus** (Erzsébet királyné útja 18, 06 83/510 450) is a small and friendly modern hotel, located between the town centre and the lido, with a reputable terrace restaurant. If you'd prefer a place down by the lake, try the **Hotel Hullám** at Balatonpart 1 (06 83/312 644), a pre-war establishment with airy, high-ceilinged rooms.

There are many bars and restaurants on and around **Kossuth Lajos utca**, the main street, catering to the student population.

Keszthely is a good base from which to venture up the lake towards Badacsony, a scenic wine centre with volcanic hills, or the cute little village of Szigliget with its 14th-century castle ruins. Hévíz is also close at hand, a resort built around Europe's largest thermal lake. *See p213* **Radioactive recreation**. This north-west tip of Balaton has become more accessible to UK visitors thanks to the launch of a Ryanair flight from London Stansted to FlyBalaton airport at Sármellék in 2006.

Tourinform Keszthely

Kossuth Lajos utca 28 (06 83/314 144/www. keszthely.hu). **Open** *Oct-May* 9am-6pm Mon-Fri; 9am-12.30pm Sat. *June-Sept* 9am-8pm Mon-Fri; 9am-12.30pm Sat, Sun.

Siófok

Siófok, the first big lakeside town you'll hit by car or rail from Budapest, is Balaton's sin city: big, loud, brash and packed in high season. Although it's the lake's largest resort – Greater Siófok stretches for 15 kilometres along the shore – there isn't much in the way of sightseeing.

Siófok's Petőfi sétány strip runs for two kilometres. Here you'll find big Communist-era hotels, bars with oom-pah bands, amusement arcades, topless places, video game arcades, parked cars blasting out pop techno, a reptile house full of scary snakes. and an endless procession of Hungarian, German and Austrian tourists.

The **Roxy** at Szabadság tér 4 is a decent brasserie where the drinks are well made. **Flört** (Sió utca 4, 06 20/333 3303, www.flort.hu) is one of Hungary's best nightclubs: two dancefloors (one techno, one tacky), some excellent DJs, a succession of bars on different levels of the barn-like main room, and a roof terrace overlooking the Sió Canal. Its main rival is the **Palace** (06 84/350 698), just out of town. Both clubs host big-name house and techno DJs.

By the strip are tacky diners and food stalls. The **Diana Hotel** (Szent László utca 41-43, 06 84/315 296) has a fine restaurant with excellent *fogas*. The **Janus** (Fő utca 93-95, 06 84/312 546), now part of the Best Western chain, is a good hotel, if pricey. On the strip itself, the **Hotel Napfény** (Mártirok utca 8, 06 84/311 408) is cheaper, with spacious rooms and balconies.

Tourinform Siófok

Víztorony (06 84/310 117/www.siofoktourism.com). **Open** *Oct-May* 9am-6pm Mon-Fri; 9am-noon Sat, Sun. *June-Sept* 8am-8pm Mon-Fri; 9am-noon Sat, Sun.

Radioactive recreation

Tucked away from the bright lights of Balaton, **Hévíz** is a phenomenon all of its own. Europe's largest thermal lake has been attracting bathers since medieval times. It took the enlightened aristocrat, György Festetics, the local landowner famed for the palace of the same name at nearby Keszthely, to channel the lake into a bathhouse before tourism became popular here in the 19th century. Five hotels were built in the 1860s, and by the 1890s Hévíz was a spa destination for the well-to-do.

The post-war authorities built high-rise hotels and tourist-oriented restaurants around the lake, but still Hévíz retains a certain character. Bathing takes place all year round and in winter the lake steams dramatically. The deep blue, slightly radioactive warm water is full of Indian water lilies and middle-aged Germans floating around with rubber rings. Best of all, the pointed wooden bathhouse complex set on stilts stretches right out into the middle of the lake. Hévíz is a health centre as well as a tourist resort – the main spa hospital still lines the western shore.

Recently modernised, upmarket hotels also offer treatments based around the water's curative effects on rheumatic and locomotive disorders. At the top end are the **Carbona** (Attila utca 1, 06 83/342 930, www.carbona.hu), and **Rogner Dorint Hotel Lotus Therme** (Lótuszvirág utca, 06 83/500 500, www.rogner.co.at/rogner), and the two neighbouring Danubius hotels, the **Hévíz** (Kossuth utca 9-11, 06 83/341 180) and the **Aqua** (Kossuth utca 13-15, 06 83/341 090), both with numerous pools and services detailed on www.danubiusgroup.com. The **Hotel Európa Fit** (Jókai utca 3, 06 83/501 100, www.europafit.hu) is of a similar ilk.

There are numerous pensions, guest houses and smaller hotels as well; see www.heviz.hu for details. The tourist office at Rákóczi utca 2 (06 83/341 348) is surrounded by tourist restaurants – but none stands out.

To access Hévíz from Keszthely, it's a 15-minute bus journey from stop no.4 on Fő tér. From FlyBalaton airport (www.flybalaton.hu) at Sármellék, a bus awaits arrivals on the thrice-weekly Ryanair flight (www.ryanair.com) from London Stansted, before making the 25-minute journey to Hévíz. Alternatively, a FlyCar (www.flycar.hu) minibus to Hévíz takes 20 minutes and costs Ft1,400, Ft2,300 return.

Trips Out of Town

Eger

Wine, fierce women and Gypsy song.

With a **castle** that was the scene of a historic victory, a quaint downtown designed for walking and a rich tradition of making and drinking wine, Eger has plenty to offer visitors.

Located 128 kilometres (80 miles) north-east of Budapest, the town is at the foot of the low, rolling Bükk Hills, ideal for fishing, hunting and camping. They also produce the grapes that make wines like Hungary's best known Egri Bikavér (Bull's Blood), a hearty, dry red blend of local wines, along with sweet, white Tokaj dessert wine. Nearby **Tokaj**, an hour's drive from Eger, is also lined with cellars.

Inside Hungary, Eger is best known as the place where a small, outnumbered group of Magyars held off 10,000 invading Ottomans during a month-long seige in 1552. The Turks came back and finished the job 44 years later, but the earlier siege of Eger has been fixed in the nation's imagination by Géza Gárdonyi's 1901 adventure novel *Egri csillagok* ('Eclipse of the Crescent Moon'). Gárdonyi's version, which has the brave women of Eger dumping hot soup on the Turks, is required school reading, and his fiction seems almost to have replaced the actual history. There's a statue of the author within the castle, and a **Panoptikum** featuring wax versions of his characters. Copies of the novel are on sale all over town, and there's a **Gárdonyi Géza Memorial Museum**.

The castle was later dynamited by the Habsburgs in 1702. What remains is big, but there's not too much to see. Still, it's a nice place for a stroll and it affords a fine view over Eger's baroque and flatblock-free skyscape. Tours, available in English on site, offer a recap of the battle's history and a chance to see the interior of the battlements. You can just walk around, or visit the castle's various exhibits, most of which are closed on Monday.

Another place for a great view is atop the one minaret left from the Turkish occupation, though the ascent of the stairs inside is rather long and claustrophobic. Located at the corner of Knézich utca and Markó Ferenc utca, this is one of the northernmost minarets in Europe. The mosque that was once attached is gone.

Eger's baroque buildings are splendid, most notably the 1771 **Minorite church**, centrepiece of Dobó tér. The **Basilica** on Eszterházy tér is an imposing neo-classical monolith, crowned with crucifix-brandishing statues of *Faith,*

Hope and Charity by Italian sculptor Marco Casagrande. Designed by József Hild, who also designed the one in Budapest, this cathedral has a similarly imposing façade that looks all the larger due to the long flight of steps from the square below. The statues of Hungarian kings and apostles along these steps were also made by Casagrande. The **Lyceum** opposite, now a teachers' college, has a 19th-century camera obscura in its east tower observatory that projects a view of the entire town.

Small and with a pedestrianised centre, Eger is ideal for strolling. You could easily do the town in a day, but it's a relaxing and rewarding overnighter. The **Senátor Ház Hotel** at Dobó tér 11 (06 36/320 466) is comfortable and well situated. The **Minaret Hotel** at Knézich Károly utca 4 (06 36/410 233) is cheaper.

Although you can find commercial wine cellars downtown, the local vintages are most entertainingly sampled just out of town – at **Szépasszonyvölgy**, the Valley of Beautiful Women, a horseshoe-shaped area of dozens of wine cellars, with tables scattered outside. The offerings here, from small, private cellars, are not necessarily Eger's best, but the wine is very cheap. Gypsy fiddlers entertain drinkers, and parties come to eat, dance and make excessively merry. Try to get there by the afternoon, as most places will close by early evening. Out of high season, it can be quiet on Sundays and Mondays; the valley bustles during a two-week harvest festival in September. It's a 25-minute walk from Dobó tér or a short cab ride. It can be difficult to find a taxi back – try calling City Taxi (06 36/555 555).

In town, the **Dobos Cukrászda** at István utca 6 is a historic old coffeehouse and restaurant open early enough for breakfast. To dine on traditional Hungarian fare, head for the **Fehérszarvas Vadásztanya** (Klapka út 8, 06 36/411 129) and its wild boar specialities.

Tourinform Eger

Bajcsy-Zsilinszky utca 9 (06 36/517 715/www. eger.hu). **Open** *16 Sept-14 June* 9am-5pm Mon-Fri; 9am-1pm Sat. *15 June-15 Sept* 9am-6pm Mon-Fri; 9am-1pm Sat, Sun.

Tourinform Tokaj

Serház út 1 (06 47/352 259/www.tokaj.hu). **Open** *16 Oct-14 Apr* 9am-4pm Mon-Fri; 10.30am-2pm Sat. *15 Apr-15 Oct* 10.30am-6pm Mon-Fri; 10.30am-2pm Sat.

Trips Out of Town

Pécs

European Capital of Culture between Budapest and the Balkans.

Pécs, 'the Gateway to the Balkans', is getting an infrastructural overhaul before its role as European Capital of Culture in 2010 (*see p216* **Jeux Sans Frontières**). By then, the M6 motorway from Budapest will be in place and the recently opened Pécs-Pogány airport will be handling more traffic than just infrequent arrivals from Germany and charters to Corfu. A ring road around Hungary's fourth-largest town and pedestrianised culture zones within it are foretastes of the transformation that the prestigious 2010 event might bring.

The historic sites of Pécs' attractive old town, the curious architecture, the clutch of interesting art museums and the nightlife, fuelled by a large student population, all recommend Pécs as the main contender if you're making only one foray out of Budapest.

Romans settled here and called their town Sopianae – the name of a Hungarian cigarette brand. The town prospered on the trade route between Byzantium and Regensburg; King István established the Pécs diocese in 1009, and Hungary's first university was founded here in 1367. Then came the Turks in 1543, pushing the locals outside the walls that still define the city centre and flattening the place. Thus, as in the rest of Hungary, little pre-Turkish stuff survives.

Signs of the historic struggle between Magyars and Muslims are evident in the **Belvárosi Plébániatemplom** (Inner City Parish Church), which dominates the town's main square, Széchenyi tér. Under the Ottomans, an ancient Gothic church that once stood on the square was torn down and the stones were used to make the **mosque of Pasha Gazi Kassim**. After the Turks left, Jesuits converted the mosque to its present state, which is decidedly un-church-like: the ogee windows, domed and facing Mecca, are at variance with the square's north-south orientation. The minaret was demolished in 1753, but inside the church, on the back wall, are recently uncovered Arabic texts. As if to counter this influence, the main interior decor features a grand mural depicting Hungarian battles with the Turks. Outside, the statue of János Hunyadi, the Hungarian leader who successfully thwarted an earlier Turkish invasion, sits on horseback in the square.

The **mosque of Pasha Hassan Jokovali** is at Rákóczi utca 2. The most intact Ottoman-era structure in Hungary, this was also converted into a church, but in the 1950s the original mosque was restored. Excerpts from the Koran on the mosque's plaster dome have been recovered, and next door is a museum of Turkish artefacts. Hungary's only active mosque, built more recently, is located about 30 kilometres south, in the small town of Siklós, also home to a restored castle.

On Dóm tér stands the four-towered, mostly neo-Romanesque **Basilica of St Peter**. The choir, the crypt, the west side of the nave and the two western towers were built in the 11th century, the two eastern towers were added about a century later. Highlights include stunning frescoes, the red marble altar of the Corpus Christi Chapel and incredible wall carvings on the stairs leading to the crypt. Nearby Szent István tér has Roman ruins and a small park with cafés and a market.

Káptalan utca, a small street running east off Dóm tér, is packed with museums and galleries. At no.2, in a building built in 1324, is the museum of **Zsolnay** tiles, the colourful ceramics you see on top of Budapest's more extravagant

Széchenyi tér in the heart of **Pécs**.

buildings from the turn of the century and in Pécs on top of new buildings too. The Zsolnay factory is in Pécs, and this building houses some unusual Zsolnay pieces, though the best of the collection is probably what's visible from the courtyard. Across the street, at no.3, is the Magyar Op-artist **Victor Vasarely museum**, in the house where he was born. Underneath this house is the **mining museum**. Nearby, at Janus Pannonius utca 11, is an interesting museum of works by **Tivadar Csontváry**. Hungary's answer to Van Gogh, Csontváry made haunting paintings using vivid colours.

The **Santa Maria** at Klimó György utca 12, built into the city walls, is a good spot for lunch. The slightly more expensive **Aranykacsa**,

at Teréz utca 4 (06 72/518 860), cooks fantastic duck – its speciality – and other Hungarian fare.

Király utca, off Széchenyi tér, is a good stretch for a bar crawl, and there are DJ clubs here too, such as **Bázis** (no.11). The nearby Labirintus (Megyeri utca 53) also hosts live acts. Get a copy of the free *Pécsi Est* for listings.

The best hotel in Pécs is the art nouveau and elegant **Palatinus**, located at Király utca 5 (06 72/889 400). The **Hotel Fönix** at Hunyadi út 2 (06 72/311 680), north of Széchenyi tér, is just as central and cheaper.

Tourinform Pécs
Széchenyi tér 9 (06 72/213 315/www.pecs.hu). **Open** 8am-5.30pm Mon-Fri; 9am-2pm Sat.

Jeux Sans Frontières

Liverpool, Cork... and now Pécs, Hungary's first prestigious European Capital of Culture, hosting in 2010. Under the slogan 'The Borderless City', Pécs has played up its position at the crossroads between Central Europe and the Balkans – it's a short drive over the border to Croatia, over another to Serbia, and there's a daily train service to Sarajevo. Pécs' partner host Szeged is less than 20km from Romania.

The other motto for 2010 is 'five'. Known as 'Five Churches' in Latin, German and Slovak, Pécs ('five' in other Slavic languages) has created five key projects linked with the event. Most prominent (and most expensive) will be the creation of a Zsolnay Cultural Quarter around the factory complex responsible for the bright, iconic porcelain and ceramic decorations of the late 19th century – as seen in Budapest on Matthias Church or in the Museum of Applied Arts. Back then, a significant expanse of land

was given over to living quarters for workers' families, restaurants, a park, school and nursery, as well as the factory buildings. Within the park was a series of art nouveau sculptures. Much is in a state of disrepair, to be transformed by 2010 with a museum of industrial history, a design centre, workshops, bars, restaurants and sundry places of entertainment. The main new cultural venue will be a 1,000-capacity Music and Conference Centre, to host an improving local Pannon Philharmonic Orchestra and, during 2010, classical, jazz and rock concerts. There will also be a Choir Olympics, a competition between amateur choirs around the world. Nearby, a regional library and information centre will be built. Along a 'Museum Street' especially created for it, a Grand Exhibition Space will be added to the Old Town Hall; this will complement the fifth cultural element, the revival of public squares and parks, itself broken down into five elements: wells, squares, streets, parks and playgrounds.

The basic overall cost for these projects is some 144 million euros and, this being Hungary, there has been no end of squabbling behind the scenes. Three years before the event, none of the main figures responsible for establishing the project remain – István Tarrósy, Tibor Kiss and Méhes Márton among them. Another, Gábor Freivogel, looked set to jump ship in June 2007 when he declared to a Dutch newspaper: 'Common sense left this town years ago'.

Directory

Features

Sikló.

Directory

Getting Around

By air

Ferihegy airport is 20km (12.5 miles) south-east of Budapest on the E60. There are three modern terminals next to each other: Terminal 1, and the adjacent Terminals 2A and B. The newly renovated Terminal 1 (269 9696) is for budget flights. Terminal 2A is for Malév flights; 2B is for all other airlines. For details on arrivals and departures call the central number 296 7000 (English spoken) or check www.bud.hu.

Airport Minibus Shuttle

296 8555. **Open** 5am-1am. English spoken.
This is the best way into town. For Ft2,300 (Ft3,900 return), a minibus will take you to any address within the Budapest city limits. Buy a ticket at the LRI counter in the arrivals hall, tell staff where you're going, then wait ten minutes for a driver to call your destination after they've planned their route. To be picked up from town and taken to either terminal, call a day in advance. Accessible for wheelchair users.

Public transport

Take the no.200 bus (accessible for wheelchair users) from all three terminals to Kőbánya-Kispest metro station and the blue M3 metro from there for the cost of one public transport (BKV) ticket for each leg (Ft230 from the airport newsagent). Last buses from the airport are at 11.45pm. Last metro leaves at 11.10pm, or there's also the 909 night bus from the station.

Taxis from the airport

Zóna taxi (www.zonataxi.eu) operates from outside the arrivals area. They have fixed fares for four zones with a maximum fee for each, but if the taxi meter shows less you do not need to pay the whole amount given for that zone. Prices are between Ft3,000 and Ft4,300, the city centre in zone 2 at Ft4,100. The return journey is Ft3,000 from zones 1-2 and Ft3,500 from zones 3-4. Another option is to call any of the companies recommended (*see p220* **Taxis**).

Airlines

Air France

East-West Business Center, VIII.Rákóczi út (483 8800/airport 296 8415/www.airfrance.com/hu). M2 Astoria/tram 47, 49. **Open** 8.30am-5pm Mon-Fri. **Credit** AmEx, DC, MC, V. **Map** p249 F6.

Austrian Airlines

2nd floor, Millennium Center, V.Pesti Barnabás utca 4 (999 4012/airport 268 9601). M3 Ferenciek tere/M1 Vörösmarty tér/tram 2/bus 7. **Open** 9am-5pm Mon-Fri. **Credit** AmEx, DC, MC, V. **Map** p249 E6.

British Airways

East-West Business Center, VIII.Rákóczi út 1-3 (777 4747/airport 296 6970/www.british airways.hu). M2 Astoria/tram 47, 49/bus 7. **Open** 10am-noon, 1-4pm Mon-Fri. **Credit** AmEx, DC, MC, V. **Map** p249 F6.

EasyJet

00 44 870 600 0000/ www.easyjet.com.

Jet 2

00 44 871 2261737/www.jet2.com.

KLM

East-West Business Center, VIII.Rákóczi út 1-3 (373 7737/ airport 296 5747/www.klm.hu). M2 Astoria/tram 47, 49/bus 7. **Open** 8.30am-4.30pm Mon-Fri. **Credit** AmEx, DC, MC, V. **Map** p249 F6.

Lufthansa

IX.Lechner Ödön fasor 6 (411 9900/airport 292 1970/www. lufthansa.hu). Tram 2. **Open** 9am-5pm Mon-Fri. **Credit** AmEx, DC, MC, V. **Map** p249 G9.

Malév

XIII.Váci út 26 (235 3222/airport 296 9696/www.malev.hu). M3 Lehel tér. **Open** 9am-6pm Mon; 9am-5pm Tue-Fri; 9am-4pm Sat, Sun. **Credit** AmEx, DC, MC, V. **Map** p246 F2.
Malév's 24-hour information service for both terminals is on 296 7000. Ticket reservations can be made on 235 3888, 06 40 212 121 or at www.malev.hu.

Ryanair

00 44 871 246 0000/ www.ryanair.com.

Wizz Air

470 9499/www.wizzair.com.

By bus

If arriving by bus, you'll be dropped at **Népliget bus terminal** (IX.Üllői út 131, 382 0888, 465 5656, M3 Népliget, 6am-6pm Mon-Fri, 6am-4pm Sat, Sun; no English spoken). There are left luggage facilities here.

Volánbusz/Eurolines

Ticket office Népliget bus terminal, Üllői út 131 (219 8080/219 8063/www.volanbusz.hu). M3 Népliget. **Open** 8am-5pm Mon-Fri; 10am-3pm Sat. **Credit** AmEx, DC, MC, V.
The main international carrier, with connections to all major European cities.

By train

Budapest has three main train stations: **Déli** (south), **Keleti** (east) and **Nyugati** (west), all with metro stops of the same name. The Hungarian for a main station is *pályaudvar*, often abbreviated to *pu.*. Keleti station serves most trains to Vienna, Bucharest, Warsaw, Bulgaria, Turkey and north-western Hungary. Déli station also serves Vienna and Austria, as well as Croatia, Slovenia and south-eastern Hungary. Nyugati station is the main point of departure for Transylvania and Bratislava. Services can get moved around according to season, so always double-check your departure station before you travel.

Trains are cheap and reliable. The fastest, Intercity, require a seat reservation (Ft520). Leave reasonable time to buy your ticket. You can also buy tickets from the conductor with a small levy. Yellow departure timetables are posted at the main stations. 'R' means you must reserve a seat. Avoid *személy* trains, which stop at all stations. *Gyors* (fast) trains are one class down from Intercity.

MÁV Information
24hr info line 4049 4949/371 9449/www.mav/hu/www.elvira.hu. National enquiries (6am-midnight daily) 461 5400. International enquiries (6am-midnight daily) 461 5500.
You can also try calling one of the stations listed below.

MÁV Railbus
Platform 6, Keleti station (353 2722/www.railbus.hu).
Railbus offers transfers from railway stations to the airport. For prices and reservations call the 24-hour line on 06 70 455 0345.

Déli station
I.Alkotás út (355 8657). M2 Déli pu./tram 18, 59, 61. **Open** 24hrs daily. **Map** p245 A5.

Keleti station
VIII.Baross tér (313 6835). M2 Keleti pu./bus 7. **Open** 24hrs daily. **Map** p247 J5.

Nyugati station
VI.Nyugati tér (349 0115). M3 Nyugati pu./tram 4, 6. **Open** 24hrs daily. **Map** p246 F3.

Public transport

The Budapest transport company (BKV) is cheap and efficient, and gets you close to any destination. The network currently consists of three metro lines, trams, buses, trolleybuses and local trains. In summer there are also BKV Danube ferries. Maps of the system are available at main metro stations. Street maps also mark the routes. Due to the construction of metro line 4 there will be temporary changes in routes until 2009. Look out for signs at bus and tram stops or see www.bkv.hu/angol/home/index.

Services start around 4.30am and finish around 11pm; there's a limited night bus network along major routes. Tickets can be bought at all metro stations, and at some tram stops and newsstands. A single ticket (*vonaljegy*) is valid for one journey on one type of transport (except for ferries, which have a separate system, and buses that go beyond the administrative boundary of Budapest). So if you change from metro to tram, or even from metro line to metro line, you have to punch a new ticket, unless you use a transfer ticket (*átszállójegy*) or a metro transfer ticket (*metro átszállójegy*). If you're staying for more than a day, the easiest option is to buy a ten-ticket (*tíz jegy*) booklet, stamping as you go, without tearing off any of the tickets (inspectors do spot checks at barriers).

One-day, three-day, weekly, fortnightly and monthly passes are also available from metro stations, although you'll need a photograph to obtain anything except a one-day or three-day pass. Take your photo to a main metro station to be issued with a photopass. You should ask for a *napijegy* (one-day), *turistajegy* (three-day), *hetijegy* (weekly), *kétheti*

bérlet (fortnightly) and *havibérlet* (monthly). All these tickets run from the day of purchase, apart from the monthly, which is valid per calendar month. There is also a 30-day pass (*harmincnapos bérlet*) – only valid from the day of purchase. Inspectors bearing red armbands are common and can levy on-the-spot fines of Ft2,500.

Prices
Single ticket – Ft230
Single ticket from bus driver – Ft260
Transfer ticket – Ft380
Metro ticket for 3 stops – Ft180
10 tickets – Ft2,050
20 tickets – Ft3,900
Day – Ft1,350
3-day – Ft3,100

Passes (with photo)
Week – Ft3,600
2-week – Ft4,800
Month – Ft7,350
30-day – Ft7,350

BKV information
Free infoline *06 80 406 611.*

Budapest card
Two- and three-day cards work as BKV passes for an adult and a child under 14, as well as providing free admission to 60 museums, half-price sightseeing tours and discounts in certain restaurants, baths and shops. Ask for a free brochure at the main metro stations or at tourist information offices.

Budapest card for 2 days – Ft4,700
Budapest card for 3 days – Ft5,600

Metro

The Budapest metro is safe, clean, regular and simple. There are three lines: yellow M1, red M2 and blue M3. These connect the main stations and intersect at Deák tér. The renovated M1 line, originally constructed for the 1896 Exhibition, was the first underground railway in continental Europe. The other lines, constructed post-war with Soviet assistance, still have Russian trains.

Directory

At rush hour, trains run every two to three minutes (the length of time since the last train is shown on a clock on the platform). Single tickets, three-stop, five-stop and metro transfer tickets can be purchased from either the ticket machines or ticket office in the stations. Ticket offices close at 8pm. After that, knock on the station's office door to get a ticket. Reluctant clerks are often more reliable than ticket machines. Validate tickets in the machines at the top of the escalators and in Deák tér passageways when changing lines.

Buses, trams & trolleybuses

There's a comprehensive bus, tram and trolleybus network. Timetables are posted at all stops. The main bus route is line 7, connecting Bosnyák tér, Keleti station, Blaha Lujza tér, Astoria, Ferenciek tere, Móricz Zsigmond körtér and Kelenföld. The Castle bus (Várbusz) goes from Moszkva tér round the Castle District and back. Buses with red numbers are expresses that miss certain stops.

Night buses have three-digit numbers starting with 9; a reduced but reliable service follows the main daytime routes. Handiest are the 906 following the Nagykörút, the 914 following the blue M3 metro line, and the 907 from Kelenföld station to Örs Vezér tere, following the M2 route. On main routes, buses run every 15 minutes.

The most important tram routes are lines 4 and 6, which follow the Nagykörút from Moszkva tér to Fehérvári út and Móricz Zsigmond körtér respectively; line 2, which runs up the Pest side of the Danube; and lines 47 and 49, which run from Deák tér to Móricz Zsigmond körtér and beyond into deepest Buda.

Suburban trains (HÉV)

There are four HÉV lines. The main one runs from Batthyány tér via Margaret Bridge to Szentendre. A normal BKV ticket is valid as far as the city boundary at Békásmegyer, with an extra fee thereafter. First and last trains from Batthyány tér are at 3.50am and 11.30pm, and from Szentendre at 3.45am and 11.10pm. Other lines run from Örs vezér tere to Gödöllő, Vágóhíd to Ráckeve, and Boráros tér to Csepel.

Danube ferries

BKV Danube ferries offer a river ride that's cheap when compared with the various organised tours. The local service runs from May to the beginning of September, between Pünkösdfürdő north of the city and Boráros tér at the Pest foot of Petőfi Bridge, stopping at most of the bridges, Vigadó tér and Margaret Island. Fares vary between Ft220 and Ft700 for adults and Ft150 and Ft350 for children. Boats only run once every couple of hours, with extra services laid on at weekends. Timetables are posted at all stops.

Boats to Szentendre, Visegrád and Esztergom on the **Danube Bend** leave from Vigadó tér (*see p206*).

There are also any number of sightseeing tours down the Danube, by day and night, with commentaries, Gypsy bands or dinner-and-dance. *See p60* **Budapest by boat**.

Ferry information

Vigadó tér terminal (V. Vigadó tér, 318 1223/www.mahart.hu). Or try the BKV information line – *see p219*.

MAHART Passnave Sightseeing Boat

Vigadó tér terminal (V. Vigadó tér, 484 4013/www.mahart passnave.hu).

Eccentric conveyances

Budapest has a bizarre range of one-off forms of public transport. For the price of a BKV ticket the **cog-wheel railway** runs up Széchenyi-hegy. It runs from the Hotel Budapest, two stops from Moszkva tér on trams 56 or 18. Last train down is at 11.30pm.

Across the park from the cog-wheel railway is the terminal of the narrow-gauge **Children's Railway** (*gyermekvasút*; 397 5392), which wends its way through the wooded Buda Hills. It was formerly the Pioneer Railway, run by the Communist youth organisation; many of the jobs are still done by children. Trains leave every hour between 9am and 5pm and tickets cost Ft450 (return Ft900) for adults and Ft300 (return Ft600) for children.

Another way up into the hills is the **chairlift** (*libegő*; 391 0352) up to Jánoshegy – at 520 metres the highest point in Budapest. Take the 158 bus from Moszkva tér to the terminus at Zugligeti út. The chairlift station is a short walk across the road. It costs F500 one-way (Ft1,000 return), Ft400 for students and Ft200 for children, and runs 10am-5pm Mon-Fri, 10am-6pm Sat, Sun. There are cafés at the top, and you can walk to Erzsébet lookout tower or the Jánoshegy stop on the Children's Railway.

Tamer but more central, the **funicular** (*sikló*) takes a minute to run up from Clark Ádám tér to the Castle District. This runs from 7.30am to 10pm (closed every second Monday morning) and a one-way ticket costs Ft700 for adults, Ft400 for children.

The **Nostalgia Train**, an old-fashioned steam engine, chuffs from Nyugati station up the Danube Bend on Saturdays in summer. *See p166*.

Taxis

Taxis in Budapest have yellow number plates and yellow taxi signs on them. Rates vary from cheap to outrageous but an average journey across town with a reliable company should not cost more than Ft1,500. Try and stick to cabs displaying the logo of one of the companies mentioned below. Others often have doctored meters or will take you by the scenic route. Sadly nearly all taxis parked by Keleti or Nyugati stations are in a cartel and their drivers have little shame in charging exorbitant prices. Also avoid cars hanging around outside main hotels and tourist spots. For a taxi to and from **Ferihegy airport**, *see p218*.

The reliable **Fötaxi** has cabs with checked patterns on their doors and can be spotted from a distance thanks to their oval-shaped lights – although some rogue cabs have adopted similar markings. Calling a taxi is the safest and easiest method. Most dispatchers can speak English and the cab will be there in five to ten minutes. Even though taxi companies have different tariffs, which comprise a basic fee, a fee per kilometre and a waiting fee, there's a price ceiling for all.

To give a rough idea, average tariffs at reliable companies are: basic fee Ft300; fee per km Ft210; waiting fee Ft48 per min. A receipt should be available on request. Say *'számlát kérek'*. A small tip of rounding up to the nearest Ft100-Ft200 is customary but not compulsory. Simply indicate the amount you'd like to pay – or the amount of change you'd like to get back – as you hand over the money.

Reliable companies include:

Budataxi (233 3333)
City Taxi (211 1111)
Fötaxi (222 2222)
Rádió Taxi (777 7777)
Tele5 (555 5555)

Driving

Budapest has all the traffic problems of most modern European cities with a few extra ones thrown in for good measure. Hungarian driving is not good. Hungarians have constant urges to overtake in the most impossible places, lack concentration and jump traffic lights. Many vehicles are of poor quality. Roads can be even worse.

There's been a huge influx of Western cars in recent years, increasing traffic levels around Budapest and daytime parking problems. Practically all the bridges and central streets are jammed in rush hour. Talk of restricting traffic hasn't yet amounted to much. If you can't find your car where you left it, it doesn't necessarily mean it's been stolen. Your vehicle may have been towed for illegal parking (*see p222* **Parking**).

● Seatbelts must be worn at all times by everyone in the car.
● Children under eight must be in a child safety seat. If a child can't be fitted into a safety seat, special cushions (*ülésmagasító*) should be used, so the child is lifted up enough to fasten the seatbelt. Children under 12 or under 150cm are not allowed to travel in the front seat without a safety seat.
● Always make sure you carry your passport, driving licence, vehicle registration document, motor insurance and *zöldkártya* (exhaust emissions certificate) for cars that have been registered in Hungary. Don't leave anything of value in the car.
● Headlights are compulsory by day when driving outside built-up areas. It's also recommended that you use them in the city at all times.
● Priority is from the right unless you're on a priority road, signified by a yellow diamond on a white background.

● Watch out for trams in places such as the Nagykörút where the passengers alight in the middle of the road.
● Speed limit on motorways is 130kph, on highways 110kph, on all other roads 90kph unless otherwise indicated, and 50kph in built-up areas. Speed traps abound, with spot fines that vary greatly.
● The alcohol limit is zero per cent and there are many spot checks, with severe penalties. Take a taxi if you're drinking.
● You're not allowed to speak on a mobile phone while driving unless you're using a speakerphone or hands-free set.

Breakdowns

A 24-hour breakdown service is provided by the **Magyar Autóklub**, which has reciprocal agreements with many European associations. English and German are usually spoken, but if not they will ask you for the model (*típus*), colour (*szín*) and number plate (*rendszám*) of the vehicle, and also the location.

City Segély
(342 4564/06 20 933 1330).
Open 24hrs daily.
No credit cards.

Magyar Autóklub
(345 1800/24hr emergency 188).
Open 24hrs daily. **No credit cards** but they will accept a credit letter from affiliated organisations.

Car hire

It's advisable to arrange car hire in advance. When asking for a quote, check whether the price includes *ÁFA* (VAT). You have to be over 21 with at least a year's driving experience. A valid driver's licence is required and a credit card is usually necessary for the deposit. There's an insurance charge and varying rates of mileage. Most companies have desks at both airport terminals.

Directory

Avis

*V.Szervita tér 8 (318 4158/
airport terminal 1 296 8680/
airport terminal 2 296 6421/
www.avis.hu). M1, M2, M3
Deák tér.* **Open** 7am-6pm
daily. **Credit** AmEx, DC,
MC, V. **Map** p249 E5.

Budget

*I.Krisztina körút 41-43 (214
0420/airport terminal 1 296
8842/airport terminal 2 296
8197/www.budget.hu). M2 Déli
pu..* **Open** 8am-8pm Mon-Fri;
8am-6pm Sat, Sun. **Credit**
AmEx, DC, MC, V.

Europcar

*V.Deák Ferenc tér 3 (328
6464/airport terminal 1 421
8373/airport terminal 2 421
8370/hotline 421 8333/
www.eurent.hu). M1, M2, M3
Deák tér.* **Open** 8am-6pm daily.
Credit AmEx, DC, MC, V.
Map p249 E5.

Hertz

*Vecsés, Hertz utca 2 (296 0999/
airport terminal 1 296 8466/
airport terminal 2 296 7171/
www.hertz.hu).* **Open** 8am-5pm
Mon-Fri. *Airport* 8am-10pm daily.
Credit AmEx, DC, MC, V.
Other locations: Hotel Marriott,
V.Apáczai Csere János utca 4 (266
4361). **Open** 7am-7pm daily.

Parking

More and more areas have
parking meters, so look for the
signs that show you've entered
a zone where you have to pay.
Little red bags (popularly
known here as Santa bags)
behind the wipers of other
cars are another indication.

Check signs for hours
(usually 8am-6pm weekdays,
8am-noon Sat). After that
parking is free. Tickets are
valid for one to three hours.
Tickets can be purchased at
the meters but you'll need to
have change, or a parking card
that can be bought in advance
in denominations of Ft5,000,
Ft10,000 and Ft30,000. The
disadvantage of using a card
is that certain cards are only
accepted in certain areas.
Parking can also be paid for

over the phone – you'll need to
register by clicking on to
www.emert.hu/ENindex.php.

If you forget to buy a ticket
or it exceeds the time covered,
you might find a red bag under
your wiper. In this case you
need to pay the bill you find in
the bag. The fine increases if
you don't pay it within three or
six days. You can pay it at the
parking meters. Find 'extra fee'
and 'paying the demanded
amount' in the menu and you'll
get a receipt. If you pay at the
meter, you must forward the
copy of the receipt via fax or
post to the customer service
office of the company to which
the area belongs. You can also
pay the fine at any post office.

In more serious cases you
might find your car clamped
or towed away. For wheel-
clamping release, about
Ft10,000, call the number
displayed on a parking meter
nearby. Cars that have been
towed away can be traced by
phone (307 5208, 383 0700).

In Budapest you can use the
parking attendant controlled
areas (V.Március 15 tér or
under Nyugati station flyover)
or these car parks:

Car parks

V.Szervita tér 8. V.Aranykéz utca
4-6. VII.Nyár utca 20. VII.Osvát
utca 5. VIII.Futó utca 52.

Petrol

Most filling stations are open
24 hours a day. Unleaded petrol
is *ólommentes*. Stay away from
fuel marked with a 'K' as this is
for lawnmowers and Trabants.
Nearly all petrol stations accept
credit cards and sell tobacco
and basic groceries.

Cycling

Budapest is becoming more
cycle-friendly, although air
pollution is high and drivers
generally unwary. Several
establishments around
Budapest will rent you a
bicycle and give you a tour –
or you can just ask for a map
of the increasing number of
routes and find your own
way. Road standards can
vary; some of the smaller
ones are poorly marked. For
more details, *see p199* **Life
in the narrow lane.**

Budapestbike.hu

*VII.Wesselényi utca 18 (06 30 944
5533 mobile/www.budapestbike.
hu). M1, M2, M3 Deák tér.* **Open**
10am-8pm daily. **Map** p249 F5.

Yellow Zebra

*V.Sütő utca 2 (266 8777/www.
yellowzebrabikes.com). M1, M2,
M3 Deák tér.* **Open** *Nov-Mar*
10am-6pm daily. *Apr-Oct* 8.30am-
8pm daily. **Map** p249 E5.

Travel advice

For up-to-date information on travel to a specific country
– including the latest news on safety and security, health
issues, local laws and customs – contact your home
country government's department of foreign affairs.
Most have websites packed with useful advice for
would-be travellers.

Australia
www.smartraveller.gov.au

Canada
www.voyage.gc.ca

New Zealand
www.mft.govt.nz/travel

Republic of Ireland
foreignaffairs.gov.ie

UK
www.fco.gov.uk/travel

USA
www.state.gov/travel

Resources A-Z

Addresses

When addressing an envelope in Hungarian, write the name of the street first followed by the house number. Street is *utca*, often abbreviated to *u* on street plates, envelopes and maps. This shouldn't be mixed up with *út* (*útja* in the genitive), which is road or avenue – unless it's a *körút*, which means ring road. *Tér* (genitive *tere*) is a square, *körtér* is a roundabout. Other Hungarian thoroughfares include *köz* (lane), *fasor* (alley), *sétány* (parade), *udvar* (passage or courtyard) and *rakpart* (embankment).

Envelopes should show the four-figure postcode, in which the middle numbers stand for the district; for flats, the floor number is given in Roman numerals, followed by the flat number. On street plates, the district is written in Roman numerals, with the building numbers within the block immediately underneath.

Age restrictions

In Hungary, the age of consent is 14 and people officially come of age at 18. Until then you're not allowed to buy cigarettes and alcoholic drinks or get a driving licence without parental permission.

Business

The Hungarian market has long been liberalised and open to foreign competition. State-owned companies have nearly all been privatised. Foreign-owned companies and individuals can buy property – but only a Hungarian citizen is permitted to own farmland.

It is also becoming easier to enforce contracts, as the company court system gets more effective.

Local business revolves around personal contacts. Western investors still find their Hungarian counterparts fixated on bleeding short-term benefit out of long-term business ventures. Westerners, especially those involved in small- and medium-sized business, should be wary of entering deals that require far-sighted local partners.

Accounting & consulting firms

Deloitte & Touche

VI.Dózsa György út 84C (428 6800/fax 428 6801/www.deloitte. com). M1 Hősök tere/bus 20, 30. **Open** 8am-7pm Mon-Fri. **Map** p247 J2.

Ernst & Young

XIII.Váci út 20 (451 8100/fax 451 8199/www.ey.com). M3 Lehel tér. **Open** 7.30am-7pm Mon-Fri.

KPMG

XIII.Váci út 99 (887 7100/ fax 887 7101/www.kpmg.com). M3 Forgács utca. **Open** 9am-7pm Mon-Fri.

PriceWaterhouse Coopers

VII.Wesselényi utca 16 (461 9100/fax 461 9101/www.pwc global.com). M2 Astoria/bus 7. **Open** 8.30am-5.30pm Mon-Fri. **Map** p249 F5.

Commercial banks

Central-European International Bank (CIB)

II.Medve utca 4-14 (457 6800/fax 489 6500). M2 Batthyány tér/bus 11. **Open** 8.30am-4pm Mon, Tue, Thur; 8.30am-6pm Wed; 8.30am-2.30pm Fri. **Map** p245 B3.

Citibank

V.Szabadság tér 7 (374 5000/fax 374 5100/www.citibank.hu). M3 Arany János utca/M2 Kossuth tér. **Open** 9am-5pm Mon-Thur; 9am-4pm Fri. **Map** p249 E4.

K&H Bank

V.Vigadó tér 1 (328 9000/fax 328 9696/www.khb.hu). Tram 2. **Open** 8am-5pm Mon; 8am-4pm Tue-Thur; 8am-3pm Fri. **Map** p249 D5.

OTP Bank

V.Nádor utca 16 (473 5000/fax 473 5996/www.otpbank.hu). M2 Kossuth tér/bus 15. **Open** 8am-4pm Mon-Fri. **Map** p246 D4.

Conventions & conferences

Major hotels offer conference facilities too (*see pp35-51*).

Budapest Convention Centre

Budapest Kongresszusi Központ *XII.Jagelló utca 1-3 (372 5700/fax 466 5636).* Tram 61/bus 8, 12, 112. **Open** varies. **Map** p248 A7.

Regus Business Centre

V.Regus House, Kálmán Imre utca 1 (475 1100/fax 475 1111/ www.regus.com). M2 Kossuth tér/tram 2. **Open** 8.30am-6pm Mon-Fri. **Map** p246 E3. Short-term leases and various multilingual secretarial services.

Couriers & shippers

DHL Hungary

XI.Kocsis utca 3 (06 40 454 545 mobile/fax 204 5555). Tram 18, 41, 47. **Open** 8am-6pm Mon-Fri. **Credit** AmEx, MC, V.

Federal Express

Airport Business Park Building C5, Vecsés, Lőrinci utca 59 (06 29 551 901/fax 06 29 551 972/ www.fedex.com/hu). **Open** 8am-7pm Mon-Fri. **Credit** AmEx, V.

Hajtás Pajtás Bicycle Messenger

VII.Damjanich utca 42 (327 9000/ www.hajtaspajtas.hu). Bus 30/ trolleybus 75, 79. **Open** 24hrs daily. **No credit cards.** The fastest couriers in town, with 100 riders and five dispatchers to get round a gridlocked city. Also delivers in Hungary and abroad.

Lawyers

Allen & Overy/ Déry & Co

Madách Trade Center, VII.Madách Imre utca 13 (483 2200/fax 268 1515). M1. M2, M3 Deák tér. **Open** 8am-8pm Mon-Fri. Map p249 E5.

Baker & McKenzie/ Martonyi & Kajtár

VI.Andrássy út 102 (302 3330/ fax 302 3331). M1 Hősök tere. **Open** 9am-5.30pm Mon-Fri. Map p247 H2.

CMS Cameron McKenna/Őrmai & Partners

Ybl Palace, V.Károlyi Mihály utca 12, 3rd floor (483 4800/fax 483 4801). M3 Ferenciek tere/bus 7. **Open** 9am-6pm Mon-Fri. Map p249 E6.

Köves Clifford Chance Pünder

Madách Trade Center, VII.Madách Imre utca 14 (429 1300/fax 429 1390). M1, M2, M3 Deák tér. **Open** 8am-8pm Mon-Fri. Map p249 E5.

Money

Hungary's currency is the forint. It is fully convertible. In May 2007 the exchange rate was Ft250/€1, Ft370/£1. Hungary is not expected to adopt the euro until 2010.

Because of policies aimed at gradually bringing Hungary into the eurozone, the forint should appreciate slightly against the euro over the next couple of years. In other words, the euros may actually buy fewer forints in the near future – although there is also local inflation to be accounted for.

Credit and debit cards connected to half-a-dozen global clearance systems can be used to withdraw forints at thousands of ATMs around Hungary. Wire transfers are quickly and easily arranged – but expect a one-day delay.

Cheques (except travellers' cheques) are pretty much non-existent in Hungary. They cannot be cashed in less than three weeks, and only then at grievous personal expense. Foreigners are free to open a bank account in Hungary in almost any currency with the minimum of hassle.

Office hire & business centres

At mid 2007 prices, top-quality office space in Budapest costs €12-€21 per square metre per month. The following offices have English-speaking staff.

Biggeorge's International

Buda Square Irodaház, III.Lajos utca 48-66 (225 2525/fax 225 2521). Bus 6, 60, 86. **Open** 8am-7.30pm Mon-Fri.

Colliers International

XII.Csörsz utca 41 (336 4200/ fax 336 4201). Tram 61/bus 105, 112. **Open** 8am-6pm Mon-Fri.

Cushman & Wakefield, Healey & Baker

Deák Palota, V.Deák Ferenc utca 15 (268 1288/fax 268 1289). M1, M2, M3 Deák tér. **Open** 8.30am-6.30pm Mon-Fri. Map p249 E5.

Jones Lang LaSalle

Alkotás Point, XII.Alkotás utca 50 (489 0202/fax 489 0203). Tram 61. **Open** 9am-6pm Mon-Fri. Map p245 A6.

Recruitment agencies

Antal International

II.Moszkva tér 8 (336 2414/ fax 336 2029). M2 Moszkva tér/ tram 4, 6. **Open** 9am-5pm Mon-Fri. Map p249 A3.

Grafton Recruitment

V.Károlyi Mihály utca 12 (235 2600/fax 235 2601). M3 Kálvin tér/M3 Ferenciek tere/bus 7. **Open** 8.30am-6pm Mon-Thur; 8am-5pm Fri. Map p249 E6.

TMP Worldwide

XI.Bartók Béla út 14 (235 0377/ fax 235 0378). Tram 18, 19, 47, 49. **Open** 9am-5pm Mon-Fri.

Relocation services

Settlers Hungary

XII.Maros utca (212 5017/ fax 212 5146/www.settlers.hu). M2 Déli pu./tram 59, 61. **Open** 8.30am-5pm Mon-Thur; 8.30am-4pm Fri.

This company will help with all aspects of moving to Budapest as a foreigner: international schools, car registration, setting up medicals, official stamps, obtaining tax numbers and customs clearances.

Useful organisations

American Chamber of Commerce

V.Deák Ferenc utca 10 (266 9880/ fax 266 9888). M1, M2, M3 Deák tér. **Open** 9am-5pm Mon-Fri. Consultations by appointment only. Map p249 E5.

British Chamber of Commerce

V.Bank utca 6 (302 5200/fax 302 3069). M3 Arany János utca. **Open** 8.30am-5pm Mon-Fri. Consultations by appointment only. Map p245 E4.

British Trade & Investment Section

V.Harmincad utca 6 (266 2888/ fax 429 6360). M1 Vörösmarty tér/M2, M3 Deák tér. **Open** 9am-5pm Mon-Fri. Consultations by appointment only. Map p249 E5.

Budapest Stock Exchange

Budapesti Értéktőzsde *VI.Andrássy út 93 (429 6857/ fax 429 6899). M1 Kodály körönd.* **Open** 10am-3pm Mon-Fri. Not open to the general public. Map p249 G3.

Hungarian Chamber of Commerce

Magyar Kereskedelmi és Ipari Kamara *V.Kossuth Lajos tér 6 (474 5101/ fax 474 5105). M2 Kossuth tér.* **Open** 8.30am-4.30pm Mon-Thur; 8.30am-2pm Fri. Map p246 D3.

Hungarian Investment & Trade Development Agency

Magyar Befektetési és Kereskedelemfejlesztési Kht.

VI.Andrássy út 12 (472 8100/fax 472 8101/www.itd.hu). M1 Bajcsy-Zsilinszky út. **Open** 8am-4.30pm Mon-Thur; 9am-2pm Fri. **Map** p246 E4.

Hungarian National Bank

Magyar Nemzeti Bank
V.Szabadság tér 8-9 (428 2600). M2 Kossuth tér/M3 Arany János utca/tram 2. **Open** 8am-1pm Mon-Fri. **Map** p246 E4.

Ministry of Economics & Transport

Gazdasági és
Közlekedési Minisztérium
V.Hold utca 17 (475 3434/fax 475 3435). M2 Kossuth tér/M3 Arany János utca. **Open** 9am-4.30pm Mon, Tue, Thur; 9am-5pm Wed; 9am-2pm Fri. **Map** p246 E4.

US Embassy Commercial Service

Bank Center Building, V.Szabadság tér 7 (475 4090/ fax 475 4676). M3 Arany János utca/M2 Kossuth tér. **Open** 6am-5pm Mon-Fri. **Map** p246 E4. The Information USA office also organises a regular commercial database for interested parties, open 11am-5pm Tue, Thur, by appointment only.

Customs

Coming into Hungary, items of clothing or objects that could be deemed to be for personal use remain exempt from duties.

Arriving from an EU country, apart from Romania and Bulgaria, individuals over 17 years old are also allowed to bring in 800 cigarettes, 200 cigars, 400 cigarillos or 1000 grams of tobacco, as well as 90 litres of wine, ten litres of spirits and 110 litres of beer, and 250ml of perfumes.

Arriving from Romania, Bulgaria and outside the EU, individuals over 17 years old are allowed to bring in 200 cigarettes, 50 cigars, 100 cigarillos or 250 grams of tobacco, one litre of wine, one litre of spirits and five litres of beer, and 250ml of perfumes.

Merchandise up to a value of 175 euros is allowed in duty free. There's no limit to the amount of foreign currency you can bring in. It's forbidden to bring in drugs or arms.

On exit the limits are:

● wine – 1 litre
● spirits – 1 litre
● 250 cigarettes, 100 cigars or 250 grams tobacco

When leaving the country, non-EU citizens are able to reclaim the sum of the value added tax on most items (except, for example, antiques, works of art and services) bought in Hungary. The total value of the items should exceed 175 euros and the goods should be taken out of

the country within three months of purchase. For VAT refunds keep the receipt you get when purchasing an item (ask for an '*ÁFAs számla*') and get it stamped by the customs officers at the border or the airport. At the airport you have to show the item to the officer, so make sure you keep it in your hand luggage. Get an *ÁFA visszaigénylő lap* (VAT refund form), which will contain all the necessary information. A claim has to be made within six months. Note that EU citizens can no longer reclaim ÁFA on goods purchased in Hungary. For further customs information, contact 470 4119, 470 4121, vam.info@vpop.hu.

Disabled

On public transport many older buses have been replaced by low-floored ones, as have most trams on the busiest lines 4 and 6. The M1 metro line is also accessible, as is the airport minibus.

There is also a special transport bus arranged through the **Hungarian Disabled Association**, who can provide a helper. The Museum of Fine Arts, Museum of Applied Arts and others in the city are all now accessible.

Average monthly climate

Month	High temp (C°/F°)	Low temp (C°/F°)	Rainfall
Jan	7/45	2/36	53cm
Feb	10/50	2/36	43cm
Mar	13/55	4/39	49cm
Apr	17/63	6/43	53cm
May	20/68	9/48	65cm
June	23/73	12/54	54cm
July	25/77	15/59	62cm
Aug	26/79	16/29	42cm
Sept	23/73	12/54	54cm
Oct	20/68	8/46	60cm
Nov	14/57	4/39	51cm
Dec	7/44	3/37	59cm

Directory

New buildings and stretches of street are being designed with the disabled in mind.

There are also a limited number of special trips available, such as the one to Lake Balaton by train once a week. For more details call:

Hungarian Disabled Association

MEOSZ
III.San Marco utca 76 (388 5529/388 2387/fax 454 1144). Tram 1. **Open** 8am-4pm Mon-Fri.

Drugs

Even though the law doesn't explicitly prohibit the 'use' of drugs, everything else – producing, selling, buying, offering and obtaining – is illegal. If caught with a small amount of drugs, you can be sentenced to two to nine years' imprisonment. If it's a first-time offence and you're not dealing to minors, you might escape with a fine, compulsory rehabilitation treatment or a warning. For a large amount of drugs, the punishment is anything from five years to a life sentence, depending on whether the drugs were for personal use or for peddling. Small amounts are defined as:
Amphetamines 1-10 grams
Cocaine 3-8 grams
Ecstasy 10-20 tablets
Grass 10-100 grams
Hashish 10-100 grams
Heroin 1-6 grams
LSD 5-15 pieces
Methadone 200 pieces
Large amounts are defined as 20 times the small amounts.

If the police consider you suspicious, they have the right to stop and search; if you're driving, they can give you a compulsory urine and blood test. You have the right to ask for a lawyer or call your own. In a drug-related emergency call 104. Doctors must observe laws of confidentiality. For more details and drug-related legal advice see **TASZ** or www.drogriporter.hu.

CAT

XIII.Hollán Ernő utca 40 (320 2866). Tram 2, 4, 6. **Open** 6-10pm Mon-Fri; 4-8pm Sat, Sun. **Map** p246 D2.
CAT's risk-reducing programme provides clean needles, as well as counselling and information on medication and rehabilitation.

Drog Stop Hotline

06 80 505 678 mobile.
Open 24hrs daily.

Kék Pont Drug Consultation Center

215 7833/06 30 490 2840 mobile.
Open *Telephone enquiries* 10am-6pm Mon-Fri.

TASZ

Hungarian Civil Liberties Union
VIII.Víg utca 28 (209 0046/279 0755). Tram 4, 6. **Map** p250 H6.

Electricity

The current used in Hungary is 230V, which works with UK 240V appliances. If you have US 110V gadgets, bring the transformers with you. Plugs have two round pins, so bring an adaptor for any other plug.

Embassies & consulates

American Embassy

V.Szabadság tér 12 (475 4400/ after office hours for US citizens only 475 4703/fax 475 4764/ www.usembassy.hu). M2 Kossuth tér/M3 Arany János utca. **Open** 8am-5pm Mon-Fri. **Map** p246 E4.

Australian Embassy

XII.Királyhágó tér 8-9 (457 9777/ fax 201 9792/www.ausembbp.hu). M2 Déli pu.. **Open** 8.30am-4.30pm Mon-Fri.

British Embassy

V.Harmincad utca 6 (266 2888/ fax 266 0907/emergency number 06 70 335 5564 mobile). M1 Vörösmarty tér/M2, M3 Deák tér/tram 2. **Open** 9am-5pm Mon-Fri. **Map** p249 E5.

Canadian Embassy

II.Ganz utca 12-14 (392 3360/ 392 3390). Tram 4, 6. **Open** 8.30am-4.30pm Mon-Fri.

Irish Embassy

Bank Center, V.Szabadság tér 7 (301 4960/fax 302 9599). M2 Kossuth tér/M3 Arany János utca/tram 2. **Open** 9.30am-12.30pm Mon-Fri. **Map** p246 E4.

New Zealand Consulate

VI.Nagymező utca 50 (302 2484/ fax 311 8092). M1 Opera/M1 Oktogon. **Open** 9am-5pm Mon-Fri. **Map** p246 F4.

Romanian Embassy

XIV.Thököly út 72 (384 8394/fax 384 5535). Bus 7. **Open** 8.30am-noon, 2-6pm Mon, Tue, Thur, Fri. **Map** p247 K3.

South African Embassy

II.Gárdonyi Géza út 17 (392 0999/fax 200 7277). Bus 11. **Open** 9am-12.30pm Mon-Fri.

Emergencies

For hospitals, *see p227* **Health**. For **helplines**, including poisoning, *see p229*.
Ambulance **104/331 9133**
Emergency breakdown **188**
Fire **105**
General emergencies **112**
Police **107**

Gay & lesbian

Information

GayGuide.Net Budapest

06 30 932 3334 mobile/ http://gayguide.net. **Open** *Phoneline* 4-8pm daily.
Founded by a group of expats, the site offers an up-to-date gay guide with accommodation, a gay tour and general city information. It operates a phone line all year round and promises to reply to every email within 48hrs. You can subscribe to its mailing list or place a classified ad on the web page to make contacts.

HEAT

www.pararadio.hu
Fiksz Rádió 98 FM.
Para Radio's popular online show.

Ki-más

www.fikszradio.hu
Fiksz Rádió 98 FM.

Mások

*1461 Budapest, PO Box 388
(266 9959/www.masok.hu).*
Hungary's main gay magazine,
published monthly and available
in gay venues around the city
and at newsstands downtown.

Other groups
& organisations

Habeas
Corpus Jogsegély

*1364 Budapest, PO Box 31 (06
30 996 5666 mobile/www.habeas
corpus.hu).* **Open** 4-6pm Wed.
A group addressing the legal
issues of sexuality in Hungary.

Háttér Support Society
for Gays & Lesbians

Háttér Baráti
Társaság a Melegekért
*1554 Budapest, PO Box 50 (office
329 2670/helpline 06 80 505 605
mobile/www.hatter.hu).* **Open**
6-11pm daily.
'Background' is the main gay and
lesbian organisation in Hungary. It
offers information and counselling,
and runs an HIV/AIDS prevention
project and a self-help group.

Labrisz
Lesbian Society

*VI.Király utca 58, buzzer 13
(321 9351/www.labrisz.hu).*
Open 6-9pm Mon, Thur.
This group runs meetings and
educational programmes.

Öt Kenyér

*1461 Budapest, PO Box 25
(www.otkenyer.hu).*
This Catholic gay group
has regular meetings. Email
otkenyer@otkenyer.hu or call
06 30 459 8167 or 06 70 540 9342.

Szimpozion
Circle of Friends

*1553 Budapest, PO Box 50
(06 30 595 8174 mobile/
http://szimpozion.fw.hu).*
Provides support for the gay,
lesbian, bisexual and transgender
community through educational
projects, leisure and sports.

Vándor Mások

*1463 Budapest, PO Box 926
(www.gay.hu).*
Gay and lesbian hiking group.
Events and excursions are
published in *Mások* magazine.

Health

In 2007 Hungary introduced
a fee of Ft300-Ft600 for every
consultation. You may also
be obliged to pay 30 per cent
of the cost of examinations.
Most doctors will speak some
English. Emergency care is
provided free to EU citizens,
although it's probably wise
to take out some extra medical
insurance as well. Those
working here should get a TB
(social security) card through
their employer to obtain free
state health treatment, and
register with a local GP.

Accident &
emergency

In an emergency, go to the
casualty department of the
nearest hospital. Make sure
you take a Hungarian speaker
and some form of ID. For
emergency numbers, *see p226.*

Ambulances

The emergency number is 104,
but this may be Hungarian-
speaking only. If you call 331
9133, you should find an
English speaker. Companies
listed below offer private
ambulance services.

American Clinics
International

*I.Hattyú utca 14 (224 9090/www.
firstmedcenters.com). M2 Moszkva
tér.* **Open** 8am-7pm Mon-Thur;
8am-6pm Fri; 8.30am-1pm Sat.
24hr emergency service. **Credit**
AmEx, MC, V. **Map** p245 A3.

Főnix SOS Ambulance

*XII.Diós árok 1-3 (200 0100). Bus
28, 128.* **Open** 24hr emergency
service. **Credit** AmEx, MC, V.

IMS

*XIII.Váci út 184 (7.30am-8pm
Mon-Fri 329 8423; 8pm-7.30am
8pm-7.30am Mon-Fri, 24hrs Sat,
Sun 250 9160/fax 349 9349
/www.imskft.hu). M3 Gyöngyösi
út/night bus 950.* **Open** 7.30am-
8pm Mon-Fri. 24hr emergency
service. **Credit** AmEx, MC, V.

Complementary
medicine

There are several Chinese
doctors who offer acupuncture
and massage therapies.
The Homeopathic Doctors'
Association website offfers
a list of English-speaking
practitioners.

Dr Funian Yu

*VII.Bethlen Gábor utca 8 (342
2772). Bus 7/trolleybus 75, 79.*
Open *by appointment only* 7am-
noon, 2-6pm 6pm. **Credit** MC, V.
Map p247 J4.
Chinese acupuncture service at a
fraction of Western prices.

Homeopathic
Doctors' Association

*II.Margit körút 64B (225 3897/
fax 225 3898/www.homeopata.
hu). Tram 4, 6.* **Open** 2-6pm Mon;
9am-1pm Wed. **No credit cards.**

Contraception
& abortion

Condoms are easily available
at pharmacies, supermarkets
and many 24-hour corner
shops. Abortion is legal and
widely used. Birth control pills
can be bought at pharmacies
with a doctor's prescription.
Refer to a local doctor or
gynaecologist. To avoid
undesired pregnancies,
medicinal treatment is
available within 72 hours
after conception. For details
on the nearest clinic, call
06 30 30 30 456 (mobile).
You will need a Hungarian
speaker to get through.

Dentists

Although Hungary can
provide adequate state dental
care, most people go private if
they can. Prices are reasonable
compared to the West, as
evidenced by the amount of
Austrians who come over the
border for treatment and
beautification. English is
spoken in all the clinics
listed below.

Dental Co-op

*XII.Zugligeti út 58-60 (398 1028/
06 30 228 3199 mobile). Bus 158.*
Open 8am-8pm Mon-Fri.
Credit MC, V.

SOS Dental Clinic

*VI.Király utca 14 (267 9602/269
6010/06 30 383 3333 mobile/
www.sosdent.hu). M1, M2, M3
Deák tér.* **Open** 24hrs daily.
Credit AmEx, MC, V.
Map p249 E5.

Super Dent

*XIII.Dózsa György út 65 (239
0569/www.superdent.hu). M3
Dózsa György út.* **Open** 9am-7pm
Mon, Wed-Fri; 2-7pm Tue. *X-rays*
8am-6.30pm Mon-Fri (by
appointment on 451 0506).
Credit MC, V.

Doctors

For **American Clinics
International** and **IMS**,
see p227.

Medicover
Westend Klinika

*Westend Business Center, V.Váci
út 22-24 (465 3100/hotline 06 80
329 677 mobile). M3 Nyugati pu./
tram 4, 6.* **Open** 7am-7pm Mon-
Fri. **Credit** AmEx, MC, V.
Map p246 E2.
24hr emergency service for
Medicover members.

Professional
Orvosi Kft

*V.Múzeum körút 35, 3rd floor,
no.6 (317 0631/fax 317 2035).
M3 Kálvin tér/tram 47, 49.* **Open**
by appointment 8am-8pm Mon-Fri.
No credit cards. **Map** p249 F6.

Opticians

If you're in urgent need, the
easiest way to get a new pair
of contact lenses, have your
glasses repaired or get your
eyesight tested is to drop in at
any of the **Ofotért** or **Optirex**
chain stores located around
the city, where you can receive
a full-scale ophthalmological
service of good standard.

Eye tests can also be
performed here by qualified
doctors or optometrists. *See
also p227* **Ambulances**.

Ofotért

*V.Károly körút 14 (317 6313/
www.ofotert.hu). M1, M2, M3
Deák tér.* **Open** 10am-6pm Mon-
Fri; 10am-2pm Sat. **Credit** DC,
MC, V. **Map** p249 D5.
Other locations: II.Margit körút
4 (212 2980); V.Bajcsy-Zsilinszky
út 16 (317 2883); V.Szent István
körút 19 (473 0150); VIII.Rákóczi
út 28 (268 1139).

Optirex

*Campona Bevásárlóközpont,
XXII.Nagytétényi út 27-47 (424
3210/www.optirex.hu). Tram 47
to terminus, then bus 3, 14 or
114.* **Open** 10am-8pm Mon-Fri;
10am-6pm Sat; 10am-4pm Sun.
Credit MC, V.
Other locations: V.Szent István
körút 11 (312 6676); XI.Bartók
Béla út 22 (466 5966).

Pharmacies

Pharmacies (*gyógyszertár*
or *patika*) are always marked
with an illuminated green
cross. Opening hours are
generally 8am-6pm or 8am-
8pm Mon-Fri, with some also
open on Saturday mornings.
Some English is spoken at
most pharmacies. The
following locations are open
24 hours daily.

Déli Gyógyszertár

*XII.Alkotás utca 1B (355 4691).
M2 Déli pu./tram 18, 59, 61/bus
21, 102, 139/night bus 960.*
Map p245 A5.

Mária Gyógyszertár

*XIII.Béke tér 11 (320 8006).
M3 Árpád-híd/tram 14/bus
4, 20, 30, 32/night bus 901.*

Óbuda Gyógyszertár

*III.Vörösvári út 86 (368 6430).
HÉV to Árpád-híd/tram 17/bus
18, 37, 60, 137/night bus 923.*

Szent Margit
Gyógyszertár

*II.Frankel Leó út 22 (212 4311).
HÉV to Margit-híd/tram 4, 6,
17/night bus 906, 923, 931,
960.* **Map** p245 C2.

Teréz Gyógyszertár

*VI.Teréz körút 41 (311 4439).
Tram 4, 6/night bus 906.*
Map p246 F3.

STDs, HIV & AIDS

The incidence of AIDS remains
at a relatively low level in
Hungary, although this may
soon be on the increase with
the influx of foreigners,
a general lack of public
awareness and high local
promiscuity levels. With
Hungary's admission to the
EU, the law that HIV-positive
people be centrally registered
has been repealed. If your
result is positive and a second
test is required, you will be
offered the option of going to
Szent László Hospital – in this
case, you have to give up your
anonymity to receive a health
insurance number. For an
anonymous second test, you
can also go to Vienna. The
website www.anonimaids.hu
provides details.

AIDS hotline

338 2419. **Open** 8am-3pm Mon-
Thur; 8am-1pm Fri.

Aids-Hilfe Wien

*Mariahilfer Gürtel 4, Vienna 6
(00 43 1 59937/wien@
aidshilfe.at).* **Open** 4-8pm Mon,
Wed; 9am-1pm Thur; 2-6pm Fri.
Test results one week later, but
must be collected in person.

Anonymous AIDS
Advisory Service

Anonim AIDS
Tanácsadó Szolgálat
*XI.Karolina út 35B (466 9283).
Tram 61.* **Open** 5-8pm Mon, Wed;
9am-noon Tue, Fri. **Map** p248 A6.
Free anonymous AIDS and STD
tests. English spoken.

PLUSS

*1570 Budapest, PO Box 184
(455 8193/www.pluss-hiv.hu).*
Support group for people with
HIV and AIDS.

Skin & Genital Clinic

Bőr és Nemikórtani Klinika
*VIII.Mária utca 41 (266 0465/
266 0468). M3 Ferenc körút.*
Open 8am-11pm Mon-Fri.
Map p249 G7.
Free anonymous AIDS tests.
The above numbers are for the
central switchboard – ask for
AIDS test information.

Directory

Helplines

Alcoholism

Alcoholics Anonymous
251 0051. **Open** 3-6pm daily.

Domestic violence

NaNE – Women United Against Violence
06 80 505 101 mobile.

Poisoning

Heim Pál Kórház
210 0720/333 5079 (children).

Péterfy Sándor Kórház
322 3450/321 5215 (adults).

ID

Hungarian law requires you to carry photographic ID or passport with you at all times – although you'll rarely be checked. If you lose your passport, report it to the police station nearest you, then go to your embassy for them to provide an emergency one. For **Police stations**, *see p232*.

Insurance

All EU citizens are entitled to free emergency treatment. Taking out travel insurance, covering this and lost or stolen valuables, is always wise.

Internet

Most downtown shopping malls (*see p141*) will have a cybercafé, and there are Wi-Fi hotspots in town. Refer to www.hotspotter.hu (*ingyenes* is free; *térítés* is pay-for).

Internet cafés

Electric Café
VI.Dohány utca 37 (413 1803/ www.electriccafe.hu). M2 Blaha Lujza tér/M2 Astoria/bus 7. **Open** 9am-midnight daily. **Rates** Ft200/hr. **No credit cards. Map** p249 F5.

Tutorials, games, CD burning, photocopying, printing and digital picture downloading are also available.

Private Link
VIII.József körút 52 (334 2057/ www.private-link.hu). Tram 4, 6/night bus 906. **Open** 24 hours daily. **Rates** Ft700/hr. **No credit cards. Map** p249 G6.
Large, functional operation with 54 terminals. Photocopying, scanning and CD burning are also available.

Yellow Zebra
V.Sütő utca 2 (266 8777/www. yellowzebrabikes.com). M1, M2, M3 Deák tér. **Open** 8.30am-8pm daily. **Rates** from Ft100/15min. **No credit cards. Map** p249 E5.
CD burning, digital picture downloading, scanning and printing. Bike rental too.

Left luggage

24-hour left-luggage facilities are available at **Nyugati** and **Keleti** stations (*see p219*). Lockers are also provided.

Legal help

For legal assistance, contact your embassy for a list of English-speaking lawyers (*see p224* **Business**).

Libraries

Municipal Ervin Szabó Library

Fővárosi Szabó Ervin Könyvtár *VIII.Szabó Ervin tér 1 (411 5052).* M3 Kálvin tér. **Open** 10am-8pm Mon-Fri; 10am-4pm Sat. **Map** p249 F7.
From late 2007, the British Council Library will be relocated here, offering excellent magazine, periodical, and English-teaching sections, plus a huge video library. Membership for one year is Ft3,600, for six months Ft2,400.

National Foreign-Language Library

V.Molnár utca 11 (318 3688). M3 Ferenciek tere. **Open** 10am-8pm Mon, Tue, Thur, Fri; noon-8pm Wed. Closes 4pm in summer. **Map** p249 E6.

Open to anyone. Membership for one year Ft2,800; day ticket Ft350. Good periodicals section and helpful staff.

National Széchényi Library

I.Buda Palace Wing F (224 3848). Várbusz from M2 Moszkva tér. **Open** 10am-8pm Tue-Sat. **Map** p248 C5.
Hungary's biggest public library – it claims to have every book both written in Hungarian, and about Hungary and Hungarian issues published in any foreign language. Also stocks academic papers, periodicals and offers inter-library services. Useful for research but you can't check books out. Take some form of ID for entry.

Lost property

If you lose something, enquire at the police station in the area where you lost it (*see p232* **Police stations**). Take along a Hungarian speaker, especially if you need a statement for insurance purposes.

Airport

Ferihegy airport lost luggage terminal 1 296 5449, 296 5278; terminal 2 296 5965, 296 5966. Airport minibus lost luggage 296 5967, 296 5968. You can try tracing your luggage at: www.worldtracer.aero.

Public transport

BKV Lost Property Office
Talált Tárgyak Osztálya *VII.Akácfa utca 18 (461 6688).* M2 Blaha Lujza tér. **Open** 8am-5pm Mon, Tue, Thur; 8am-6pm Wed. **Map** p249 G5.

Rail

For items left on trains, go back to the station, find the office *'ügyelet'* and be persistent but pleasant; it can get results. Try calling Déli (375 4376), Keleti (314 5010) and Nyugati (349 0115).

Media

Daily newspapers

Blikk
Top-selling daily with more than 700,000 readers. Usual tabloid fare of crime, page three girls and sports, but less malicious in political and celebrity coverage than its British counterparts. Owned by Ringier.

Expressz
Daily classifieds newspaper. An absolute must if you're looking to rent or rent out a flat.

Magyar Hírlap
Hírlap has been going since 1968. Aligned with dissident intellectuals and now with the liberal Free Democrats (SZDSZ), it has a liberal attitude and a sharp focus on economy and finance. Colourful and easy on the eye as well.

Magyar Nemzet
Last bastion of the non-extreme right among daily newspapers. It is said to have close links with the centre-right party FIDESZ. Also allegedly propped up by politically sympathetic backers.

Nemzeti Sport
Hungary's leading daily sports paper – its international results coverage is second to none in the world. Owned by Ringier.

Népszabadság
The closest thing that Hungary has to a paper of record. *Népszabadság*, once the mouthpiece of the Communists and still closely aligned with the Hungarian Socialist Party, now ranks second behind Blikk in terms of overall readership. Owners include France's Ringier and Germany's Bertelsmann.

Népszava
Old organ of the Communist trades unions, *Népszava* remains close to the left but survives only through the largesse of various sponsors.

Világgazdaság
A truly professional publication covering business, economic and financial news. Owned by Germany's Axel-Springer.

English-language

The international press is available at **A Világsajtó Háza** (*see p141*). Copies of the *Budapest Sun* and other freebies can be found at major hotels and the airport.

Budapest Business Journal
Formula-driven coverage of Hungarian corporate and economic news.

Budapest Sun
Owned by Britain's Associated Newspapers, the *Sun* transplants provincial British tabloid style to Budapest. It features decidedly unambitious news articles, naive and insular coverage of the expat community, poor film listings and lots of 'escort service' ads.

The Hungarian Quarterly
Academic journal in English with essays on Hungarian history, politics and culture, plus book, film and music reviews. Usually available in downtown bookstores.

Hungary Around the Clock
Subscriptions info@kingfish.hu
An English-language digest of each day's news covering politics, economics, business and finance. Compiled from Hungarian press and faxed or emailed to subscribers by 7am each business day.

Listings

Pesti Est, Exit
These two useful pocket-sized weekly freebies are available around Budapest every Thursday. The established *Pesti Est* offers the more comprehensive service, including separate listings for English-language films – although the reviews are in Hungarian. *Exit* is far sharper about nightlife.

Pesti Műsor
What's on weekly (Ft249) available every Thursday with comprehensive listings; also features events outside Budapest. Now published in a renewed format to try to compete with the leading freebies.

Magazines

168 Óra
Weekly, consisting mostly of interviews. Maintains a liberal slant, yet has managed to enrage every government since its founding in the 1980s.

Heti Világgazdaság (HVG)
Hungary's answer to the *Economist*. The most influential weekly for more than two decades, HVG is owned by its employees and is largely politically independent. One of the few publications in Hungary that aspires to non-partisan, hard-hitting journalism. Online version has English section (www.hvg.hu).

Magyar Narancs
Hungary's only alternative newspaper has extensive coverage of minority issues, in-depth news features and extensive listings.

Radio

There are three state-run stations. **Kossuth Rádió** (540 MW) is the national station, offering a gabby yet informative mix of talk and music. **Petőfi Rádió** (98.4 FM) provides the regular inane background of Hungaropop, sport and occasional political discussion. **Bartók Rádió** (105.3 FM) plays the highbrow card, with classical music, poetry and dramas.

Apart from broadcasts propped up by the state, almost every local music station plays commercial pop.

The main alternative station is **Tilos Rádió** (90.3 FM). Tilos began as an anti-regime pirate broadcast under Communism. Today, it's still non-profit with no ads, surviving on state support and listener donations. Another alternative is **Rádió C** (88.8 FM), the radio station for Roma, with music and talk shows of interest to the Roma community. There is also one all-news station, **Infó Rádió** (95.8 FM).

BBC World Service

BBC frequencies change every six months. For the most up-to-date frequencies see www.bbc.co.uk/worldservice/schedules.

Rádió Café

On 98.6 FM, Rádió Café features English-language chat show on Tuesdays at 8pm.

Television

Cable TV

Each district in Budapest has a separate arrangement for cable TV. The Netherlands' UPC dominates the Hungarian market. Cable packages tend to include some English-language channels, such as CNN, BBC World, SkyNews, CNBC, Eurosport and Cartoon Network/TCM.

Duna TV

Satellite channel aimed at serving the substantial ethnic Hungarian minorities in neighbouring countries. Heavy on cultural and documentary programming.

MTV1

The flagship of state-owned broadcasting. That sucking sound is public money going down the toilet in order to spread propaganda for whatever party is in government. The quality of its news division has been substantially improved, but don't expect it to be impartial.

MTV2

Second state-owned channel. Offers more documentary, cultural and public service programming, but often simply broadcasts what MTV1 is airing.

RTL Klub

Majority-owned by Luxembourg/Germany-based CLT-UFA. Same programming mix as TV2 but with higher local production quality. The news broadcasts rely more on the tabloid approach.

TV2

Majority-owned by Scandinavian Broadcast System with a local group holding a minority interest. Airs a predictable mix of news, mostly dismal foreign films and locally produced trash, including the latest wave of game shows and voyeur TV.

Money

The Hungarian unit of currency is the forint, usually abbreviated as HUF or Ft – the convention we've used in this guide. Forint coins come in denominations of Ft1, Ft2, Ft5, Ft10, Ft20, Ft50 and Ft100. Notes come in denominations of Ft200, Ft500, Ft1,000, Ft2,000, Ft5,000, Ft10,000 and Ft20,000. The euro will not be introduced until at least 2010.

ATMs

There are cash machines all over town. Apart from those on the Cirrus and Plus systems, allowing you to draw on a foreign bank account or credit card, there are also exchange machines, swapping foreign banknotes for forints. American Express has a 24-hour machine and both **Nyugati** and **Keleti** stations have round-the-clock exchange facilities (*see p219*).

Banks & foreign exchange

Most banks open at 8am and close at 3pm, 4pm or 5pm Monday to Friday; some are open on Saturday morning. Apart from cash and travellers' cheques, banks can advance money on a credit card. ATM and exchange machines are available around the clock at most banks.

Banks may give better rates than change kiosks, but do shop around – rates can vary. Travellers' cheques can be changed at banks and change kiosks, though often at a worse rate than the cash equivalent.

Bureaux de change

IBUSZ Bank

V.Ferenciek tere 10 (485 2700/ www.ibusz.hu). M3 Ferenciek tere/ tram 2/bus 7. **Open** 9am-6pm Mon-Fri; 9am-1pm Sat. **Map** p249 E6.

Interchange

V.Kigyó utca 2 (266 6814). M3 Ferenciek tere/bus 7. **Open** 24hrs daily. **Credit** AmEx, MC, V. **Map** p249 E6.
Other locations: Keleti station (open 24hrs daily; 342 7913); Nyugati station (open 6.30am-8.40pm daily; 332 0597).

M&M Exclusiv Tours

V.Váci utca 12 (267 0591). M1 Vörösmarty tér/M2, M3 Deák tér. **Open** 9am-6pm Mon-Sat; 10am-6pm Sun. **No credit cards. Map** p249 E5.
Other locations: V.Nyugati tér 6 (311 1610).

Credit cards

Credit cards are accepted in thousands of outlets. The most widely accepted cards are American Express (AmEx), Diners Club, Euro/Mastercard and Visa.

Lost/stolen credit cards

American Express 484 2639
Diners Club 268 8888
Mastercard 06 80 201 2517
Visa Global 06 80 17682

Opening hours

Opening hours vary according to the type of shop. Most are open from 10am to 6pm Monday to Friday, and 10am to 1pm on Saturday. Shopping malls usually open daily at 10am and close at 9pm. Supermarkets, greengrocers and bakeries usually open at 7am and close between 6pm and 8pm Monday to Friday, and 1pm and 3pm on Saturdays. '*Rögtön jövök*' means that the owner will be back in five minutes – maybe. Many shops stay open later on Saturdays and on Thursday evenings. Non-stops are small 24-hour corner shops where you can buy basics and booze; almost every district will have one. Most restaurants close by 11pm or midnight, bar closing times vary. For **Public holidays**, *see p235*.

Directory

Police stations

Unless you commit a crime, you shouldn't have much contact with the police, but they can stop you and ask for ID. If you're robbed or lose something, report it to the police station nearest the incident. Take a Hungarian speaker. It's only worth the bother if the item was valuable, or your insurance company needs the forms.

You can report a crime on the Central Emergency Number (112) or to the police (107). In case you can't get through to an English-speaking dispatcher, you can try the English-language hotline (438 8080).

Police headquarters

XIII.Teve utca 4-6 (443 5500).
M3 Árpád-híd/tram 1/bus 26, 32, 106, 120, 133.

Police stations

V.Szalay utca 11-13 (373 1000).
M2 Kossuth tér.
VII.Dózsa György út 18-24 (461 8100). Bus 20, 30/trolleybus 74.
VIII.Víg utca 36 (477 3700). M2 Blaha Lujza tér/tram 4, 6/bus 99.

Postal services

The Hungarian postal service is reasonably efficient. Letters from the UK take about four working days to arrive. Post boxes are square and red with post horn and envelope symbols. Some people take their letters to the post office, where staff will affix the stamp and post it for them – post offices even offer a range of cards to choose from. Expect to queue, especially at Christmas.

Most post offices are open from 8am to 7pm on weekdays. There are no late-night branches in central Budapest, but the one at Keleti station (VIII.Baross tér 11C) is open 7am to 9pm Monday to Friday. There is a 24-hour post office at the Fogarasi út branch of Tesco (XIV.Pillangó utca 15).

Letters weighing up to 30g cost Ft62 to send within Hungary. A letter weighing up to 20g to European countries costs Ft180 and to anywhere else in the world Ft200; up to 100g costs Ft330 and Ft420 respectively. Priority postage (*elsőbbségi*) brings an extra fee depending on the weight of the letter. Postcards (*képeslap*) cost Ft140 to European countries and Ft150 to overseas.

To send something registered (*ajánlott*) costs an extra Ft600.

Poste restante letters go to the office at Nyugati station. For courier services and express mail, *see p223* **Business**.

Sending packages

You can send a package weighing up to 2kg as a normal letter, which costs slightly less than if you send it as a package. Otherwise, a package weighing up to 5kg costs Ft8,250 overland to European countries, Ft10,000 by air; to overseas, the cost will be Ft11,550-Ft13,200 and Ft18,000-Ft22,000 respectively. Tie your package with string and fill out a blue customs form (*vámáru nyilatkozat*) from the post office. Sending anything worth over Ft10,000 is so complicated it's not worth the bother. Special boxes are sold at the post office. Post offices provide a booklet in English detailing charges; otherwise try www.posta.hu.

Religion

According to the most recent Hungarian census carried out in 2001, of the 1.7 million people living in Budapest 45.5 per cent are Roman Catholic, 12.6 per cent are Protestant, 2.6 per cent are Lutheran, 1.6 per cent are Greek Catholic and 0.5 per cent are Jewish.

The rest belong to minor churches or none. Many churches around town have services in English.

Anglican services

St Columbia Church of Scotland, Presbyterian Chaplaincy

VI.Vörösmarty utca 51. M1 Vörösmarty utca. **Map** p246 G3.
Presbyterian services on Sundays at 11am.

Catholic services

International Baptist Church

Móricz Zsigmond Gimnázium, II.Törökvész út 48-54. Bus 11.
Services on Sundays from 10.30am.

International Church of Budapest

III.Kis Korona utca 7 (06 27 304 460 mobile/06 70 218 2607 mobile/www.church.hu).
M3 Árpád-híd/HÉV to Árpád-híd/bus 6, 86.
Multi-denominational worship in English and children's ministry on Sundays at 10.30am.

Jesuit Church of the Sacred

Jézus Szíve templom
VIII.Mária utca 25 (318 3479).
M3 Ferenc körút/M3 Kálvin tér/tram 4, 6. **Map** p249 G7.
Catholic mass in English on Sundays at 5pm.

Páduai Szent Antal Plébánia

II.Pasaréti út 137 (200 2623).
Bus 5, 29.
Catholic mass in English on Sundays at 4pm.

Jewish services

Central Synagogue

VII.Dohány utca 2. M2 Astoria/ M1, M2, M3 Deák tér/tram 47, 49/bus 7. **Map** p249 F5.
Services take place at 9am Sat; 6pm Mon-Fri, Sun. *See also p96* **Walking Jewish Budapest**.

Jewish Community Centre

VII.Síp utca 12 (413 5526).
M2 Astoria/tram 47, 49/bus 7. **Open** 10am-4.30pm Mon-Thur; 10am-1.30pm Fri, Sun.
Map p249 F5.
Summer services in Hebrew.

Safety & security

Budapest is a relatively safe city. Look out for pickpockets and purse-snatchers around the tourist spots of Váci utca, the Castle District, Heroes' Square and at stations. Be careful if walking alone at night around the ill-lit outlying areas of town or District VIII around Rákóczi tér, and consider phoning a taxi (*see p221*) if necessary.

You are obliged by law to carry some kind of ID on you at all times and the police make spot checks, especially in places where expatriates tend to congregate. In most other places, it is pretty unlikely that you'll be checked.

Smoking

Hungarians are heavy smokers. Smoking is banned on all public transport, on trains, in theatres and cinemas, but allowed in almost all restaurants, most of which have non-smoking areas. Bars and cafés are often thick with cigarette smoke.

Study

Language classes

Centre for Advanced Language Learning
Idegennyelvi Továbbképző Központ
*VIII.Rigó utca 16 (459 9648/
www.itk.hu).* Tram 4, 6.
Map p250 H6.
This independent non-profit institution is organised under the Eötvös Lóránd University (*see right*). One of its tasks is to assess knowledge of Hungarian language and culture for examinations.

European Language School
Európai Nyelvek Stúdiója
*V.Múzeum körút 39 (317 1302).
M3 Kálvin tér/tram 47, 49.*
Map p249 F6.
Individual Hungarian tuition at all levels, structured to suit the student; Ft3,400 per 45-minute lesson. No group tuition.

InterClub Hungarian Language School
*XI.Bertalan Lajos utca 17 (365
2535/www.interclub.hu).* Tram
47, 49/bus 86. **Open** *Office* 9am-
5pm Mon-Thur; 9am-4pm Fri.
Map p249 E8.
Language school specialised in Hungarian courses for foreigners.

Katedra Language School
*VII.Madách tér 4 (327 8383/
www.katedra.hu).* M1, M2, M3
Deák tér. **Open** *Office* 8am-8pm
Mon-Fri; 9am-noon Sat. **Credit**
DC, MC, V. **Map** p249 E5.
Intensive and standard courses at Ft29,990 for 40 lessons.

Universities

Budapest Technical & Economic Sciences University
Budapesti Műszaki és Gazdasági Egyetem (BME)
*XI.Műegyetem rakpart 3 (463
1111).* Tram 4, 6, 47, 49/
bus 86. **Map** p249 E8.
Established in 1782, the BME has more than 9,000 students studying at seven faculties that include Architecture and Chemical, Electrical and Civil Engineering. The education is highly practical, and BME is among the few Hungarian institutions whose diplomas are accepted worldwide.

Budapest University of Economic Sciences & Administration
Budapesti Közgazdaságtudományi és Államigazgatási Egyetem (BKE)
*IX.Fővám tér 8 (482 5000).
Tram 2, 47, 49.* **Map** p249 F7.
An independent institution since 1948, the BKE issues diplomas in International Economics and Business, and Political Studies.

Central European University (CEU)
*V.Nádor utca 9 (327 3000/fax
327 3001/www.ceu.hu).* M3
Arany János utca. **Map** p246 D4.
Founded by George Soros, the CEU offers postgraduate courses. Departments include History, Legal Studies, Gender Studies, and Political and Environmental Sciences.

Eötvös Lóránd University
Eötvös Lóránd Tudományegyetem (ELTE)
*V.Egyetem tér 1-3 (411 6500/411
6700).* M2 Astoria/tram 47, 49.
Map p249 E6.
The largest and oldest Hungarian university was founded in 1635, moved to Buda in 1777, then to Pest in 1784. Today, there are 12,000 students at the Faculties of Humanities, Sciences, Law and the Institute of Sociology.

Semmelweis University of Medicine
Semmelweis Orvostudományi Egyetem (SOTE)
*VIII.Üllői út 26 (459 1500/
www.sote.hu).* M3 Ferenc körút/
tram 4, 6. **Map** p250 H7.
The Semmelweis has been in its current form since 1955, when the faculties of Pharmacy and Dentistry were incorporated. Ignác Semmelweis, who discovered the cause of puerperal fever, taught here in the 1800s.

Telephones

Phoning home is easy, but there are no cheap hours for making international calls.

Dialling & codes

For an international call dial 00, wait for the second purring dial tone, then dial the country code and number: Australia 61, Canada 1, Eire 353, New Zealand 64, South Africa 27, UK 44, USA 1.

To call other places around Hungary from Budapest, or to call Budapest from the rest of the country, you have to dial 06 first, wait for the second tone, and then follow with code and number. You also have to dial 06 before calling mobile phones, which are commonplace in Hungary.

To call Hungary from abroad, dial 36 and then 1 for Budapest. For a provincial Hungarian town or a Hungarian mobile from abroad, dial 36 and then the number without the initial 06.

Public phones

Most public phones take cards, costing Ft800 for 50 units or Ft1,800 for 120, on sale at post offices and newsagents. Coin phones in bars take Ft10, Ft20, Ft50 and Ft100 coins; a local call should cost Ft60.

To get a cheap international rate you might consider using a Neo Phone or TeleCard, available at post offices, petrol stations and newsstands.

Mobile phones & pagers

If you need a phone but your flat doesn't have one – which is not an uncommon occurrence – mobile phones or pagers are your best bet. GSM companies currently operating in Hungary include:

Pannon GSM

VII.Károly körút 3A (1220/ www.pannongsm.hu). M2 Astoria/ tram 47, 49. **Open** 9am-8pm Mon-Fri; 9am-2pm Sat. **Credit** DC, MC, V. **Map** p249 F6.

T-Mobile Magyarország

V.Petőfi Sándor 12 (1430/www. t-mobile.hu). M3 Ferenciek tere. **Open** 9am-7pm Mon-Fri. **Credit** AmEx, MC, V. **Map** p249 E6.

Vodafone

Westend City Center, VI.Váci út 1-3 (1270/288 1270/www. vodafone.hu). M3 Nyugati pu./tram 4, 6. **Open** 10am-9pm Mon-Sat; 10am-6pm Sun. **Credit** MC, V. **Map** p246 E2.

Faxes

Some post offices have a fax service, but this involves a lot of form-filling. Most major hotels also have fax services.

Time

Hungary is on Central European Time, which means that it's one hour ahead of GMT, six ahead of US Eastern Standard Time and nine ahead of US Pacific Standard Time.

Tipping & VAT

There are no fixed rules about tipping in Hungary but it's customary to leave about ten to 15 per cent for waiters in cafés and restaurants. Round up the amount to the nearest couple of hundred forints.

Some restaurants add a ten per cent service charge, in which case don't feel obliged to give any tip – just round up the bill. If you'd like to leave something, simply tell the waiter as you pay either how much your rounded-up amount comes to or how much change you'd like back. Saying *köszönöm* (thank you) as you hand over a note means you are expecting them to keep all the change. The same rule applies to taxi drivers. It's also customary to tip hairdressers, beauticians, car mechanics, cloakroom attendants, repairmen, changing room attendants at baths and pools, and doctors and dentists.

Value Added Tax (*ÁFA*) is 20 per cent and included in the price of goods and services. *See p225* **Customs**.

Toilets

There are public toilets at various locations around town, for which you'll have to pay a small fee (usually Ft50-Ft100) to an attendant. Look for WC or Toilette signs: *Hölgyek* (Ladies) and *Urak* (Gents). The quality of toilets in the more down-market bars leaves a lot to be desired. It's often easier to pop into a smarter bar or a fast-food restaurant, although they might also charge a fee if you are not a customer.

Tourist information

The best place for tourist information is **Tourinform**, with terminals around town. **IBUSZ** is the most useful for accommodation. **Express** is a student travel agency.

Express

V.Semmelweis utca 1-3 (266 6188). M2 Astoria/bus 7. **Open** 8.30am-4.30pm Mon-Fri. **No credit cards. Map** p249 F6. Friendly staff, flights, student cards and youth hostel cards.

IBUSZ

V.Ferenciek tere 10 (485 2767/ 485 2768). M3 Ferenciek tere. **Open** 9am-6pm Mon-Fri; 9am-1am Sat. **Credit** AmEx, DC, MC, V. **Map** p249 E6. Hungary's oldest tourist agency can book rooms, organise tours and provide information, plus the usual travel agency services. **Other locations**: Westend City Center, VI.Váci út 1-3 (450 1477).

Tourinform

V.Sütő utca 2 (24hr phone 438 8080/06 80 630 800 mobile/ www.budapestinfo.hu). M1, M2, M3 Deák tér. **Open** 8am-8pm daily. **Map** p249 E5. Staff are helpful and multilingual, and can provide information on travel, sightseeing and entertainment options. **Other locations**: I.Szentháromság tér (488 0475); VI.Liszt Ferenc tér 11 (322 4098); Ferihegy airport (438 8080).

Visas & immigration

Nationals of EU member countries can enter Hungary with their valid national passport or national ID card. It is no longer necessary for the passport to be valid until six months after the date of entry into Hungary. Those wishing to stay longer than three months should register with the Hungarian Immigration and Nationality Office for a European Economic Area Residents' Permit for Citizens. More details can be found at www.bm-bah.hu.

Citizens of the United States, Canada, Australia, New Zealand and most other European countries (apart from Albania, Serbia & Montenegro, Turkey and the

Ukraine) can stay in Hungary for up to 90 days without a visa; only a passport is required. Citizens of South Africa require a visa. In theory, non-EU citizens who wish to stay longer than 90 days need a residence visa. In practice, they can skip into a neighbouring country and get their passport stamped for another three months.

Residence visas are obtained from the Hungarian consulate in your country. The issuing process may take up to two months. Residence visas are valid for one year and must be renewed prior to their expiration dates. For a second year you must apply for a separate residence permit, which is valid for another year. You may then be eligible to obtain a residence permit for a longer period.

For a residence visa you need a work permit, a legal permanent residence, an AIDS test, a chest X-ray, numerous value stamps that you buy at post offices, several forms and passport photos, your passport and official translations of every foreign language document with stamps on them.

If you're not working in Hungary, but would like to live here, then you should apply for the residence visa based on your financial status, which means that you'll need to prove, with the assistance of a recent bank account statement, that you have the wherewithal to reside in Hungary without having recourse to work.

To obtain Hungarian citizenship, for foreigners who have no Hungarian spouse or parents, the process can take up to eight years. You must have already had a residence visa for one year and a residence permit for two years. Then you can apply for an immigration certificate, a process which takes about a year. After four years of

holding an immigration certificate, you can then apply for a Hungarian passport.

If you have Hungarian parents, you can apply for a local passport. If you're married to a Hungarian, you can apply for an immigration certificate after you've lived in Hungary with a residence permit or visa for three years, and have been married to the Hungarian person for three years. *See also p236* **Working in Budapest**.

Water

The water in Hungary is clean and safe to drink. In some old houses there are still lead pipes, so run the tap for a few minutes before drinking.

Weights & measures

Hungary has its own system for measuring out solids and liquids. A *deka* is ten grams; a *deci* is ten centilitres. In a bar, for example, you might be asked whether you want *két deci* or *három deci* (0.2 or 0.3 litres) of whatever drink you've just ordered. Wine in bars (but not in restaurants) is priced by the *deci*. At a fruit stall, if you want 300 grams of tomatoes, you'd ask for 30 dekas – *harminc (30) deka paradicsomot*.

When to go

Although Budapest can be icy cold in winter and infernally hot in summer, the climate is Continental and generally agreeable. *See p225* **Average monthly climate**.

Spring

Average temperature 2°C-10°C in March; 11°C-22°C in May. May is probably the most pleasant month in the city, before the influx of tourists

begins. Winter attire gets discarded, though rain showers can sometimes dampen spirits.

Summer

Average temperature 16°C-32°C. Most Hungarians leave Budapest for the Balaton or their weekend house. It can get very hot, especially during July. If there's a breeze off the Danube, it's pleasant – if not, you can expect a pall of pollution.

Autumn

Average temperature 7°C-20°C. The weather is lovely in September, but it starts to get cold in October when everything moves inside and the heating gets turned on.

Winter

Average temperature -4°C to 4°C. Winters are cold and quite long, but not unbearably so: the air is very dry and central heating good. Snow falls a few times, often giving Budapest a different light. Smog can descend if there's no breeze to blow away the fumes from the coal used for heating.

Public holidays

New Year's Day; 15 March, national holiday; Easter Sunday; Easter Monday; 1 May, Labour Day; Whit Monday; 20 August, St Stephen's Day; 23 October, Remembrance Day; 25, 26 December, Christmas.

There's usually something open on most holidays apart from the night of 24 December, when even the non-stop shops stop. New Year's Eve is very lively, as is St Stephen's Day on 20 August, with fireworks launched from Gellért Hill. Note that public disturbances on national holidays may drag on into 2008 (*see p24*).

Directory

Women

Although men and women are equal by law in Hungary, there are countless problems – from wage differentials to sexual harassment at work, unfair division of labour and domestic violence. Women's organisations have been set up to help solve these problems, but 'feminist' is still an dirty word in Hungary. The values imposed upon the traditional division of labour by the Communist regime meant that women not only had to stick to their traditional roles, they were also suddenly expected to work eight hours a day outside the home. Thus were the problems of 'emancipation' solved in Hungary in the post-war era.

As fathers were not expected (and until 1982 were not allowed) to stay at home with their children as primary carers, women's careers suffered. Women also did all the housework, teaching children traditional roles.

With the modern-day women's movement, this is slowly starting to change. Abortion is now legal and accessible, women's wages are slowly rising, sexual harassment and wife beating are more often reported and punished by law, and more men do the housework. But the old values still surface, as do sexist jibes and odd looks if a woman enters a bar alone.

Association of Hungarian Women

Magyar Nők Szövetsége
VI.Andrássy út 124 (331 9734).
M1 Hősök tere. **Open** 11am-4pm
Mon-Fri. **Map** p247 H2.
Now independent, this was the original Communist-era association, so don't expect it to be particularly radical. It has 45 member organisations and 10,000 members striving for equal opportunity and participation. The president is Judit Thorma.

FATIME Feminist Working Group

FATIME Feminista
Munkacsoport
Budapest 1519, PO Box 336.
Formed in 2004, FATIME regularly publishes the online feminist magazine *FemiDok* (www.femidok.hu), with English-language content.

NaNE – Women United Against Violence

NaNE – Nők a Nőkért
Együtt az Erőszak Ellen
Budapest 1447, PO Box 502
(helpline 06 80 505 101 mobile/
www.nane.hu). **Open** *Helpline*
6-10pm daily.
Rape and domestic violence are low-profile issues in Hungary. There's no law against marital rape and little sympathy for rape victims. NaNE gives information and support to battered and raped women and children, campaigns for changes in law, and challenges social attitudes to violence.

International women's associations

North American Women's Association of Budapest (NAWA)

II.Kuruclesi út 13B
(www.awa.org.hu). Bus 29.
Membership required. Contact Cheryl Burchill (06 20 920 8242 mobile, cherylburchill@hotmail.com), or chair Andrée Schouten (ajschouten@hotmail.com).

Professional Women's Association of Budapest (PWA)

The PWA organises meetings from 7pm on the second Monday of every month. These events are open to any professional women working in Budapest. For further information, contact 06 30 358 3450 (mobile).

Working in Budapest

UK, Irish and certain EU nationals now have the right to live and work in Hungary without a permit. For more information, check the Hungarian embassy website of your country or refer to http://ec.europa.eu/eures/home.jsp?lang=en.

Non-EU citizens coming to Hungary to work must already have a work permit and a residence visa, except for company directors who need the relevant Hungarian corporate documents. You must start the process in your home country, because you will need a residence visa from the Hungarian embassy there.

The work permit is your employer's responsibility. You need to provide translated certificates and diplomas, and a translated medical certificate. Only documents translated by the Országos Fordító Iroda (www.offi.hu) are accepted. The medical certificate involves having a chest X-ray and a blood test. The employee submits the work permit to the Hungarian embassy in his or her home country. *See also p234* **Visas & immigration**.

Central Hungarian Regional Labour Centre

Közép-magyarországi
Regionális Munkaügyi Központ
VIII.Kisfaludy utca 11 (303 0722).
Tram 4, 6. **Open** 8.30am-4pm
Mon-Wed; 8.30am-1pm Thur, Fri.
Map p250 G7.

Országos Fordító Iroda

VI.Bajza utca 52 (428 9600).
M1 Bajza utca. **Open** 8.30am-4pm
Mon-Thur; 8.30am-12.30pm Fri.
Map p247 G2.

Settlers Hungary

XII.Maros utca (212 5017/
fax 212 5146/www.settlers.hu).
M2 Déli pu./tram 59, 61. **Open**
8.30am-5pm Mon-Thur; 8.30am-4pm Fri.
Can help with work permits.

State Public Health & Medical Administration

Állami Népegészségügyi és
Tiszti Orvosi Szolgálat (ÁNTSZ)
XIII.Váci utca 174 (465 3800).
M3 Gyöngyösi utca. **Open**
8am-3pm Mon-Fri; 8am-noon Fri.

Vocabulary

Nowhere else in Europe will the traveller be confronted with as great a linguistic barrier as in Hungary. Basic words bear no resemblance to equivalents in any major European language.

The good news is that pronunciation of common words is easy – and the long ones, such as *viszontlátásra*, ('goodbye') can be shortened (*viszlát*). *Köszönöm*, thank you, is used as *köszi*. *Szervusz* is an all-purpose greeting, more formal than *szia*, meaning both hello and goodbye.

For menu terms, *see p114*.

Pronunciation

The stress is always on the first syllable. Accents denote a longer vowel. Double consonants are pronounced longer (*kettő, szebb*). Add 't' to nouns if they are the object of the sentence: 'I would like a beer' is *egy sört kérek* (*sör + t*).

a – like 'o' in hot
á – like 'a' in father
é – like 'a' in day
í – like 'ee' in feet
ö – like 'ur' in pleasure
ü – like 'u' in French *tu*
ő, ű – similar to ö and ü but longer
sz – like 's' in sat
cs – like 'ch' in such
zs – like 's' in casual
gy – like 'd' in due
ly – like 'y' in yellow
ny – like 'n' in new
ty – like 't' in tube
c – like 'ts' in roots
s – like 'sh' in wash

Useful expressions

Yes *Igen*
No *Nem*
Maybe *Talán*
(I wish you) good day *Jó napot (kívánok)* (formal)
Hello *Szervusz; szia* (fam)
Goodbye *Viszontlátásra*
How are you? *Hogy van?* (formal); *hogy vagy?* (familiar)
I'm fine *Jól vagyok*
Please *Kérem*

Thank you *Köszönöm*
Excuse me *Bocsánat*
I would like *Kérek...* (an object)
I would like (to do something) *Szeretnék...* (add infinitive)
Where is...? *Hol van...?*
Where is the toilet? *Hol van a wc?* (wc vay tzay)
Where is a good/not too expensive restaurant? *Hol van egy jó/nem túl drága étterem?*
When? *Mikor?* **Who?** *Ki?*
Why? *Miért?* **How?** *Hogyan?*
Is there...? *Van...?*
There is none *Nincs*
How much is it? *Mennyibe kerül?*
We're paying separately *Külön-külön fizetünk*
Open *Nyitva*; **closed** *zárva*
Entrance *Bejárat*; **exit** *kijárat*
Push *Tolni*; **pull** *húzni*
Men's *Férfi*; **women's** *női*
Good *Jó*; **bad** *rossz*
I like it *Ez tetszik*
I don't like it *Ez nem tetszik*
I don't speak Hungarian *Nem beszélek magyarul*
Do you speak English? *Beszél angolul?*
What is your name? *Mi a neve?*
My name is... *A nevem...*
I am (English/American) *(angol/amerikai) vagyok*
I feel ill *Rosszul vagyok*
Doctor *Orvos*
Pharmacy *Patika/gyógyszertár*
Hospital *Kórház*
Ambulance *Mentőautó*
Police *Rendőrség*

Getting around

Railway station *Pályaudvar*
Airport *Repülőtér*
Arrival *Érkezés*
Departure *Indulás*
Inland *Belföldi*
International *Külföldi*
Ticket office *Pénztár*
I would like two tickets *Két jegyet kérek*
When is the train to Vienna? *Mikor indul a bécsi vonat?*
Here *Itt*
There *Ott*
Towards *Felé*
From here *Innen*
From there *Onnan*
To the right *Jobbra*
To the left *Balra*
Straight ahead *Egyenesen*
Near *Közel*/**far** *Messze*

Accommodation

Hotel *Szálloda*
A single room *Egyágyas szoba*
A double room *Kétágyas szoba*
Per night *Egy éjszakára*
Shower *Zuhany*
Bath *Fürdőkád*
Breakfast *Reggeli*
Do you have anything cheaper? *Van valami olcsóbb?*
Air-conditioning *Légkondicionálás*

Time

Now *Most*
Later *Később*
Today *Ma*
Tomorrow *Holnap*
Morning *Reggel*
Late morning *Délelőtt*
Early afternoon *Délután*
Evening *Este*
Night *Éjszaka*
(At) one o'clock *Egy óra (kor)*

Numbers

Zero *Nulla*
One *Egy*
Two *Kettő* (note *két*, used with an object: *két kávét* **two coffees**)
Three *Három*
Four *Négy*
Five *Öt*
Six *Hat*
Seven *Hét*
Eight *Nyolc*
Nine *Kilenc*
Ten *Tíz*
Eleven *Tizenegy*
Twenty *Húsz*
Thirty *Harminc*
Forty *Negyven*
Fifty *Ötven*
Sixty *Hatvan*
Eighty *Nyolcvan*
Ninety *Kilencven*
One hundred *Száz*
One thousand *Ezer*

Days of the week

Monday *Hétfő*
Tuesday *Kedd*
Wednesday *Szerda*
Thursday *Csütörtök*
Friday *Péntek*
Saturday *Szombat*
Sunday *Vasárnap*

Directory

Further Reference

Books

Biography, memoir & travel

Fermor, Patrick Leigh *Between the Woods and the Water/A Time of Gifts* In the 1930s Fermor hiked from Holland to Istanbul, stopping off in Hungary along the way. These evocative memoirs are the result.
Márai, Sándor *Memoir of Hungary 1944-48* Insightful memoir by exiled Magyar author.
Pressburger, Giorgio & Nicola *Homage to the Eighth District* Authentic and touching recollections of Jewish society before and during World War II.

Children

Dent, Bob *Budapest for Children* Slim volume full of suggestions for keeping the little ones entertained.
Gárdonyi, Géza *Eclipse of the Crescent Moon* Boys' Own adventure about the 1552 Turkish siege of Eger.
Molnar, Ferenc *The Paul Street Boys* Juvenile classic of a boys' gang in a District VIII building site.

Food & drink

Gundel, Károly *Gundel's Hungarian Cookbook* The best Hungarian cookbook, by the man who modernised Magyar cuisine.
Lang, George *The Cuisine of Hungary* Detailed study of local gastronomic development.
Liddell, Alex *The Wines of Hungary* A useful introduction to the art of Hungarian viticulture.

History, architecture, art & culture

A Golden Age: Art & Society in Hungary 1896-1914 Colourful compendium, with works by the Hungarian greats. Drab essays.
Búza, Péter *Bridges of the Danube* Everything you could ever want to know about Budapest's famous bridges, with occasional absurd asides.

Crankshaw, Edward *The Fall of the House of Habsburg* Solid and solidly anti-Hungarian account of the dynasty's demise.
Garton Ash, Timothy *We the People* Instant history by this on-the-spot Oxford academic.
Gerő, András *Modern Hungarian Society in the Making* Collection of essays on the last 150 years of Hungarian political, social and cultural history. Excellent piece on Széchenyi.
Hanak, Peter & Schorske, Carl E *The Garden and the Workshop: Essays on the cultural history of Vienna and Budapest* Comparative cultural history of the Golden Age in the two capitals of the Austro-Hungarian Empire.
Heathcote, Edwin *Budapest: A Guide to 20th Century Architecture* Portable, clear and concise guide.
Kontler, László *Millennium in Central Europe: A History of Hungary* The most thorough account in English of the Magyars.
Lendvai, Paul *The Hungarians: A Thousand Years of Victory in Defeat* Not as comprehensive as Kontler, but a great read.
Litván, György *The Hungarian Revolution of 1956: Reform, Revolt and Repression 1953-1963* Blow-by-blow accounts of the 1956 Uprising.
Lukács, John *Budapest 1900* Extremely readable and erudite literary and historical snapshot of Budapest at its height. The best book about the city's history and culture currently in print.
Taylor, AJP *The Habsburg Monarchy 1809-1918* Terse history of the Habsburg twilight.

Language

Payne, Jerry *Colloquial Hungarian* More entertaining than most language books, drawing on interesting dialogues.

Literature

Ady, Endre *Neighbours of the Night: Selected Short Stories* Prose pieces somewhat stiffly rendered in English, but at least they translate – unlike his gloomy but stirring poetry.

Bánffy, Miklós *They Were Counted/They Were Found Wanting/They Were Divided* Acclaimed Transylvanian trilogy recalls the lost world of Hungarian aristocracy as it falls apart.
Bierman, John *The Secret Life of Laszlo Almasy* Subtitled *The Real English Patient*, this is the true story of the Hungarian desert adventurer whose controversial life was used by Michael Ondaatje as the basis for his bestselling novel and screenplay.
Eszterházy, Péter *A Little Hungarian Pornography/Helping Verbs of the Heart/The Glance of Countess Hahn-Hahn/She Loves Me/Celestial Harmonies* One of Hungary's most popular contemporary writers, Eszterházy's postmodern style represents a radical break with Hungarian literary tradition.
Fischer, Tibor *Under the Frog* Seriously funny and impeccably researched Booker-nominated romp through Hungarian basketball, Stalinism and the 1956 revolution.
Kertész, Imre *Fateless/Kaddish for a Child Not Born* Accounts of the Holocaust and its effects by the 2002 Nobel Laureate for Literature.
Konrád, George *Stonedial* Covering the period of the Soviet occupation into the 1990s.
A Feast in the Garden Highly autobiographical novel leading from village to Holocaust to communist tyranny.
Kosztolányi, Dezső *Skylark/Anna Édes/Darker Muses, The Poet Nero* Kosztolányi, who wrote these novels in the 1920s, was probably the best Magyar prose writer of the last century. Responsible for the Hungarian translation of *Winnie-the-Pooh*.
Krasznahorkai, László *The Melancholy of Resistance* This tale of events in a tiny village is the basis for the film *Werckmeister Harmonies*.
Örkény, István *One Minute Stories* Vignettes of contemporary Budapest: absurd, ironic, hilarious.
Rubenstein, Julian *Ballad of the Whisky Robber* Punchy crime fiction based on the true story of the prolific, whisky-sodden bank robber and folk hero Attila Ambrus, set in 1990s Budapest.

Index

Note: Page numbers in **bold** indicate section(s) giving key information on a topic; *italics* indicate photographs.

Accommodation

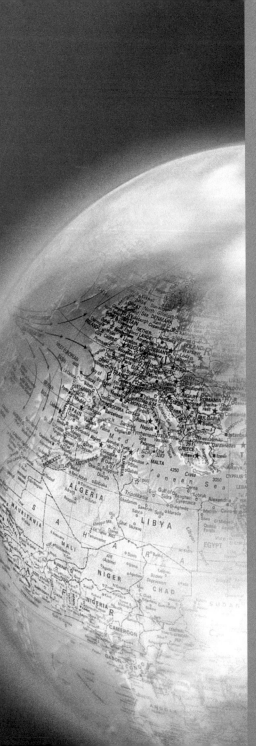

Place of interest and/or entertainment	■
Railway & bus stations	■
Parks	■
Hospitals/universities	■
Area name	VÁR
District number	XII
Metro station	Ⓜ

Maps

**OUR CLIMATE NEEDS
A HELPING HAND TODAY**

Be a smart traveller. Help to offset your carbon emissions
from your trip by pledging Carbon Trees with Trees for Cities.

All the Carbon Trees that you donate through Trees for Cities
are genuinely planted as additional trees in our projects.

Trees for Cities is an independent charity working with local
communities on tree planting projects.

www.treesforcities.org   Tel 020 7587 1320

Trees for Cities
Charity registration number 1092154

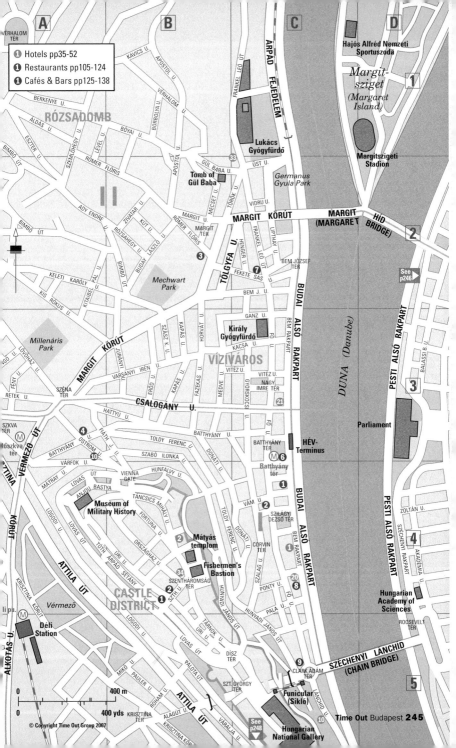

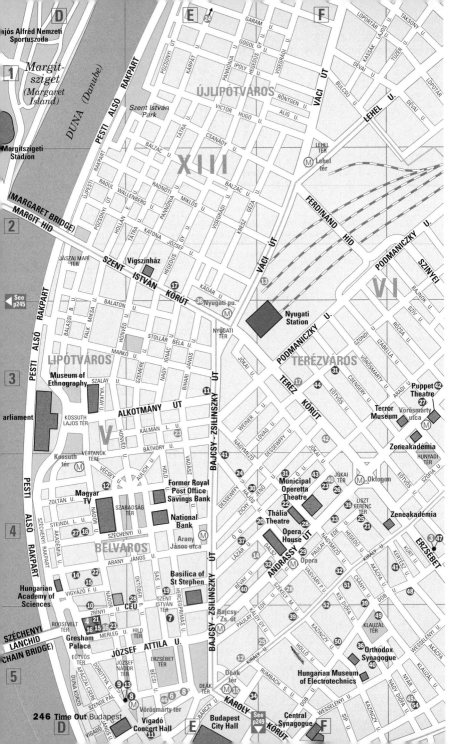

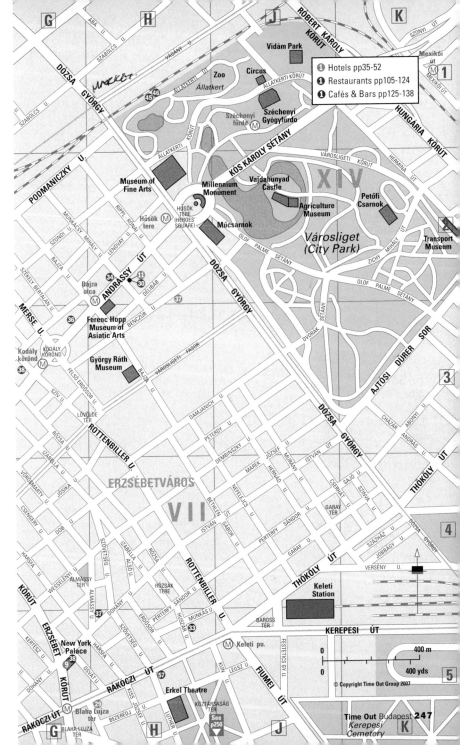

See p250

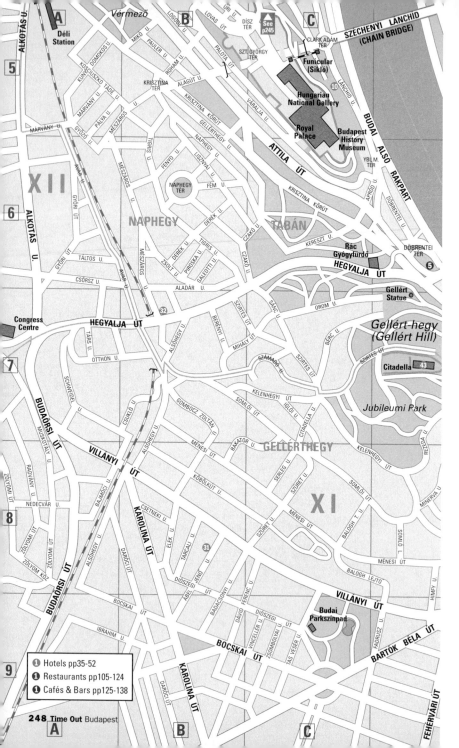

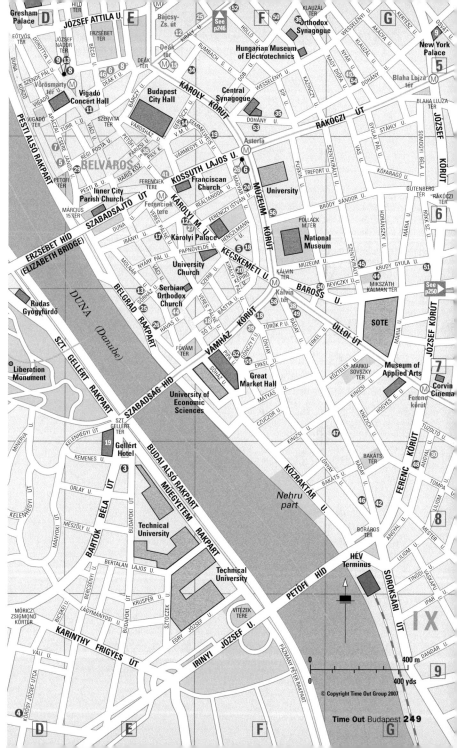

© Copyright Time Out Group 2007

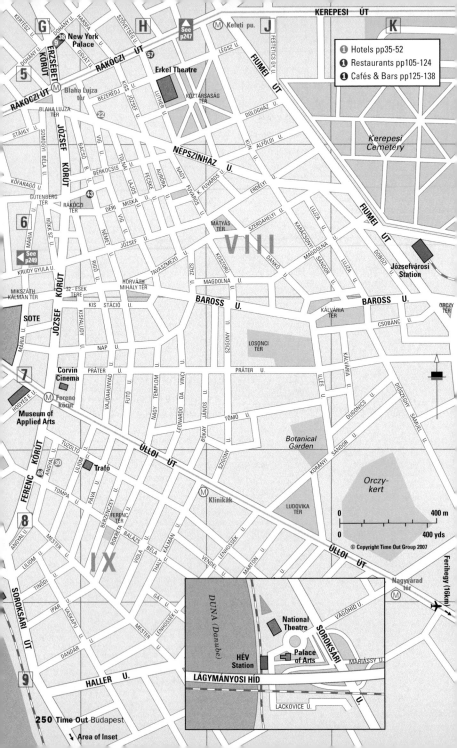

KEREPESI ÚT

G **H** J **K**

Kertész U.

Dohány U.

New York
Palace

Hansa u.

Szövetség u.

5

ERZSÉBET KÖRÚT

Dohány U.

Osváth u.

RÁKÓCZI ÚT 57

Kelett pu.

RÁKÓCZI ÚT

FESTETICS GY. U.

See p247

Légszi u.

FIUMEI ÚT

Erkel Theatre

LUTHER

KÖZTÁRSASÁG TÉR

Blaha Lujza tér

Blaha Lujza
tér

BEZEREDJ U.

KISS JÓZSEF U.

DOLOGHÁZ U.

KUN U.

ALFÖLDI U.

Kerepesi
Cemetery

STÁHLY U.

SOMOGYI BÉLA U.

JÓZSEF

KÖRÚT

VIG U.

BACSÓ B.

TOLNAI LAJOS U.

22

NÉPSZÍNHÁZ U.

FECSKE U.

AURÓRA U.

NAGY FUVAROS U.

FUVAROS U.

ERDÉLYI U.

LUZSA U.

FIUMEI ÚT

KÖFARAGÓ U.

BÉRKOCSIS U.

GÜTENBERG TÉR

RÁKÓCZI TÉR

DÉRI MISKA U.

VIG U.

43

NÉMET U.

JÓZSEF U.

MÁTYÁS TÉR

SZERDAHELYI U.

KARÁCSONY S.

MAGDOLNA

LUZSA U.

DOBOZI U.

Józsefvárosi
Station

6

MÁRIA U.

RÖKK SZ. U.

See p249

KRUDY GYULA U.

RIGÓ U.

TAVASZMEZŐ

ZSZÚ U.

KOSZORÚ U.

DANKÓ U.

MAGDOLNA SÁNDOR

LUZSA U.

VIII

MIKSZÁTH KÁLMÁN TÉR

KÖRÚT

JÓZSEF

32-ESEK TÉRE

HORVÁTH MIHÁLY TÉR

KIS STÁCIÓ U.

MAGDOLNA U.

BAROSS U.

SZIGONY U.

KÁLVÁRIA TÉR

BAROSS U.

ORCZY TÉR

SOTE

KISFALUDY U.

NAP U.

LOSONCI TÉR

KÁLVÁRIA

CSOBÁNC U.

7

HŐGYES E. U.

Corvin
Cinema

PRÁTER U.

VAJDAHUNYAD U.

TEMPLOM U.

LEONARDO DA VINCI U.

JÁNOS U.

PRÁTER U.

ILLÉS

DUGONICS

DIÓSZEGHY

SZÁMEL U.

Ferenc
körút

NAGY

FUTÓ U.

BÓKAY

TÖMŐ U.

Museum of
Applied Arts

FERENC

KÖRÚT

TÚZOLTÓ U.

ANGYAL U.

48

30

LILIOM

Trafó

PÁVA U.

ÜLLŐI ÚT

SZIGONY U.

Botanical
Garden

KORÁNYI SÁNDOR

Orczy-
kert

TOMPA U.

BERZENCZEY U.

FERENC TÉR

BOKRÉTA U.

BALÁZS U.

Klinikák

LUDOVIKA TÉR

0   400 m

0   400 yds

© Copyright Time Out Group 2007

8

ANGYAL U.

MESTER U.

LILIOM U.

VISKI U.

BÉLA U.

KÁLMÁN

THALY U.

VENDEL U.

LENHOSSÉK U.

MÁRTON U.

Ferihegy (16km)

Nagyvárad
tér

IX

TINÓDI U.

IPAR U.

VÁSKAPU U.

GÁT U.

MESTER U.

LENHOSSÉK U.

VÁGÓHÍD U.

SOROKSÁRI

MARIÁSSY U.

9

SOROKSÁRI ÚT

DANDÁR U.

HALLER U.

LÁGYMÁNYOSI HÍD

LACKOVICE U.

ÚT

DUNA (Danube)

National
Theatre

HÉV
Station

Palace
of Arts

SOROKSÁRI

1 Hotels pp35-52

1 Restaurants pp105-124

1 Cafés & Bars pp125-138

↘ Area of Inset

Street Index

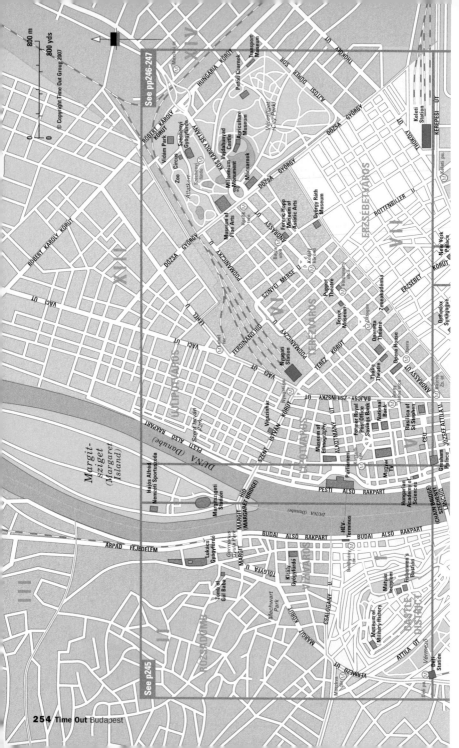

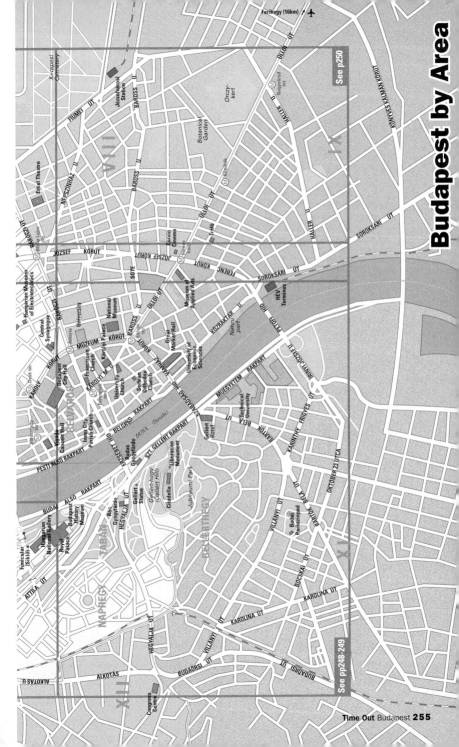

See p250

See pp248-249

Ferihegy (16km)

Kerepesi Cemetery

Erkel Theatre

Józsefvárosi Station

Orczy-kert

Botanical Garden

Hungarian Museum of Electrotechnics

Central Synagogue

University

National Museum

Museum of Applied Arts

HÉV Terminus

Budapest City Hall

Franciscan Church

Károlyi Palace

University Church

Great Market Hall

Serbian Orthodox Church

University of Economic Sciences

Nehru park

Inner City Parish Church

Pesti Concert Hall

Rudas Gyógyfürdő

MÜEGYETEM RAKPART

Technical University

Gellért Hotel

Hungarian National Gallery

Budapest History Museum

Royal Palace

Rác Gyógyfürdő

Gellért Statue

Liberation Monument

Gellért-hegy (Gellert Hill)

Citadella

Jubileumi Park

Budai Parkszínpad

Funicular (Sikló)

TABÁN

NAPHEGY

GELLÉRTHEGY

Congress Centre

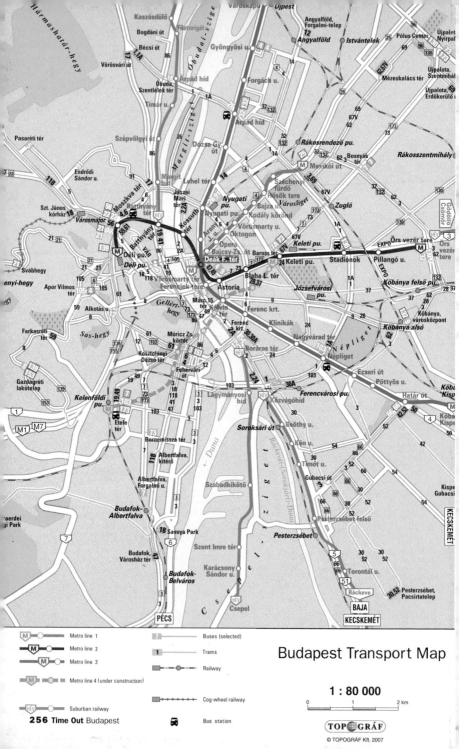

Budapest Transport Map

1 : 80 000

0   1   2 km

© TOPOGRÁF Kft. 2007